Unreal Engine 4.X By Example

An example-based practical guide to get you up
and running with Unreal Engine 4.X

Benjamin Carnall

BIRMINGHAM - MUMBAI

Unreal Engine 4.X By Example

First published: July 2016

Production reference: 1260716

Published by Packt Publishing Ltd.
Livery Place
35 Livery Street
Birmingham B3 2PB, UK.

ISBN 978-1-78588-553-2

www.packtpub.com

Credits

Author
Benjamin Carnall

Reviewer
Matt Matte

Commissioning Editor
Amarabha Banerjee

Acquisition Editor
Reshma Raman

Content Development Editor
Parshva Sheth

Technical Editor
Gebin George

Copy Editor
Joanna McMahon

Project Coordinator
Ritika Manoj

Proofreader
Safis Editing

Indexer
Tejal Daruwale Soni

Graphics
Abhinash Sahu

Production Coordinator
Aparna Bhagat

About the Author

Benjamin Carnall is an enthusiastic and dedicated programmer whose love for problem solving led him to the world of game development. He relishes opportunities to learn new and interesting ways to create gameplay experiences for others. Ben began his journey with Game Development in 2012, after he graduated from Media Design School with a diploma in interactive gaming. He then went on to graduate from the same university with a bachelors of software engineering in 2014. Since then, Ben has immersed himself in the Game Development community of New Zealand—starting out as a programming contractor and working on various titles around Auckland. He then began to work as a lecturer at Media Design School and taught Graphics programming for games, Physics programming for games, and Sony PlayStation development at the bachelors level. Most recently, Ben has been working as a programmer for the studio Aroura44, developing a title called Ashen.

I would like to thank so many people for supporting me during the authoring of this book. Thanks to the wonderful people around me, I remained fed and happy while endeavoring to put into words the jumble of information that knocks around in my head.

Thank you to my parents for making sure I stayed healthy and well fed. Thank you to my lovely Emily, for keeping my morals high and my smile wide. Thanks to the team at Epic for making such an awesome engine! Without them I would not be writing this now. Thanks to my editor, Parshva Sheth, for working through this with me, we made it! And finally, I'd like to thank you, the reader, for taking a chance with this book and for jumping into the world of game development!

About the Reviewer

Matt Matte is the founder of Full Metal Jacket Games, and he was recently featured on Unreal Engine's Spotlight Projects section with their Tron- inspired VR game. Matt is the official Seattle Unreal Engine Rep and the organizer of the largest Unreal Engine Meetup in the world, with over 800 members. He's published three games with Unreal Engine. The latest game released in August 2016 is Monkey Land 3D: Reaper Rush.

Matt has over 10 years of experience in Unreal Engine, starting with building mods in the Unreal Engine 3 editor and then moving on to UDK and UE4 to build completely original titles. He's an expert Unreal developer and technical artist that specializes in setting up characters, both controlled by a player and Artificial Intelligence, including rigging and creating animations, setting up physics with the PHAT editor, animation blueprints, and blending, AI behavior trees, and synchronized special effects. He's created games with Blueprints only and a hybrid of both C++ and Blueprints.

His primary focus is on virtual reality games. F.M.J. Games has won two Seattle VR Hackathons for best graphics and experience. They also won the Peoples Choice Award for NASA's 2015 Space Apps Challenge, all with UE4 and its powerful real-time rendering. They've been awarded new VR hardware by Epic, Oculus, and Valve for their accomplishments in VR design.

Matt has reviewed the blueprints and code in this book and tested that they work and are fully functional. Contact Matt through `www.fmjgames.com` for anything Unreal Engine game development related.

www.PacktPub.com

eBooks, discount offers, and more

Did you know that Packt offers eBook versions of every book published, with PDF and ePub files available? You can upgrade to the eBook version at www.PacktPub.com and as a print book customer, you are entitled to a discount on the eBook copy. Get in touch with us at customercare@packtpub.com for more details.

At www.PacktPub.com, you can also read a collection of free technical articles, sign up for a range of free newsletters and receive exclusive discounts and offers on Packt books and eBooks.

https://www2.packtpub.com/books/subscription/packtlib

Do you need instant solutions to your IT questions? PacktLib is Packt's online digital book library. Here, you can search, access, and read Packt's entire library of books.

Why subscribe?

- Fully searchable across every book published by Packt
- Copy and paste, print, and bookmark content
- On demand and accessible via a web browser

Table of Contents

Preface

Unreal Engine 4 is a cutting-edge game development engine that has revolutionized the way developers pay for engine licenses. Instead of forking out millions of dollars to access this first class engine, developers can use it completely free of charge, until they find themselves with a profitable product on their hands.

Unreal Engine 4 provides a rich AAA development toolset with cutting-edge technical features to anyone who is keen to develop great games. The engine has been developed in C++, and not only are we able to leverage the power of C++ for our projects, but we also have access to the entire engine source! This book will start you on your journey toward mastering UE4's toolset and becoming a proficient C++ UE4 developer!

What this book covers

Chapter 1, Introduction to Unreal Engine 4, takes you through the installation of UE4, creating new UE4 projects, and an introductory overview of the main engine editor.

Chapter 2, Blueprints and Barrels – Your First Game, introduces you to the world of Blueprint Visual Scripting. You will leverage the Blueprint system of UE4 to create your first UE4 game project, called Barrel Hopper.

Chapter 3, Advanced Blueprint, Animation, and Sound, covers some of the more advanced Blueprint concepts, and it also concludes the development of the Barrel Hopper project by showing you how to include animation and sound in your projects.

Chapter 4, Unreal Engine, C++, and You, introduces you to the concepts and syntax that will be encountered when working with C++ and Unreal Engine 4.

Chapter 5, Upgrade Activated – Making Bounty Dash with C++, will expand on your knowledge of C++ with UE4, by taking you through the development of a purely C++ implemented game project!

Chapter 6, Power Ups for Your Character, Power Ups for the User, guides you in creating a UE4 C++ plugin, and it also introduces you to some advanced UE4 C++ concepts. This chapter concludes the development of Bounty Dash!

Chapter 7, Boss Mode Activated – Unreal Robots, will introduce you to UE4's extensive AI toolset by taking you through the creation of the Boss Mode game project.

Chapter 8, Advanced AI and Unreal Rendering, covers some of the advanced concepts of UE4's AI system; it will also introduce you to UE4's material editor and rendering system!

Chapter 9, Creating a Networked Shooter, breaks down and explains all the networking systems included in UE4. This chapter will have you create your own networked First Person Shooter, which you will be able to play over LAN with your friends.

Chapter 10, Goodbyes and Thank yous, will show you how to package your project for distribution and testing, and it also covers a brief summary of what has been learned before concluding the book!

What you need for this book

- Processor: Quad-core Intel or AMD, 2.5 GHz or faster
- Memory: 8 GB RAM
- Video Card: DirectX 11 compatible graphics card Unreal Engine 4.10.*

Who this book is for

Unreal Engine by Example was written for keen developers who wished to learn how to fully utilize Unreal Engine 4 to make awesome and engrossing game titles. Whether you are brand new to game development or a seasoned expert, you will be able to make use of this engine with C++. Experience in both C++ and other game engines is preferred before embarking on the Unreal by Example journey; but with a little external research into the basics of C++ programming, this book can make a complete game development novice into an Unreal Engine developer!

Conventions

In this book, you will find a number of text styles that distinguish between different kinds of information. Here are some examples of these styles and an explanation of their meaning.

Code words in text, database table names, folder names, filenames, file extensions, pathnames, dummy URLs, user input, and Twitter handles are shown as follows: "It is now time for the famous `Hello World`."

A block of code is set as follows:

```
#include "BMBossCharacter.h"
#include "BehaviorTree/BlackboardComponent.h"
#include "BehaviorTree/BehaviorTree.h"
```

New terms and **important words** are shown in bold. Words that you see on the screen, for example, in menus or dialog boxes, appear in the text like this: "Then create a new **Blackboard** asset from the same category."

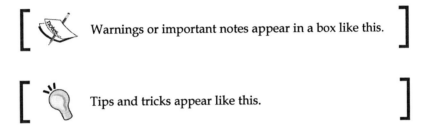

Warnings or important notes appear in a box like this.

Tips and tricks appear like this.

Reader feedback

Feedback from our readers is always welcome. Let us know what you think about this book—what you liked or disliked. Reader feedback is important for us as it helps us develop titles that you will really get the most out of.

To send us general feedback, simply e-mail feedback@packtpub.com, and mention the book's title in the subject of your message.

If there is a topic that you have expertise in and you are interested in either writing or contributing to a book, see our author guide at www.packtpub.com/authors.

Customer support

Now that you are the proud owner of a Packt book, we have a number of things to help you to get the most from your purchase.

Downloading the example code

You can download the example code files for this book from your account at
`http://www.packtpub.com`. If you purchased this book elsewhere, you can visit
`http://www.packtpub.com/support` and register to have the files e-mailed
directly to you.

You can download the code files by following these steps:

1. Log in or register to our website using your e-mail address and password.
2. Hover the mouse pointer on the **SUPPORT** tab at the top.
3. Click on **Code Downloads & Errata**.
4. Enter the name of the book in the **Search** box.
5. Select the book for which you're looking to download the code files.
6. Choose from the drop-down menu where you purchased this book from.
7. Click on **Code Download**.

You can also download the code files by clicking on the **Code Files** button on the
book's webpage at the Packt Publishing website. This page can be accessed by
entering the book's name in the **Search** box. Please note that you need to be
logged in to your Packt account.

Once the file is downloaded, please make sure that you unzip or extract the folder
using the latest version of:

*   WinRAR / 7-Zip for Windows
*   Zipeg / iZip / UnRarX for Mac
*   7-Zip / PeaZip for Linux

The code bundle for the book is also hosted on GitHub at `https://github.com/`
`PacktPublishing/Unreal-Engine-4X-By-Example`. We also have other code
bundles from our rich catalog of books and videos available at `https://github.`
`com/PacktPublishing/`. Check them out!

Downloading the color images of this book

We also provide you with a PDF file that has color images of the screenshots/
diagrams used in this book. The color images will help you better understand
the changes in the output. You can download this file from `https://www.`
`packtpub.com/sites/default/files/downloads/UnrealEngine4XByExample_`
`ColoredImages.pdf`.

Errata

Although we have taken every care to ensure the accuracy of our content, mistakes do happen. If you find a mistake in one of our books—maybe a mistake in the text or the code—we would be grateful if you could report this to us. By doing so, you can save other readers from frustration and help us improve subsequent versions of this book. If you find any errata, please report them by visiting http://www.packtpub.com/submit-errata, selecting your book, clicking on the **Errata Submission Form** link, and entering the details of your errata. Once your errata are verified, your submission will be accepted and the errata will be uploaded to our website or added to any list of existing errata under the Errata section of that title.

To view the previously submitted errata, go to https://www.packtpub.com/books/content/support and enter the name of the book in the search field. The required information will appear under the **Errata** section.

Piracy

Piracy of copyrighted material on the Internet is an ongoing problem across all media. At Packt, we take the protection of our copyright and licenses very seriously. If you come across any illegal copies of our works in any form on the Internet, please provide us with the location address or website name immediately so that we can pursue a remedy.

Please contact us at copyright@packtpub.com with a link to the suspected pirated material.

We appreciate your help in protecting our authors and our ability to bring you valuable content.

Questions

If you have a problem with any aspect of this book, you can contact us at questions@packtpub.com, and we will do our best to address the problem.

1
Introduction to Unreal Engine 4

Welcome to *Unreal Engine 4 by Example*! During the course of this book you are going to learn how to utilize **Unreal Engine 4 (UE4)** to create high-quality games using C++. This chapter will show you how to install the engine, introduce you to the engine's **User Interface (UI)**, show you how to create new projects, and give you a rundown of what to expect from this book. The purpose of this chapter is to give you a general idea of how this book will be formatted and how to get the most out of your *Unreal Engine 4 by Example* experience.

The chapter will cover the following points:

- Navigating this book and what to expect
- Installing UE4
- Creating new UE4 projects
- Navigating UE4's User Interface
- Creating a basic actor and adding components
- Opening and exploring the examples provided by Unreal

Navigating this book

First off, it should be stated that the use of C++ features heavily in the later stages of this book. It is strongly advised that you already have some experience with writing in C++ or a similar low-level language before embarking on this journey.

This is a *By Example* book, meaning that you will be taught how to use UE4 via the breakdown and explanation of previously created UE4 game projects. These projects have been created specifically for this book with your education in mind! Each project will be taught over two chapters, the first will include the core concepts and features needed to implement the title. The second will delve into the advanced or more complicated components of each project. By the end of each project you will have learnt core UE4 functionality plus some very interesting polish techniques.

By the end of this book you should find yourself well on your way to becoming a skilled Unreal Engine developer capable of using C++ and the provided Blueprint system to utilize Unreal Engine's rich feature set to create polished game titles.

Game Projects you say?

Yes, game projects! By the end of this book you will have created four unique game projects that will all include their own polish features. These projects culminate with the creation of your very own multiplayer first-person shooter!

During the course of this book you will create the following game projects:

- **Barrel Hopper**: A homage to the original Donkey Kong, this project will be created entirely using Blueprint and will introduce you to the high-level systems used when creating games with UE4.

- **Bounty Dash**: Our take on an endless runner, this project will be your first look into C++ with UE4. We will be expanding on some of our content created for Barrel Hopper and really start to unlock the potential of UE4.

- **Boss Mode**: For this project we will be expanding on your C++ technical skill set by creating an engagement with a game boss controlled by **Artificial Intelligence (AI)**, which will be visually detailed by taking advantage of UE4's in-depth rendering and shading functionality.

- **Network Shooter**: This will be the culmination of your journey with this book and your UE4 education. You will be creating a networked first-person shooter that lets you create a game you can play with your friends through a Local Area Network.

Installing Unreal Engine 4

The version of Unreal Engine we will be using for this book is Unreal Engine 4.11.0. You may use any 4.11.# engine version as long as your version number exists within the 4.11 family. If you have already installed Unreal Engine 4.11 you can skip this section and jump straight to *Creating your first project*. First things first, you need to sign up as an Unreal Engine developer. Navigate to `https://www.unrealengine.com` in your browser and select the **GET UNREAL** option located in the top right-hand corner of the web page.

This will then redirect you to the login/sign-up page for a UE account. If you do not have an account, follow the steps presented in the page to create one. This account will integrate you into the Unreal Development community. Through this account you can get Unreal Engine news, updates, and developer support.

Once this is done you will be directed to the downloads page, choose the OS that you will be developing on (MAC, Windows) and you should see the download begin for an Epic Games Launcher installer. The Epic Game Launcher is the portal for all Unreal Engine versions and you will use this application to install, manage, and launch the engine version you wish to use.

Once the Epic Games Launcher has been successfully installed, run it and it will prompt you to log in with the account credentials you previously set up with Epic. If everything has gone according to plan you should be presented with the Unreal Engine launcher. From the launcher you will need to navigate to the **Unreal Engine** tab located in the top left-hand side of the window. From here you can see **News**, **Learning Resources**, and **Marketplace Content** for the engine. I advise you to take your time to explore each of the options available to you, however we will be focusing on the **Library** section.

By selecting the **Library** element on the list on the left-hand side of the window you will be presented with any currently installed engines as well as any Unreal projects you have already created. There will be an **Add Versions** button near the top of the window.

Pressing this button will present you with a light-colored engine node, click the drop-down arrow next to the engine version number and be sure to select 4.11.0. Once this is done, hit **Install**. The launcher will now handle downloading and installing your new engine version!

While the engine is installing I would strongly suggest you spend some time exploring `https://www.unrealengine.com`. The website is a great place to find video tutorials, learning resources, and the Unreal Engine Wiki. You do not need to utilize these resources to follow this book, however the content they have provided is very informative and will definitely help you on your journey to becoming a proficient Unreal Engine developer. Once the engine has been installed, hit **Launch** and you are ready to go!

[Tip: If you hit the drop-down arrow next to launch you can create a shortcut for the engine version.]

Creating your first project!

It is now time for the famous `Hello World`, but this time it will be `Hello Unreal`. With your engine version launched you will be presented with the **Unreal Project Browser**. This browser features two tabs, **Projects** and **New Project**, select **New Project**. The first thing you can see in this tab is a large selection of icons under two more tabs, **Blueprint** and **C++.** We will be selecting the **Blueprint** tab and we will be creating a **Blank** project, your selection should appear as follows:

Under this section you will see three dropdown boxes titled **Desktop/Console,** **Maximum Quality,** and **With Starter Content**. We will leave these as they are for now but this is where you can swap your target platform for the project, change the graphics quality, and whether or not you would like to use the starter content provided by Epic. Below these options you will see fields to populate the directory where you wish to create the project and what the name of the project will be. We shall title this project `Hello Unreal`. Once this is done, click the green **Create Project** button and the engine will finally launch.

Navigating the Unreal Engine UI

Welcome to the Unreal Engine User Interface! It can be a bit overwhelming at first but, fear not, all will be explained. By the end of this book you will be very familiar with the layout and workings of this engine view. Now, for the sake of brevity, I will hand your Unreal education over to the Epic team for a short moment. In the top right-hand corner of the window next to the name of the project you should see a grey academia cap flashing green.

Clicking this cap will start a short tutorial that will familiarize you with the engine's layouts and panels. I am leaving this up to Unreal as the introductory tutorials are succinct and efficient at bringing you up to scratch with the editor layout and camera controls. This gives us more time to get to the juicy learning!

Once you have completed this introductory tutorial you will be guided to the tutorial home panel. Here you will be able to find a list of simple tutorials that will help familiarize you with the different features of the engine, could you please complete the two tutorials under the **Basics** category. Feel free to utilize the other tutorials during the course of the book. I will likely be covering almost all of the topics covered in the tutorials but they may prove useful as an additional learning resource. Now that Epic has taught you how to view its engine, it is now time to teach you how to use the engine!

Creating a basic actor

At this point you should have a world that looks similar to this:

What we are going to do now is remove the table, statue, and chairs from our level and replace them with our own actor. The purpose of this is to show you how we can create new actors and add components from within the editor without having to navigate to other areas of the engine. You can remove actors by clicking on them and hitting the *Delete* key, right-clicking on them and selecting **Edit | Delete** from the dropdown menu, or by finding the actor in the **World Outliner** and performing the same steps.

Once the table and chairs have been removed, we need to add an actor to the world that we wish to build upon. To do this we need to place an element from the **Modes Panel** in the top left-hand side of the window. As stated in the introductory tutorial, the **Modes Panel** is where you can find all of the tools that you will need to perform construction actions within the editor. The five tabs you can interact with are **Place**, **Paint**, **Landscape**, **Foliage**, and **Geometry Editing**.

These options will be explored during the course of this book but, for now, we are concerned with the **Place** tab. The **Place** tab is where you can find all of the editor objects that can be dragged and dropped into the level. Here you can find things such as basic geometry primitives, BSPs, visual effects, and numerous processing volumes.

[If you wish to see detailed documentation for each of the editor objects, click the small question mark on the right-hand side of the object name.]

From the list on the left-hand side of the panel, select **Basic**; this will show you a selection of simple objects that can be dragged into the world. We want to drag an **Empty Actor** into the world.

Objects, Actors, Pawns, and Characters

Unreal Engine utilizes a specific naming convention for the objects that can be created and built upon within the editor. There are **Objects**, **Actors**, **Pawns**, and **Characters**. Each name represents an expanded level of functionality. In general, you can think of Actors as whole items or entities such as a power up or boost pad, where an object is usually a small part or **Component** with specialized functionality. For example, a whole car could be an Actor but the engine within the car would be considered an Object. Pawns and Characters I will detail in later chapters. The term object(s) will be used to refer to things in our levels but when required I will use the capitalized Actor or Object when specification is required.

Select our new actor now by clicking on it within the viewport. With the **Empty Actor** selected in our world we are presented with a few new visual elements. The first is the transform widget; the transform widget provides us with the ability to translate, rotate, and scale objects within our world. You can swap the functionality of your transform widget by pressing the *W* key for translation, the *E* key for rotation, and the *R* key for scale. Alternatively, in the top right-hand side of the **Viewport** panel you can click and select the appropriate transform icon. We can also select the globe icon in the same corner to swap between world and local space transformation. Simply put, world space transformation will present a transform axis in line with the world. Local space will present a transform axis in line with the object (based on the objects arbitrary forward).

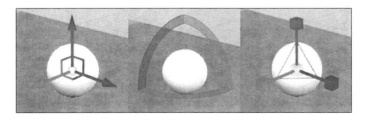

If you are ever curious to see the world space axis, it can be found in the bottom left-hand side of the screen, denoted by a simple line widget. This can be used to orient yourself while using the 3D camera/building levels.

Adding components to your Actor

You will notice that, if you try to scale or rotate the empty actor, nothing happens. That is because, at this point, the empty actor only contains a `DefaultSceneRoot` component. A component is an Object that is owned by other Unreal Engine 4 objects (usually Actors, Pawns, or Characters) that provide different functionalities/features to the object. In this case our actor owns a `DefaultSceneRoot` component allowing us to translate, rotate, and scale the object.

Why then does scaling and rotating do nothing? Well, right now we have no 'visual' components included in our actor and by that I mean any components that contain geometry that will visually represent the object in the game world. Without a visual reference, the orientation or size of the empty actor has no context, only the location of the object in 3D space could be of any use, thus we have the ability to translate.

This brings me to the second visual element; on the right-hand side of the window is the **Details** panel. This panel is used to show all information about any selected object within our world. From the **Details** panel we can manipulate exposed member data, add and remove components, and edit component properties. There are a few other tricks the **Details** panel offers us but I will expand upon those later on in the book.

You can also change the name of objects in the details panel. Right now our object is called **Actor**, we should change this to a more specific name, let's use `Hello Sphere`. Now we need to add a visual reference to our Hello Sphere. Under the **Details** panel you can see a green **Add Component** button; clicking this button will bring up a list of pre-built components we can add to our actor. We would like to add a **Sphere** to our actor, it can be found under the **Basic Shapes** section of the dropdown. You can either use the search bar provided to find specific components or scroll down the list until you find what you require.

The component hierarchy

Once you have added the sphere mesh to our `Hello Sphere` actor you will see a new element in the **Details Panel, component hierarchy**. We still have our `DefaultSceneRoot` component but now, directly under it, we have our sphere mesh. This brings up a very important point: Component parenting.

Within the **Details** panel you will notice that the sphere mesh component is indented slightly and directly beneath our `DefaultSceneRoot` component.

This is called parenting; our sphere mesh is now a child component of our `DefaultSceneRoot` component. This means that any scaling, rotation, or translation we apply to our `DefaultSceneRoot` will be applied to our sphere as well. However, any transformations we enact on our sphere mesh will not be applied to our `DefaultSceneRoot`. You can change the hierarchy of an object's components by clicking and dragging them up and down the list. The top-most component will be the Root Component and will dictate the transform of all subsequent components.

Ignoring this can lead to disjointing of child components and can be fairly troublesome. I encourage you to now translate the `Hello Sphere` with the `Sphere component` selected in the details panel, then again with the `DefaultSceneRoot` component selected instead. You will notice that, upon the second translation, the Sphere Mesh maintains its relative distance from the location of the `DefaultSceneRoot` component. It is because of this that I would strongly advise to only apply transformations to child objects when you wish those transformations to remain constant, relative to the parent.

If you wish to move everything within an object instance you may select the `ObjectName` (Instance) element within the hierarchy.

Modifying components

Now translate the Hello Sphere to the same location that the table and chairs originally occupied. We are going to add some `Flash` to our `Hello Sphere`. We are going to add two more components to the actor; a **Text Render** component and a **Particle System** component. We will then use the **Details** panel to modify the properties of these components to achieve our desired visual result.

First, let's modify the text. After adding a Text Render component, select it in the component hierarchy. You will see that the bottom section of the **Details** panel will change. This section is where you can modify the component's properties. You will notice that you can also get access to the component's transform properties here, this is so you can perform exact transformation changes to an object without having to use the transform widget.

Underneath the **Transform** and **Materials** sections we will see a section titled **Text**. It is here that the main properties for our Text Render component exist. The first thing we need to do is change the text so it says something meaningful. Let's change the **Text** field to `Hello World` then change the **Horizontal Alignment** field to `Center`.

Your Text section of the details panel should look something like this:

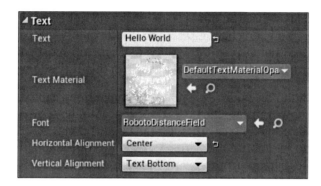

3D transformation and axis

Unfortunately the 3D text is partially penetrating the sphere mesh. To fix this we will be applying a translation to the Text Render component. We wish to apply this translation to the Text Render child component as we want this translation to remain the same regardless of the position of our actor. Instead of using the widget we can use the Transform section of the **Details** panel. You will notice a 3x3 field matrix under the Transform section. The top row represents the location of the component in 3D space, the second row the rotation, and the bottom row the scale. We want to move our 3D text vertically by a small amount and reduce the scale of our sphere so that our text sits above our sphere mesh.

3D game engines will use an arbitrary 3D co-ordinate system to accurately gauge the transformation of objects in 3D space. These co-ordinate systems are made up of three axis — X, Y, and Z. We gauge the direction of the co-ordinate axis by the direction in which the axis increases in a positive manner.

To better understand how axis work, we will take your position as a developer as a reference. If you were to see your own Unreal axis set, you would see a red axis (the X axis) extend outwards from your chest towards the screen. This is because the X axis in Unreal Engine increases in a positive manner forwards into the screen. In a similar fashion you would see a green axis extend out of your right-hand side (the Y axis), and finally you would have a blue axis extending upwards from your head (the Z axis). As an example, imagine the chair in the following screenshot is the chair you are sitting in:

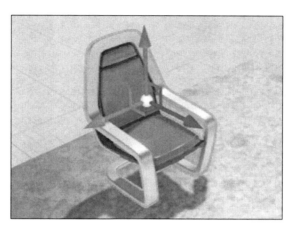

We need to translate the text component 30cm positively along the Z axis. To do this, ensure that you have the Text Render component selected in the component hierarchy and simply change the third field in the top row of the **Transform** section of the **Details** panel to 30.0. However, our text render component is still intersecting with the sphere, we now need to scale down or shrink our sphere mesh component.

To scale down the sphere, make sure the Sphere Mesh component is selected in the component hierarchy, then press *R* to bring up the Scale Transform widget. You'll notice, as you hover your mouse over the different sections of the widget, that they will change to a yellow color. This means that if you were to press and hold the left mouse button, any movement of the mouse will result in a scale change on that axis. To scale the sphere along all axis uniformly, there is a small white box in the widget where all the axis meet. If your mouse is situated over this box, all of the axis will change to a yellow color. With this white box selected, click and drag the mouse to scale the sphere to half the size it was before. Or, alternatively, change all of the values in the bottom row of the transform matrix to 0.5.

This will move our text render component up and out of our smaller sphere mesh, resulting in something that looks like this:

Adding the Unreal factor

Our little sphere has come a long way, however we need to add something to our actor to make it stand out. This brings our other new component into focus, the **Particle system**. Particle systems are components that allow us to attach previously created particle effects to our actors. The creation of these particle effects and a more in-depth description will be detailed in the *Boss Mode Activated* chapter.

For now, we can use the new component's **Details** panel to modify which particle effect we would like to use and how it is transformed. With the Particle System component selected in the hierarchy, select the **Template** dropdown field in the **Particles** section and select P_Fire. This will use the P_Fire particle system template for the particle component. You may notice that the particle system is quite large initially; I scaled the system to about 1/3 of the original size. You can do this by using the scale widget or the transform field in the **Details** panel with the particle system component selected.

We are not done yet, Unreal Engine boasts a very flexible and feature-rich renderer. One of the most commonly used features is the **Material system**. Materials are pre-built visual effects we would like to apply to our surfaces. Materials encompass all surface details such as textures, color, and physical properties such as roughness and luminescence. The creation of Materials along with an in-depth description is covered in the *Boss Mode Activated* chapter. For now we can use a pre-made material for our Sphere Mesh. With the Sphere mesh component selected, click the dropdown field under the **Materials** section of the **Details** panel. Search in the list for M_Metal_Burnished_Steel. You'll notice that when the material is selected, the appearance of the sphere will change. You now see something similar to this:

And that is it! We are done setting up our game world for the Hello World project. Now you can click the large play button in the **Toolbar** at the top of the Editor window and fly around your new game world! You will notice at the top of the screen there are a few options, these in-editor play options will be explained in the next chapter *Blueprints and Barrels*. Congratulations on making your first Unreal Engine project Hello Unreal! All of the concepts presented in this project will be expanded on in much more detail in the following chapters. What you have learned here is only the beginning; there are many more interesting features and techniques yet to come.

Pre-Built projects as a learning resource

Now that you are comfortable creating and modifying your own projects, it is important to learn how to interact with the Unreal Learning tools to download pre-built projects so you may learn from other people's work.

Epic releases example projects that you can navigate and explore to learn about the different faces of the engine. If you open the **Epic Games Launcher** application and return to the **Unreal Engine** tab, you will notice in the list on the left-hand side of the screen a Learn element. Selecting this element will open up the **Learn** page of the **Epic Game Launcher**. From this page you can get access the engine documentation, video tutorials, community wiki and, most importantly, the example projects. If you scroll down, you will see a section titled Engine Feature Samples. This section holds all of the example projects that you can download to see how Epic Games implements the different feature sets of the Unreal Engine. The one in particular I would like to draw your attention to is the **Content Examples** project.

The **Content Examples** project features a set of levels that demonstrate the use of many of the Engine's features. If at any point the uses of the Engine's components seem unclear, you may be able to find an example of that component's implementation in this project. Once the project has been downloaded it will appear in the **Library** section of the **Unreal Engine** tab.

Summary

Well done on taking your first steps towards becoming an Unreal Engine developer! I hope you look forward to learning from this book and continuing your game development adventures with Unreal Engine 4. In this chapter you have learned how to install the engine, navigate its unique interface, and you have made your first Unreal Actor! The next chapter *Barrels and Blueprints* will expand on the skills you just have learned to create your first UE4 game project! You will be recreating a version of the classic arcade game Donkey Kong©. The chapter will have you learn more about interfacing with the engine editor, how to create a workflow with Unreal Engine, and how to work with the Blueprint visual scripting system.

2
Blueprints and Barrels – Your First Game

Welcome to **Blueprints** and **Barrels**! During this chapter, you will be introduced to the **visual scripting** system called Blueprint. This system will be your first entry point toward creating customized functionality and content, using UE4. This chapter will show you the basics of how to create and work with Blueprints to achieve the same level of freedom that any other text based scripting language can provide. You will also expand on the engine navigational skills you learned in the previous chapter as we delve into the more complicated facets of the **Editor** panel and how you can communicate between the different components of the engine. You will learn all this by creating your very first UE game project, **Barrel Hopper**.

This chapter will cover the following points:

- Creating Blueprints
- Navigating the Blueprint GUI
- How to find Blueprint functions
- Basic coding functionality with Blueprint (logical nodes, objects, and events)
- Game mode Blueprints
- Using UE4's world outliner
- Basic level creation and blocking
- Blueprint collision
- Adding physics dynamics to objects in a world
- Creating a Blueprint character
- Controlling a character through Blueprint
- Debugging Blueprints

Creating your first Blueprint

Now, it is time to create your first Blueprint. Instead of jumping straight into a new project, I can't think of a better place to create your first Blueprint than our `Hello World` project. It is time to give our `Hello Sphere` an upgrade! The first thing we need to do is create a Blueprint from our actor. To do this, we need to select the `HelloSphere` actor by clicking on the **Actor** in the viewport or selecting the `HelloSphere` name in the **World Outlier**. This will populate our **Details Panel** with the appropriate options. Just next to the **Add Component** button, there is a **Blueprint/Add Script** button, click on this now:

You will be prompted to save the Blueprint we are about to create in some folder within our **Content Browser**. For now, save the blueprint in the Content folder directly. Name this Bluerpint **HelloUnrealBP** and press the green **Create Blueprint** button.

The Blueprint window

You will have been presented with an entirely new window, the Blueprint window. This will be your work area whenever you are editing or creating Blueprints. The Blueprint window boasts a new layout of panels and visual sections:

1. **Components**: Located in the top left-hand side of the window, this panel functions in exactly the same way as the top of the **Details** panel in the editor window. You can use this panel to add and remove components.

2. **My Blueprint**: Located directly under the **Components** panel, this panel is responsible for all of the different technical members of the Blueprint. This is where you can find your **Event Graphs**, **Events**, **Functions**, **Macros**, **Variables**, and **Event Dispatchers**. Each of these elements will be described in detail throughout the chapter.

3. **Details**: This panel functions exactly the same way as is it did in the editor window. This panel exposes all of the publicly exposed properties of your currently selected component within the Blueprint.

4. **Toolbar**: The toolbar is located in center of the screen at the top and features a set of large clickable buttons. These buttons will be explained in the next paragraph.

5. **Viewport**: This viewport section is responsible for showing the current physical arrangement of the blueprint in 3D space. This section will also be used to navigate the graphs or functions that are created with the Blueprint system. These other panels can be seen as tabs along the top of the viewport window. By default, **Viewport**, Construction Script, and **Event Graph** are shown.

Working with Blueprints

When creating Blueprints, you are frequently going to want to test your recent changes and additional functions as intended. You will also want to make sure that you have minimal errors, warnings, or bugs. The way you will do this is by interfacing with the previously mentioned **Toolbar**. The buttons featured on the **Toolbar** allow you to perform varying actions that assist with having your Blueprint execute in a test environment. Each button performs the follows:

1. **Compile**: This compiles the current Blueprint and will output any errors or warnings. You can specify various parameters for Blueprint compilation that will adjust if the file is saved and how Blueprint compile errors are handled. These parameters can be found by navigating to **Editor Preferences | Content Editors | Blueprint**.

2. **Save**: This saves the Blueprint.

3. **Find in CB**: This opens the content browser and navigate to a selected asset. This lets you locate any assets included in your Blueprint within your content browser. This can be useful if you wish to edit these assets midway through working with a Blueprint.

4. **Class Settings**: This opens a **Details** panel that is responsible for all of the Blueprint Properties such as the Blueprints Parent class, thumbnail appearance, and any *interfaces* the Blueprint is concerned with. These options will be covered when we look at advanced blueprint functionality.

5. **Class Defaults**: This opens a **Details** panel that is responsible for the default values of all of the *publically* exposed variables that can be found in the Blueprint and its components. This lets you specify what state you would like these variable to be in when an instance of this Blueprint is created in a game.

6. **Simulation**: This runs the Blueprint as a simulation. The simulation takes place within the Blueprint viewport. This lets you witness how the Blueprint will function within the game without having to create an instance in the level and running the game.

7. **Play**: This runs the current project, and functions in the same way as the play button within the editor window. The main difference is the drop-down window located next to the Play button. This lets you select the in-Editor Blueprint instance you wish to scrutinize for debugging. Note that this kind of playing in the editor is known as a **PIE** (**Play In Editor**) session

All of these options provide you the ability to debug and run your Blueprints while working on them in your project.

 Once you are familiar with the engine and you no longer need the tabs describing the title of each panel. You can right-click on the tab and select the **Hide Tab** option, so you can maximize available screen space.

Blueprint elements

Each Blueprint will include and be composed of certain elements, these elements can be found under the **My Blueprint** panel. Each of these elements will be used by you to create the custom functionality that you require from your Blueprint.

Graphs

Blueprint Graphs are the canvas with which you work to create blueprint functionality. It is within these graphs that you will place and connect your Blueprint nodes. **Event Graphs** house the *Events* that will be fired during a Blueprint's application lifetime. These events can be things like the *Tick* event that will be called every frame or the `ActorBeginOverlap` event that will be called when the Blueprint object is overlapping another. Blueprint functions and Macros will also be constructed using the graph system; however, these graphs will be independent.

Functions

Blueprint functions are a means of wrapping frequently used functionality or functionality that you wish to expose to other objects These functions act in a very similar way to standard C++ functions. You may also specify an encapsulation level when working with Blueprint functions (public, protected, and private). Blueprint functions allow you to specify both input and return parameters.

Macros

Similar to functions but are only internally facing, meaning that they can only be called from within the *Blueprint itself*. Macros are predominantly used for grouping sets of simple instructions that will be called very frequently. The major difference between Blueprint functions and Blueprint macros is that macros are *inlined* when the Blueprint is compiled. As UE4 is a C++ based engine, all blueprints are eventually compiled down into generated C++ that can be then again compiled into executable binary. When I state that the Macros are inlined, I am speaking of traditional C++ inlining to the macro function itself it its generated C++ form.

Variables

Blueprint variables allow you to create data types that can store information. These variables are very similar to **Class Member Variables** in C++. You can specify an encapsulation level and default values for Blueprint variables. It is also important to note that, for every component included in a blueprint, there will be a corresponding variable that will act as a reference to the component. This allows you to access components form within your blueprint graphs.

Event dispatchers

Event dispatchers allow you to bind events to one another. For example, if you wanted some functionality to be performed in Class A when an event in Class B is fired, you can do that using Event dispatchers; or similarly you can set up these delegate relationships within single objects as well. We will cover these in detail at the end of the chapter. This is very similar to **Delegates** in C++ and C#.

Modifying the Hello Sphere Blueprint

Double-click on the `HelloUnrealBP` to open it. Now, you should be able to see our spherical friend front and center within the **Viewport**. You will also notice that the components we added to our `Hello Sphere` can be found in the **Components** panel and as variables in the **My Blueprint** panel. This is so that we can get references to our components within our **Blueprint Graphs**.

Our goal is to have it, so we can approach our Hello sphere and the 3D text will change from **Hello World** to **Hello Player**. To do this, we are going to need to add another component, work with the Blueprints **Event Graph**, and utilize an **Event**.

The first thing we need to do is provide a volume we can use to detect other overlapping actors. To do this, we need to add a `SphereCollision` component via the **Add Component** button in the top-left corner of the Blueprint window. Do this now, and name it `SphereCollision`. With the new component selected in the **Components** panel, you should be able to see the collision sphere visualized within the viewport. Scale the sphere volume via the in viewport widget (like we did in Chapter one), so it is approximately 3.5x bigger than our sphere mesh. You should be presented with something that looks similar to this:

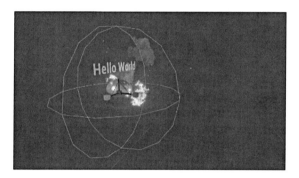

The next thing we need to do is ensure that this component will generate **overlap events**. With the sphere collision component selected address, the **Details Panel** on the right-hand side of the Blueprint window. Under the **Collision** section, you will see a series of options, one being a checkbox titled **Generate Overlap Events**, with this checkbox ticked, this Blueprint will fire the `ActorBeginOverlap` event within the event graph when it overlaps another object also signaled to generate either hit or overlap events. It is important to note that both offending bodies must be set to generate these events or nothing will occur.

Working with Blueprint graphs

Now, we need to modify the Blueprints **Event Graph**. This will be your first attempt at creating custom functionality with Blueprints. Open the **Event Graph** either by double-clicking on the **Event Graph** element under the **Graphs** section of the **My Blueprint** panel, or selecting the **Event Graph** tab above the **Viewport** panel. You should see a graph with three slightly translucent **Event Nodes** underneath comment bubbles. These are currently disabled events. They have been presented to you by default as they are the most commonly used events; however, until functionality has been appended to these nodes, they will not be triggered.

You should see a node titled **Event ActorBeginOverlap** as follows:

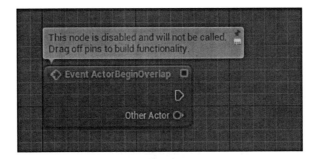

This is the event that will be triggered when other objects overlap our `SphereCollision` component. To enable this node, we need to append functionality to the node. We can do this by left-clicking on the hollow white arrow on the right-hand side of the node and dragging off into the grid, then releasing the left mouse button. Upon releasing the left mouse button you will be presented with a list of available *functions*, *events*, and *logical nodes*. This list is your access point into the Blueprint node library as well as any custom functions, events, or Macros you have created within the Blueprint itself. Functions in blueprint appear in the form of *Nodes*, which are a visual representation of the function within our graph.

This list will be context sensitive by default, meaning that you will only see options that are concerned with the **Critical Execution Path** and are related to the Blueprint. This path is the order in which your nodes will execute and it can be denoted by a white line that runs between nodes connected via white arrows. The question is what function do we need to call to change our text? What we need to do is, set the **text parameter** on our `TextRender` component. As our list is context sensitive and we have a `TextRender` component included in our blueprint, we can assume that we will be able to find the function we desire. Given that, simplistically, we wish to **Set Text** let's try searching for that. By typing or clicking in the search box at the top of the list, we will be able to perform a keyword search for our function.

By typing **Set Text**, we are presented with the following options:

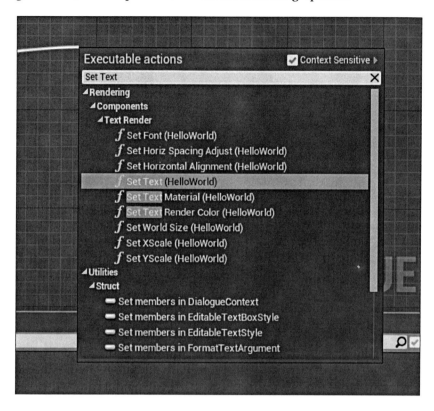

As you can see, the context sensitive search has provided us with all of the functions that we can call that either partially include the phrase Set Text or are related to the TextRender component. You will also notice that all of the function calls also have (Hello World) following the function name, this means that if you select that function it will already be set up to affect our HelloWorld TextRender component that we included in the Blueprint. Select this option now. You will see something similar to this:

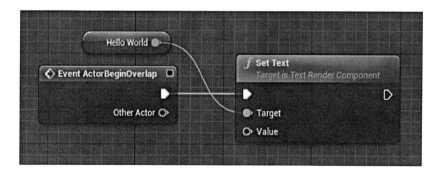

Compiling Blueprints

Congratulations! You have created your first Blueprint function! As you can see, two of our nodes are linked via the white line. This means that the Set Text function will be hit immediately after the event ActorBeginOverlap has been triggered. You will notice that the event has one pin titled **Other Actor** on the right hand side of the node, whereas our Set Text function node has two pins titled **target** and **value** on the left-hand side of the node. These are the node's inputs and outputs. Inputs act in exactly the same way as function parameters do in C++ and are found on the left-hand side of the node. This means that those pins are for data that you wish to pass into a function or node, whereas pins on the right are the resultant output of a function or node and are similar to output parameters or a return type in C++.

As you can see, the target pin has already been populated for us. Our **Context Sensitive** node search has provided us with a Set Text function that has already set our TextRender component to be the target. The small node titled hello world is our visual representation of the reference we have to the component. This reference can be found as a variable under the **MyBlueprint** panel. Select this small node and press the *Delete* key. You will notice that the Target pin is now empty, and in its place, the field has been populated with the word **self**. This means that when no input is specified for this pin, it will default to use a self-reference, that is, a reference to the blueprint you are working from.

On trying and compiling the blueprint by clicking on the **Compile** button in the **Toolbar** panel, you will see that there are two errors preventing successful compilation in the **Compiler Results** panel, which can be found at the bottom of the Blueprint window:

> ⊘ This blueprint (self) is not a TextRenderComponent, therefore ' 🔾 **Target** ' must have a connection.
> ⊘ The current value of the ' 🔾 <u>Value</u> ' pin is invalid. 'Value' must have an input wired into it ('by ref' params expect a valid input to operate on).
> ❗ [0076.18] Compile of Hello_Sphere_Blueprint failed. 2 Fatal Issue(s) 0 Warning(s) [in 216 ms]

Each time you compile a blueprint, you will receive a verbose report of any errors or warnings within your blueprint. You may double-click on these report lines to take you to the area of the Blueprint where the error occurs. The first error states that the default parameter of the Target input pin self, meaning a reference to the blueprint we are working from, is not of a compatible type with the function input pin. This makes sense as the Blueprint we are working from is not of type TextRender component. The second states that the value of the Value pin is invalid. This is because we have not specified any input value for this pin. The final line is a summary of the compilation, including compilation time in milliseconds.

Using Blueprint variables

The first thing we need to do is replace the `HelloWorld TextRender` component reference we deleted. To do this, we can click and drag the variable from the **MyBlueprint** panel into the graph, then select **Get** from the drop-down menu. You can then click and drag the pin on the right-hand side of the reference node and connect it with the `Target` input pin on the `Set Text` function node. While you have the `HelloWorld` reference pin dragged, you can see a small box underneath the marker. This will inform you of the action that will take place upon releasing the pin.

> When clicking and dragging variables from the **MyBlueprint** panel, you can hold *Ctrl* to spawn a `get` node or *Alt* to spawn a `set` node.

The next thing we need to do is populate our `Value` pin with the text value that we want to appear when a player moves within our `Sphere Collision Volume`. To do this, we need to summon our function search widget, you can do this by right-clicking on blank space within the graph. We need to search for a `Make Literal` function; these functions are utility functions that allow the creation of temporary variables during Blueprint execution. Specifically, we require a `MakeLiteralText` node. Select this option from the search window and type `Hello Player` in the `Value` box on the left-hand side. Then, connect the **Return Value** pin to the **Value** pin on the `Set Text` Node. Now, Compile! No errors or warnings should present and the compilation will be successful.

Now, we can run our project and see the fruits of our labor! After pressing the Play button in the main editor window we will possess a flying first person avatar, fly close to our hello sphere and you will see the text change!

Utilizing the Blueprint palette

We are nearly done with our Hello World Unreal project. There are still a few basic facets of Blueprint usage that have yet to be covered. We are going to extend the functionality of our `HelloSphere` so that it can say hello directly to the **object** that has entered its bounds. To do this, we will need to get the name of the object that has overlapped with the `HelloSphere`, prefix that name with `Hello` and convert the resultant string to a format the `Value` input pin will comply with. We should also change the text back to `hello world` when the object leaves the bounds of our sphere.

We will be finding our desired blueprint functionality in a different way than before: we will use the **Palette Panel**. To bring up the Palette panel, select **Window | Palette** from the drop-down menus located at the top of the screen underneath the tab banner. This will bring up the Palette panel on the right-hand side of the Blueprint window. This panel acts as a search directory for Blueprint library nodes. Nodes found in this panel will not be context sensitive, meaning you will have to populate all input pins yourself. At the top of the **Palette** panel, you can see any nodes that you have specified as a favorites. The bottom half is the search directory titled **Find a Node**. Here, you can specify a class you wish to search for within for the node, and a search bar where you can enter the keywords for your node search.

The first thing we need to do is ensure that our text will reset upon leaving the bounds of our sphere collision volume. To do so, we will need to utilize another event, similar to the `ActorBeginOverlap` there is an `ActorEndOverlap` node. We can find this by searching for it in our **Palette** or by right-clicking on graph. If you used the **Palette** to search for the function to create the node all you need to do is select the desired function from the list and click and drag it into the graph.

With our `ActorEndOverlap` node now in the graph, all we have to do is replicate the previous functionality we created for our `ActorBeginOverlap` event yet instead of using `Hello Player` as our literal value we can use `Hello World!`. You can copy paste blueprint nodes if you wish. All lines and associations will be preserved. I would advise you to keep copy pasting of nodes to a minimum. If you are finding yourself copy pasting functionality quite frequently, it is likely you would be able to wrap the functionality into a blueprint function.

Blueprint meta-data and string manipulation

Now, to create the functionality to print the name of the object that has overlapped our bounds, we are going to need to retrieve two more function nodes and adapt our `ActorBeginOverlap` functionality. Retrieve `GetObjectName` and `Append` now. We will use these two nodes to complete our functionality. As you can see, the `GetObjectName` node takes in an object reference (remember our Unreal Object Hierarchy), which is the base type of all Unreal Objects. This input pin is used to specify which object we wish to get the name from. This kind of information is known as meta-data and is usually present in large polymorphic inheritance chains.

We are going to drag the **Other Actor** pin from our `ActorBeginOverlap` node to this input pin. This will retrieve the name from our overlapping actor as a string. It is important to note that our collision functions `ActorBeginOverlap` and `ActorEndOverlap` all expect the colliding object to be of type **actor**, that is, because `UActor` is the base class from which all objects that can move or be physically present in a scene should inherit from and `UActor` inherits from `UObject` allowing us to make the conversion.

Now that we have our offending actor's name, we need to prefix the resultant string with `Hello` via our `Append` node. By default, our append node will have two input pins, **A** and **B**, in short the resultant string will be whatever value is plugged into **A** plus whatever value is plugged into **B**. For our purposes, we wish to plug our offending actor's name into **B** and leave **A** unconnected, but type `Hello` in the field box provided this will result in `Hello` **B**. Ensure `Hello` is followed by a space.

On the right-hand side of our `Append` node, we have an output pin for the resultant string. There is something else on this node; however, there is an **Add Pin +** button. This is because our `Append` node has an `expandable number of input pins`. By clicking this button, we will add a **C** input pin; do this now. We now have an extra input pin on the left-hand side of the node, the resultant string will now be *A+B+C*. Fill the provided text field for **C** with `!` to add some extra enthusiasm.

We are now going to plug the resultant string from this append node into the input pin provided by the `Make Literal Text` node. You will notice that `string` and `text` are two different types. With the `string` output pin, click and drag the mouse over the input pin for the `MakeLiteralText` node. You will see that the little box by the mouse that shows what will happened upon releasing the pin is not a green tick but a box stating **Convert String to Text**.

This means that upon releasing the left mouse button the Blueprint will create a **conversion node** that takes in a `string type` and outputs a `text type`. This is very similar to **conversion** in C++. However, conversions between types in Blueprint could be concealing more complicated functionality as some types may require additional steps to convert between. With this step complete, you should see something similar to this:

The node arrangement for the `ActorEndOverlap` event will appear as follows:

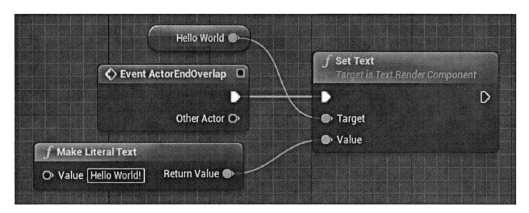

Now, run your project and encroach on our spherical friend you will see the text change to something along the lines of **Hello DefaultPawn_1!** Then upon leaving the spheres bounds, it will change back to `Hello World`! Well done, you have completed your first Blueprint! Now that we have created a `hello world` project and a `hello world` blueprint, I think it is time we sank our teeth into your first unreal game project Barrel Hopper! We will be expanding our Blueprint skillset and learning some new editor tricks. We can finally close our `hello world` project!

Creating the Barrel Hopper project!

We are going to create our Barrel Hopper project the same way we created our Hello World project. Load the UE4.11 clients and create a new project that is a **Blank Blueprint project** titled **Barrel Hopper**. For this project, we are going to need a few things. We are going to need a **Character** that can move around and jump, a camera that provides us a side on view, barrels that can spawn and will despawn the player when collided with, and a level for all of these elements to exist in.

Creating our Character

We are going to be creating our first UE Character. To construct our character, we will create a new Blueprint that inherits from the UE4 UCharacter class. UCharacters are designed to be possessed and controlled by various controllers while utilizing UE character movement and physics backend. As UCharacter is at the bottom of the UObject hierarchy, it is the most developed of the objects, inheriting all of the parent object's public or protected functionality. The relationship between UCharacters and the engine will be described in more detail in *Chapter 4, Unreal Engine, C++, and You*.

Before we create the character, we need to set up our file hierarchy in the **Content Browser** so that our assets are organized in a logical manner. To create folders simply *right-click* on the folder hierarchy on the left-hand side of the **Content Browser** panel and select **New Folder**. Create a folder now titled **Barrel_Hopper**, and within that folder, create one titled **Character**. Every time we make a new category of object, it is a good idea to add a folder in the content browser that will let you group assets together that are associated with that category of object. You should have a hierarchy that looks similar to this:

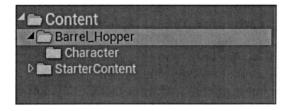

To create the character blueprint, select the newly created **character** folder and right-click within the large area in the center of the panel. This opens up a menu of objects that we could create within this folder as new content. Click on the **Blueprint** option now. This will open the blueprint creation wizard; from here, you can select which class you would like to inherit from to create the Blueprint. For our purposes, we wish to create a character so select the **Character** option. This will create a new blueprint within our `Character` folder, name this character `BH_Character`. If is not already, open this blueprint now.

As you can see our `BH_Character` blueprint is void of any functionality and only has a few components. The `Capsule` component will act as the root component and will be used as the **colliding volume** for the character. The `Arrow` component is an in editor tool that shows us which way our character's forward vector points while being placed in a scene. The `Mesh` component is used to visually represent our character; at the moment, we have no mesh specified so nothing is shown.

Finally, the last component present is the `CharacterMovement` component. This component is responsible for all character movement and the variables that dictate how the character will move through the 3D world. You will also note that all of these components are specified as inherited that is because these components exist in the `UCharacter` code created base class that our new `BH_Chracter` blueprint inherits from.

I would strongly suggest looking at the Details panel each time you encounter a new component so that you may better understand the workings of the component and how you can manipulate it for your needs. Do this now for the `CharacterMovement` component; we will be changing a few of these variables later. As you can see, we have the ability to set the walking speed of the character, how much gravity affects the character, and other movement based variables.

Bringing our character to life

Currently, we only have a shell for a character that we need to fill to fully realize our **Barrel Hopper Character**! The first thing we need to do is attain the assets that we require to visualize and later animate our character. To do this, we are going to transfer some of Unreal Engine's provided content to our blank project. While keeping our current project open, create another new blueprint project. This time we want to create a project from the **Side Scroller template**. We are going to be migrating their mannequin assets to our current content folder. To do this, we need to navigate to the folder we wish to migrate from the new `Side Scroller` project via the **Content Browser**.

In our case, we need to navigate to **Content | Mannequin**. Right-click on the **Mannequin** folder and choose the **migrate** option. This will prompt you to select the content folder you wish to migrate these assets too. Direct this path to the content folder of our Barrel Hopper project. Your content folder should be located at (Project Directory) \BarrelHopper\Content\.

> If you do not know where your content directory of Barrel Hopper is, you can right-click on any of the assets in the **Content** browser and select Show in Explorer. Then, copy and paste the path from the search bar at the top.

Once you have migrated the files, return to your original project to find that the migrated mannequin folder can be found within our content browser. Now, all we need to do is tidy up our content browser by moving around some of the assets. Under **Mannequin | Character**, there should be three folders **Materials**, **Mesh**, and **Textures**. Highlight these folders by shift clicking them, then click and drag the folders into our **Character** folder. You will be prompted to choose, **copy**, or **move** the folders; select the move option. We will be returning to our Mannequin folder to later retrieve the animation assets we require in *Chapter 3, Advanced Blueprint, Animation, and Sound*.

Giving our character a mesh

Now that we have the visual assets we require for our character, we can begin to construct our character blueprint. From within the Blueprint window for our BH_Character, select the Mesh component. In the **Details** panel, you will see a drop-down field for **Skeletal Mesh**. Using this drop-down field, select SK_Mannequin. You will see that, when the mesh is brought into our Character blueprint, the mesh sits too high within our capsule and is facing the wrong way.

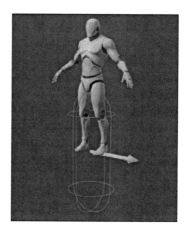

You will also notice that the capsule is just too small for our new mesh. We could scale the mesh so that it fits within the capsule, but that will not always work. Instead, you can change the width and height of the Capsule component so that it encompasses the character mesh vertically and is roughly 1.5x wider than the **chest** of the character. In this instance, we only want our colliding volume to encompass the core body of the character, we do not require rough collision on body extremities such as **arms**. To do this, select the capsule component and adjust the **Capsule Half Height** and **Capsule radius** variables found under the **Shape** section.

To fix the mesh displacement issue, select the Mesh component and use the transform widgets to bring the mesh down so that the heels of the feet are in line with the bottom of the capsule (~ -85cm on the z-axis) and rotate the mesh so that it is facing down the direction of the Arrow component. Your finished alignment should look something like this:

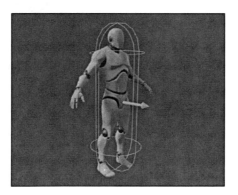

You can adjust the 'step' amount for rotations and translation using the transform widget via the numbered button next to the orange grid in the top right hand of the viewport. Clicking on the orange grid will disable snapping all together, and you will have free range of movement.

Creating the character's camera

We need to add a camera to our character blueprint, so we can have our viewport update with our character's movements. This requires two new components—a Camera component that will act as the main camera for our game scene, and a SpringArm component that will be used to position the camera appropriately in 3D space. Add these two components to the Blueprint now. Ensure that they are child components of the Capsule component as we wish their positions to update relative to the capsule component. Also ensure that the Camera component is a child of the SpringArm component, as we will be using the spring arm to position and rotate the camera.

With the `SpringArm` component selected, check the **Details Panel** for the property titled **Arm Length**, and set this to **550cm** now. As you can see, our camera is pushed back away from our character. We need to ensure our spring arm is positioned so that the camera will maintain a side on view as our character traverses the world. Pitching the camera up slightly as well will provide a better view of our level to the end user.

We can do this by setting variables in the **Transform** section of **Details** panel. Set the Y value (Pitch) of the transform **Rotation** property now to **-2.5 now**. Also, underneath arm length, there is a vector property titled **Socket offset**, set the Z component of this offset to be **75cm**. This will displace the camera upwards along the z-axis. You will see something similar to this:

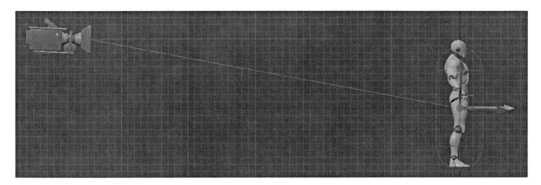

As you can see, from within the Blueprint Editor Viewport, our camera does not currently take a side on view of the Character. That is ok. In the world we are about to create, we need to ensure that the camera continues to look down the **x-axis** regardless of the character's current rotation. We will then limit the character's movement, so it can only move along the axis that is at right angles with the look direction of the camera. With both of these constraints in place, we will have a suitable side scrolling environment. To ensure that our camera does not rotate with our character, select the `SpringArm` component, within the **Details** panel for this component. Under the **Camera Settings** section, there are three checkboxes: **inherit yaw**, **inherit pitch**, and **inherit roll**. Uncheck all of these checkboxes and save the blueprint. We also need to ensure our character does not inherit its rotation from its owning controller. What controllers are and how to use them will be covered later in this book. For now, select **BH_Character(Self)** from the **Components** panel. Then within the **Details** panel, uncheck the property **Use Controller Rotation Yaw**; it can be found in the **Pawn** section.

Game modes and how to make them

Game Modes in Unreal Engine are a set of instructions that inform the engine which objects to use for things such as the **players default pawn** (default character to use), the **game rules**, and what state objects to use for processes such as **HUD**, **Player states**, and **Game states**. We will not only be creating custom game modes but also custom objects for each of the game mode classes. To create a game mode, simply open the blueprint wizard by right-clicking on the appropriate content browser folder and choose to create **Game Mode Blueprint**.

As we are creating a new category of objects, I would also advise creating a Game_ Mode folder in our content browser. Name this new game mode BH_GameMode and save it within the new Game_Mode folder. When you open the game mode blueprint, you will be presented with the standard Blueprint window. You will notice that this object does not have many components, only itself and a default scene root. This is because game modes will not be placed in the scene, they are simple objects that we will set as an engine parameter and do not require a physical form within a 3D scene.

By selecting the BH_GameMode(Self) component, you will see the **Details** panel houses and the aforementioned game mode classes. Under the **Classes** section, in the **Details** panel, you can see a field titled **Default Pawn Class**. Click on the drop-down field and select our BH_Character. This drop-down list will automatically populate with any objects that can be used as **Default Pawns**. We will eventually be setting most of these class references to our custom objects, but for now, everything else can remain as is. What we have just done is create a game mode that informs the engine that when a controllable player is spawned into a world to use our BH_Character object by default.

All we need to do now is set the game mode in the engine so that when we press the **Play** button our BH_Character is used instead of the free flying first person avatar. To do this, go to the **Edit** drop-down menu at the top left hand side of the **Editor** window; from this window, select **project settings**. This will bring up a **Project Settings** window. This is where you can set a multitude of options on both your current project and the engine itself.

On the left-hand side of the panel is a list of categories, one of which is **Maps & Modes**; choose this now. Here, you can set which Map to use, how Local multiplayer will be laid out, and the **Default Game Mode**. We are only concerned with the latter at this stage. Under the **Default Modes** section, you can see a **Default Game Mode** field, click the drop-down menu, and select our BH_GameMode.

Now, navigate back to the main level editor window and select the `Player Start` object within the scene. This will be where our player spawns. Rotate this Player Start object to 90 degrees on the z-axis. This will rotate the Player Start so that the arrow is pointing up the y-axis. Now, press play and you should see our new character standing side on to the camera!

Creating and receiving input events

Now that we can see our character in the game world, it is time to get him moving! We are going to create some input events via our project settings, then receive those events in our `BH_Character` Blueprint. Let's start by setting up some input axis mappings and input action mappings. These mappings simply bind an input, that is, a key press or mouse change, to an axis event or action event that we can receive in our objects. Axis mappings should be used when you wish to receive varying levels from an input, these are most commonly used for analogue inputs such as joysticks and mouse movements. Whereas action mappings should be used when you wish to input from something that has no variable movement, for example, a button or key press.

Creating the input Events

Sometimes, you may need to create action or axis mappings that receive input from multiple sources. You may need to create an axis mapping for aiming that can take in input from **both** the mouse and analog sticks. In our case, we will be creating an action mapping for jumping and an axis mapping for moving. Open the **Project Settings Window** again via **Edit | Project** settings. Address the list of categories on the left-hand side. This time select **Input**, which is under the **Engine** section. This will show the input settings for our current project.

You create mappings by clicking on the white plus (+) next to the desired mapping category. Press the white plus next to the **Action Mappings** field now:

You may need to click on the small arrow next to **Action Mappings** to expand the category. You should see a filed titled `NewActionMapping_0` rename this mapping to **Jump** now. Now, press the small arrow next to this field. We can now map an input to this mapping. This means, when we press the specified input, in our case it will be the *space bar*, an action event tilted `InputAction Jump` will trigger in Blueprints that has included the new mapping in its event graph.

Just underneath the mapping name is a small drop-down followed by four modifiers. Clicking this dropdown will open a search for inputs, in this search type **Space Bar** and select the corresponding input. The modifier checkboxes specify whether or not the modifier key must be pressed for the input to register. You should see something like this:

Now, we need to make an axis mapping for movement, just below the **Action Mappings** category is **Axis Mappings**. Again, click on the small plus on the right-hand side of this category; then, expand the field. Name this new mapping to **Move**. By default, only one input field is present. For movement, however, we need two; one for each direction of movement along a given axis, in our case left and right along the y-axis. Fortunately, as our game Barrel Hopper only has a movement on one plane due to its side scrolling nature, we only require input for horizontal movement. Thus, one axis mapping with two inputs. If we were dealing with a game with complete 3D movement, we would require two more mappings for each axis we would like to move along.

Press the small white plus sign, next to the **Move** mapping. This will provide another input field. This time our input fields are followed by a value called **scale**. This scale parameter is the value that will be parsed through the function when the input device is at full input (analog stick fully pressed in one direction). Despite our key presses having no range of variable output, we will still be using key presses for our input, we may at some point wish to provide controller support without having to create a new mapping, and then in turn not needing to edit all of our Blueprints! Set the first input to *A* and set the **scale** to **-1.0**, and set the second input to *D* and the **scale** to **1.0.** You should see something similar to this:

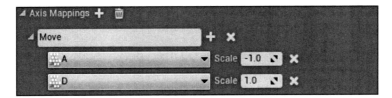

Receiving input events

All we need to do now is receive our newly created events in our character. Luckily, the `CharacterMovement` component largely handles the output from these events. Open the `BH_Character` blueprint and navigate to the event graph, use either the **Pallet** or the right-click on menu to find our newly created axis mapping `InputAxis Move` and our newly created action mapping `InputAction Jump`. You will find the axis mapping under **Input | AxisEvents** and the action mapping jump under **Input | ActionEvents**. Create both of these nodes now. As you can see our `InputAxis Move` node outputs a **float** axis value (this will exist between 1.0 and -1.0, thanks to our scale values in our `Move` mapping). We need to plug this floating point value into some meaningful function to get our character to move.

The function we can use is `AddMovementInput`, find this node now. This node takes in a **Target**, which is the `Pawn` to be moved, a **World Direction** to move in, a **Scale Value** to move by, and a **Force** Boolean we can tick to always force movement. Leave the **Target** pin as the default self-reference, connect the **Axis value** pin to the **Scale Value** input pin, and leave **Force** unchecked. For the **World Direction,** we are going to use the right vector of our `Camera` component! To do this, drag the reference to our `Camera` component into the graph, create a `get` node, click and drag from this node's output pin to bring up the context sensitive function search. Search for the `Get Right Vector` node. This will create a function node that outputs the right vector of the `Camera` component. Plug the output vector pin from this `Get Right Vector` node into the **World Direction** input pin of the `AddMovementInput` node.

Now, run the project! When you press *A* and *D* you should move left and right relative to the direction the camera is looking in! You will notice that our character does not currently turn to face the direction it is moving in. To fix this, check the checkbox titled **Orient Rotation to Movement** in the `Character Movement` component's details panel.

Jumping is even easier, return to the `BH_Character` Blueprint. If you have not already created the `InputAction Jump` node, do it now. Action mappings will fire a pressed event when the input is pressed and then will fire a release event when the same input is **released**. Drag from the pressed pin of our `InputAction Jump` node and from the context sensitive search find the function node `Jump`. Do the same from the released pin, but instead find the function node `Stop Jumping`. These functions will inform the Character Movement component when it should initiate a jump action and if it should stop the jump action early; in games, this can be used to create jump actions that jump higher if the input is held down. Your current Blueprint layout should look something like this:

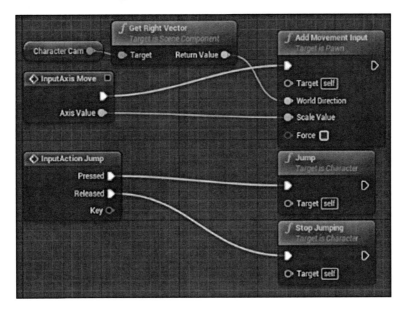

Tweaking the character movement component

You will notice that, if you jump with your character now, there is no air control at all. You may have also noticed that the character turns fairly slowly, these are small but very significant factors that can affect the general feel of your game. Most of the time these slight changes are influenced by a single movement property.

Thankfully, our Character Movement component has all of our movement properties grouped in a similar place. This is where the **Details** panel for the Character Movement Component comes into play. Each section of this **Details** panel is responsible for a different area of 3D movement. The first two we are concerned with are **Character Movement (General Settings)** and **Character Movement: Jumping / Falling**. It is within these sections that you will find the parameters that drive specific parts of character movement such as turn rate, fall speed, air movement, and gravity influence.

To give our character a better movement feel, we are going to change some of these variables. The first one we are going to modify is the **Gravity Scale**. One of the best ways to prevent a character from feeling floaty in a game world is to increase the jump and fall speed of the character. Change the **gravity scale** to **2.0**; it can be found under the **General Settings** section of the Character Movement component **Details** panel. This will make our character accelerate downwards faster when falling.

Under the same section you will find **Rotation Rate**; change the yaw of Rotation rate to **720**. This will make our player rotate much faster when moving from left to right. **Orient Rotation to Movement** is already checked, so we can leave that property alone. Under the **Jumping / Falling** section of the **Details Panel** change the **Jump Z velocity** to **1000.0**, the air control parameter to **0.8** and we will be done! You can tweak these parameters later to change how your character moves through 3D space later if you wish. For now each section should look similar to this:

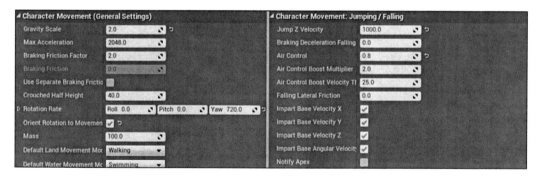

Now, run the project again and test how those small changes have modified the feel of moving our character. In the next section of this chapter, we will be creating the game world within which we will be moving around. Feel free to tweak these values once the level has been created to adjust the movement to your liking.

You can tell when a variable has been changed from its default value when there is a small yellow undo arrow on the right-hand side of the variable field

Building the level!

UE provides a very in-depth and multi-use editor. From this editor, developers are able to create amazing and high-detail levels, the combination of editor tools present in UE4 creates a developer environment where the most limiting factor is the imagination! For the scope of this chapter, we will be using a limited tool set of the editor to act as an introduction to building levels with UE4. Each of the game projects you will create during the course of this book will require a new approach to building levels. This chapter will teach you the fundamentals of level creation and manipulation while teaching you some tricks to make position world geometry a breeze. We are going to take the default level arrangement from this:

To a more realized gameplay level, like this:

For this process, we are going to be creating a new level. To do this navigate to **File | New Level** and select the option default. Save this level as `Barrel_Hopper_Map`.

Camera tips and tricks

It's time for us to learn about the various camera and viewport tricks that we can use when working with levels to make creating interesting world environments that is much easier.

Camera settings

There is nothing worse than spending hours placing objects in a 3D scene, only to find that once the camera has moved, everything is out of alignment! It is important to constantly check how the world geometry appears from multiple angles, as you are positioning your assets in a scene. This is particularly important when placing blocking volumes that prevent players from accessing areas of your map you do not wish them too.

In the top left-hand corner of any viewport are a series of view buttons. They look like this:

Clicking on the downward arrow opens up a drop-down menu that has a large selection of settings that you can apply to your viewport camera. Here, you can set things such as **Field of View** and **Far View Plane**, if you would like to have runtime statistics like Frames per Second displayed and many more camera-specific options. Most of these options will be explored over the course of the book.

One of the most important buttons on this bar is the one that currently says **Perspective**. It is this button that allows you to swap between camera perspective types, with the default being 3D perspective view. The other options for this button are the available orthographic views. What this means is that these view modes allow you to change how your world is viewed through the Editor window. If you select the **Front** option, it will change the camera from a perspective camera affected by **FOV** to an **orthographic** camera that looks in the opposite direction of the world's x-axis. This is very important to a level designer, as you are able to view the layout of your game world without a FOV bias from multiple angles.

The button titled **Lit** allows you to specify the rendering mode through which you would like to view your world. Do you want to see the level unaffected by postprocessing? Do you want to see your level unaffected by lights? All of these options are here. It is important to use these options to remove **visual clutter** when dealing with levels that are heavily affected by post-processing and visual effects.

The final option allows you to specify which objects you would like to see in your viewport. If you want to view your entire world without any of your currently placed static meshes or BSP volumes, you can specify this here. It is also through this option that you can specify specific post-processing effects that you wish to view your world with.

Controlling the camera

On top of the basic camera controls there are a couple more advanced methods of camera manipulation. One of the control techniques covered in the tutorial that you saw when you opened Unreal for the first time was focusing. Pressing *F* will move the camera, so the currently selected object is front and center in the screen. There are some object-specific camera controls that expand this concept. You can press and hold *ALT* while pressing the left-mouse button to orbit the focused object; if you do the same thing while pressing the right-mouse button, you are able to dolly in and out from the object. You may also pan the camera up, right, left, and down by holding the middle mouse button.

For a complete list of in editor controls address `https://docs.unrealengine.com/latest/INT/Engine/UI/LevelEditor/Viewports/ViewportControls/index.html`.

Creating the level

At the moment, our newly created map has a **Player Start**, a **Sky sphere**, a **light source**, some **atmospheric fog** and a **floor**. We are going to change this level to match something similar to the preceding image. Through this process, we are going to learn some level construction tips, what **BSP geometry is**, and how we can use them, as well as how we can apply and modify **materials**. In the game **Barrel Hopper**, we will be getting the player to scale sloping ramps to reach the top of a level while trying to jump over barrels that are rolling down the ramps. We need to construct a level that accommodates these gameplay requirements.

Blocking geometry

The first thing we are going to do is roughly place our level geometry that we will later be replacing with static mesh actors; this is called **blocking**, and we are going to do this using **Geometry Brushes**. This process allows us to estimate the level geometry without having to create custom mesh assets in a third party tool such as Maya or 3DsMax. Fortunately, the Geometry Brush that we are going to use to **block** our level can be converted to static mesh actors, so we will be able to create our entire level using UE 4.

To ensure our World Outlier remains tidy and organized before we begin create a folder structure, we can group similar objects in our 3D world. Do this by clicking the small + folder button in the top right-hand corner of the **World Outliner** panel. Create three folders now, **Lights**, **Geometry Brushes**, and **Visuals**. Match the folder structure show here:

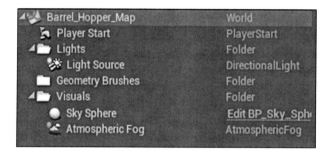

Whenever we create a new **Geometry Brush** ensure that it is categorized under the similarly named folder in the **World Outlier**. Now what we need to do is select the static mesh actor titled **Floor** and delete it. We are going to be creating all of our level geometry from scratch.

Geometry Brushes and how to use them

We are going to use **Geometry Brushes** to block our scene. These brushes are used by UE 4 to add geometry to a scene that has prebuilt behavior like collision, tessellation, and material tiling. They can be used by developers to effectively block a 3D scene then be converted to static mesh assets for later optimization of the 3D scene. The reasons this is beneficial to developers is the huge amount of time saving this process can afford the level designers. It also eliminates a major development hold up the level designer can continue to create without having to wait for assets from the 3D modelers.

From the **Modes** panel on the left-hand side of the Editor window, ensure that the place mode is active and navigate to the **BSP** section. Here, you can see a list of basic primitive types such as **Box**, **Cone**, **Cylinder**, and so on. From this list, click and drag the **Box** option into the 3D scene. Congratulations, you just created your first **Geometry Brush**! As you can see, it is currently called **Box Brush** in the world outlier. Change this now to **Floor Brush**.

Currently with the brush selected, you should see a Details Panel that contains a **Transform** section, a **Brush Settings** section, and an **Actor** section. If you see something different, but you can see that the brush object is obviously highlighted, it means that you have selected a single face on the brush. I will come back to this later. If this is the case, deselect the brush and then select the brush again by clicking on it once.

The section that we are most concerned with is the **Brush Settings** section. It is here that we can change the **proportions** of the brush.

It is important to use the **Brush Settings** section to modify the proportions of the brush as opposed to using the scale of the object through the transform properties. The reason being that when we change proportions using **Brush Settings**, the way a material will appear on the surface of the brush will be preserved. If we were to use the scaling tools, we would have to adjust the UV's of the brush. A UV is simply how we choose a specific pixel from a texture when it is mapped to a surface. When a surface is scaled, the UV's are stretched resulting in the texture stretching as well.

Placing the geometry

For now, we can ignore the other settings. The first thing we need to do is ensure our floor brush is centered in our world at the 3D co-ordinates of 0, 0, 0; we will call this **origin**. We then need to proportion our brush, so we can use it as the floor in our 3D world.

We can do this by changing the **Brush Settings**. Change the **X** value of the brush to **5000cm**, the **Y** value to **5000cm**, and the **Z** value to **25cm**. Next, we need to position the brush. Change **Transform Settings** so that all numbers along the **Location** row are **0**. This will shift our floor to **origin**. Now, because our brush is now 25 units in height, we should adjust the location of the brush so the top side of the brush is flush with the zero plane. To do this, simply change the **Z** value of the location row in the **Transform Settings** to **-12.5cm**. You should now be presented with something similar to this:

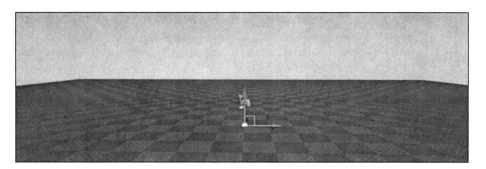

Converting a geometry Brush to a static mesh

The next thing we should do is place a **Brush** in our scene that we can use to represent the size and scale of our character, so we have a persistent visual reference for when we construct our level. To do this drag another **Box Brush** into the scene. This time proportion the brush using the Brush setting to the following — **X 100cm**, **Y 100cm**, and **Z 200cm**. We are using these dimensions as that is roughly the bounds within which our character occupies. Now, we are going to make this box a static mesh actor and place it in the scene. This will create a mesh object that the character will be able to pass through and our camera will not collide with. To do this, select the brush and under the **Brush Settings** section click on the white drop-down arrow at the bottom of the section to expand the option list. You will be presented with these options:

Press the **Create Static Mesh** option now and save the resultant mesh under the `Barrel_Hopper` folder. You will notice that our Brush has been replaced with a `static mesh`! We will use this mesh as an *approximation volume* when building the rest of the level. Now is a good time to update our folder hierarchy in our Content browser, as it currently contains a `Mesh` and a `Level` with no containing folder. Add two new folders to our content browser: **Levels** and `Static_Meshes`. Place the new mesh under the `Static_Meshes` folder and place our new `Barrel_Hopper_Level` in the **Levels** folder. Create a similar `Static_Meshes` folder in the **world outlier** and place the new mesh under this folder. From this point forward, I will leave organizing your **content browser** and **world outlier** up to you for the sake of brevity.

Now, we need to create the walls and the ramps the barrels are going to roll down. Let's start by creating the walls. Drag a new **Box Brush** into the world. This time proportion this Brush using the brush settings with **5000cm** on the **X**, **25cm** on the **Y**, and **5000cm** on the **Z**. Then, you can place the brush using the location settings at: **X 0cm**, **Y -1100cm**, and **Z 2500cm**.

Applying materials to geometry brushes

We can then duplicate this brush and use it for our other wall; but before we do that, we want to apply a material to our brush. Now, we need to select a face of the brush, do this by holding *Ctrl* and *Shift* then clicking on a face of the brush. This will present you with a new section list in the Details panel that has properties specific to single face of the brush.

We need to ensure that we select all faces of the brush before applying the material, so it is applied to all faces. Do this by clicking on the select dropdown under the **Geometry** section and then by clicking **Select all adjacent faces**. This will select all faces of the currently selected brush. With all of the faces selected, click the dropdown under the **Surface Materials** section and find and select **M_Brick_Clay_ Beveled**. The entire brush should now appear to be made of beveled clay bricks!

To **duplicate** our wall brush we can do one of two things, we can copy paste the element via our **world outlier** or we can hold *Alt* while transforming the brush using the in-viewport transform widget. Do this now by holding *Alt* and translating the wall brush along the y-axis using the green arrow of the translation transform widget. You will notice that the original brush remains in place and you have instead dragged a duplicate of the brush off the original. Position this brush at **X 0cm, Y 1100cm**, and **Z 2500cm** using the **Transform** settings of the new brush now. While you are at it, you should also apply the `M_Brick_Clay_Beveled` material to the floor brush now as well!

 If you ever want to have an object you are trying to move snap to an underlying surface, press the *End* key.

With both of our walls in place, the **light** from our **light source** is being obstructed and our world is beginning to look quite dark. To remedy this, we need to place a **Skylight** in the scene. A Skylight is an object that captures the color of your world outside a distance threshold from the Skylight's position and applies that as a uniform light within the scene. As we have a skybox with a light blue ambient color, the Skylight will provide a light to the scene that matches this color. Click on and drag a **Skylight** into the scene from the **Modes Panel** in the **Place Tab** under the **Lights** section. You should now see something that looks like this:

Level building and trigonometry!

We are starting to form the basic bounds of our level! You may have notice that we are starting to cut off large chunks of our **brush geometry** from the player; we will deal with this later. For now, we need to construct our **ramps**! This will require yet another **Box Brush**. Drag a new **Box Brush** into the scene. We want this brush to be roughly three-fourth of the length between our two walls, so there is a 550 cm space between the edge of the ramp and the wall. This will ensure that our barrels can fall through the gap, and our player can jump up to the next ramp. We also want our ramp to be sloped so that our barrels will roll down towards the climbing player. Let's use 15 degrees.

We can use some basic **trigonometry** to figure the length of our ramp. If the ramp is sloped at an angle of 15 degrees and our adjacent side length is *1650 (3/4 of 2,200)*. Then, the length of our ramp is roughly 1708 as *1650/cos(15) = 1708*. We can increase this to 1800 so that we have some leeway for our player, and so the ramps are easier to place in our level.

With our new length of ramp, we can angle and place this ramp. Using the **transform settings**, place our first ramp at: **X 0, Y -240,** and **Z 200**. Make sure that the rotation of the ramp is set to **15** in the **Roll** value (the first column). From here, all we need to do is **duplicate** the ramp, **raise** it by an amount, and **inverse** the Y position and the Roll angel. The separation for each ramp that I used is 655. I based this number off of the height if the character block out mesh we made earlier, which is 200 units and accounted for the total height of the ramp being 442 (also calculated using basic trig, this time 1650 * Tan(15)). This number was then rounded to 655.

Before duplicating the ramp brushes, ensure that you apply M_Brick_Clay_Beveled to all of the brush faces. Now, select the first ramp brush, duplicate it, and then transform the brush by 655 units on the z-axis. Now, you need to flip the rotation of the ramp and position it correctly along the y-axis. As our ramps will alternate symmetrically, you can simply inverse the Y value of the location transform and the Roll value of the Rotation Transform. Your second Ramps Transform matrix should look like this:

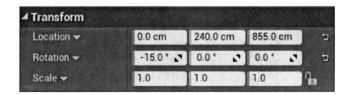

Repeat this process until you have six ramps and can see something similar to this:

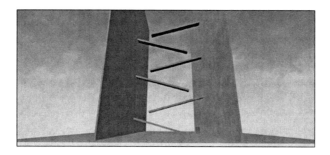

We are nearly done with blocking our level! All we need to do now is close off our play area with a roof and a back wall! This is very easily done as we can use a duplicate of our floor brush as the roof, and we can use a duplicate of one of the wall brushes as the back wall. Set the floor brush duplicates position to $-$**X 0, Y 0,** and **Z 4360**. Yaw the wall brush duplicate by 90 and set its position at $-$**X 950, Y 0,** and **Z 2500**. You should now have something that looks very similar to this:

We are done on blocking your level! If you aren't happy with the way your level is lit, try adjusting the **Light source** directional light to your liking. If you find that all of the shadows in your level have the word preview repeated through them; it means you need to rebuild your lighting. To do so, click on the drop-down arrow in the **Build** icon under the **Toolbar** panel and select **Build Lighting Only**:

Now that we have blocked our level, we can add the other assets to our scene so we can start to form the gameplay of Barrel Hopper!

Getting our barrels rolling

With our level **blocked** out we can begin to place our **Gameplay-centric** actors into the level and add the appropriate functionality to them. In this case, we will be creating the **barrels**. We are going to need to create a barrel object that rolls with physics, destroys the player when the two collide and destroys itself when it reaches the bottom of the level. We are also going to have to create an object that handles spawning these barrels at certain intervals.

The first thing we need to do is create a new blueprint that inherits from Actor called **BH_Barrel**. It is going to be a physics-driven actor that will be one of the key elements in the game world, so create this new blueprint now. BH_Barrel will start with the same default components we are used to seeing when working with a new actor. We need to add a visual component to our BH_Barrel. Add a **Cylinder shape** via the **Add Component** button now. The **Cylinder** will be used as our Barrel Mesh. Let's make an attempt to have our grey scale cylinder look a bit more like a barrel by applying the M_Wood_Floor_Walnut_Worn material to the mesh. You can do this by selecting the Cylinder component and modifying **Element 0** under the **materials** section in the **Details Panel**. Also, rotate the Cylinder component around the y-axis by 90 degrees so lays on its side. You should be presented with something similar to this:

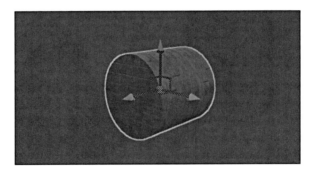

Applying physics to objects

Adding **physics dynamics** to an object in UE 4 is actually quite simple given a basic 3D shape. In the case of our Barrel, we already have the perfect shape, a cylinder! What we are going to do is enable physics simulations on our `Cylinder` component. We can do this by selecting the component and navigating to the **Physics** section of the **Details** panel. At the top of the section is a checkbox titled **Simulate Physics**, tick this now. Bam! You have applied physics dynamics to this object! The UE physics layer will now handle all interactions between this object and other physical objects in a 3D scene given the right collision settings.

There are a few more steps we need to take before we are ready to spawn our `BH_Barrels` in the game world. We also need to **constrain** our barrel so that is does not move in an undesirable way. Because we are creating a **side scroller**, we only want freedom of movement on a certain plane. In our case, it is the **YZ plane.** The axis along which the character can move (x-axis and z-axis) are also the only axis we wish our physics bodies to have freedom of movement along. To constrain our body in this way, expand the **Constraints** field under the **Physics** section of the **Details** panel and select **YZPlane** from the drop-down list titled mode. The Physics section of the Cylinder's Details panel should appear as follows:

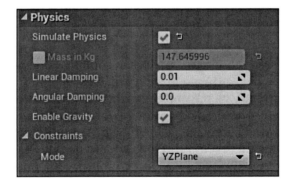

Barrel spawners and Blueprint timers

Now, we need to create the object that will **spawn** the `BH_Barrels`, so they can roll down the ramps and act as hazards to the player trying to reach the top of the level. This will be a simple object that only consists of the default components. However, we will be utilizing a new **event** in the graph of this blueprint. We will be using **Event Tick** to set up a timer so that this object spawns a new barrel whenever a certain threshold of time is reached.

Creating Blueprint variables

Create a new Blueprint that inherits from `Actor` now, and call it **BH_Barrel_Spawner**. We are not going to add any new components to this object, so you can immediately navigate to the **Event Graph**. To set up our timer, we are going to create two new **variables** of type `float`. To create these variables, click on the small white plus next to **Variables** in the **My Blueprint** panel. By default, the Blueprint will create new variables of type `boolean`. Click on the white plus twice now and call the first variable `barrelTimer` and the second `timeSinceLastBarrel`. We need to change the type of these variables to be `float`. We can do this by selecting the variables within the **My Blueprint** panel under the **Variables** section and addressing the **Details** panel. The **Variable Type** property can be changed via the provided dropdown. Change the type of both of these variables to `Float` now, which is denoted by a green bar symbol in the dropdown.

From this details panel, we are also able to modify the various properties of the variable. You will note that we are able to set the **Default Value** of this variable. The value we provide here will be the value that is used upon object creation. This means we can specify a time in seconds that we wish to use as the rate at which barrels will spawn. For now, set the default value to **3.0**. Create another float variable now and name it `timeSinceLastBarrel` and set the **Default Value** to `0`.

Event tick

Now, we are going to use those two variables in combination with **Event Tick** to create our timer. The `Event Tick` node is provided by default in the event graph; however, it should currently be translucent as there is no functionality being extended from the node. The `Event tick` node outputs a `float` variable called **Delta Seconds**. This variable represents the time in seconds since the last frame, meaning that every time this event is hit it provides you with the change in time in seconds since the **last** time the event was hit. We can accumulate the value of this variable over time to gauge how much time in seconds has passed in total. What we are going to do is accumulate delta seconds into the variable `timeSinceLastBarrel`; then, when the value saved within is larger than our `barrelTimer` value, we will spawn a `BH_Barrel`.

The first thing you need to do is add **Delta Seconds** to `timeSinceLastBarrel` and then save the result back into `timeSinceLastBarrel`. You can do this by creating a `get` reference to `timeSinceLastBarrel`, then dragging a line off of the output pin from the reference, and then search for **float + float**. This will give you a + node with two green inputs and one green output. By default, one of the input pins is populated by `timeSinceLastBarrel`. Plug **Delta Seconds** into the other input pin. From the output pin, click on and drag off another line, and this time, search for **Set Time Since Last Barrel** and parse in the result of the + node.

Now, we need to check if our accumulated value is larger than our timer value. To do this, drag from the output pin of the Set node we just created and summon the **float > float** node. This node features two float input values, the top input will be compared against the bottom, that is, **is top > bottom**. This node will output a Boolean variable that will be the result of this condition. What we need to do is plug this value into a branch node. Before we go into branch nodes, lets quickly check your Blueprint is coming along in the right direction. At the moment, you should see something similar to this:

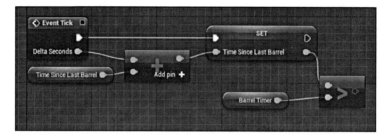

Branch nodes

Branch nodes act in a very similar way to `if` statements in C++. Drag off from the output pin of the > node and search for **Branch**. This will present you with a new type of node. This is a **logical node** and can affect the **critical execution path**. As you can see, it takes in a Boolean input as well as the execution path but outputs two execution path options. One for when the input pin has a value of `true`, and another when the input value is `false`. From the true execution path option, drag out a line and search for Spawn Actor From Class. This node will spawn our `BH_Barrel`. The node itself takes in a few inputs they represent the following:

- **Class**: The type of object you wish to spawn. Set this to `BH_Barrel` now.

- **Spawn Transform**: The transform we wish the object to have upon spawning. Summon a node called `GetActorTransform` and plug the orange output pin into this input.

- **Collision Handling Override**: This is an `enum` that represents how the object will handle collision if it is spawned inside another object. Leave this as default.

- **Instigator**: A reference to a pawn that is responsible for damage caused by the spawned actor. Leave this one blank.

Finally, drag another execution line from this node and then set our `timeSinceLastBarrel` variable back to zero via a set node. Your second half of the graph layout should look similar to this:

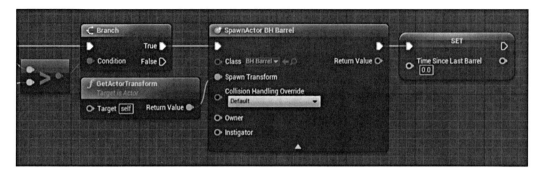

Now, let's drag `BH_Barrel_Spawner` into our level and see if they work! Return to the Editor window and place one spawner about 450 units above where each ramp meets a wall. With all of the spawners in place, press the **Play** button in the **Toolbar** panel then immediately press the Eject option that appears. This will let you fly around your level mid-simulation without being constrained to the **Default Player Pawn**. You should be able to see a legion of barrels being spawned every 3.0 seconds! You will also notice a very immediate problem. There is nothing that can get rid of our barrels, so they just keep building up!

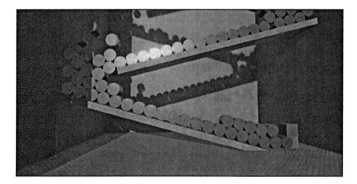

Trigger volumes and destroying Actors

What we need to do is place some trigger volumes in the scene that will destroy any barrel that enters its bounds. A trigger volume is an area in 3D space that will fire an event if any actor overlaps the 3D volume. We will be creating volumes that are cuboid in shape. From the **Place** tab of the **Modes** panel, navigate to the **Basic** section. From here, you will see an object called **Box Trigger**, click on and drag a box trigger into the scene now. Call this new trigger **BH_BarrelKiller**.

Then, click on the **Blueprint/Add script** button. This will create a new Blueprint titled BH_BarrelKiller_Blueprint. Again, we are not going to be adding any components to this new blueprint. We are only going to be extending functionality from the Event ActorBeginOverlap node.

What we need to do is check if the actor that has just overlapped our new trigger volume is of type BH_Barrel. If it has, we need to destroy the actor! Doing this is easy. Drag a line from the **Other Actor** output pin featured on the ActorBeginOverlap node and search for a function titled GetClass. This node has an output pin that is the class type of the object that is parsed into the node. We can use this class type output pin to determine if the object is of type BH_Barrel.

Drag a line from this class output pin and search for *Equal (Class) or type = for short*. This will spawn a class comparison node that will check if the top class input is equal to the bottom class input. By default, the top input pin will be populated with the class pin we just dragged from; the bottom pin we will not connect. Simply select BH_Barrel from the provided drop-down list. The comparison node will have a Boolean output pin that will represent the result of the comparison; if the comparison was resolved to be true, we want to destroy the overlapping actor.

We will do what we did in our timer and create a branch node from this Boolean output. From the true execution path, search for a node called DestroyActor. This node takes in an actor to destroy. For this input pin, we will drag the Other Actor reference from the Event ActorBeginOverlap node. Instead of dragging this pin directly, we are going to keep our graph tidy by utilizing something called a **reroute node**. It is simply something we can use to steer the paths of our graph lines. After dragging from the output pin of the ActorBeginOverlap node type reroute and select the **Add Reroute node...** option. Use these reroute nodes to create a clean path from the Event node to the final Destroy Actor function node. I create a path that looked like this:

You will notice that you can have multiple lines from an output pin. This is because this reference can be accessed by multiple things along the execution path.

> If you want to remove all lines from a pin in one go simply hold *Alt* then click on the pin you would like to remove lines from. Similarly, if you want to shift multiple lines to a different reference, hold *Ctrl* and then click and drag from the pin.

Debugging our Blueprints

Much like C++ code, UE allows us to debug our Blueprints. This is a very useful tool that Unreal has provided for us. Let's take our BH_BarrelKiller_Blueprint as an example. We have just created a node cluster that performs functionality based on a logical check. If we were developing in C++ code and our desired functionality was not taking place, we would place breakpoints throughout the areas of code we wish to investigate, so we can closer inspect our game state at runtime. We can perform the same debugging functionality with Blueprints. We have scripted some blueprint functionality that should only destroy actors when they are of type BH_Barrel. So, let's place a breakpoint on our Destroy Actor function node by right-clicking on the node and selecting **Add breakpoint**. Nodes with breakpoints can be denoted by a small red circle in the top left-hand corner of the node.

Now place an instance of our BH_BarrelKiller at the base of our first ramp and run the project! Eventually our breakpoint will be hit and you will be presented with something that looks like this:

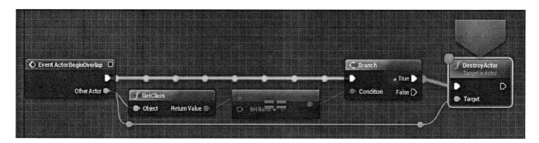

The giant red arrow denotes the node on which the breakpoint was hit. You will also notice that the execution path has been highlighted and features a series of nodules translating toward the node. This is used to show you which execution path is currently being taken! This is very important when working with blueprints as the number of execution paths that stem from one event can become quite numerous; this highlight shows you exactly what order your node set was executed in.

Another useful tool that is provided to us is the preservation of runtime debug values. In other words, the variable states and temporary variable states are preserved when a breakpoint is hit, and you can inspect each value to see if the correct values have been stored. Given our current breakpoint, we are interested in two variables. The first being the type that was returned from the Get Class function, and second being the Boolean result of our comparison node. If you hover your mouse over the purple class input pin on our comparison node, you will see runtime debug information about that value. As shown here:

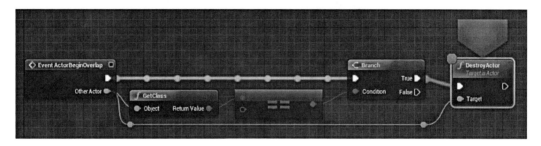

As you can see, the value is currently set to BH_Barrel.BH_Barrel_C, which means the class type is of our BH_Barrel Blueprint, which is exactly what we are looking for. You can also see the result of our comparison node by hovering over the input pin on our branch node. You will see that it has been set to true, which is why our true execution path from the branch node has been hit.

The final debugging tool that will be covered this chapter is the **Debug Filter**, which can be found in the **Toolbar** panel at the top of the Blueprint window next to the **Play** button. This filter allows you to isolate one Blueprint object you wish to test for debugging. Perhaps, only one of your Blueprint instances is not working. If you know the name of the object in the world outlier, you can specify the name here and you will only receive debugging output relevant to the specified object, this includes breakpoints!

Masking our destruction with particles

With our new trigger volume created, place one BH_BarrelKiller_Blueprint at the end of each ramp so that the volume is floating in mid-air but is touching the edge of the ramp as seen here:

Now, run the project again and watch as our barrels destroy themselves when they reach the end of each ramp! Right now, it is quite jarring to have the barrels simply disappear when they are removed. We can fix this with a simple particle effect played upon the destruction of the barrel. Open the **BH_Barrel** blueprint again. We are going utilize a new event node called Event Destroyed. Navigate to the event graph and search for this new event node. The event will be triggered every time an actor of this type is destroyed. Thankfully, the DestroyActor function we are using in our **BarrelKiller** object will trigger this event!

Drag a line from the execution arrow and search for a function node called **Spawn Emitter at location**. This node takes in an emitter template to spawn, a location to spawn the emitter at, a rotation to spawn the emitter with, and a Boolean titled **auto destroy**. The last parameter means the emitter will destroy itself upon completing the particle simulation. Set **Emitter Template** to **P_explosion** via the provided drop-down menu.

Setting the location is going to be tricky as our Mesh does not have a world location. If we were to use the location of our DefaultSceenRoot component, it would play the particle effect at the Barrels original spawn location. What we can do is attach a scene component as a child of our cylinder mesh! Remember the object hierarchy we covered in *Chapter 1, Introduction to Unreal Engine 4*? If the new scene component is a child of the Cylinder mesh, it will translate with the Mesh as it rolls down the ramp! Create a new scene component via the **Add component** button and call it **Barrel_Scene** now. Then drag this new component onto the Cylinder mesh component in the **components** panel to child it to the Cylinder component.

Now returning to our event graph, the value we are going to plug into the **Location** input pin of the `Spawn Emitter` node is the **world location** of our new `Barrel Scene` component. Drag a get reference to this new component from the **variables** section of the **My Blueprint** panel. Drag a line from the reference output pin and search for the `GetWorldLocation` function node. This will output a world vector you can use as valid input for the **Location** input pin. We can leave the rotation values as the default provided, but ensure that auto destroy is checked; otherwise, our spawned emitters will never destroy themselves, and we will have a similar issue to the one we were having with our never ending barrels!

After the Spawn Emitter at Location node, drag the output pin of this node **Return Value**, which is a reference to the newly spawned emitter and search for a function titled **Set Active**. This will ensue that the emitter is set to activate upon spawn if it is not already specified by the emitter by default. Here, there is two Boolean input pins titled **New Active** and **Reset**. Check both of these. You should be presented with something similar to this:

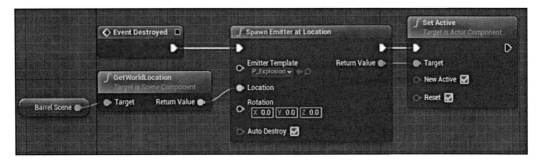

Run the project again, and you will see explosions where there was once nothing! It is quite enjoyable to watch the barrel detonate at the end of the ramps. The next thing we need to do to complete basic gameplay required for Barrel Hopper is kill the player!

Respawning the player

One of the key elements of `BarrelHopper` is punishing the player for unsuccessfully jumping over a barrel. What we need to do is reset the player to the default starting position every time it is hit a by a barrel. The goal is for the player to reach the top of the level in the shortest amount of time possible. In this chapter, we are going to create a rudimentary respawn system that utilizes Event **Delegate**. What we want to do is have our game mode respawn our player after a certain amount of time when the `OnDestroyed` event is fired from within our `BH_Character`. We are going to have to detect collisions with our barrels, destroy our actor, and then ensure that the desired respawning functionality takes place. We will do this via a delegate.

To begin, open the BH_Gamemode blueprint we created earlier in the chapter and navigate to the event graph. We need to graph some functionality that will get the Player Character reference, cast the Player Character to the BH_Character type, and then **bind** the OnDestroyed event of the BH_Character to a custom event in the game mode. Next, right-click on the event graph and type **Add Custom Event**. This will create a new event node in the graph, rename this node to **Character_Respawn** now. You will notice that on the top right-hand of the event node is a little red square. We will come back to this later.

Next, drag an execution line from the Event BeginPlay node that is present by default in the event graph; then, search for the function **Cast To BH_Character**. This function will attempt to cast from any provided object to our BH_Character. The node has one input pin for the object you wish to cast from, and one output pin for the resultant BH_Character reference. You will notice that the node has two execution path pins: One for a successful cast and another for a failed cast. Before we go any further, we need to provide this cast with a target. Right-click on the graph and search for the node **GetPlayerCharacter**. This node takes in a player ID (0 by default) and outputs a reference to a character object. Plug this output reference into the cast node. This cast will be successful as our BH_Character inherits from character.

Drag a line from the output reference of our cast node and search for the **Bind Event to OnDestroyed** node. This will provide you with a node that has an execution path input pin, a reference to the target input pin, and a small red square input pin called **Event**. Remember the similar looking small red square on our custom event Character_Respawn we made earlier? We are going to join these pins together, thus, binding them. Now, whenever OnDestroyed is hit in our BH_Character, Character_Respawn will also be hit in our game mode. You graph should look similar to something like this:

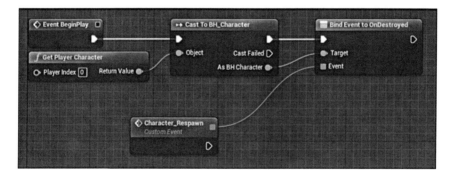

This kind of binding is known as a delegate. `Character_Respawn` is now a delegate of the `OnDestroyed` event. Simply put, delegates are triggered for execution when the owning function or event is triggered. We are able to bind multiple delegates to a single event if we wish. This means we can have different objects execute functionality based off of one event.

Delay nodes

Now, we need to create some functionality for this newly bound event to execute. Let's start by creating a **delay** node. It is used to stall execution along an execution path for a given period of time. To create one, simply right-click on the event graph and search for **Delay**. Connect the execution pin from our `Character_Respawn` event to that of the `Delay` node. Then under the **duration** value input **1.5** as we wish for the player have a respawn timer of **1.5** seconds. The next thing we need to do is spawn a new character. To do this create a **SpawnActor From Class** node; this time specify the class type to be `BH_Character`.

Now, we have encountered our first problem, how are we going to specify which transform to use for our player start? Easy, we can set it to the initial position of our player when it is created for the first time. For now, create a variable in the `BH_GameMode` blueprint titled `spawnTransform` that is of type `transform`. Then, get a reference to this variable in your graph, and plug it into the **Spawn Transform** input pin of our spawn actor node.

Player controllers

The next thing we need to do is ensure that our player can control the new character we just created. This introduces you to a new concept **Player Controllers**. The only reason we can control our `BH_Character` is that by default at game start up, our character is assigned our **Player Controller**, meaning that any input we provide to the game through the keyboard or mouse is sent to our `BH_Character`. In a single player game such as Barrel Hopper, this is easy as there is only one Player Controller. In local-multiplayer games, this can become a much bigger challenge as there is a Player Controller for each player connected to the game.

For now, all we need to do is find a node called **Get Player Controller** that takes in a player index and returns the associated controller. We can leave the input index at 0 as there is only one player. Drag a line from the output pin and search for a function node called Posses. This node will take in a **target**, which is the player controller and **In Pawn**. This will then direct any inputs from the target controller to the provided pawn. Plug the output reference pin from our **Spawn Actor BH_Character** node and plug it into this in pawn pin. Your complete functionality should look like this:

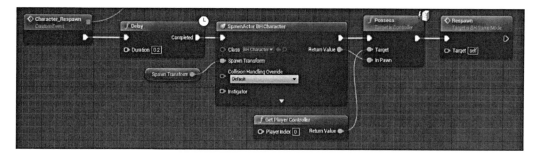

The last thing we need to do in our BH_Gamemode is ensure that this newly created character has its OnDestroyed event bound to the Character_Respawn event in the game mode as the Begin Play event we used previously will not be called again. This is easy to solve. Simply create another custom event within our game mode, and call it respawn. Have the event node for our respawn have its execution path feed into the functionality that trails our Begin Play event. Next, call the new respawn event at the end of the Character_Respawn functionality chain. This ensures that our new character's OnDestroyed event is bound to the Character_Respawn event. You can see the call to the respawn event in the preceding image. The graph around our being play event now looks like this as well:

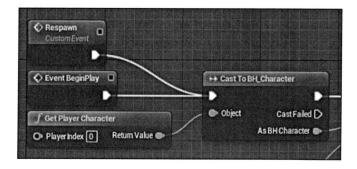

Hit Events

Now, we have to detect for barrel collisions from within our player. To do this, all we need to do is utilize an event called `Event Hit`. This event functions in a very similar way to **OnActorBeginOverlap**. The only difference is this event is called when a physical collision takes place. It is important that we use this event when dealing with collisions between `BH_Character` and `BH_Barrel`, as both objects contain rigid physics bodies that will not allow for penetration; thus, no overlapping. The process that will follow Event hit is nearly identical. We will be taking the other output pin from Event hit which is a reference to the offending actor and checking to see if it is of type barrel. If this is true, we can destroy our character! The required functionality can be seen here:

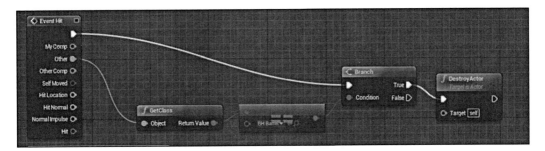

All we have left to do is set the value of that `spawnTransform` variable when our character is created for the first time. To do this, all we have to do is get the game mode in our `BH_Character`, cast it to `BH_Gamemode`, and then set the `spawnTransform` variable to the `transform` of the `BH_Character`. Do all of this when event `beginPlay` is hit, and you can ensure that the transform specified is that of the first spawn location. You can see the required functionality here:

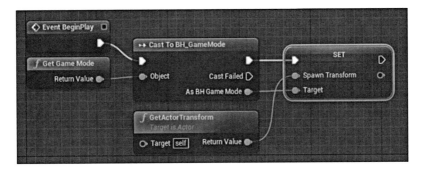

Now, run the project and enjoy the base game of what is `Barrel Hopper`!!

Summary

Great job! You made it this far! You are now familiar with the basics of Blueprint and level creation. You created a blueprint character from scratch that you then brought to life through input events and the character movement components. You learned about the Blueprint window and a large portion of the intricacies and details of that new work environment. You summoned prebuilt nodes via the context sensitive search and blueprint pallet. You created your very own custom functionality using blueprint and how to debug that functionality! You have learned how to utilize brushes to block out level approximations so that you can get onto developing the game. You created a legion of rolling barrels that can bring doom to the players of `Barrel Hopper`. You have actually done quite a lot so far and there is much more to come!

In the next chapter, you will learn all about the animation system provided by Unreal and how you can utilize these systems through Blueprint and provided Editor tools. You will learn how to load and play sounds in the 3D. You will also learn how to bind animation events and triggers to sounds and other actions within the blueprint! We will also be providing that final layer of polish to `Barrel Hopper` to turn it from a basic game loop to a polished mini-game! I look forward to showing how to do all of this and more in the next chapter!

3
Advanced Blueprint, Animation, and Sound

Well done on reading through till this Chapter. We will be learning how to animate our character using the very powerful *animation and sound tools* included in UE4. By the time the chapter is through, the character that we have created for Barrel Hopper will be moving around in well-blended articulated motion. UE4 provides an in-depth and easy-to-use animation pipeline that takes your characters from stoic, silent, statues to dynamic living features of the game world. The tools of this pipeline are very similar to Blueprint in nature yet very different in practice. You will learn how to master these tools so that you may bring true justice to the sounds and animations provided to you by artists, thus bringing your game characters to life.

During the course of this chapter, we will also explore the 3D sound functionality provided by Unreal as well as learn how we can utilize the sound system in conjuncture with the animation system to create animation-driven sound effects such as footsteps. These animations and sounds will require information from the game world—this chapter will also teach you how to communicate between the game world and these other components of the engine.

The chapter will cover the following points:

- UE4 animation pipeline and how to export animation assets
- Working with UE4 animation tool
- Creating events and loops with animation montages
- Creating animation graphs and how to apply these graphs to in-game characters
- Receiving queues from the game world/character state to play the correct animation

- Loading and modifying sounds

- Playing sounds in 3D space

- Working with the animation montage tool to create animation-driven sounds

- Advanced blueprint techniques

- Creating and utilizing basic HUD and font objects

Cleaning up shop

We left off with our Barrel Hopper project, having just implemented some *respawning logic*. In its current state our project is a basic **prototype** at best. During the course of this chapter we will be refining our previous implementations as well as adding new layers of polish via the inclusion of animation and sound effects. However, before we do this, we should clean up the functionality we already have in place.

As it is now, when our player dies we leave nothing in charge of the main camera. You may have noticed that, upon player collision with a barrel, the camera will disjoint and show a default view of the world's origin. We need to append to the functionality we created as an **event delegate** so that, when our player is destroyed, the game mode creates a new camera and sets it as our main view target. We can then interpolate from this new camera to our Player camera upon respawn to create a nice, clean respawn effect. Before we do this, I think now is a great time to introduce you to some new concepts that let you organize your Blueprint graphs.

Logic flow

Unreal Engine's Blueprint system features a few nodes whose sole purpose is to control the execution flow of the blueprint. They will divert or navigate the critical execution path to flow in a desired direction or sequence. You have already experienced this at a small level using a branch node that will dictate the execution flow path based on the state of a `bool` value, and the reroute node that lets you clean up your Blueprint graph lines. The other flow control nodes provided by Unreal are as follows:

- **Branch Node**: This node will execute one of two paths based on the state of an input `bool`.

- **Do N**: Will only allow an execution path to enter a specified number of times. Execution count can be reset by an execution input.

- **Do Once/Do Once Multi input**: This node only allows a specified execution path to happen once.

- **FlipFlop**: Will execute one of two paths in an alternating fashion every time execution passes through the node.

- **ForLoop**: This node will act as a traditional `for` loop, a very common iteration structure used across most programming languages. You can specify a first and last index and an execution path for the loop, and one once the loop has completed.

- **ForLoopWithBreak**: As previous, but you may break out of the iteration logic early by navigating the execution flow to a break node.

- **While Loop**: Will remain in loop until a `bool` input is set to `false`.

- **Gate**: This node will continue the execution flow until it has been flagged to close, at which point the flow will stop at the Gate node.

- **MultiGate**: Similar to the previous bullet, however allows you to specify multiple execution flow outputs that can be chosen via an integer index.

- **Sequence**: Allows you to create a sequence of execution paths that will be fired in order.

Using a sequence

Before we begin to create the respawn camera functionality, we will implement a *sequence* to maintain a tidy Blueprint Event graph. As stated previously, the sequence node allows us to create a series of execution paths that will be executed in order. This allows us to associate similar functionality with a given sequence path. In our case we will be creating two groupings of functionality. One to spawn a new camera that can be used while our character is respawning, and another to respawn our character after a certain amount of time has passed. We have already created a basic implementation of the latter in the previous chapter.

Create a sequence node now and ensure that it has two output execution paths. They should be titled **Then 0** and **Then 1**. Place this node directly after the `Character_Respawn` event and connect the execution path to the input pin, then append the player respawn functionality we created in the last chapter from `Delay` onwards to the **Then 1** output execution path. You should see something similar to this:

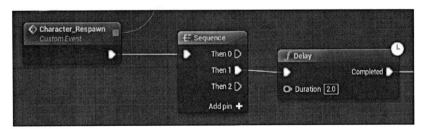

We will now create our camera spawn functionality and append it to the **Then 0** output pin. This means that our camera spawn functionality will execute, *then* our player respawn functionality.

Creating custom cameras

We are going to be creating something called a camera actor then setting this to be our Target View. Camera actors are not cameras in themselves but are an in-world object that owns a camera component. Setting a camera actor as the Target View will use this camera component as the camera through which the player views the game world. You can use any actor that owns a camera component as a target for the view.

Where do we spawn the camera?

We are going to use the SpawnActorFromClass node to create our camera actor. However, just like in previous instances of using this node, we need to provide a *transform* for the actor to use at spawn. We need this transform to be that of the character's camera upon his untimely barrel-related demise. To do this we can create a transform variable in BH_GameMode called CameraAtDeath and ensure we set this from our BH_Character when the OnDestroyed event is hit.

Do this now. Summon the Destroyed event in BH_Character, use the GetGameMode function node to return a reference to the current game mode, cast this reference to BH_GameMode, then set the CameraAtDeath transform to that of the *player's camera* (reference name CharacterCam) via the GetWorldTransform function. The functionality should appear as shown in the BH_Character Blueprint:

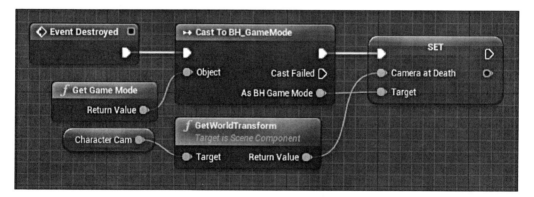

Spawning the camera object

With the transform of the character's camera at death attained, navigate back to the BH_GameMode Blueprint, and we can now create our camera spawn functionality. Do this now by finding a SpawnActorFromClass node and setting the class to CameraActor, then transform to the CameraAtDeath variable and leave the rest as defaults. Be sure to connect this new node to the **Then0** execution output from the sequence node.

To save out our camera so we may have a reference to use in future, create a CameraActor reference variable in the **MyBlueprint** panel called GameModeCamera, and set the value of this reference to the output of the SpawnActorFrom Class node we just created. Before we do this however, we should be sure that we do not leave any floating camera objects around the world and clutter our memory. We need to first check whether there is already an existing game mode camera populating that reference. If there is, we need to destroy it, *then* assign the newly created camera.

We can do this by using an IsValid node. This node will take in an object reference and output two execution paths, one if the reference is valid, and another if it is not. Spawn one of these nodes now and parse the GameModeCamera to the input labeled InputObject. From the **IsValid** path, spawn a DestroyActor node and parse the GameModeCamera reference to it. Then connect both the execution output of the DestroyActor node and the **IsNotValid** path to the **Set Node** for the GameModeCamera reference. This means that if there is a valid camera actor populating the GameModeCamera reference, then destroy that actor (thus freeing-up memory) and set the new camera actor, otherwise we avoid that functionality and assign the new camera actor to the reference.

Setting the Target View

To ensure that our new camera maintains consistent view properties with our previous camera, we are going to need to change one of the new camera's **default properties**. To do this, drag a line from our GameModeCamera reference and search for GetCameraComponent. Now we need to drag a line off the resultant camera component reference and set the bool ConstrainAspectRatio property to false. This will mean the new camera preserves the aspect ratio of the current viewport.

We need to set this camera actor as the **Target View**. Do this via the SetViewTargetWithBlend node. This node takes in a reference to the actor we would like to use as a target, a reference to the player controller who's view we will be changing, a blend time that will dictate how long the blend will take between views, a Blend function type, a Blend Exponential value, and a bool flag that will lock the last frame of the camera when blending.

Plug our new camera actor into the **NewViewTarget** input and use
`GetPlayerController` with a player index of zero to get a `PlayerController`
reference for the **target** input. We can leave the rest as default for now as we wish to
have the view target swap happen instantaneously. You should see something that
looks similar to this:

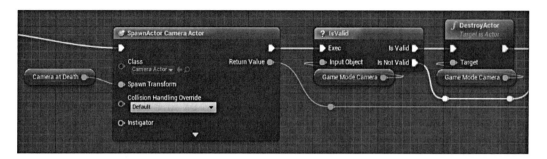

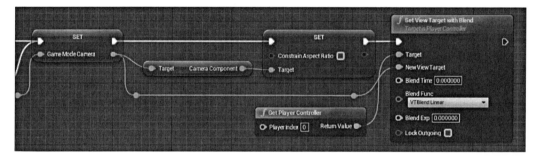

Respawning the player with a Blueprint function

Now that we have our new view, we want the player to witness the aftermath of
their death for a short time before respawning the character and setting the view
back. The reason for this will become clear later in the chapter when we cover
animation. The delay node we have created will do this for us. Feel free to adjust the
respawn time, meaning the delay node length, to your liking. Immediately following
the delay node, we have our previously created respawn functionality. We will be
modifying this to include some new camera manipulation functionality so we can
smoothly translate from the respawn camera back to the player camera.

Creating the Blueprint function

To keep the functionality following our sequence node tidy, we should create a **blueprint function** within which we can group the player's respawn functionality. Create the function now by pressing the small white plus next to the **Functions** category in the **MyBlueprint Panel** and title it `RespawnPlayer`. If you wish to rename the function later, simply right-click the function you wish to rename and select **rename** from the dropdown. With the new function selected, you will see some new fields in the **Details** panel on the right-hand side of the window.

It is in this panel where you can specify a description for the function, a category for the function to be grouped under, keywords to be used when searching for the function, a compact node title (similar to the AND and XOR nodes), an access specifier that will set the encapsulation level for the function, and a `bool` representing whether the function is pure (meaning it will not require an execution path, for example `GetPlayerController`). It is also where you will specify any inputs or outputs for the function node. We can leave these all as defaults for now. Open the new function by double-clicking `RespawnPalyer` in the **Details** panel.

You will be presented with a new graph space that represents the *work area* for this function. Unlike the event graph, you will see only one entry point for the graph. The purple node titled **Respawn Player** will fire when the function is called. You will also notice you *cannot* summon event nodes within a function graph, you may call events thus triggering them, but you cannot *define* the functionality of an event node like you can from within an event graph. This is because function graphs must only contain functionality that specifically pertains to the function itself. What we are going to do is cut our player respawn functionality starting from the `SpawnActor BH_Character` node and ending at the `Respawn` event call node that we have in our event graph, and paste it into the `RespawnPlayer` function graph and reconnect the critical execution path. You should see something similar to this.

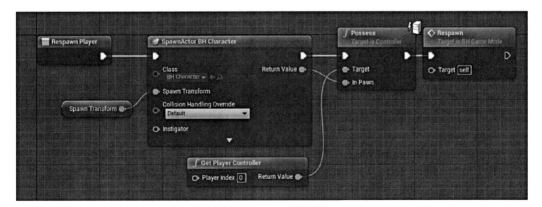

You may have noticed the strange icon located on the top right-hand corner of the Possess node. This simply means this function will only be executed on the **server authority**, something that we will cover later on in the book when we address networking.

The only issue with this current node set-up is that the moment we possess the newly spawned character, the target view will be overridden and the new character's camera will be used. This removes any possibility for us to do a nice blend between view targets. In our case we would like to have the target view *cubically interpolate* between the death camera and spawn camera views. To do this we will have to re-set our target view back to the GameModeCamera we made earlier, with a blend time of zero specified, then immediately set the target view back to our character camera again, however this time we specify a 1.0 second blend using VTBlendCubic specified for the blend function. This will produce a smooth transition effect from the camera we created when the player died, to the camera location when the player spawns.

To do this, summon a SetViewTargetWithBlend node and set the current PlayerController as the **Target**, the GameModeCamera as the **New View Target**, and leave the rest as defaults. Then summon another SetViewTargetWithBlend node, this time instead of using the GameModeCamera as our **New View Target** we are going to use the Player Character we just spawned! We can get a reference for this character by using the GetPlayerCharacter node and specifying an input index of zero. Because UCharacter inherits from UActor we are able to specify our new character as a valid input for the SetViewTargetWithBlend node. This time we will not be leaving the rest of the values as default. Specify 1.0 for the **Blend Time**, VTBlendCubic for the **Blend Func**, leave **Blend Exp** as zero, and check the **Lock Outgoing** bool. You should end up with a node arrangement that looks like this:

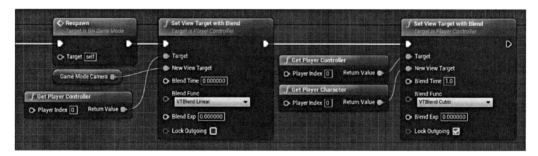

Awesome! Now the respawn functionality is complete. We will be making small edits to the BH_GameMode blueprint regarding respawning later on in the chapter. For now, we are going to be looking into Unreal Engine's animation systems.

Animation with UE4

Animation is a very effective way to establish the traits of a character. From the sleek movements of an assassin to the lumbering gait of a giant, the way the character moves and gestures is a core feature of that character's identity. UE4 offers a robust and easy-to-use workflow for animating characters. The following sections will illustrate how to set up a rudimentary animation implementation for the BH_ Character. As it stands, our character is frozen in one pose. By the end of this section the BH_Character will be running, jumping, and falling in articulated motion.

Animation Conventions

Before we begin to break down the workflow of animation within UE4, it is important to establish a few animation conventions. These conventions are relevant among all animation workflows. In video games, animations are essentially a series of frames that are interpolated at real time to create the illusion of motion. Game developers have implemented multiple techniques to mask this interpolation so that there is no discernible skip between poses, leaving us with what appears to be smooth and natural motion.

If you think of a stop motion movie, animators will move figures within the scene a very small amount every frame to make it seem as though the characters are moving. A similar thing is happening during game animations. An animator will have created a series of animation **key frames** using a third-party tool. These frames will then be interpolated between at real time and a resultant pose will be calculated.

The way an animator articulates this motion is through the use of a skeleton. A skeleton is a collection of bones the animator can move to create the motion of a character. Each bone in a skeleton is bound to a section of geometry of the character mesh. When a certain bone moves, the bound geometry will also move. This means the animator can bring an otherwise static object to life. If the categories were to be broken down, it would look like this:

- **Animation**: A collection of frames that contain a character at varying stages of a given motion that will be played in sequence.
- **Skeleton**: The rig/frame the animator used to create the animation. This skeleton must be present in-engine for the animations to work as intended.
- **Frame**: A key frame or single frame of time within the animation.
- **Pose**: The resultant stance of the character given the amount of real time that has passed since the animation has begun play. Poses may be the result of two frames of animation that have been interpolated between to compensate for real-time precision, for example a pose between Frame 30 and Frame 31.

- **Blend**: A Blend is the transition between animations. You can swap from one animation to another via a Blend. The Blend will dictate how this transition takes place over time. You may want the transition to be instantaneous or you may want the character to blend between two animations smoothly over time.

Animation Blueprints

Much like our standard Blueprints, UE4 offers another workflow tool called Animation Blueprints. It is with these Animation Blueprints that we establish the state machine for the character's animation, set up our animation graph, and create an animation event graph. These core features are responsible for the following:

- **State Machine**: Animation state machines are a visual representation of the logic behind a character's animation state. It is from these state machines that you will determine what animation to play given the character's current physical state, for example is the character moving? Play the running animation. Is the character falling? Play the falling animation.

- **Animation Graph**: This animation graph utilizes the same node-based visual scripting system that is implemented in Blueprint. These graphs are responsible for the blending and merging of poses. A great example is blending the state machine pose for a character, such as the running or idle pose, with a hit reaction animation pose. The result will be the original running or idle pose influenced by the hit reaction pose, this will have that hit reaction animation look different for each character state, saving our animator a lot of time.

- **Event Graph**: Very similar to a Blueprint Event graph, this will be used to create blueprint functionality for animation-related events. This graph will have access to the owning character Blueprint. This means we can call functionality in our character blueprint based off of events that take place in our animations, and attain variable information from the character to dictate animation logics.

Importing and exporting animation assets

When creating animation flows for a character, you first need to obtain some animation assets. Loading and exporting animations into UE projects is very easy. Simply navigate to the animation asset that your artist has provided (.fbx file format is ideal) and either import this asset or click and drag from your file explorer into the content browser panel. During this process the animation asset creation wizard will open. This will ask you to choose a skeletal mesh to associate these animations with, plus some other import options. To export animations, simply right-click on the animation you wish to export within the UE content browser and hit export.

Thankfully the mannequin assets we borrowed included a set of animations that we can use to articulate our character. Navigate back to the content folder you migrated these assets to (**Content | Mannequin**) and open the animation folder. Inside you will find an animation blueprint, a **Blendspace**, and seven animation assets denoted by a green border. Select only the animation assets and move them to the `BH_Character` folder, we will be recreating our own versions of the animation Blueprint and Blendspace.

Creating your first animation Blueprint

When creating any animation asset within Unreal, the skeleton is the asset that creates a common association. This is important as our animation blueprint needs to know of this association so all of the assets we reference within the Blueprint are relevant to the target skeleton. Let's create the animation Blueprint for our character now by right-clicking in the content browser. Choose the parent class to be `AnimInstance` (this is the base class from which all animation blueprints inherit). For the target skeleton, select **UE4_Manniquin_Skeleton**. This will ensure that any assets that we are able to reference from within the animation blueprint also use the same skeleton. Name this new animation blueprint `BH_Character_AnimBP`.

> You can right-click the skeleton asset itself and select an option from the create dropdown to automatically establish the skeleton association with the new asset.

Navigating animation Blueprints

Open this new animation blueprint; you will be presented with the **Animation Blueprint** window. There are a few new panels here that you will not have seen before, a new toolbar layout, and a new type of graph. The elements of this new window are detailed as follows:

1. **Toolbar**: Located at the top of the panel, this toolbar functions in a similar way to the toolbar featured in blueprints. There are some new buttons and features to the toolbar that will be detailed in the following.

2. **Viewport**: Located on the left-hand side of the window the viewport is a key feature of the window, it is through this Viewport that you can see the resultant output pose/animation with your given animation functionality. This allows you to see real-time previews of your animation logics.

3. **Anim Preview Editor**: Located below the viewport, this panel is where you will find any variables that have been used to influence the output of the anim graph. This means you can preview the resultant animation given a certain set of variable states.

4. **MyBlueprint**: Located in the bottom-center of the window, this panel acts in exactly the same way as the **MyBlueprint** panel featured in standard blueprints. It is here that you can find any technical features of the Animation Blueprint.

5. **Asset Browser**: The asset browser occupies the same space as the **MyBlueprint** panel and can be accessed via a tab by default. In the asset browser you will find any animation assets that are associated with the target skeleton of this Animation Blueprint.

6. **Details**: This time, the details are located in the bottom-right of the window. It is here that you will be able to change any exposed settings of the selected element.

7. **Anim Graph**: This is a new type of graph that is unique to Animation Blueprints and can be found in the center of the window. This graph is responsible for all of the animation flow logic. It is here that you will be performing animation blends and summoning various nodes that dictate how the character will animate.

8. **Event Graph**: Event graphs featured in Animation Blueprints allows you to create and receive *animation-specific events*. It is also here that you can update variables contained within the Animation Blueprint that may dictate the animation of the character.

The toolbar

As stated previously, Animation Blueprints boast a few new buttons in the toolbar. These new buttons are specifically related to animation. The first are the options **Preview** and **RefPose**, which allow you to choose what you would like to occupy the Viewport. **Preview** will show you the output pose of your given animation functionality, **RefPose** will show you the base pose the animation will be blending from. The third option is titled **Record**. This allows you to record an animation sequence based on what is playing in your preview viewport. There is also a new navigation tool on the right-hand side of the toolbar panel that looks like this:

This section allows you to easily navigate between all of the assets that are relevant to this Animation Blueprint. They have been listed in a *hierarchical* order. The Skeleton is the base from which many animation assets will stem from. The Mesh is the **skeletal mesh** that you are using to preview the output from this Animation Blueprint. The Animation is the currently active animation asset associated with the given skeletal mesh, and the Graph is the Animation Blueprint itself.

The order of this hierarchy represents the polymorphic order of the animation pipeline. You can have *multiple* skeletal meshes that are based off of one skeleton. You can have multiple Animations based off of one skeletal mesh. This means that you can have one Animation Blueprint that can be used for multiple skeletal meshes and Animations, given that they use the same target skeleton.

Populating the Animation graph

Currently in our new `BH_Character_AnimBP` there will be no functionality present in the **anim graph** apart from the `FinalAnimationPose` node. This node takes in a new pin type that we haven't seen before. The pin is represented by the outline of a standing person. This pin is of type pose. Animation nodes will take in one or more poses and output a pose to then be fed into subsequent animation nodes. `FinalAnimationPose` itself is the end of the animation chain. The pose that is parsed into this node will be the pose that is used for this frame. Currently your **anim graph** will look like this:

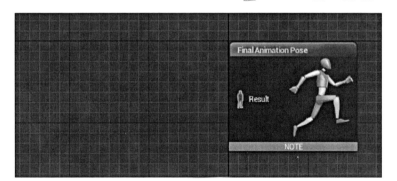

What we need to do is create some functionality that outputs a pose to this node. We are going to be creating a **state machine**. As stated previously, a state machine will determine an output animation based on various state variables that are related to the character in some way. We need to create a state machine that will handle outputting the correct animation based on the character's current movement state.

To create a new state machine, right-click in the **anim graph** and search for **add new state machine**. Selecting this option will create a state machine node. With the node highlighted, you will notice that the Details panel in the bottom right-hand side of the window has updated to provide the appropriate fields. Rename this node to `Character_Locomotion` now, as this node will handle the animation based on the character's current locomotion. Drag from the output pose pin and connect it to the input pin on the `FinalAnimationPose`.

If you compile the blueprint, the compiler will output some warnings. They are all associated with the state machine currently being empty; we need to fill this state machine with relevant functionality. Double-click the state machine node now.

Working with state machines

With the `Character_Locomotion` state machine open you will now see another nearly blank graph with only a small node titled **Entry** in the center. State machine graphs are different to Blueprint graphs as the nodes that are created and the connections between them are represented differently. This is because, as opposed to the visual plotting of functionality, this is the visual plotting of **logic flow**.

State machine graphs are made up of **State Nodes** and **Transition Lines**. A State Node is a node the represents a logic state that can be assumed, they are usually responsible for playing an animation associated with the state. A Transition Line is an association between states that represents the ability for one state to transition to another based on a rule.

The `Entry` node present does exactly as is titled. This node will be the entry point when this state machine is queried for the output pose. What we need to do is create a new State Node and connect it to this entry node. The first state that we should create when working with a locomotion state machine is an Idle State. That is because, by default, the first state node that is connected to the entry node will be responsible for the default pose of that state machine. In other words, if none of the other transition rules resolve to be true, this state will be the one that is responsible for playing the animation. In the case of locomotion, if a character is doing nothing, we wish them to play an idle animation.

State nodes

To create new state nodes, simply right-click on the graph and select **Add State**. This will create a new state node titled `state` by default. If you select this state it will be bordered by an orange outline and the Details panel will update. If you look at the Details panel now you will see that you can rename the state node, change this now to `Idle`. You will also notice that, in the Details panel under the **Animation State** section, you can also specify event names that you wish to trigger when that state is entered. This is a very powerful tool as you can have other functionalities execute upon an animation state change. If you specify any non-null names in these fields, an `AnimNotify` event will be created with the entered name that can be summoned in the Animation Blueprints event graph.

Transition Rules

The next thing we need to do is create a transition between the entry node and the new `Idle` state node. Do this now by clicking and dragging from the small arrow present in the `Entry` node to the `Idle` node we just created. This will create a white arrow. As this is the transition from the entry node to this first state node, we will not be creating any transition rules, meaning this transition will take place every time. Usually transitions also include a rule that must evaluate to `true` before the transition takes place. Create another state node now and title it `JumpBegin`. Click and drag from the outside edge of the `Idle` node onto the `JumpBegin` node, another arrow will be created but there will also be a small white circle with a bi-directional arrow within. Your graph should look similar to this:

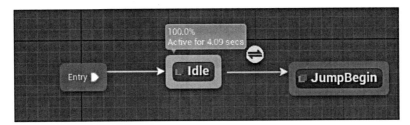

The small white circle represents a transition rule. Select this transition rule now so that it is highlighted, then address the Details panel. You will notice that this transition rule has many properties that can be changed to affect not only how the transition takes place, but also how the blend between the two state animations takes place. Double-click on the circle now. You will be presented with a new graph that has a single result node that takes in a `bool` titled `CanEnterTransition`. Simply, if the `bool` value that is parsed to this node resolves to `true`, the transition will take place. We want this value to be `true` when the character is jumping, and `false` when it is not.

We need to receive information from our character. We can do this from the Animation Blueprint Event Graph. Save this information in a relevant variable then check the state of this variable from within this transition. How do we do that? Member variables. Within the **MyBlueprint** panel, add a new `bool` variable and name it `IsInAir?`. Then drag a visual reference to this variable into the transition rule graph and plug it into the `CanEnterTransition` input pin. Alternatively, a much easier way to create variables on the fly is to drag a line from the `CanEnterTransition` input pin and then select **Promote To Variable** from the suggested list. This will create a new member variable automatically, saving the hassle of having to do it through the **My Blueprint Panel**. With the new variable created we can change the state of this `bool` value in the **event graph** for this AnimBP and it will affect this transition rule.

An important thing to note is the navigation bar at the top of the graph; it looks like this:

> BH_Character_AnimBP > AnimGraph > Character_Locomotion > JumpBegin (state)

The purpose of this bar is to show you how nested you are within the animation graph. Currently we are looking at the `JumpBegin` state, which is in our `Character_Locomotion` state machine, which is in our `AnimGraph`! This is very useful as it allows us to easily transition back to any of the other graphs by clicking on the option in the navigational bar. There are also backwards and forwards arrows on the left-hand side of the bar.

Playing animations from within states

Playing animations from within state nodes is very easy, simply double-click the state node and you will be presented with another `FinalAnimationPose` node. This node will output the final pose for this state to the state machine that will then be outputting that pose to the **anim graph**. Double-click the **Idle State** node now. The animation we want to play here is the `ThirdPersonIdle` animation. You can summon this animation into the graph by one of two ways. The first is by right-clicking in the graph and searching for **play ThirdPersonIdle**. The second is by looking in the asset browser for the correct animation then clicking and dragging the correct item into the graph. With the play `ThirdPersonIdle` node in the graph, click the output pose pin and drag it to the `FinalAnimationPose` input pin. Compile the blueprint now. With this connection made, you will see that the preview pose within the viewport has updated to the idle animation! You will also notice in the **AnimPreviewEditor** panel we can now see the `IsInAir?` variable we created earlier. We can now check and uncheck this variable to preview how our state machine will function.

Finishing our state machine

To finish our state machine, we simply need to add two more states and three more transitions. The main purpose of these states is to complete our jump loop. We have our jump loop in three different animations: we have a jump begin animation, a jump in air loop animation, and a jump land animation. The reason for this is we do not know how long the character will be in the air for, therefore the number of times in the air loop plays depends on the amount of time the character is in the air while jumping. Once the character has landed again we can then finish our jump loop and play the jump end animation.

Add two new states to our machine now, call them JumpLoop and JumpEnd. Also create transitions between JumpBegin and JumpLoop, JumpLoop and JumpEnd, and then JumpEnd and Idle. This has now created our closed state machine loop. If the character is not jumping it will be in an idle pose. Your state machine should look similar to this:

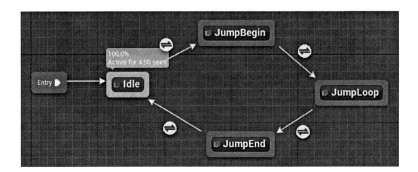

Now that we have the shell of our state machine, let's begin filling our states with the appropriate animations and our transitions with the appropriate conditional checks. Start by adding and connecting the play ThirdPersonJump_Start node to the JumpBegin state graph. The rule we will create between JumpBegin and Jumploop will be using information that utilizes the current animation that is playing. What we will be doing is checking whether the ThirdPersonJump_Start animation is 80% of the way through playing. If it is, we wish to transition to the JumpLoop state, initiating a blend between the jump begin and the jump loop animations.

Double-click the transition node between JumpBegin and JumpLoop. Within this transition graph we can utilize the context sensitive search to find the function we need. Right-click inside the graph and search for the function **Time Remaining (ratio) (ThirdPersonJump_Start)**. You can simply search for the keyword ratio to find this node. As we are in the transition between a state that plays the ThirdPersonJump_Start and another, the ratio function found will automatically observe the appropriate animation.

This node will return the time remaining in the animation as a fraction. This value will be of type float. Take the result of this node and then search for a float less than float node (<). Plug this value into the top input then in the bottom input type 0.2. This less than node will return true when the animation has less than 20% of the animation play time remaining. Your node arrangement should appear as follows:

The next step is to play the jump loop animation from within the JumpLoop state. Do this now by adding and connecting the Play ThridPersonJump_Loop node to the state graph. Now go back out into the state machine graph and under the **AnimPreviewEditor**, tick the **IsInAir?** checkbox. You should see the character transition from an idle pose to the jump begin animation, then to the jump loop!

There is a small problem though, the transition between the jump begin and jump loop animations looks a little janky. The issue here is the jump begin animation is **looping** and starting the second loop before the transition blend begins with the jump loop animation. Even though we specified that the animation should transition before the animation ends, when you specify an animation to loop (which is set to true by default), the engine will blend the last few frames of the animation with the first few frames of the animation to create a smooth loop.

To fix this, open the JumpBegin state and select the Play ThirdPersonJump_Start node. Selecting this node will populate the Details panel with properties that are associated with this animation node. Under the settings category there is a **Loop Animation** checkbox. Uncheck this now and re-preview our animation sequence by checking the **IsInAir?** variable, you will see the transition is now much smoother! However, when you uncheck the variable, nothing happens, the character remains in the jump loop. That is because we have yet to specify our JumpLoop to JumpEnd transition rule.

Do this now by opening the transition between the two states. This time, instead of checking the IsInAir? variable directly, parse the value of this variable to a NOT node. This node will return true when the provided input is false. Plug the output from this NOT node into the CanEnterTransition input pin. You also need to provide the JumpEnd state the play ThirdPersonJump_End node, do this now. Also ensure that the play ThirdPersonJump_End node has the loop animation property (found in the Details panel) unchecked.

The last thing you need to do is specify the transition between the JumpEnd state and the Idle state. Use the same ratio node transition rule we used when specifying the transition rule between JumpBegin and JumpLoop. Now compile the Animation Blueprint and test our state machine using the **IsInAir?** checkbox in the **AnimPreviewEditor** panel. You should see a transition similar to this:

The Animation Blueprint Event graph

Despite our preview viewport showing a correct sequence, if we are to run the game, our character will still not animate at all. There are two reasons for this. This first is that we have not assigned the IsInAir? variable to anything relevant yet, the other is that we have not informed our BH_Character to use the BH_Character_AnimBP. We can do this now by opening the BH_Character blueprint, selecting the Mesh component from within the **Components** panel, and changing the **Anim Blueprint Generate Class** field under the **Animation** section of the Details panel to BH_Character_AnimBP.

Now that we have associated our character with our custom Animation Blueprint, we can retrieve data from the owning character in the Animation Blueprint event graph and set our IsInAir? variable. Navigate back to the BH_Character_AnimBP and open the **EventGraph**. By default, you should see two translucent nodes, one is Event Blueprint Update animation. This event will be called every frame (similar to Event Tick in standard blueprints). This node will also provide the current delta time (time since last frame).

The other node is a pure node called TryGetPawnOwner. This will try and get the pawn that owns this animation instance. As our BH_Character inherits from UCharacter, which in turn inherits from UPawn, and our BH_Character_AnimBP inherits from anim instance, this node will work perfectly, we will just have to do some casting if we want access to BH_Character-specific functionality.

The first thing we are going to do is ensure that our `TryGetPawnOwner` node returns a valid reference. This is similar to checking the validity of pointers in C++. We can do this easily by finding the node `IsValid`. This node takes in a reference to a `UObject`, if the reference is valid one execution path will be fired, if it is not, the other will. This is a very powerful tool as it allows us to ensure that we only carry out object-dependent functionality if that object is valid.

Click and drag from the `TryGetPawnOwner` output pin and search for `IsValid?`. This will summon the node and automatically assign the output reference to the input of the new node. From the `IsValid` path summon a set node for our `IsInAir?` variable. We only want to do this if our `Pawn` reference is valid, otherwise we will try and access data that has yet to be created and we will either see an in-game crash or runtime error.

As the `UPawn` class is responsible for the movement objects of any given pawn or pawn child class, we don't require a cast of this reference. From the `TryGetPawnOwner` reference, click and drag a line and search for the function `GetMovementComponent`. This will return the movement component that is associated with the owning pawn. As you have seen with our `BH_Character`, the movement component is responsible for all movement variables and parameters. We can query whether the character is currently falling by dragging a reference from the `GetMovementComponent` output pin and searching for the function `IsFalling`. This function will return a `bool` representing the falling state of the character. Set our `IsInAir?` value to the output `bool`. Your graph should look similar to this:

Now we can run our project and our character will idle and jump accordingly!

Getting our character running

Despite being able to stand still and jump properly, our character is currently having a hard time running. When we move across our map, he simply slides. What we want to do is have our character run instead. Not only do we want the character to run but we also want the character to transition from standing to walking to running, smoothly. One of the best ways to do this is by using a **BlendSpace**.

A Blendspace allows you to set up a graph of animations you wish to transition between. The axis of this graph will represent a value that you provide to the Blendspace. When plotting the animations along the axis, you are saying that, when the provided value is X, I would like the animation at position X to be of full weighting, meaning that you want that animation to entirely dictate the motion of the character's mesh. This also means that you can have an animation A at value X on the graph and an animation B at value Y on the graph. Let's say that X is 100 and Y is 200. If the value you provide to the Blendspace is at 150, the output pose will be influenced 50% by animation A and 50% by animation B.

This is perfect for our running example. We use the character's speed as the value we will be parsing to the Blendspace. We can have an idle animation at value 0 (we won't be moving in this case), a walk animation at value 90, and a run animation at value 375. This means that, as our character increases in speed, the weighting of the output pose will transition smoothly between these three animations, resulting in a gradual change of the stance and running intensity of the character.

Working with Blendspaces

Blendspaces are another animation asset, however unlike Animation Blueprints, they themselves are classified as animations, meaning that you will be introduced to a new workspace, The animation workspace. As we are only concerned with one axis (speed), we need to create a one-dimensional Blendspace. Do this now by right-clicking in the content browser and creating a **Blendspace 1D** object, it can be found under the animation field. Name this BH_Idle_Run_BS1D. Double-click the Blendspace now to open it.

You will be presented with the animation window. There are a few new panels to work with here, they are detailed as follows:

1. **Skeleton Tree**: Located in the top left-hand corner of the window, this panel shows you the current skeleton hierarchy of the animation asset you are working with.

2. **Anim Asset Details**: Located underneath the Skeleton Tree panel. This panel is similar to the details panel in Blueprints and allows you to modify specific parameters of the current animation asset you are working with.

3. **BH_Idle_Run_BS (Blendspace name)**: Located in the bottom-center of the window this area shows the workspace for the Blendspace itself. It is here where you will be establishing your axis values and plotting your animation points. Note that the name for this section will change depending on the animation asset.

4. **Asset Browser**: Located in the bottom-right corner of the window this panel shows you the animation assets associated with the same skeleton that you can reference in this asset.

5. **Details Panel**: Though unpopulated at the moment, this panel is used predominantly when setting up `anim` notifies in standard animation assets. This will be covered later in the chapter.

6. **Viewport**: This panel shows the current output of the animation asset and some other statistical information about the skeletal mesh.

The toolbar at the top of the window has also changed slightly. You can now import and export animations directly from the toolbar. You can also create another animation assets from here.

Creating the running Blendspace

The first thing we need to do is set up our workspace. Under the **BH_Idle_Run_BS** panel there is a checkbox titled **display editor vertically**. Check this now if you wish. I prefer to have the display appear this way so I can maximize visible information in the panel. The next thing we need to do is set up our axis. Right now our single axis has no label and the range is from 0 to 100. We need to rescale our axis so that it goes from 0 to 370 and label it **Speed**. We can keep the number of divisions the same as we wish to have our walk animation play when our character is moving at roughly ¼ of its maximum speed. Do this now by filling in the corresponding fields within the panel then press the apply parameter changes button. Your parameters field should look like this:

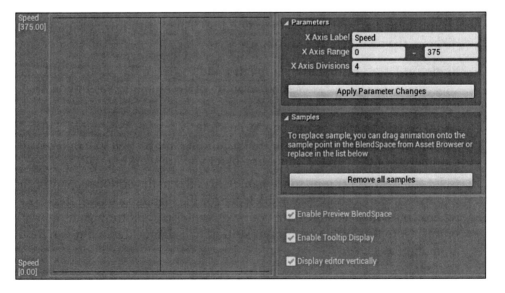

Now that our axis has been set up, the next thing we need to do is provide the graph with animations. You can only plot animations at division points. This is so that the Blendspace can correctly interpolate between animations based on the current value and the difference between divisions. Click and drag the `ThirdPersonIdle` animation from the **Asset Browser** onto the bottom of the graph. You should be presented with a small node on the axis at the very bottom of the graph. This means that when our speed value is zero, the idle animation will play.

Do the same for the `ThirdPersonWalk` animation but drop this animation node at the first division. You can preview the output animation of a Blendspace by clicking in the Blendspace graph and hovering your mouse over the axis between these two nodes. This will use the value your mouse is currently at on the axis for the Blendspace weighting.

The next thing we need to do is drag and drop the `ThirdPersonRun` animation onto the top of the Blendspace graph. This means that at speed 0, the character will idle, at speed ~90, the character will walk, and at speed 375, the character will run. The Blendspace itself will handle the interpolation between these animations when the speed value deviates from these axis points. Your final Blendspace graph should look like this:

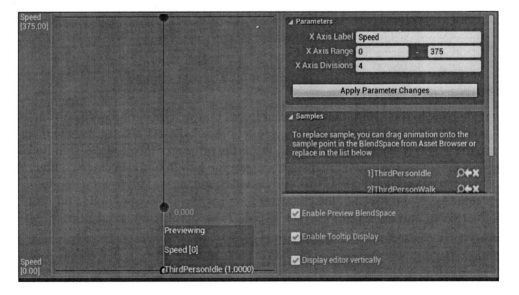

Utilizing the running Blendspace

Now, where do we call this Blendspace so we can get its output pose to influence our character animation? We are going to replace the play Idle animation in our idle state of the locomotion state machine with this Blendspace! This is a great example of combining animation assets within the UE4 animation pipeline to achieve polished results. We can use the state machine to dictate which animation asset we will be utilizing, then use the specific functionality of the Blendspace1D to add another level of polish to our character movement.

Open the BH_Character_AnimBP now and navigate to the Idle state node. Delete the play animation node that is there currently and search for the BH_Idle_Run_BS1D node, (keyword Blendspace). This will summon a node that takes in a float value representing the speed value we have specified in our Blendspace axis, and outputs a pose. Plug the pose output into the FinalAnimationPose node of this state graph. We do not currently have a value we can plug into the speed input pin. However do the same thing we did with our IsInAir? variable and create a member variable of type float called Speed, we will later assign a value to this variable in the Anim Blueprint Event Graph. Create this member variable now and assign it to the input pin of the Blendspace node. Your functionality should appear as follows:

Navigate back to the Animation Blueprint Event Graph. Drag another line off the TryGetPawnOwner node and search for a function called **GetVelocity**. This will return the Velocity Vector of the player. From the output of this node, search for a function called VectorLength. This will output the length of the vector as a float. As the character's velocity vector is un-normalized, it means we can use the length of this vector to get the speed of the character in cm/s. Summon a set node and plug this float value into the input pin. Your event graph should appear as follows:

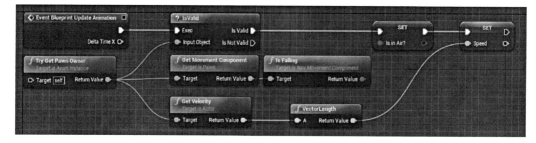

Now, when you run the project, our character will animate when we jump and run! Great work!

Creating your first sound scape

Sound in games is one of the most important tools that you can leverage to enhance the immersion and enjoyment a player has with your title. UE offers a very easy-to-use sound toolset that we are going to be learning how to utilize. We will be learning how to create 3D sound queues, how to trigger sound effects based off of animation `ques`, and how to add global sound volumes to your game scenes.

Importing sounds and sound cues

The first thing we need to do is import the sounds that we will be using to create our ques. All raw sound assets must be added to your content folder then used to create a `Sound Cue` object. Sound cues allow you to play sounds from within Blueprints, codebase, and animations at runtime. These objects also allow you to apply any modifications to how our raw sound file is played back during runtime. This means we can perform sound modifications such as modulation, oscillation, attenuation, Doppler effects, and much more from within the engine.

We are going to utilize these sound cues and other UE4 sound functionalities to add explosions to our barrels, footsteps to our character, background noise to our scene, and a groan for when our character kicks the bucket. Import the sounds `deathsound.wav` and `footstep.wav` provided with this textbook (ensure to create the appropriate organizational folders to contain the new sounds). Then create two sound `ques` objects titled `BH_Footstep` and `BH_Death`. We can create sound `ques` by right-clicking in the content browser and selecting **Sounds | Sound Cue**.

Working with sound cues

Like many of the UE objects, sound cues feature a graph-like workspace that you can drag and drop nodes into, which will be linked via some path. In a similar way that animation graphs have an output pose node, sound cues have an output sound node that looks like this:

Unlike most graphs you encounter when working with Unreal, there will only be one type of pin. This means that all nodes that you work with will take in the same type for input and output. In this case the pins are of type *sound*. While working with sound cues you will pass this `sound` reference through nodes that perform the sound modification mentioned previously.

Open the `BH_Footstep` sound cue now. You will be presented with an empty graph featuring the previous node. You will notice that the layout for this workspace is much simpler than what we have encountered previously. You have a **Viewport** panel that shows you the sound `ques` workspace. A **Details** panel on the left-hand side of the window shows you any properties of the currently selected node. A **Palette** panel on the right-hand side of the window acts as a search directory for sound cue modification nodes.

Again you are presented with a **Toolbar** at the top of the window that provides you with Sound Cue-specific functionality. This time you are presented with three new buttons, **Play Cue**, **Play Node**, and **Stop**. **Play Cue** will play the cue in its entirety, taking into account the entire sound modification chain up to and including the output node. The **Play Node** button will allow you to play the sound modification chain up to a specific node. This is a very powerful debugging tool as you will be able to test how a sound plays before being parsed into the next modification node.

Sound modification

We need to summon a node that allows us to play the `footstep.wav` sound file we imported earlier. This is very similar to the way we played animations from our state machine earlier in the chapter. Right-click in the graph somewhere and search for a node titled `Wave Player`. This is the node that will play the raw sound file specified in the **Details** panel. Select this new `Wave Player` node and address the **Details** panel, change the **Sound Wave** element to **footstep** by selecting/searching for the appropriate asset via the dropdown menu provided. Plug the output of this node into the output node and press the **Play Cue** button. You will hear a sound similar to that of someone walking on the ground. Now if you press that play cue button multiple times you will notice that the sound always plays the same way. As we are creating a footstep sound cue, we need this sound to vary slightly each time it is played otherwise the player may find the sound to be monotonous and repetitive.

We can now utilize one of the aforementioned sound modification nodes. From the **Pallet** on the right-hand side of the window, find the **Modulator** node. This node will take a sound input then randomly vary the pitch and volume of this sound so the output of this node sounds slightly different every time it is played. How much modulation takes place is dependent on the ranges specified in the **Details** panel of the modulator node. I used 1.0 as a minimum and 1.5 as a maximum for both pitch and volume.

Ensure that all of the connections between nodes have been made, and repeatedly press the **Play Cue** button. You will notice that the sound varies slightly each time it is played. If this is not immediately apparent, select the wave player node, then use the **Play Node** button instead to hear the sound again without modification. The difference will be immediately noticeable.

Our death sound cue can remain very simple. No modification is required as the sound will be played only at the point of the player's death, which will happen far less frequently than the player's footsteps. Simply summon the wave player node, select the **death.wav** asset via the **Details** panel, and parse the output to the Output node.

Playing sounds via animation notifications

Now that we have created our sound cues we need to play them at the correct time. For our footstep sound we are going to use an *animation notify* to determine when the sound is played. This means we can perfectly sync the sound cue to the foot striking the floor in the animation. To do this we are going to need to add a *play sound notify* to the animation asset that we are using for our run. We are going to have to add a similar notify to our walk animation as well, as both feature in the **Blendspace** we are using to drive the locomotion of the character.

Working with animation assets

Open the **ThirdPersonRun** animation, you will be presented with a window arrangement very similar to that of the Blendspace we made earlier. The main difference is the information that is presented in the **ThirdPersonRun** tab in the middle-bottom of the screen. You will notice that there is a new set of information being presented here and it looks like this:

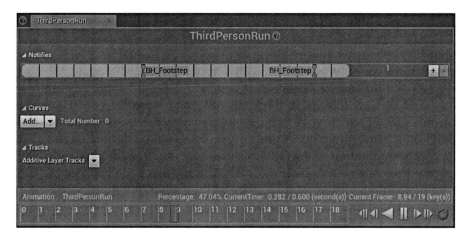

Notifies

The section at the top of the panel titled **Notifies** is where you can place notify markers along a time bar. These markers will enact some form of functionality when the animation reaches the specified point along the presented bar during runtime. The vertical lines on the bar represent the key frames of the animation. While the animation is playing, a small red line indicates the current play position of whatever animation is being previewed. This means you can play or scan the animation until a desired visual pose is seen (in our case, the moment the character's foot hits the floor), then address the **notifies** bar for the position of the red line, this is where you should place the notification.

Animation Notifies can be of three different types; play sound notify, play particle effect notify, or custom notify, which will be associated with a similarly named event that can be summoned in the event graph of an Animation Blueprint. The two notifies seen in the previous example are play sound notifies titled by the sound cue that is used at that notify point.

Curves

The next section titled **Curves** allows you to create something called a data curve. By default, the curves value progresses as the time of the animation progresses. For example, address the following image:

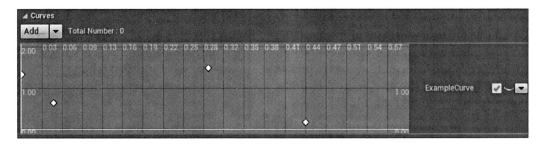

The previous curve shows that, as the animation plays, the value of ExampleCurve will vary between roughly 1.6 and 0.3 with a maximum value of about 1.9. The vertical red line represents the position at which time point the preview animation has reached. If we were to retrieve the value of this curve at this point, it would return around .99. These curves can be useful to generate meaningful data based on the progression of an animation. A great example would be if there were a *sweet spot* within a combat animation. You could use these curves to affect the damage amount that is received by an enemy. As the animation approaches the *sweet spot* in time, the curve's value would increase, then decrease as the animation progresses past this *sweet spot*. You could then use this value as a scalar when calculating attack damage.

Additive layers

The next section **Additive tracks** allow you to modify the current animation from inside UE as part of an **Additive Layer**. This means that you can take the existing animation and use an additive layer to produce an adjusted version of the animation. You can also create a separate, new animation with its own motion that is based on an original, utilizing the record animation button in the **Toolbar**.

> Implementation of these additive layers is not within the scope of this book; however you can address the online documentation at `https://docs.unrealengine.com/latest/INT/Engine/Animation/AnimHowTo/LayerEditing/index.html` for more information.

Statistics bar

At the very bottom of the animation panel is a statics bar that shows you in-depth metrics for the given animation. This panel can be very useful to ascertain animation data at a given point so you may record the metrics to be used in logics. This bar also boasts the buttons that you can use to navigate the animation that you are working with. You can play in forward time and in reverse. You can also traverse the animation frame by frame via the buttons immediately next to the play/reverse buttons. There is also a red loop button that lets you turn looping on and off within the preview. These are preview controls and will have no effect on the animation during runtime.

Placing the animation notifies

We need to add two notifies to your current **Notify** bar for the **ThirdPersonRun** animation. To do this we are going to navigate the animation using the frame-by-frame buttons at the bottom of the panel. We need to find the frames that each foot falls on the floor, it is at these key frames that we will be placing the play sound notifies. Navigate to Frame 6 of the animation by either scrubbing the red bar along the animation timeline or by pressing the **To Next** button in the controls.

You should see this in the preview window:

Now address the Notifies bar, you will see the vertical red line is overlapping one of the black dividing lines. Right-click on the red line now and select **PlaySound** from the **AddNotify** dropdown. This will add a new notify to the track titled PlaySound. With this notify selected (the notify marker will go from red to yellow), address the **Details** panel in the top right-hand side of the window. Here you can choose whether you want to modify the pitch or volume of the sound, whether you wish the sound to follow the parent, namely have the sound follow the character as it moves, and whether you would like to attach the sound emitter to a bone.

Select the Sound dropdown and search for the **BH_Footstep** cue we created earlier, then set the **volume multiplier** to 0.1 as we do not wish for the footsteps to dominate the sound scape. Then set the **pitch multiplier** to 1.8 as we want the footfalls to sound light. Create the exact same notify at key frame 16 for the other foot. When you play the animation within the preview panel you will hear sounds playing as the player's feet hit the ground! As we also use the **ThirdPersonWalk** animation in our running Blendspace, we need to add the same notification to the footfalls of the walk animation. They key frames are 8 and 24.

You may also add the footstep sounds to the **ThirdPersonJump_Start** animation at frame 1. To make the effect more prominent and punchier, you can set the Volume multiplier to 0.5 and have two notifies staggered directly after each other as seen in the following:

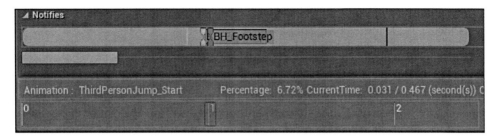

Finishing our soundscape

We need to do a few more things before the soundscape of Barrel Hopper is finished. We need to have the barrels play an explosion noise when they detonate, we need to have the player groan when they die, and we need to have some music looping in the background. These are all fairly easy to establish and will take simple world objects or calls to the sound queues.

Exploding barrels

Thanks to the starter content being included in our blank project, we have access to a couple of the Unreal provided assets, one them being an explosion sound cue. We simply have to play this sound cue when the barrel object receives its OnDestroyed event. Navigate to the BH_Barrel Blueprint. We are going to append to the functionality following the Event Destroyed node. From the Set Active node, drag a new execution path and search for **Play Sound at Location**. This node takes in a vector location and a reference to the cue we wish to use. For the **Sound** parameter, search in the dropdown menu for **Explosion Cue**, and for the **Location** parameter use GetWorldLocation with the BarrelScene component as the target. Your new functionality should appear as follows:

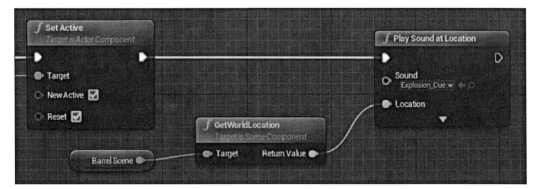

This functionality will play the `Explosion_Cue` at an emitter positioned at the same place as the `BarrelScene` component.

Players death rattle

Now we need to create similar functionality for our `BH_Death` cue from within our `BH_Character` Blueprint. Navigate to the blueprint and find the `OnDestroyed` event. Append a `PlaySoundAtLocation` node to the existing functionality. For the **sound** input, search for `BH_Death` from the dropdown menu, and for **Location** input use the `GetActorLocation` function with self as the target. This will mean that, when the play is destroyed, the death sound cue we created earlier will play.

Looping level sound

Creating persistent looping level sound is much easier to implement than it is for your sound designer to create non-pervasive background sound. All we need to do is create an **Ambient Sound** object, place it somewhere in the scene, and inform the object which que to play. We can do this by searching for the **Ambient Sound** object in the **Modes Panel** of the **Editor** window. Click and drag this object into the scene and, with it selected, address the **Details Panel**. Here you can change **Sound** parameter under the **Sound** section to `Start_Music_Cue`. This will use the ambient sound track that Unreal uses for the starter content level.

Now play the game, interact with the world, and behold the glorious soundscape we just created.

Adding the finishing touches to Barrel Hopper

Now that we have explored the basics of animation and sound with UE4, we can finish polishing our Barrel Hopper project. We are going to be adding a session timer to the HUD, a gameover screen, and ragdoll physics to our character so that when the player runs into a barrel, the character will go limp and hilarity will ensue.

Ragdolls and Event dispatchers

Let's start by adding ragdoll physics to the character upon death. The reason we are starting here is to implement the ragdoll. We are also going to have to implement an event dispatcher. An event dispatcher allows us to bind a collection of events that will trigger when the single event dispatcher is executed. This means we can execute all bound functionality across multiple blueprints from one call to the event dispatcher. This is similar to the **Event Delegate** we currently use in the BH_GameMode but allows us to bind events to a dispatcher that has no explicit functionality of its own.

We are also going to have to create a custom event in the BH_Character to bind to this **Event Dispatcher**, which will replace the functionality following Event Destroyed. We cannot use OnDestroy as the moment we call the Destroy function, the mesh will disappear and we will not be able to see the character ragdoll. Instead we will use this new custom event and a delay node to destroy the character.

Create an event dispatcher now by adding one to the **MyBlueprint Panel** of the BH_Character blueprint. Call this dispatcher **DeathDispatcher**. Then create a new custom event in the BH_Character event graph titled **Kill**. We are going to be transferring all of the Event Destroyed functionality to the new Kill event. We then have to bind this event to our new DeathDispatcher. We will do this in exactly the same way as we set up our delegate association in *Chapter 2, Blueprints and Barrels – Your First Game*. Be sure to delete the old Event Destroyed node and the subsequent functionality we just copied.

Navigate to the BeginPlay event node within the BH_Character Blueprint and you will see our old functionality that we created to set the spawn transform of the player. Append this functionality with a BindEventToDeathDispatcher node. This node can be found using the **pallet** or the context sensitive search. Now bind this to the Kill event by joining the red square pin in the top right-hand corner of the Kill event node to the red square pin in the bottom left-hand side of the Bind Event to DeathDispatcher node. Your finished arrangement should appear as follows:

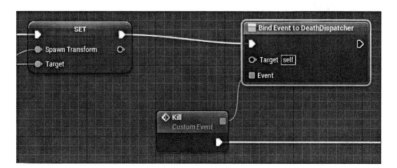

Now we need to also make sure that we bind the correct event in the BH_GameMode and that we call the correct dispatcher when our player hits a barrel. Do this now by searching for the `Call DeathDispatcher` node and replacing the previous `Destroy` call that we had at the end of the `Event Hit` functionality in our BH_Character event graph. Then in our BH_GameMode, replace `BindEventToOnDestroy` with `BindEventToDeathDispatcher`. You will see these changes in the BH_Character Blueprint:

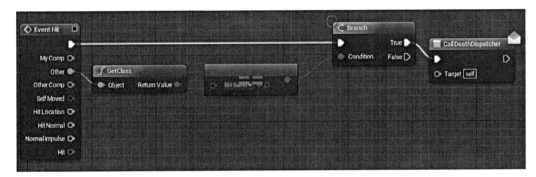

And this in the BH_GameMode Blueprint:

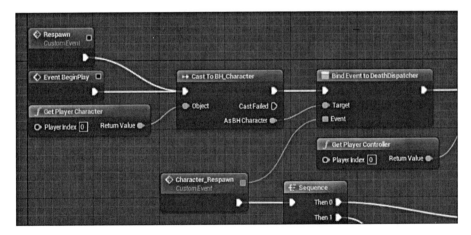

Now run the game and ensure that nothing has changed and our character dies and respawns as before. With this change in place we are now free to add our ragdoll functionality to the `Kill` event without worrying about our character deleting itself before the player's view has moved to the respawned character.

Enabling ragdoll on the character mesh is actually quite simple as the skeleton's physics asset has already been created for us. If you are unfamiliar with this asset, it's called **SK_Mannequin_PhysicsAsset** and it will have been migrated with the skeleton mesh. Open the asset now and you will be presented with this view:

Each of those capsules surrounding the player acts as physics bodies that are constrained by joints. They will act as the driving manipulators for the bone positions of the mesh. The result, a limp ragdoll that allows for the motion of the skeletal mesh! Usually these assets have to be created by hand, one capsule at a time, when the mesh is imported into the engine. These assets must be created if you would like to utilize physics simulations for the character mesh.

To enable ragdoll on the character mesh, simply drag a reference node into the **Event Graph** for the Mesh object. Drag a line off of the reference pin and search for the SetSimulatePhysics node, then check the bool **simulate** parameter. To ensure that the mesh ragdolls properly and collides with surrounding physics volumes, be sure to set the collision preset on the Mesh component to Ragdoll, the setting can be found in the **Details** panel with the Mesh component selected. The arrangement can be seen as follows:

The next thing you must do is disable the collision on the `Capsule collider` as we no longer want objects in the world to collide with this component. You can do this by dragging a visual reference to the `capsule component` into the **Event Graph**, then searching for the `SetCollisionResponsesToAllChannels` node. Set the target to be the `capsule component` reference then set the **New Response** parameter to `Ignore` via the provided dropdown. Append this new ragdoll functionality to the `Kill` event functionality.

The last thing we have to do is ensure that we destroy the actor after a period of time. Summon a delay node, append this to the ragdoll functionality, then set the duration of the delay node to 3.0 seconds. Directly after this delay node, call `Destroy` actor. This means that, when the player dies, the camera will stay long enough over the dead character to see it ragdoll for a time, then after the camera moves back to the spawn position for the next character, the old character will delete itself. Your finished kill event functionality will look similar to this:

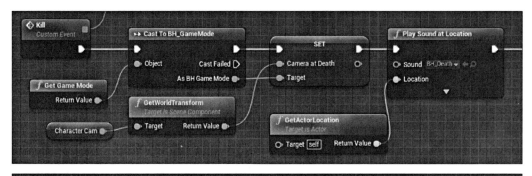

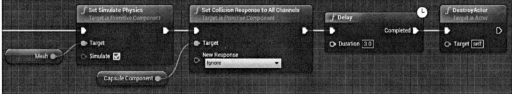

Now play the scene, deliberately kill the character by running into a barrel, and see the character mesh flail around, similar to what can be seen in the following:

Creating a basic HUD

Now that we have all of our visual polish features in place, we can create a **HUD** that will show how long the player's current run attempt is. This HUD will also complete our game loop and allow the player to see their final time upon reaching the top of the level. We will also offer the player the choice to exit the game upon completion or to reset to the start position. To do this we are going to have to create two new objects, a `BH_HUD` object and a `BH_Winner` object. `BH_HUD` will inherit from the Unreal Engine `HUD` object and the `BH_Winner` will inherit from the `trigger box` object in a similar way to our `BH_BarrelKiller` objects.

Making the HUD object

Our `BH_HUD` object is going to be responsible for drawing the in-game HUD as well as the end game screen. This means we are going to be creating two functions, one called `DrawInGame` and one called `DrawEndGame`. We will need to call either function based off of a bool that represents whether or not the player has reached the end of the level. Create a `BH_HUD` object now by opening the blueprint wizard, be sure that the parent class of the blueprint is of type `HUD`.

In the **MyBlueprint** panel of our `BH_HUD` blueprint we are going to be adding two functions, `DrawInGame` and `DrawEndGame`. Then we are going to add a `float` variable titled `PlayerAttempt`, a `Font` reference titled `ScreenFont`, and a `bool` value titled `GameWon`. Do this now. In the event graph of the `BH_HUD` there will be an event titled `EventRecieve DrawHUD`, this event will be called by the engine when the renderer deems it necessary to draw the HUD. From this event create a `branch` node based off of `GameWon`. From the `True` Branch call `DrawEndGame`, and from the false Branch call `DrawInGame`. Great! The shell of our HUD object has been created. Now we need to add meaningful functionality to the two draw functions. Before we move on, use these images to ensure you have set up the `BH_HUD` blueprint properly, your graph should appear as follows:

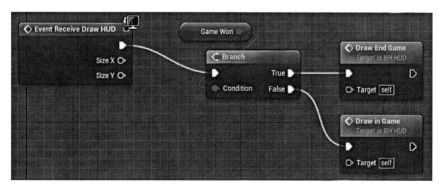

And your **MyBlueprint** panel will look like this:

Drawing the in game HUD

Open the DrawInGame function graph by double-clicking on the entry in the
Functions sections in the **MyBlueprint** panel. We need to draw the player's current
run attempt to the screen. We can do this via a function called DrawText. We need
to figure out how we can position this text so it appears at the top-center of the
screen. We can do this by getting our viewport dimensions, dividing the width
value by two, then subtracting the width of our text that will be drawn to the screen
from this value. This calculation will give us an X position to draw the text that will
compensate for the width of the text string so that the text always appears in the
center of the screen.

This is easily done with the following node arrangement:

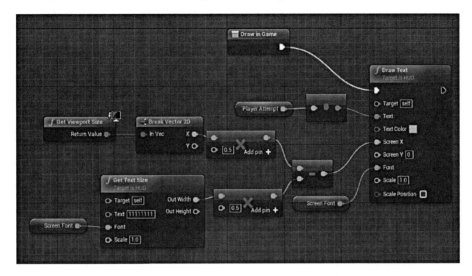

As you can see, we are using the PlayerAttempt variable we added earlier to determine what is to be drawn. We are then getting our viewport dimensions via a pure function, dividing the x component by two (or multiplying it by 0.5), then subtracting the resultant X value by the string text length multiplied by the width of a character using our provided font. The font type as of yet has not been specified, but we will get that later. You will notice that the Y value has been set to zero for the screen text as we wish the text to be flush with the top of the screen.

Now to add functionality to DrawEndGame. This will be slightly different as we need to draw a few additional lines, and we need to have the following text appear:

This is going to require more of the same calculations we did for the in-game text but we are going to position the text in the center of the screen. The arrangement of nodes appears as follows:

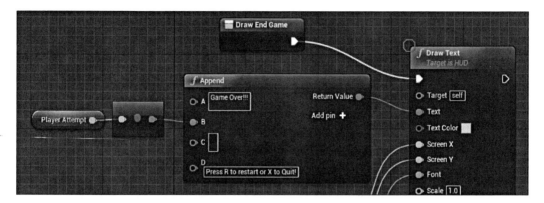

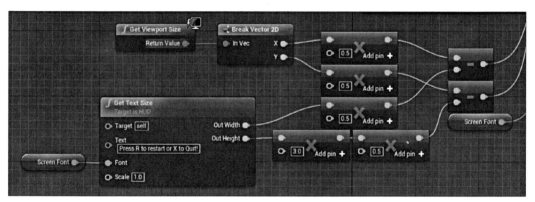

As you can see, the functionality is very similar to that of DrawInGame. This time however, we are also taking into account the **vertical scale** of the text as we wish for it to appear in the center of the screen. Also, instead of drawing three lines of text to the screen, we can instead create one big string that includes new line characters and draw that to the screen instead. To do this, simply hold shift when you press return to add a new line character to a text field. When taking the height into account, it's important to multiply the height by 3 as there are 3 lines of text that we are using for the end game scene. There will be a small margin of error as this does not account for the vertical spacing of the lines.

Making the font

Font objects are very easy to create and are done so in the same way as traditional Unreal Engine objects. Right-click in a content browser folder and create a font object found under the **User Interface** dropdown. Create a new font now and call it BH_Font. Open this font now. You will be presented with a new window, the font editing window. Here you can specify which installed font you wish to use. You can use any installed font file for this. You can also specify how the font is cached in memory as well as a default font size and name.

In our case, we need to press the **Add font** button that can be found in the **Composite Font** panel at the top of the window. This will then prompt you to name the font, select an installed font you wish to use, and which hinting algorithm to use with the font. Hinting of fonts is an algorithm used when rendering a font so that the outline of a font lines up with a rasterize grid (pixel grid). This makes the font appear smoother and removes visual artifacts when rendering a font to the screen. We can leave all of these values as default for now as our font will be nothing special.

We need to ensure our font is of a correct base size. The reason we will adjust the size of the font and not scale it from the DrawText node is because this way the font will maintain resolution. If we were to scale the font up using the DrawText node, it will appear pixelated. To adjust the size of the font, change the **Legacy Font Size** under the **Runtime Font** section in the details panel to 24. Now navigate back to our BH_HUD object and be sure to set the default value of our font reference screen to BH_Font.

Parsing information to and setting the HUD

To make sure we populate the PlayerAttempt variable with the correct value, we need to be able to increment that value while the player is alive and has yet to reach the end of the level. To do this, we simply need to increment this value from inside the BH_Character blueprint via the Tick event. We can do this by navigating to the Event Tick node in the BH_Character event graph. To get the HUD object we have created, simply use the GetPlayerController node to get a reference to the player controller, then from the output reference search for the function GetHUD. Cast this reference to BH_HUD. Now all we need to do is get the PlayerAttempt value from this BH_HUD reference, increment by the Delta Seconds variable that has been parsed via the Event Tick node, then set the PlayerAttempt variable with the result.

This can be done with the following arrangement:

The next thing we need to do is ensure we use our new BH_HUD object as the HUD for the game. This can be done back in the **Details** Panel of the BH_GameMode. We can set the HUD class parameter under the **Classes** section of the **Details** Panel of BH_GameMode to ensure that our new HUD object is used.

An end goal for the player, the chapter, and the project

Now all we need to do is create and flesh out the BH_Winner object. This object is simply going to dictate when the player reaches the end of the level, pause the game at this time, inform the HUD to end the game, and bring up the Game End text.

Start off by creating a blueprint that inherits from Trigger Volume. Call this blueprint BH_Winner. Address the blueprint **Viewport** and select the Collision Component. Make sure that the **Box Extent** settings in the **Shape** section of the **Details** panel is set to 96 across all axis. This will ensure that this box occupies 96cm³ of space in the scene.

We simply need to append functionality to the ActorBeginOverlap. Drag a line from the input OtherActor from the Event ActorBeginOverlap node. Call GetClass on this input reference via searching for it using the context sensitive search. Check that this class is equal to the BH_Character class by creating a class comparison node. Do this by searching for == after dragging a line from the purple class output pin. Create a branch node based off of this comparison operation. Now we need to get the HUD again and cast it to the BH_HUD. Do this in the same way we did when setting the PlayerAttempt variable. Instead, this time we will be setting GameWon to true then pausing the game by using the SetGamePaused function node.

The node arrangement appears as follows:

The only thing we have left to do is ensure that our game mode can receive input then when the player presses *R*, the game will restart or if the player has reached the end, press *X* to close the game.

This is very simply done by navigating to the event `Begin Play` in the `BH_GameMode`. From the functionality following this node, append one more node. Search for the **Enable Input** node. This node will take in a reference to the player controller you wish the object to receive input from. In our case we want our game mode to receive input from the default player controller (the keyboard) so we will use the `GetPlayerController` node and specify index 0, then plug the resultant player controller reference into the **Player Controller** parameter of the Enable input node.

Next, summon two input event nodes x and R. You can do this by simply searching for **X** in the **pallet** or context sensitive search. This is the other way to receive input events from within blueprints. It saves you having to create an input mapping, however you will not be able to change this input to something else without modifying the graph, like you can with an input mapping.

From the R event, summon a node called `RestartGame`. This node will reset the game to default values and positions. From the X event, check whether the game is paused by searching for the pure function `IsGamePaused`, then use a branch node to check whether this `bool` value resolves to true. If so, summon the node `QuiteGame`. This will take in a reference to a specific player and a quit preference. Leave both of these as default. The node arrangement should appear as follows:

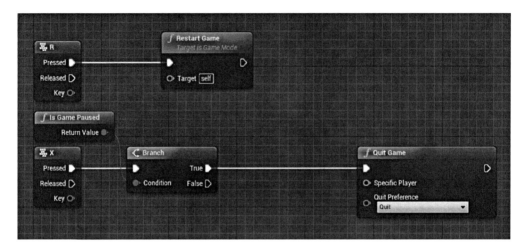

Summary

We are done! Congratulations! You have finished your first Unreal Engine By Example project. You have gone from creating a small empty scene with a simple flaming sphere to a fully-fledged mini-game! Over the course of this chapter, you learnt about event dispatchers and how to tidy up your code graph using logical flow nodes. You have been introduced to the animation and sound toolsets provided by UE4, and you have added a HUD to the Barrel Hopper project. You are progressing well.

In the next chapter we are going to begin our journey by covering the fundamentals of using C++ and UE4. I look forward to guiding you through your first C++ Unreal Engine project!

Unreal Engine, C++, and You

Welcome to Chapter 4! Well done on working through to this point, we are finally ready to open Pandora's box and bring C++ into our Unreal Engine workflow! Unreal Engine has been designed specifically to allow game developers to utilize C++ to its full extent when creating content. By the end of this chapter, you will be able to leverage the low-level nature of C++ to create in-depth functionality that maximizes the potential of UE4. In fact, from this point forward, C++ will be our main avenue when it comes to creating functionality. If you do not already have a basic understanding of, or experience with, C++, I strongly recommend brushing up on the C++ programming language and Visual Studio 2015 IDE before continuing with this book.

This chapter will introduce you to the concepts and syntax that you will encounter when working with C++ and UE4. The relationship they have created between codebase and engine is robust and involved, this chapter will act as an introduction to the workings of this relationship. Through the remaining chapters we will continuously build on this knowledge so that you may master C++ with UE4. However, with power comes responsibility: C++ is a low-level language by nature, therefore by using it you are also exposing your projects to vulnerabilities brought about by buggy and incomplete code. The code provided in this and the following chapters will take steps to show you how to avoid these vulnerabilities.

In short, this chapter will cover the following points:

- Why you should use C++ with Unreal Engine 4
- How UE4 utilizes polymorphism and virtual inheritance
- How to create an UE4 C++ project
- How to read UE4 C++ code
- What is a pre-compile stage and how does Unreal Engine 4 utilize this?

- What are UE macros?
- How to write functions in C++ that the engine can see
- How to create C++ objects that can be seen by UE
- How to write C++ functions that need to be defined in Blueprints

UE and C++

UE was designed specifically with C++ development in mind. In the history of UE, you traditionally only had access to `UnrealScript`; unless you paid a great deal of money to become an UE developer. `UnrealScript` is a scripting language developed by the Engine team to allow you to create high-level content that would interface with the Engine. The purpose of this script was to provide a layer of abstraction between the developer and engine. You could say that Blueprint has largely replaced `UnrealScript` as the primary scripting tool for UE. UE4 is unique in that it provides immediate and direct access to C++ source and development to all users.

The engine itself was written in C++ and to get access to this source all you need to do is sign up to GitHub and register your GitHub login with your Unreal developer account. Through GitHub you will then be able to download and compile the latest version of the engine source. This design of *made with and for* C++ means that C++ should be your first option when developing with the engine. This chapter will not only detail when and why you should use C++ over Blueprint, but also when you should leverage the communication between the two to enhance the efficiency of your UE workflow.

Visual Studio is the IDE you must use when working with UE. Fear not though, installing the latest version of the engine also includes an installation of the 2015 community edition of Visual Studio. The engine also provides many Visual Studio integration tools that synergize the IDE with the engine. The steps to properly set up your Visual Studio with Unreal Engine can be found here at `https://docs.unrealengine.com/latest/INT/Programming/Development/VisualStudioSetup/index.html`.

The previous tutorials and guides are a fantastic resource to expand any knowledge you gain over the course of this book.

Why use C++

C++ is a very powerful programming language with many low-level tools that you can utilize as a developer. If you are already familiar with the language you will know of the advantages it provides when it comes to memory management, generic codebase via templated programming, and the power of **OOP (Object Oriented Programming)** using virtual inheritance and polymorphism. If you are unaware of those concepts I would strongly suggest that you go do some separate research on C++ and how to use it, as these concepts will be assumed as known when covering further topics. I find the following website to be a great resource for introductory C++ concepts—`http://www.cplusplus.com/doc/tutorial/`.

Knowing how to use C++ with UE4 is essential to becoming a skilled and competent UE developer. This knowledge will allow you to fully utilize the power and limitless potential of UE. This is not hyperbole either, as not only can you use C++ to create content on a project-by-project basis, but you may also edit and add to the engine's C++ source code to create core engine functionality and adaptions you feel are lacking by default.

The biggest advantage of using C++ as your main development tool instead of Blueprint is *stability*. During the course of a project, you may wish to update engine versions to gain access to up-to-date iterations of engine functionality. If the implementation of your project is heavily based in Blueprint, this upgrade can lead to very serious build-stability issues. As Blueprint is constantly changing and updating with each iteration of the engine, large, core portions of Blueprint may be subject to change.

This happens far less frequently in code and, when it does, it is much easier to debug so that you may make amendments to fix any issues that arise. With regards to debugging, using C++ allows us to debug UE code much the same as you would any other Windows application codebase. We are able to place break points, utilize the call stack, scrutinize memory states, observe variable states at runtime, place data break points, and any other C++ debugging features we are used to.

Another advantage is the speed at which you can implement new functionality using the various interfaces the engine provides to C++ developers. If you are already very familiar with the language, you will relish the toolset provided by the engine and begin to thoroughly enjoy your time working with it. It may even come down to development preference, I personally favor C++ when developing with the engine as that is what I am comfortable with.

Now, only using C++ to create your project is not advised as there are definitely some things that Blueprint does much better than C++. When it comes to establishing object associations and asset assignment, it is far easier to do this in Blueprint as you have the power of the Editor at your disposal. This book will teach you how to effectively combine C++ with the other toolsets of the engine to maximize your development capabilities.

Polymorphism, virtual inheritance and templates

If you do not already know what polymorphism, virtual inheritance or templates are, your C++ journey with UE will be confusing and difficult. Using the link provided previously and the power of Google I would strongly recommend learning up on these topics before continuing with this book.

All of the UE objects that you interact with will have some base established in C++ code. In turn, most of these objects will also feature virtual functionality thus extensibility via C++ code. This will be your main entry point into the Unreal codebase. For example, when you wish to create a character object in code, the first thing you will do is create a class that inherits from UCharacter, thus becoming a child class of UCharacter. This will give you access to the various interfaces, methods, and variables that make up the UCharacter base class.

Through the virtual functions featured in base classes we will be able to have the engine invoke and execute our own custom functionality in-place of, or appending what exists in, the base class. Each facet of integration will be detailed as we progress through the following chapters. The first thing you will notice is that your new custom classes can be seen by the engine, meaning you can create Blueprint abstractions of your custom classes!

The other major C++ feature that UE utilizes is templatization. When adding other engine-based components and accessing Unreal Engine functionality, you will be utilizing UE's template objects and template functions. These template objects and functions extend UE4's customizable nature by providing us with generic feature sets that will be compatible with our custom C++ objects.

Hello World for C++

Before we begin to create an in-depth game project like `Barrel Hopper`, we will first return to the good old `Hello World` idea. We are going to be creating something very similar to what we created in *Chapter 1, Introduction to Unreal Engine 4* yet, this time, purely in C++! We can start by creating a new C++ project. Open Unreal Engine 4.10 via the Epic Games Launcher then select the **New Project** tab like we did before, however this time we are going to be choosing the **C++** tab. From the collection of project templates, select **Basic Code**.

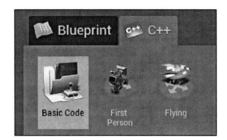

Call this project `Hello Code`. There will be a small waiting period while the engine prepares your project. Once finished you will be presented with an editor window and a Visual Studio project will have opened. The first thing we are going to do is add a new code class to our project. Do this by selecting **New C++ Class...** from the **File** dropdown located in the top left-hand corner of the main editor window.

This will open the class creation wizard. You will see that it prompts you to choose a parent class for the new object. We are going to be creating another hello sphere, this time using C++. As we are going to be creating an object that exists in the game world as an interactable and visible entity, we need to extend this object from the `AActor` base class. The reason for this will be explained soon.

Tick the checkbox **Show All Classes** in the top right-hand side of the class creation wizard then select Actor from the shown classes. You can also use the search bar provided at the top of the class creation wizard to find the desired base class. Hit the green **Next** button at the bottom of the wizard and you will be asked to name the class. Call this class `HelloSphere` then click the green **Create Class** button. The wizard will then generate an .h and `.cpp` file for us.

Exploring your first code class

You will notice that the source for the new `HelloSphere` object has been added to your Visual Studio project automatically and can be found under the source filter **Source** | `HelloCode`.

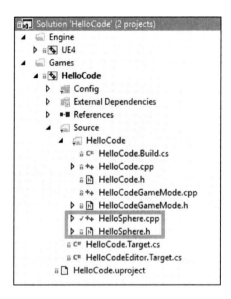

As you can see, it has been included alongside your project source files and a default `HelloCodeGameMode` object. Before we start to write anything, let's first break down what is presented to you by default so we can better understand the workings of an UE Object. Let's address the `HelloSphere.h` header file. There is not too much here to begin with, you should be presented with the following:

```
// Fill out your copyright notice in the Description page of Project
Settings.
#pragma once

#include "GameFramework/Actor.h"
#include "HelloSphere.generated.h"

UCLASS()
class HELLOCODE_API AHelloSphere : public AActor
{
    GENERATED_BODY()

public:
    // Sets default values for this actor's properties
```

```
    AHelloSphere();

    // Called when the game starts or when spawned
    virtual void BeginPlay() override;

    // Called every frame
    virtual void Tick(float DeltaSeconds) override;
};
```

Accommodating for the Unreal Build Tool

As you can see, `#pragma once` is specified by default, this is a pre-processor instruction informing the compiler to only compile this header file once when building the project. The first thing that you may notice is the include list for the header file. As you can see, the header file for the object's parent class (`AActor`) is included. Underneath this however is `#include "HelloSphere.generated.h"`. This line is very important as this allows the **Unreal Build Tool (UBT)** to generate code for our custom object.

The UBT is a very core aspect of the Unreal C++ workflow. It is through this tool that the engine is able to create associations between our custom objects and the core facilities of the engine. You may have seen something similar with other engines. The UBT does its work during something called a *Pre-Compile* stage, which makes sense as it generates code based on what is already in your object, before they are compiled by the standard compiler. How we interact with UBT will be detailed as we continue to learn about using C++ with UE4.

Pre-Compile macros and you

Unlike a standard C++ object, you will see some macros being used outside and inside the class definition. Macros are simply keywords that are swapped out for previously constructed code at compile time. In our case, these macros are going to be picked up by the UBT and replaced with generated code.

The first one that we encounter is `UCLASS()`, located just before the definition of the object. This macro is responsible for informing the engine of this object and any meta data associated with this object. As you can see, this macro includes an empty parameter list denoted by `()`, it is with this that you may also include something called *specifiers*. Specifiers act like parameters for the macro and will change how the class is interpreted by the engine. We will be utilizing these specifiers later in the chapter. For now we can leave the `UCLASS()` macro empty.

Predominantly, the presence of these macros are found in object header files with the Class definition, as it is here where you will be detailing most of the association between your code objects and UE4, which is why they are so prolific in this small 9-line class definition. The other two macros present are HELLOCODE_API, found within the class definition itself, and GENERATED_BODY().

HELLOCODE_API is used to define code set to which this object belongs and is used as an organizational tool when building the project. The macro itself will always follow the same format [ProjectName]_API, all capitalized. In this case the line class HELLOCODE_API AHelloSphere : public AActor can be interpreted as, this a class AHelloSphere that inherits from AActor publically that is part of the HelloCode project API.

GENERATED_BODY() is simply a macro that allows for code generation to be inserted within the body of the object by the UBT itself before the main compile stage.

Breaking down the rest of the header file

The rest of the object is fairly simple, it includes a default constructor AHelloSphere() and two virtual functions, BeginPlay() and Tick(). BeginPlay() is called when the actor is spawned in the level and functions in exactly the same way as Event BeginPlay in Blueprint. This function has been declared as virtual in the AActor base class, therefore we can override this function to execute our own functionality when this actor is spawned in a level. The other function Tick() is also virtual and provides us with the delta tick for the current frame via the float DeltaSeconds input parameter.

These two functions are included by default by the class wizard, as it is assumed that, at the very least, these two functions will be overridden by all custom objects that inherit from the AActor base class. Let's now look at the HelloSphere.cpp file. You are provided with basic function definitions for the default methods that were generated by the C++ class wizard.

The default constructor and include list

Before we begin to break down each of these function definitions, let's first look at the include list for this .cpp:

```
#include "HelloCode.h"
#include "HelloSphere.h"
```

As you can see, the include list for the `.cpp` of this object also includes the header file for the project (`HelloCode.h`). This provides access to the engine code base within this `cpp`, meaning we can make use of things such as object creators, object finders, and logging, among other very important features. Ok, let's now take a look at the definition for the default constructor of our `AHelloSphere` object:

```
// Sets default values
AHelloSphere::AHelloSphere()
{
    // Set this actor to call Tick() every frame.
    // You can turn this off to improve performance.
    PrimaryActorTick.bCanEverTick = true;
}
```

When working with UE objects it is within the default constructor that you will specify a majority of your object initialization functionality, as it is here that you are able to populate and initialize your object components. The reason we do this in the constructor and not in `BeginPlay()` is we wish the components to be added and initialized before our project is playing at what we could call *Editor time*. This means our object's components will be created and initialized when the project is run. We will then be able to work with these components within the editor, much like we have done so far in this book.

Within the definition of the default constructor (`AHelloSphere::AHelloSpehre()`) you will note the inclusion of `PrimaryActorTick.bCanEverTick = true`. This line flags this actor to be scrutinized for `Tick` calls. It is very important to include this line for any objects that you wish to `Tick` during runtime.

Virtual functions and calling the parent

Now let's look at the two virtual functions that have been provided by default:

```
// Called when the game starts or when spawned
void AHelloSphere::BeginPlay()
{
    Super::BeginPlay();
}


// Called every frame
void AHelloSphere::Tick(float DeltaTime)
{
    Super::Tick(DeltaTime);
}
```

You may have noticed that both of the definitions for the virtual functions include the line `Super::[FunctionName]`. This line of code executes the parent functionality of the same function. This is a very important tool as it means you are able to override parent functions without worrying about missing any core functionality that takes place in that parent call. This emphasizes the previous point of extensibility in C++. You are able to override the functions found in UE objects, call them, and write your own extension functionality.

Adding components and object creators

The first thing we want to do is add components to our new object so that we may duplicate the Hello Sphere functionality we had in *Chapter 1, Introduction to Unreal Engine 4*, Components are created via a template function titled `CreateDefaultSubobject()`. There are many object creation methods such as `CreateDefaultSubobject()` that will be used when working with the engine. One of the main reasons we will use these object creation methods is so that we utilize Unreal Engine's memory management systems.

These object creation methods will invoke UE4's memory managers, identifying and allocating the most efficient memory location for our objects. They will also register the `UObjects` we are trying to create with the **Unreal Garbage Collector**. The garbage collector automatically cleans up any `UObjects` that are no longer being referenced or have fallen out of scope. Because of this we do not have to worry about memory leaks and inefficient memory allocations.

Now let's begin writing some C++ code. We are going to be adding all of the components needed to recreate the `HelloSphere` from *Chapter 1, Introduction to Unreal Engine 4* We are going to require a `UStaticMeshComponent` for our sphere visual mesh, a `USphereComponent` so we may check for overlap events, a `UParticleSystemComponent` for our fire particles, and a `UTextRenderComponent` for our `HelloWorld` text. When adding components to an object we do not always need to include a code side handle in our class member variables. This is because `CreateDefaultSubobject()` will register our components with the base class. Unless we wish to reference a component outside of the class constructor, we can save on memory and not include a handle to the component in our class definition.

The only component that we will need access to after initialization is the `UTextRenderComponent`. We will want to change the text of the component when the default pawn overlaps the sphere component of the `AHelloSphere` actor. Navigate to `HelloSphere.h` now and add a handle to this component in our `AHelloSphere` class definition as a member variable:

```
protected:
class UTextRenderComponent* TextRenderComponent;
```

It's important to note that this has not created the component, we have merely added a handle in the form of a pointer that is of type UTextRenderComponent. We have also specified this handle to be encapsulated at a protected level as this handle will not be accessed outside of this object. You may have noticed the keyword class being used here. This is known as inline forward declaration. It is always advised to forward declare object types that may not be known to your class definition. This is to reduce including overheads in our .h files. Before we populate this handle with an initialized component, let's first create our other required components and initialize those with the appropriate values.

Navigate back to HelloSphere.cpp and within the definition of our default constructor (AHelloSphere::AHelloSphere()) add the following code:

```
// Our root component will be a sphere component that will inform us
of overlaps and collisions
USphereComponent* SphereComponent =
CreateDefaultSubobject<USphereComponent>(TEXT("RootComponent"));

RootComponent = SphereComponent;

// Assign properties to sphere component
SphereComponent->InitSphereRadius(220.0f);

SphereComponent->
SetCollisionProfileName(TEXT("OverlapAllDynamic"));
```

Here we are creating and initializing the sphere component that will be used to detect overlaps and collisions with the HelloSphere actor. As you can see, here we are utilizing the CreateDefaultSubobject() template function. This function will create a component of the templated type and return a handle to the newly created component. You can specify the component name as a parameter to this function via the TEXT macro. We are then assigning the newly created component into a temporary handle so we may access the component and change some of its properties. It is also important to note that we set the SphereComponent as our RootComponent by assigning it to the provided RootComponent variable handle.

Instead of using a **Details** panel to change properties on a component, we have instead used member functions and variables to set these values. In the previous example, we are setting the sphere radius to 220.0f via InitSphereRadius() and then setting the collision profile to OverlapAllDynamic via SetCollisionProfileName(). The latter takes in an FName representing the collision profile you wish to change to. It will make any changes to the collision settings required to match this profile. This is very similar to what you would do in the collision section of the **Details** panel.

I would strongly recommend that every time you are working with an Unreal Object for the first time, you research that object using the Unreal Engine Reference API found here at `https://docs.unrealengine.com/latest/INT/API/index.html`.

Construction helpers and object finders

The next thing we are going to do is add our static mesh component that will be used to draw the sphere geometry of the object. We need to create a `UStaticMeshComponent` and then assign it a static mesh asset we have in our content browser. Unlike Blueprint, we do not have access to the drag-and-drop functionality of the content browser to create asset associations. Instead we must use a template object provided by the `Engine.h` header file (this header is included in the `HelloCode.h` by default). This template object is called a `FObjectFinder` and is part of the `ConstructorHelpers` namespace. You can initialize this object with the type of asset you wish to find as the template type, then provide a path to the asset you wish to populate the object with as a `FName` parameter to the object constructor. The following is the code that creates the appropriate static mesh component then uses a `FObjectFinder` object to assign the correct asset. Add the following code to the default constructor definition now:

```cpp
// Create and attach a sphere mesh
UStaticMeshComponent* SphereVisual =
CreateDefaultSubobject<UStaticMeshComponent>(TEXT("SphereMesh"));
SphereVisual->AttachTo(RootComponent);

// Assign mesh to static mesh component through construction helper
ConstructorHelpers::FObjectFinder<UStaticMesh> SphereAsset(TEXT("/
Game/StarterContent/Shapes/Shape_Sphere.Shape_Sphere"));


// Adjust properties of the mesh if mesh asset was found
if (SphereAsset.Succeeded())
{
    SphereVisual->SetStaticMesh(SphereAsset.Object);
    SphereVisual->SetRelativeLocation(FVector(0.0f, 0.0f, -50.0f));
}
```

Here we have created a temporary handle (`SphereVisual`) to the `UStaticMeshComponent`. We then call `AttachTo()` on this newly created component. This function takes in a handle to the component we wish to attach to, in our case this is the `RootComponent` handle that currently points to the `SphereComponent` we created earlier. This attaching is the same as dragging one component onto another in the **Components** panel of the Blueprint Editor.

Next we create an `FObjectFinder` with the template type of `UStaticMesh` called `SphereAsset`. We then use the constructor of the `FObjectFinder` to initialize the finder with the path to a sphere asset in our content browser. This will then invoke the `FObjectFinder` to locate and assign the asset at the provided path to itself.

When providing the path to any given asset in the content browser, the easiest way is navigating to the asset in the **Content Browser,** right-clicking the desired asset, and selecting **Copy Reference**. This method can be seen as follows, along with the yielding result:

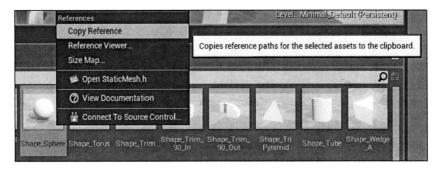

This will yield — `StaticMesh'/Game/StarterContent/Shapes/Shape_Sphere.` `Shape_Sphere`.

Everything following the object type surrounded by the (`'`) character is the path you must provide to the `FObjectFinder` constructor.

Following the construction of the `FObjectFinder` we ensure that this asset assignment was successful. We do this via the `Succeeded()` method. The `FObjectFinder` object includes the function `Succeeded()`, which returns a `bool` that represents whether the asset path provided at construction was valid and the asset has been found. If this function returns `true`, we assign the found static mesh to the `UStaticMeshComponent` we just created and adjust its relative position slightly.

We can assign the Mesh asset via the `Object` member of `FObjectFinder`. This member will be of the template type specified when creating the `FObjectFinder`, in this case `UStaticMesh`. We can use `Object` as an input parameter to the `SetStaticMesh()` function of the `UStaticMeshComponent`. We then slightly change the relative location of the sphere Mesh with `SetRelativeLocation()`, this is so that it sits in the center of our root sphere component. It is important to note that we are adjusting the relative location of the component. This means the position adjustment will be maintained as the `HelloSphere` object as a whole travels through world space.

Building the code

Alright! Now let's build our code for the first time. You may have noticed that our open Visual Studio project is not currently running our Editor (as no project instance is running). Close your UE Editor now but leave Visual Studio open. Ensure the `HelloCode` project is set as the start-up project by right-clicking on the project in the Solution Explorer and selecting **Set as Startup Project...**, also ensure that your Solution **Configuration** is set to **Development Editor** and **Solution Platforms** is set to **Win64**. You should see the following at the top of your IDE window:

Now, build the project by clicking the **Local Windows Debugger** button or pressing F5 and behold the glory of your (and Epic's) compiled code! If your project does not build cleanly, address the **Output** panel of the IDE for any errors or warnings you need to clear up.

Upon successful compilation you will be presented with the Level Editor, as you would if you had simply opened the project via the **Project Browser**. There will be one key difference however, our new `Hello Sphere` object will be included in the class lists! To see our C++ classes in the content browser there is a small button that will show or hide the sources panel. It is highlighted in the following image:

As you can see, our `HelloSphere` object can be located under the **C++ Classes | HelloCode** filter. Drag and drop our old friend into your level now and you will be presented with a sphere Mesh and sphere collider! Select this `HelloSphere` entry in the content browser and drag it into the level scene!

Adding Fire Particles and Hot Compilation

Ok, now we are going to finish creating the `AHelloSphere` object. We are going to be making edits to the code, however do not stop running the build of our project from the IDE. We are going to be Hot Compiling the following code modifications. What that is will be detailed soon. For now, let's set the `HelloSphere` on fire!

Setting the sphere on fire

We are going to set the sphere on fire by adding a `UParticleSystemComponent` to our object and then assigning this component a particle template in the same way we assigned a sphere mesh to the `UStaticMeshComponent`. Navigate to `HelloSphere.cpp` and add the following code to the `AHelloSphere::AHelloSphere()` constructor:

```
// Create the fire particle system
UParticleSystemComponent* FireParticles =
CreateDefaultSubobject<UParticleSystemComponent>(TEXT("Fire
Particles"));

FireParticles->AttachTo(SphereVisual);
FireParticles->bAutoActivate = true;

// Assign fire particle system to component
ConstructorHelpers::FObjectFinder<UParticleSystem> FireVisual(TEXT
("/Game/StarterContent/Particles/P_Fire.P_Fire"));

if (FireVisual.Succeeded())
{
    FireParticles->SetTemplate(FireVisual.Object);
}
```

We are creating the component via `CreateDefaultSubobject` as per usual. We are then attaching the newly created `UParticleSystemComponent` to the `UStaticMeshComponent` we created earlier. This is because we wish the particle system to move with the mesh when translated. We also ensure that the `bAutoActivate` member of `UParticleSystemComponent` is set to `true` as we want it to start playing as soon as the object is spawned in the level. We then use another `FObjectFinder`, this time of type `UParticleSystem`, to retrieve the `P_Fire` particle system template provided by the Unreal Starter content.

The next step is very similar to the assignment of the mesh asset to `UStaticMeshComponent`. Again we use the `Succeeded()` function to gauge the success of asset retrieval. If it succeeds, we provide the `Object` member of the `FObjectFinder` `FireVisual` to the `SetTemplate()` function of the `UParticleSystemComponent`. Because we created `FireVisual` with `UParticleSystem` as the template type, the `Object` member will be of type `UParticleSystem`, thus it is compatible as an input parameter for the `SetTemplate()` function. This is a great example of effective template use when working with C++ and UE4.

Hot Compilation

Now that we have made a change to the codebase, let's quickly demonstrate the power of Hot Compilation. Hot Compilation allows the developer to make changes to the codebase of an object without having to rebuild the entire project. To perform a hot compile, you must press the **Compile** button located in the **Toolbar** of the Level Editor. Ensure you have the `HelloSphere` object present in the viewport and then press the **Compile** button. You will notice a small popup appear in the bottom right-hand side of the screen that states **Compiling C++ Code**.... When the code compilation is successful you will see the `Hello Sphere` object in the level update to the latest version of the compiled asset! How can we tell the object has been updated? Well, it should not be aflame like so:

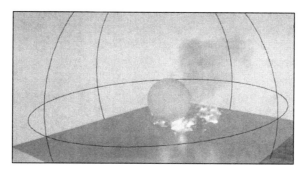

If the object has not updated properly, ensure that the code compiled successfully. If it did and the object has still not updated, simply re-drag the `HelloSphere` object into the scene and delete the original. This Hot Compilation feature is a very powerful tool as we do not have to worry about re-building the entire project whenever we make small changes to the codebase. However, large refactors or additions to the codebase will require a full re-compile from Visual Studio, especially with regards to changes made to header files, as this may have a direct impact on how the object associates with the engine. If you do experience any strange bugs after a Hot Compilation, be sure to recompile the project to see whether the bug still remains.

Hello world text and receiving events through delegates

Now it is time to finally add the 3D text that gives `AHelloSphere` a little personality. If you remember, the way we did this in Blueprint was simply by changing the text of a `TextRenderComponent` upon receiving an `OnBeginOverlap` event. We have to do this a little differently in code, instead of overriding the event function call in our `AHelloSphere` object or waiting for an event to be hit, we are going to be creating a function and binding it to the event delegate. The reason for this will be explained soon, for now let's add our `UTextRenderComponent` to the object.

Adding the 3D text

Navigate back to `HelloSphere.cpp` and, within the constructor definition
(`AHelloSphere::AHelloSpehre()`) underneath the code we just added for the
particle system, add the following code:

```cpp
// Initialize Text Render component
TextRenderComponent =
CreateDefaultSubobject<UTextRenderComponent>(TEXT("Text"));

TextRenderComponent->AttachTo(SphereVisual);

TextRenderComponent->SetRelativeLocation(FVector(0.0f, 0.0f, 110.0f));

TextRenderComponent->SetHorizontalAlignment(EHTA_Center);
TextRenderComponent->SetYScale(2.0f);
TextRenderComponent->SetXScale(2.0f);
TextRenderComponent->SetVisibility(true);
TextRenderComponent->SetText(NSLOCTEXT("AnyNs", "Any", "HelloWorld"));
```

Here we create the `UTextRenderComponent` via the `CreateDefaultSubobject()`
function, then attach it to the `UStaticMeshComponent` using `AttachTo()` and the
`SphereVisual` handle. We then change some of the properties of the text render
component. We want to have the text float above the sphere, thus we are changing
the relative offset of the text by `110.0f` on the Z axis via `SetRelativeLocation()`.
We then want to ensure that the text aligns so that it is centered around
its location in 3D space. We do this by changing the alignment type via
`SetHorizontalAllignment()` to `EHTA_Center`. We then change the scale of the text
and ensure the text is visible.

The way we set the text is fairly interesting, however we do this by using the macro
`NSLOCTEXT`. This macro creates and returns an `FText` object for us to parse into the
`SetText()` function. We only wish our text to say `HelloWorld` so why have we also
provided the strings `AnyNS` and `Any`? In short, `Any` is a key and `AnyNS` is a namespace.

`FText` as an object has been designed with localization support in mind. This means
you are able to easily localize your projects to whichever country you are building
for. Because of this, when creating an `FText` object you need to provide not only
a string value to write but also a key. The key will be used by the localization
tools to identify the text value, even after the language has changed. Meaning that
`HelloWorld` could be changed to こんにちは世界 if you were building to Japan via
the localization tools, but the key `Any` will remain the same. Namespaces are simply
used to group keys together so you may localize one namespace grouping of text but
not another. If you do not wish to use `FText` you can use an `FString` object or `FName`
object via the `TEXT` macro but this will result in a warning from the compiler.

If you want to learn more about FText and the localization tools, go here `https://docs.unrealengine.com/latest/INT/Programming/ UnrealArchitecture/StringHandling/FText/index.html`.

Ok, perform another hot compile and see the new text floating above our spherical friend:

Delegates and Events

Let's look into how we are going to be receiving the `BeginOverlap` event in our `AHelloSphere` code object. We have to add code to both our class definition in the `HelloSphere.h` file as well as the default constructor definition in the `HelloSphere.cpp`. We are going to be creating two functions `MyOnBeginOverlap()` and `MyOnEndOverlap()`. We are then going to provide these two functions to the corresponding delegates found in the `AActor` base class. Delegates are objects that act in a similar way to Event Dispatchers in Blueprint. We are able to provide multiple function handles to a delegate and have them all invoked when the delegate is instructed to broadcast.

Delegate objects are declared with a given function signature. A function signature is what defines the make-up of a function, for example the function `void Multiply(int a, int b)` has a function signature that looks like this `void function (int, int)` or `void Function ( <Param1>, <Param2>)`. Meaning a function that takes in two integer numbers as input parameters and does not return anything. You could then create a delegate called `MathDelegate` specifying this function signature at declaration. You would then be able to bind `Multiply()` to `MathDelegate` as well as any other functions with a matching function signature. When the `MathDelegate` is instructed to Broadcast `Multiply()`, any other bound functions will be invoked.

We can see the benefits of this delegate system when we utilize those provided by the AActor base class. For us to have the functionality to execute when an actor overlaps our sphere component, we need to create a function that we will bind to a delegate called OnActorBeginOverlap. We are then going to have to do the same thing with a different function for the OnActorEndOverlap delegate. The reason this has to be done via delegates instead of say, virtual functions, is so that we may have multiple functions bound to these delegates throughout the object's hierarchy, including those declared in Blueprints. You may have guessed already that whenever you add an event node to a blueprint graph you are really binding a new function to a backend code delegate of a similar name!

Let's first create the functions we are going to bind by adding the following code to the HelloSphere.h file within the class definition, just above the declaration of the UTextRenderComponent handle under the protected keyword:

```
// On Overlap implementation
UFUNCTION()
void MyOnBeginOverlap(AActor* OtherActor);

// On End Overlap implementation
UFUNCTION()
void MyOnEndOverlap(AActor* OtherActor);
```

Here we have created two functions that have the same signature void function (AActor*). This is important as this is the signature of the OnActorBeginOverlap and OnActorEndOverlap delegates. We have also encountered a new pre-compiler macro UFUNCITON(). The UFUNCITON() macro lets us inform the engine of any crucial functions that we wish the engine to know about. We may also specify any unique properties of the function via specifiers but let's not get ahead of ourselves. The UFUNCTION() macro is present here as it is required if we wish to bind these functions to any delegates.

Next we need to actually bind these functions to the aforementioned delegates. Let's do this now by adding the following code to the definition of the constructor in the HelloSphere.cpp underneath the UTextRenderComponent initialization:

```
// Bind delegates
OnActorBeginOverlap.AddDynamic(this, &AHelloSphere::MyOnBeginOverlap);
OnActorEndOverlap.AddDynamic(this, &AHelloSphere::MyOnEndOverlap);
```

What we are doing here is adding the functions we just declared to the corresponding delegates via the AddDynaminc function. This function takes in a handle to the object that will invoke the function we are binding, and a handle to the function that is to be called. We are doing this via the this keyword and the address of the respective function.

The next thing we need to do is define the functions we just bound so they perform meaningful functionality. We can do this by adding the following code to the `HelloSphere.cpp`. Note that these function definitions are outside the scope of the constructor definition:

```cpp
void AHelloSphere::MyOnBeginOverlap(AActor* OtherActor)
{
    FString outputString;
    outputString = "Hello " + OtherActor->GetName() + "!";
    TextRenderComponent->SetText(FText::FromString(outputString));
}

void AHelloSphere::MyOnEndOverlap(AActor* OtherActor)
{
    TextRenderComponent->SetText(NSLOCTEXT("AnyNs", "Any",
    "HelloWorld"));
}
```

The function `MyOnBeginOverlap()` will now concatenate an `FString` based on `Hello`, the name of the offending actor, and `!` will then convert this string to an `FText` value via `FText::FromString`. It will then set the text value of the `UTextRenderComponent` to the resultant `FText` value. `MyOnEndOverlap()` simply sets the text back to `HelloWorld` in the same way we did upon the initial creation of the `UTextRenderComponent`.

Hot compile our new changes and run the project! When you encroach on the `Hello` sphere it will greet our pawn object. You should see something similar to the following:

 If you want to learn more about delegates now, go to `https://docs.unrealengine.com/latest/INT/Programming/UnrealArchitecture/Delegates/index.html`.

Polishing the sphere

There are a few more things we need to do before our C++ `Hello Sphere` is the same as the Blueprint one we made earlier. We need to add that Unreal Factor and give our sphere that nice metallic sheen that made it glisten in the light of its own fire.

Changing materials via C++

We are going to have to change a property of the `UStaticMeshComponent` we created after we have set the mesh of the object. This is very easy to do, all we need is another `FObjectFinder` that will be able to find the material object we require, then simply set the material value of the `UStaticMeshComponent`. This can be done by modifying our original `UStaticMeshComponent` initialization code in the `HelloSphere.cpp` within the constructor definition, to appear as follows:

```
// Assign mesh to static mesh component through constructions helper
ConstructorHelpers::FObjectFinder<UStaticMesh>
SphereVisualAsset(TEXT("/Game/StarterContent/Shapes/Shape_Sphere.
Shape_Sphere"));

ConstructorHelpers::FObjectFinder<UMaterial> SphereMaterial(TEXT("/
Game/StarterContent/Materials/M_Metal_Burnished_Steel.M_Metal_
Burnished_Steel"));

// Adjust properties of the mesh if mesh was created successfully
if (SphereVisualAsset.Succeeded() && SphereMaterial.Succeeded())
{
    SphereVisual->SetStaticMesh(SphereVisualAsset.Object);
    SphereVisual->SetMaterial(0, SphereMaterial.Object);
    SphereVisual->SetRelativeLocation(FVector(0.0f, 0.0f, -40.0f));
}
```

As you can see, all we needed to do was create another `FObjectFinder` of type `UMaterial` and ensure we check the result of the retrieval of this asset alongside that of the `UMesh`, and then simply set the material via the `SetMaterial()` function. It is important to note that the first parameter of the `SetMaterial()` function is the index of the material you wish to change. This is important when setting materials of meshes that have multiple material indexes.

With the previous code in place and compiled, we can finally say hello to a finished `HelloSphere` made entirely in C++!

Extending C++ into Blueprint

Ok, now that we have implemented a purely C++ based object, let's look at the ways we can extend our code classes into Blueprint and utilize specifiers to communicate more information from our code classes to the engine.

The first thing we are going to do is extend a custom class into Blueprint! This is a very powerful feature of the engine as it allows us to write backend functionality for objects in code, but utilize all of the association tools of the Editor for things such as assigning materials, meshes, sounds, and other asset-based functionality. To successfully extend a code class into blueprint you must provide information to the engine about the class through specifiers. These specifiers act as input arguments for macros such as `UFUNCITON()`, `UPROPERTY()`, and `UCLASS()`.

Extending a class with no macro specifier support

Let's see what happens when we attempt to extend our `AHelloSphere` C++ class we just made, which exists purely in C++. The `AHelloSphere` has not specified any additional information about itself or any of the functions/properties contained within. Navigate to the `Content` folder of the Content browser and create a new `blueprint` class. For the base class, choose `HelloSphere` under the **All Classes** section. You will be presented with a new blueprint object that is an abstraction of `AHelloSphere`! Call this blueprint `BrokenBP`. Open this blueprint now and you will see the hello sphere we just created in the Blueprint Editor.

The first thing you might notice is that all of the components we added in code can be seen in the **Components** panel and that they have all been listed as **(Inherited)**, this means that the components are based in C++ code. When you select one of these inherited components, the details panel does not populate! That is because when creating the components, we neither declared the components with the `UPROPERTY()` macro in the header file of the object, nor specified any additional information about the property that would allow us to edit the component from Blueprint.

The result, none of these components may be changed in the Blueprint and they cannot be referenced in Blueprint graphs. They can't even be seen as variables in the **MyBlueprint** panel. This may be intended when creating some objects as you might wish to extend the object into Blueprint, but you do not want any of the components specified in C++ to be modified or referenced.

You may also want to view any inherited variables that exist in the C++ base class. To do this you need to select the dropdown next to the small eye icon in the **MyBlueprint** panel and select **Show Inherited Variables**.

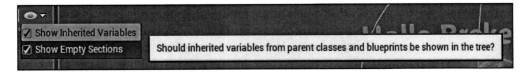

As you can see, we do not have access to the UTextRenderComponent we declared in the header file of the AHelloSphere object. This is because, as stated previously, we did not specify via a UPROPERTY() macro that we wished it to be visible or changeable in blueprint. We will get to that in a moment but first, let's try dragging an instance of this BrokenBP into our level then run the project. Upon dragging the object into the level, everything seems fine, all of the components translate with the root component and they are all drawn properly. Now let's try running the project.

Oops! We have encountered a break point, the Editor has thrown an assertion.

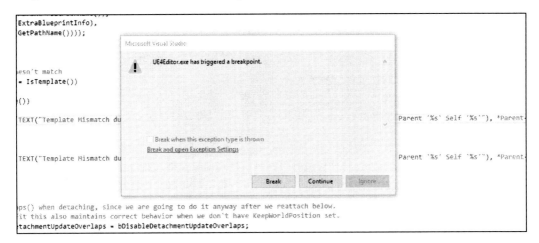

You can break at this point by pressing the **Break** button and address the position of the execution arrow. You can see from the target line of code that the reason for the break is a *Template mismatch during attachment.* Meaning that when the BP version of our code class was constructed and it attempted to attach our components to one another, this assertion was hit! The actual reason this happened is because we have not informed the engine of any of our components that we created and attached at construction. We need to do this by declaring each of the component handles in the header file with the UPROPERTY() macro. Again, we will be making changes like this very soon. First, let's hit the continue button at the top of the IDE as this break is not crucial and the project can continue play. You will notice in the following that no matter where we position our BrokenBP in the level, it is positioned very strangely during play:

The core problem that is causing all of these issues is that we have attempted to extend a C++ class into blueprint without correctly informing the engine of all of the properties that the blueprint object interacts with. The best example of this is the components themselves. It is important to note that our instances of the C++ only code class still work perfectly well in UE. It is simply this Blueprint abstraction that is broken. Fear not however! Extending C++ objects into Blueprint is very welcome and supported by UE. We just have to ensure we write code correctly to allow this to happen. Let's do this now!

Extending a class with macro specifier support

Instead of editing our original AHelloSphere, let's create a new object called HybridSphere. Do this now by creating a new C++ class via **File | New C++ Class...** and choosing Actor as the base class again. This time we are going to be creating an object that is designed specifically to be extended into Blueprint. We are going to achieve the same end result via different methods.

For one, we are not going to be assigning materials and properties to the object in C++, we are only going to be creating and attaching the components. We will leave asset assignment to the designers that work with our object in UE (or us at a later point in time)! We are however still going to be writing our overlap functionality in code, but this time we will again provide functionality so that we may override our overlap functionality in blueprint if we wish.

Defining a class with macro specifiers

Let's start by including the appropriate components, macros, and specifiers to AHybridSphere. Usually, when creating objects that are to be extended into blueprint, you must specify that it is BlueprintType in the UCLASS() macro. AActor objects are by default specified as such, we will still include this line for the sake of being explicit. We are also going to have to add a handle to each of the components we wish our AHybridSphere to own and declare them all with UPROPERTY(). The following code does just that:

```
UCLASS(BlueprintType)
class HELLOCODE_API AHybridSphere : public AActor
{
GENERATED_BODY()

public:
   // Sets default values for this actor's properties
   AHybridSphere();

    // Called when the game starts or when spawned
    virtual void BeginPlay() override;

    // Called every frame
```

```
        virtual void Tick( float DeltaSeconds ) override;

    protected:

        UPROPERTY(Category = "Components", EditAnywhere)
        class USphereComponent* Sphere;

        UPROPERTY(Category = "Components", EditAnywhere)
        class UStaticMeshComponent* Mesh;

        UPROPERTY(Category = "Components", EditAnywhere,
        BlueprintReadOnly)
        class UTextRenderComponent* Text;

        UPROPERTY(Category = "Components", EditAnywhere)
        class UParticleSystemComponent* Particles;
    };
```

As you can see, we have specified in the UCLASS() macro that this object is a BlueprintType. We have also included a handle to each component we are going to create as a member variable in our AHybridSphere class definition. The reason for this being that we need to declare each one with the UPROPERTY() macro. We do this to avoid the issues we had before when attempting to extend a code class into blueprint. The inclusion of this macro informs the engine of the existence of this property so it will feature successfully and bug free in any blueprint abstractions. It also provides us with the use of the UPROPERTY() specifiers.

The two that we have used previously are EditAnywhere and BlueprintReadOnly. EditAnywhere affords us the ability to edit the component from within our Blueprint abstractions. This means that when we create our blueprint abstraction of this C++ object, we will have access to the components properties in the **Details** panel. This is much easier than writing asset assignments and adjusting component properties from within C++. This specifier also allows us to translate, attach, and positon the component within the viewport and components panel of the Blueprint editor.

BlueprintReadOnly is only specified on the UTextRenderComponent. This specifier informs the engine that we would like to be able to read the reference to this component from within Blueprint Graphs. Meaning we can get a reference to the UTextRenderComponent and call the appropriate functions. If we wished to also write to the reference, meaning replace the UTextRenderComponent, we can specify BlueprintReadWrite.

We have also specified a category for the properties via the Category specifier. This simply groups the properties under the **Components** category and will appear so when featured in variable lists within the engine. These categories are useful for organizing function and variables lists in blueprint abstractions.

The next thing we need to do is create these components in the constructor definition. Navigate to HybridSphere.cpp and add the following code to AHybridSphere::AHybridSphere():

```
// Create the remaining components and attach to appropriate parents
Sphere =
CreateDefaultSubobject<USphereComponent>(TEXT("OverlapSphere"));
RootComponent = Sphere;

Mesh = CreateDefaultSubobject<UStaticMeshComponent>(TEXT("Mesh"));
Mesh->AttachTo(Sphere);

Particles =
CreateDefaultSubobject<UParticleSystemComponent>(TEXT("Particles"));
Particles->AttachTo(Mesh);

Text = CreateDefaultSubobject<UTextRenderComponent>(TEXT("Text"));
Text->AttachTo(Mesh);
```

As you can see, we still create our components using the CreateDefaultSubobject() template function and create our component hierarchy with AttachTo() and by setting the RootComponent. However, this time we aren't writing any code that changes the properties of these components. We are going to do all that in the Blueprint Editor. Compile this code now, we are going to make our working blueprint abstraction.

Working with code created components

Navigate to the **Content** folder of the **Content** browser again and create another blueprint object, this time specifying the base class as **HybridSphere**. Call this blueprint `FixedBP`. Ensure you have deleted the `BrokenBP` from your level and content browser, we do not wish to have any hazardous objects featured anywhere in our project. Now open `FixedBP` and you will be presented with something in the viewport that looks like this:

That is because we are yet to define any of the properties of our components. You will notice that again our components have been listed as inherited, however this time when we select them, the details panel populates. You will notice that it looks slightly different to what we are used to. The main thing to notice here is the new layout of the code component details panel. Select the **Sphere(inherited)** component now and address the **Details** panel, you will see the following:

Click the small drop-down arrow next to Sphere and you will see all of the **Details** Panel sections you are familiar with when working with **Sphere Collision** components, even though they may appear different. This is how details appear when working with code-based objects within Blueprint. Alright, let's set up our sphere. Under the Shape section of the details panel, change the Sphere radius property to `220.0f`.

Next we must scrutinize the Mesh (Inherited) component. We need to set the mesh asset to the sphere we used earlier and the material to M_Metal_Burnished_Steel. We will also have to translate the Sphere as we did before so it sits in the middle of the Sphere Collision Volume. Select the mesh component and, under the details panel, expand the Mesh section. Under the StaticMesh section you will find the StaticMesh property dropdown, set this to Shape_Sphere. Changing the material will be a little different as this time we are going to utilize a property called Override Materials. What this will do is override a material of the given static mesh. Under the **Rendering** section you will find the Override Materials property list, click the small white plus (+) to add an element, then with this element search for the M_Metal_Burnished_Steel material. You should see something similar to this in your **Details** panel:

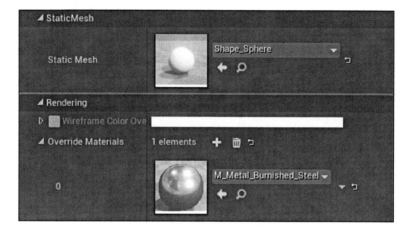

Next, to center our sphere, navigate to the **Transform** section and change the **Z** element of the Relative Location transform property to **-50.0**.

Next we must set the Particle component to the fire particle system we used before. With the **Particles (Inherited)** component selected, expand the **Particles** section of the **Details** panel and set the `Template` property to `P_Fire` via the dropdown. Finally, we have to set the properties of the **Text (Inherited)** component. Match the settings in the following screenshot then adjust the **Relative Location** property of the **Transform** section so that the **Z** element is **110.0f**:

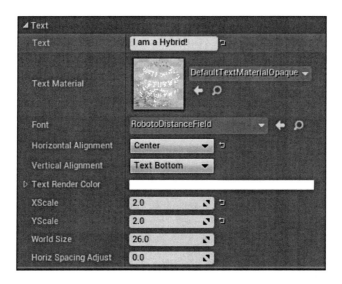

You should now see something that looks like this in the viewport:

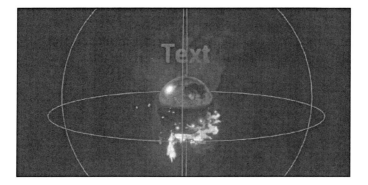

Ok, let's see how this looks in a level! Drag and drop our new `FixedBP` into the level somewhere and press **Play**. No crash! And our Blueprint object is translated to exactly where it is supposed to be.

Blueprint native events and you!

Now that we have the sphere constructed properly via the Editor, let's include the functionality that gets the AHybridSphere saying hello and goodbye. We are going to be creating this functionality a little differently this time. We are again going to be utilizing the delegate system detailed previously, but this time we are going to be writing functions that have a base functionality in code, which then may be overridden in a Blueprint if deemed necessary. This means we can create C++ functions that provide a default functionality set that will execute if no override has been defined in Blueprint. These functions are declared via the UFUNCTION() macro and the BlueprintNativeEvent specifier. Navigate to HybridSphere.h and add the following code to the AHybridSphere class definition underneath the virtual Tick function declaration:

```
// On Overlap implementation
UFUNCTION(BlueprintNativeEvent)
void MyOnBeginOverlap(AActor* OtherActor);

void MyOnBeginOverlap_Implementation(AActor* OtherActor);

// On End Overlap implementation
UFUNCTION(BlueprintNativeEvent)
void MyOnEndOverlap(AActor* OtherActor);

void MyOnEndOverlap_Implementation(AActor* OtherActor);
```

As you can see, we have created the same MyOnBeginOverlap() function, however this time we have specified that it is a BlueprintNativeEvent. That means that this event can be defined in any Blueprint abstractions. However, if it is not, look at this code class for a base implementation. You will also notice that we have included the function MyOnBeginOverlap_Implementation(). This is simply so that when we define the base implementation in our .cpp, the **UBT** knows where to look. For every BlueprintNativeEvent that you define, you must include an accompanying Implementation version of the function with the following format [FunctionName]_Implementation(Same parameter list). Without this the compiler will throw an error.

Alright, let's add the definition for our new overlap functions to the HybridSphere.cpp. We will be adding the definition to the Implementation versions of the collision functions. Navigate, to HybridSphere.cpp and add the following code:

```
void AHybridSphere::MyOnBeginOverlap_Implementation(AActor*
OtherActor)
{
    FString outputString;
```

```
        outputString = "Hello From C++!";
        Text->SetText(FText::FromString(outputString));
}

void AHybridSphere::MyOnEndOverlap_Implementation(AActor* OtherActor)
{
        Text->SetText(NSLOCTEXT("AnyNS", "Any", "Goodbye From C++"));
}
```

As you can see, it is very similar to the code we used in our `AHelloSphere` except this time we have changed the greeting to `Hello From C++`. This is so it is clear whether we are using the C++ base implementation of the `BlueprintNativeEvent` or our Blueprint Extension.

The last thing we need to do is provide these functions to the on begin and end overlap delegates! Add the following code to the constructor definition under our component creation code:

```
OnActorBeginOverlap.AddDynamic(this,
&AHybridSphere::MyOnBeginOverlap);
OnActorEndOverlap.AddDynamic(this, &AHybridSphere::MyOnEndOverlap);
```

It is important that you provide the original `BlueprintNativeEvent` function not the Implementation version of the function as the `BlueprintNativeEvent` will be calling our base implementation.

Ok, let's hot compile this code and check that it works in the level! When the compilation is complete, ensure there is a `FixedBP` object in your level, press play, and navigate towards the `HybridSphere` to be greeted from C++!

Overriding a BlueprintNativeEvent

Ok, now let's demonstrate the power of Blueprint Native Events. We are going to duplicate our `FixedBP` to create a new separate blueprint within which we can then specify our `BlueprintNativeEvent` functionality. Specifying this functionality will override our C++ base implementation and it will no longer be used when an overlap begins or ends.

Do this now by right-clicking `FixedBP` in the **Content** browser and selecting **Duplicate**, this will create a blueprint that is, by default, called `FixedBP2`. You can change this if you like or keep it as is. You will notice that all of the changes we made to the components in the Blueprint editor for the original `FixedBP` have been preserved.

Open the `FixedBP2` Blueprint and navigate to the **Event Graph**. Here we are going to be summoning two event nodes, `Event MyOnBeginOverlap` and `Event MyOnEndOverlap`. By summoning these two nodes we are effectively stating that we wish to override the C++ base implementation of these two events and use the node arrangement following these event nodes instead of the C++ base implementation. What we are going to do is set the text on our **Text (inherited)** component. Now it will be made obvious as to why we specified our `UTextRenderComponent` in `AHybridSphere` with `BlueprintReadOnly`.

Ensure that you have checked **Show Inherited variables** and, under the **Variables** section of the **MyBlueprint** panel, you will see a new category titled **Components**. Expand this now and you will see a reference to our `UTextRenderComponent` titled **Text**. Drag a reference to this component as a `get` node into the event graph and summon a `Set Text` node from it. Then summon a `make literal text` node, enter `Hello From Blueprint!` for the input to this literal node, and plug the output into the `set text` node. Connect the `Set Text` node to the `Event MyOnBeginOverlap` node. Duplicate the set text functionality and connect these new nodes to the Event `MyEndBeginOverlap` node. In the copied `make literal` text node, populate the input with `Goodbye From Blueprint!`. You should have an arrangement that looks similar to this:

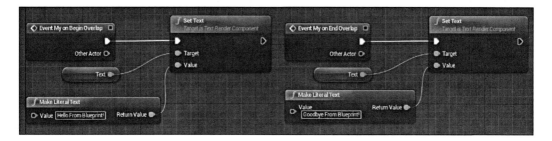

Now compile the Blueprint and drag an instance of it into the level next to our original `FixedBP` object. Ensure that there is enough space between the two of them so that we may interact with one but not the other, this should be easy as our pawn is currently flying.

Run into both in turn and you will see an output like this:

As you can see, the FixedBP2 object on the right has deferred to using the Blueprint implementation of the event where our original FixedBP object is still using the code definition, as there is no Blueprint specification provided. Keep in mind that both objects inherit from the same base class!

Summary

Congratulations! You have completed your Hello World exercise for using C++ with UE! We have learnt about the C++ workflow for Unreal Engine, how to write pure C++ objects we can then load into our levels, how to create components in C++, how to create objects in C++ that can be extended into blueprint, Blueprint native events, the Unreal Build Tool, and much more! We are going to be building on these skills in the next chapter to further hone your Unreal C++ skills when we endeavor to create your very first UE C++ title, Bounty Dash!

5
Upgrade Activated – Making Bounty Dash with C++

Welcome to Chapter 5! Well done on working through the introduction to C++ chapter! We are now going to utilize and build on those skills to produce your first C++ based Unreal Engine title, `Bounty Dash`! During this chapter, you will leverage your own technical knowledge and that of this book to create a 3D endless runner! This chapter has been designed so that we utilize as much C++ as possible, to create this project so that we may maximize your C++ learning. Once you have completed this chapter and the following, you will be well on your way to becoming a capable Unreal Engine 4 C++ programmer!

During this chapter, you are going to learn some core techniques that will provide you with the knowledge to write effective and efficient gameplay code. You will learn how to create a game character utilizing C++ and to access in level objects from C++. You will learn how to get components and metadata from objects using C++. You will use all of this knowledge to make a game with C++ and Unreal Engine! It should be noted that we are specifically taking a C++ oriented approach when developing this project, meaning that we may sacrifice development efficiency for the sake of learning. The next project started in *Chapter 7, Boss Mode Activated – Unreal Robots* will be developed with hybrid, efficient techniques in mind. In a list, we are going to be learning the following topics:

- Creating and extending the C++ basic template
- Creating character objects using C++
- Utilizing blueprint to extend C++ objects for easier asset association
- Triggering audio and animation cues in C++
- Referencing in level objects within C++ objects
- Referencing Blueprint objects in C++ with the UCLASS type

- Creating a game mode with C++
- Obtaining object metadata with C++
- Communicating with the custom C++ game mode

Creating a C++ character

Alright! Let's start the development of Bounty Dash by creating the character that we will be using for this project. Due to the nature of an endless runner, we can create a fairly simple input and movement implementation for the character. This is a great place to start with creating C++ characters, as they can quickly become complicated and involved!

Create the C++ project

Before we start building the character, we first need to create the project. Open Unreal Engine 4.10 and select the `Basic Code` project template we used for the last chapter. This time call the project `Bounty Dash`. Upon opening the project, select **New Level…** from the **File** dropdown. From the available map options, choose **Default**. This will provide us with a nice simple base to work from. Save this map as `BountyDashMap`.

The gameplay for `BountyDash` will be quite simple, there will be a seemingly infinite progression of objects that the player is running towards. The player must dodge the objects by swapping between three lanes. `Coins` will also appear periodically; the player must collect these coins to boost their score. Once a certain number of coins have been collected, the game will speed up. If the player hits an obstacle, the player will be stalled. If the player is stalled for too long in total, he will be killed by a constantly encroaching wall of death. We will definitely be expanding on these game rules as we work through the project; but for now, this a good base to work from.

The UE4 object hierarchy

As we mentioned in the previous chapters, there is a base object hierarchy that all unreal objects will inherit from. It is important to know the various stages of this hierarchy and the feature set each subsequent base class in a hierarchy brings to the table. The first thing that you must know is that all Unreal objects will inherit from the `UObject` base class. This means that every object that interacts with the engine in some way can be processed and stored generically via the `UObject` type, affording the use of the engine's generic object management systems such as the **Unreal Garbage Collector**.

When it comes to objects that exist in a level, we have already covered a brief description of objects and actors. Before we go any further with our C++ journey, a more descriptive breakdown is required. The object hierarchy for a UE4 `ACharacter` object is as follows:

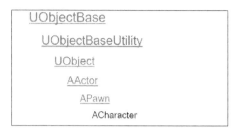

Each of the classes listed in this hierarchy add to the feature set of the object defining it as an `ACharacter`. Each of the classes featured in this hierarchy can be separated with regards to the role each class assumes. They can be broken down as follows:

- `UObjectBase`: This is the `UObject` base class from which all objects inherit. It includes generic functions that all objects will require. An example of one said function is `GetClass()`, which will return the class type of this object. This means that we are able to type check against all `UObject` classes.

- `UObjectBaseUtility`: This expands the function set that only depends on `UObjectBase`. This includes metadata functions similar to that of `GetClass()` that allows developers to get various information from their objects.

- `UObject`: This is the base class of all objects. As mentioned earlier, any unreal object will inherit from this class. Again, this class includes methods that the epic team wished all unreal objects to have.

- `AActor`: The base class for any object that can be placed or spawned in a level. `AActors` can (and will) include `Actor Components` that control how they move, render, and process. It is from this base class that we are able to make tickable actors that can be seen in levels. It is also important to note that the other main function of the `AAction` base class is the inclusion of the various networking features provided by the engine. This will be covered in *Chapter 9, Creating a Networked Shooter*.

- `APawn`: This is the base class for all actors that can be possessed and controlled by either player controllers or AI. `APawns` are the physical representations of players and creatures in levels. This provides the developers with a base class for all controllable objects, which is why a lot of the input functions we have been working with so far (in Blueprint and C++) will return or take an `APawn` reference.

- `ACharacter`: These are similar to pawns, but will include `Meshes`, collision, and in-built movement logic by default. They are responsible for all interactions that take place between a player or AI and the game world. `ACharacters` expand on the networking features mentioned in the `AActor` base class. We have already worked with a Blueprint abstraction of an `ACharacter` in `BarrelHopper`. As we know, `ACharacters` include a `CharacterMovementComponent` that will dictate how the character moves through the game world based on various movement modes.

 If you wish to find out more about the ACharacter base class and hierarch address the following API page—`https://docs.unrealengine.com/latest/INT/API/Runtime/Engine/GameFramework/ACharacter/index.html`.

Creating the Character

Alright, it's time to create our character. Start by creating the code files for the character. Open the C++ class wizard (navigate to **File | New C++ Class...**). Choose **Character** for the base class and name this new class `BountyDashCharacter`. This will create a new class of type `ABountyDashCharacter` that publically inherits from `UCharacter`. This character will need to be able to navigate between three lanes of incoming objects and coins. It will need to be able to jump and run while playing the corresponding animations. Finally, it should also include a camera that we can use as the main game camera.

What we have been given

As it was with the `AHelloSphere` object we created with the class wizard, some default functionality has been provided with the `ACharacter` base class in mind. Navigate to `BountyDashCharacter.h` now, and observer the following code:

```
UCLASS()
class BOUNTYDASH_API ABountyDashCharacter: public ACharacter
{
GENERATED_BODY()

public:
// Sets default values for this character's properties
ABountyDashCharacter();
```

```
// Called when the game starts or when spawned
virtual void BeginPlay() override;

// Called every frame
virtual void Tick( float DeltaSeconds ) override;

// Called to bind functionality to input
virtual void SetupPlayerInputComponent(class UInputComponent*
                  InputComponent) override;

};
```

There is little here that is new to you, apart from the
SetupPlayerInputComponent() function. This function is a part of the APawn
interface (which ACharacter inherits from) and allows us to bind Action Axis,
Action Mappings, and Input events to functions that we define in the class. As you
can see, it is a virtual function that we are overriding, so we may create our own
input initialization functionality. We will be doing this by calling BindAction(),
a function accessed through the UInputComponent* handle that is parsed into the
function; more on this later.

Now, navigate to BountyDashCharacter.cpp. As you can see, each of the virtual
functions declared in the header file have been defined with a simple function
body that includes the call to the parent function via the Super namespace. We will
be making edits to all of these functions during the course of this chapter; but for
now, let's begin by adding important members and methods (functions) to the
class definition.

It is also a very good idea to quickly take a look at the definition of ACharacter,
so you may familiarize yourself with the components and functions that are
provided by the base class. The two componenets we will be interacting with
are UCapsuleComponent and USkeletalMeshComponent.

What we are going to need

We are going to need to add the various member variables and functions to our
ABountyDashCharacter base class that will make up the functionality for our
main feature of the BountyDash project!

BountyDashCharacter's members

Navigate to `BountyDashCharacter.h` now; we are going to declare the public members that will be exposed to the engine and subsystems. Underneath the `GENERATED_BODY()` macro include the following members and public keywords:

```
public:
// Array of movement locations
UPROPERTY(EditAnywhere, Category = Logic)
TArray<class ATargetPoint*> TargetArray;

// Character lane swap speed
UPROPERTY(EditAnywhere, Category = Logic)
float CharSpeed;

// Audio component for obstacle hit sound
UPROPERTY(EditAnywhere, Category = Sound)
UAudioComponent* hitObstacleSound;

// Audio component for coin pickup sound
UPROPERTY(EditAnywhere, Category = Sound)
UAudioComponent* dingSound;
```

Firstly, we included an unreal template object `TArray`. It is a template container provided by UE4. This should be the default container to use when looking to store contiguous data that can be edited and referenced by the engine. The `TArray` object provides all of the functionality that we would expect from a template container. It has a similar feature set to that of STL Vector. In this case, `TArray` will contain `ATargetPoint` pointers. These `ATargetpoints` will be used to store the possible lane locations the player can move to during play. Again, we forward declared this type via the class keyword. It is important to note that this is possible as this Array is of `ATargetPoint` pointers. If the array contained whole `ATargetPoint` objects the compiler would throw an error on this incomplete type.

Next, we included the float property `CharSpeed`. This property will act as the interpolation speed with which the character can swap between lanes. This has been exposed via `EditAnywhere` as we will probably want to tweak the default value of this within the editor. Following this float value, we have two `UAudioComponent` handles. The `UAudioComponent` allows us to play sounds from our C++ classes. We included one for a sound to be played when the player hits an obstacle and another for when the player picks up a coin. We have also specified that we wish these to be editable anywhere, so we can assign these sounds from the editor.

Next, let's cover our protected members. This will include the component variables we will use to construct our camera system for the character. Add the following code to the class definition:

```
protected:
// Camera Boom for maintaining camera distance to the player
UPROPERTY(VisibleAnywhere, BlueprintReadOnly, Category = Camera)
class USpringArmComponent* CameraBoom;

// Camera we will use as the target view
UPROPERTY(VisibleAnywhere, BlueprintReadOnly, Category = Camera)
class UCameraComponent* FollowCamera;

// Player Score
UPROPERTY(BlueprintReadOnly)
int32 Score;
```

Here, we have `USpringArmComponent`. This component acts as an arm that positions the camera so that it maintains a given distance away from the character or anchor point while following some physical parameters such as drag, sway, and spring. The following `UCameraComponent` will act as the camera we use for the target view. We will be attaching the later to the former in our constructor. Both of these components have been exposed at a `BlueprintReadOnly` level, meaning blueprints will be able to call functions on these components but not replace them. Lastly, we have an `int32` that represents the score of the player. Again, we exposed this variable with `BluerpintReadOnly`, so Blueprints may read the value but not modify.

We will have two private members for this class that will only be used for internal logic. Add the following code to the class definition:

```
private:
// Data for character lane positioning
short CurrentLocation;
FVector DesiredLocation;
bool bBeingPushed;
```

The use of these members will be detailed when we begin to implement our character lane movement and collision. You will have noticed that these members have not been declared with the `UPROPERTY()` macro, that is because these members will only be used for internal logics and do not need to be engine facing.

BountyDashCharacters methods

Now that we have all of the members required for the `ABountyDashCharacter`, let's declare the methods we will be using. First up, we have the default constructor `ABountyDashCharacter()`. This has been generated by the class wizard. Again, we will use the definition of this constructor to perform a large amount of the initialization logic. Following this, we have the provided `BeginPlay()`, `Tick()`, and `SetupPlayerInputComponent()` functions. The `Tick()` function will be used to update the player's position based off the target point, and `BeginPlay()` will be used to possess control for this character and sort our array of `ATargetPoint` objects. Just below this, add the following function:

```
void ScoreUp();
```

This is a very simple function that will be called when a coin is picked up by the player. We will use it to group all of the score increment functionality. It is important to declare this method under public encapsulation, and we will be calling it form another code object. Following that, add the following code. These are the protected functions required for our character:

```
protected:
// Will handle moving the target location of the player left and right
void MoveRight();
void MoveLeft();
// Overlap functions to be used upon capsule component collision
UFUNCTION()
void myOnComponentOverlap(AActor* OtherActor, UPrimitiveComponent*
OtherComp, int32 OtherBodyIndex, bool bFromSweep, const FHitResult&
SweepResult);

UFUNCTION()
void myOnComponentEndOverlap(AActor* OtherActor, UPrimitiveComponent*
OtherComp, int32 OtherBodyIndex);
```

The first two methods `MoveRight()` and `MoveLeft()` will be bound to an input event and used to determine which target point the player needs to seek too. We have also included `MyOnComponentOverlap()` and `MyOnComponentEndOverlap()`. These two functions will be provided to the corresponding delegates so we may customize collision reactions for this character. We have to use `OnComponentBeginOverlap` as opposed to `OnActorBeginOverlap` this time as collisions will be taking place on the `UCapsuleComponent` provided by the `ACharacter` base class. We also have the generated `SetupPlayerInputComponent` function generated by the class wizard.

Constructing the Character

Now, we will flesh out some of the function definitions of `ABountyDashCharacter`, starting with the constructor `ABountyDashCharacter::ABountyDashCharacter()`. When adding code to constructor, it is always important to only include code that pertains to the construction of that object. The constructor will be executed when the object is first loaded into the engine. Meaning that an object that you are working within the editor has already had its constructor executed. This is what I like to think about when adding code to the constructor. Will the code I am about to write need to execute before this new actor is placed in the level and the game is played? If yes, then you are writing code in the right place.

We are going to be creating the camera components that are used for the target view, initializing some character movement properties so the character feels good while playing and providing the capsule component collision delegates with our custom functions. The first thing we need to do, however, is initialize the character with the required visual assets. Namely, a skeletal mesh and an animation Blueprint.

Borrowing from the old to make the new

For the purposes of this chapter, we can happily reuse the Skeletal mesh and Animation Blueprint we created for `BarrelHopper`! If you re-open the `BarrleHopper` project and navigate to the location of the `BH_Character_AnimBP` asset. Right-click on the `AnimBP` and select **AssetActions | Migrate**. You will see a list of all of the assets that will need to be migrated with `AnimBP` for the migration to be successful. Thankfully, this means that with one migration we can provide the `BountyDash` project with all of the assets, we need for a skeletal character mesh! Choose the **Content** folder of the `BountyDash` project for the destination of the migration. Once the migration is complete, you will see a new `Barrel_Hopper` folder in the content browser of the `BountyDash` project as follows:

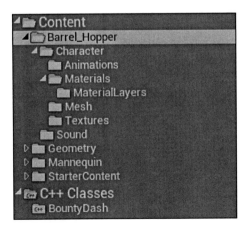

This will contain the BH_Character_AnimBP, the SK_Mannequin, and the 1D_Idle_ Run_BS, we made during the development of BarrelHopper.

Assigning Blueprints in code with generated classes

With the appropriate assets migrated, it is time to make changes to the function definitions in BountyDashCharacter.cpp. Before we begin to ensure that the included list for the BountyDashCharacter.cpp matches this:

```
#include "BountyDash.h"
#include "Animation/AnimInstance.h"
#include "Animation/AnimBlueprint.h"
#include "Engine/TargetPoint.h"
#include "BountyDashGameMode.h"
#include "BountyDashCharacter.h"
```

With those in place, you will have access to everything you need within the scope of this chapter. Now, let's begin to construct ABountyDashCharacter. Add the following lines to the ABountyDashCharacter constructor:

```
PrimaryActorTick.bCanEverTick = true;

// Set size for collision capsule
GetCapsuleComponent()->InitCapsuleSize(42.f, 96.0f);

ConstructorHelpers::FObjectFinder<UAnimBlueprint> myAnimBP(TEXT("/
Game/Barrel_Hopper/Character/BH_Character_AnimBP.BH_Character_
AnimBP"));

ConstructorHelpers::FObjectFinder<USkeletalMesh> myMesh(TEXT("/Game/
Barrel_Hopper/Character/Mesh/SK_Mannequin.SK_Mannequin"));

if (myMesh.Succeeded() && myAnimBP.Succeeded())
{
GetMesh()->SetSkeletalMesh(myMesh.Object);
GetMesh()->SetAnimInstanceClass(myAnimBP.Object->
GeneratedClass);
}
```

The preceding lines simply leverage the `FObjectFinder` template object to find and assign the skeletal mesh asset that the character will be using along with the accompanying `AnimInstance` asset. An `AnimInstance` is the base class from which all animation blueprints derive from; therefore, we are able to assign the Animation Blueprint we made earlier through the `SetAnimInstanceClass()` function. We are able to make the association between the base class and our abstracted blueprint object using the `GeneratedClass` member of the `UAnimBlueprint` object we attained through `FObjectFinder`. This `GeneratedClass` member holds the resultant C++ class that is generated upon the blueprints compilation. This means that we can associate the Animation Blueprint made in engine with the `ABountyDashCharacter` C++ object! All Blueprints feature this `GeneratedClass` member and is the main way to spawn, create, and assign blueprints using C++ code. Ensure that the paths that you provide to the `FObjectFinder` constructor match that of the paths to your assets within the project **Content** Browser.

Setting up the components

The next step to constructing the character is setting up all of the component properties so the character behaves as expected during gameplay. Start by adjusting some of the mesh and character movement properties:

```
// Rotate and position the mesh so it sits in the capsule component
properly
GetMesh()->SetRelativeLocation(FVector(0.0f, 0.0f,
-GetCapsuleComponent()->GetUnscaledCapsuleHalfHeight()));

GetMesh()->SetRelativeRotation(FRotator(0.0f, -90.0f, 0.0f));

// Configure character movement
GetCharacterMovement()->JumpZVelocity = 1450.0f;
GetCharacterMovement()->GravityScale = 4.5f;
```

We are setting the location of the mesh, so it is half way down the capsule via the `GetUnscaledCapsuleHalfHeight()` function, which will return half of the height of the capsule as it exists in component space. Note that we are using `SetRelativeLocaiton()` as we wish to make these adjustments in component space based off of the parent components transform. The next function simply rotates the character mesh by `-90.0` around the z-axis (yaw). The next thing we are doing is changing the jump velocity and gravity scale of the character movement component. We do this so that we may have a quicker jump on the character, with an increased jump velocity and gravity scale the character will jump quickly and fall quickly.

Following this, we are going to set up our cameras. First, we should create a camera boom so that the camera sits about 500 units away from the character and 160 units up. We can do this with the following code:

```
// Create a camera boom (pulls in towards the player if there is a
collision)
CameraBoom = CreateDefaultSubobject<USpringArmComponent>(TEXT("Camera
Boom"));
check(CameraBoom);


CameraBoom->AttachTo(RootComponent);


// The camera follows at this distance behind the character
CameraBoom->TargetArmLength = 500.0f;


// Offset to player
CameraBoom->AddRelativeLocation(FVector(0.0f, 0.0f, 160.0f));
```

After creating the component, you will notice that we have used the `check` macro. This macro is simply an assert. It will check that the provided condition resolves to true; if not, it will throw an assert at runtime. We then attach the `CameraBoom` to the `RootComponent` (which by default is the capsule component). We then set the length of the arm to be 500 cms long, and then position the arm 160 cm along the z-axis with `AddRelativeLocation()`. Next, we must create the camera itself and attach the camera to `USpringArmComponent`.

Every spring arm features a socket at the end of the arm. A socket is a transform that is updated with the movement of the spring arm component. A socket will maintain its relative location to whatever it is owned by at all times. With this in mind, we can attach the camera we create to this socket, and the camera will be positioned appropriately as the character moves through the world and the spring arm component updates with regards to those previously mentioned physical factors (sway, drag, and spring). We can do this with the following code:

```
// Create a follow camera
FollowCamera = CreateDefaultSubobject<UCameraComponent>(TEXT("FollowC
amera"));
check(FollowCamera);


// Attach the camera to the end of the boom and let the boom adjust to
match the controller orientation
FollowCamera->AttachTo(CameraBoom, USpringArmComponent::SocketName);


// Rotational change to make the camera look down slightly
FollowCamera->AddRelativeRotation(FQuat(FRotator(-10.0f, 0.0f,
0.0f)));
```

We attached `UCameraComponent` to `USpringArmComponet` by the `AttachTo()` function by passing a handle to the spring arm component (`CameraBoom`), and the name of the socket we would like to attach to. We can use the static member `SocketName` of the class `USpringArmComponent` as all `USpringArmComponents` have the same name for the boom socket. We then pitch the camera slightly (-10.0 degrees) so that it will look down at the character during play. Following this, we need to provide a default value for the character speed and provide the overlap functions to the `UCapsupleComponents` `OnComponentBeginOverlap` and `OnComponentEndOverlap` delegates. The following code will do that:

```
// Game Properties
CharSpeed = 10.0f;

GetCapsuleComponent()->OnComponentBeginOverlap.AddDynamic(this, &ABoun
tyDashCharacter::MyOnComponentOverlap);
GetCapsuleComponent()->OnComponentEndOverlap.AddDynamic(this, &ABounty
DashCharacter::MyOnComponentEndOverlap);
```

We are setting the `CharSpeed` value to `10.0f` as that will be the speed at which the character will interpolate between lane positions. The value is exposed with `EditAnywhere`, so if we feel it is to slow once we are testing in an editor we can change it via **Details** panel. After this, you can see that we are adding our custom collision functions to the `OnComponentBegin/EndOverlap` delegate included in the component. This is very similar to what we did in the `HelloSphere` example; yet this time, we are adding the collision methods to a delegate object in one of the owned components not the `AActor` itself.

Assuming default control

The last thing we need to do is ensure that the `ABountyDashCharacter` we place in the level is possessed by the Player Controller as soon as the game starts. Usually, this would happen automatically when we specify the default pawn in the game mode. However, we may need to adjust some of the exposed members of `ABountyDashCharacter` from the editor. We, therefore, cannot have the game mode spawn a new `ABountyDashCharacter` that is lacking these modified values. This means that we have to assume control of an already existing in level character. Add the following line to the constructor definition:

```
// Poses the input at ID 0 (the default controller)
AutoPossessPlayer = EAutoReceiveInput::Player0;
```

The preceding lines set the `AutoPossessPlayer` member of the `APawn` base class to the `enum` value `Player0`. This will ensure that when the game begins play, the default controller will possess the first `ABountyDashCharacter` we already have in the level. This affords us the ability to modify the members of our character that have been exposed with the `EditAnywhere` specifier from the editor and ensure the character we control has these properties. This is an example of something we would not have to worry about if we were going to be creating a blueprint abstraction of our player as we could simply modify the values in the blueprint object, and then assign that blueprint object type to be the default pawn.

Writing the begin Play function

Now that we have the appropriate construction functionality in place, we can write what our character is going to do at the beginning of play! We need our character to know about all of `ATargetPoints` that exist in the current game world and then add those objects to the `TargetArray` member. To do this, we need to access Game World!

Getting In-Editor objects using the Game World

One of the most important features of the UE4 programming tool set is the functionality obtained through the `GetWorld()` function. This function returns a handle to the game world that the calling class currently exists in. The handle is of type `UWorld*` and through this, we can create and destroy objects, get handles to objects already existing in the level, and obtain handles to Player Controllers. We are going to be coupling this `UWorld` handle with another UE4 template object— `TActorIterator`. This object, when specified with a type, will return an iterator that you can increment to provide access to all actors of that type within a game world. You must initialize `TActorIterator` with a game world context. Add the following code to `ABountyDashCharacter::BeginPlay()` underneath `Super::BeginPlay()`:

```
for (TActorIterator<ATargetPoint> TargetIter(GetWorld());
     TargetIter; ++TargetIter)
{
TargetArray.Add(*TargetIter);
}
```

We are creating a for loop with the initialization section used to create a `TActorIterator` object of type `ATargetPoint` called `TargetIter`. We also pass a reference to the world we wish to scrutinize to the object constructor via the `GetWorld()` function, which is part of the `AActor` interface. The condition of the `for` loop checks that the iterator is still valid, and each iteration of the loop we increment the iterator with `++TargetIter`. The resultant loop will create the iterator upon entry, increment the iterator each time the loop iterates until it is invalid. This will iterate over every `ATargetPoint` actor that exists in the game world.

For each `ATargetPoint` we encounter, we add it to the `TargetArray` via the `Add()` function. We need to dereference the iterator when passing the `ATargetPoint` into `Add()` to access the contained `ATargetPoint*` handle.

Sorting TArrays with Lambdas

The next thing we need to do in `BeginPlay()` is ensure that our `TArray` of `ATargetPoints` is sorted properly. We do not know in which order `ATargetPoints` have been found by `TActorIterator` we implemented earlier. We require these points to be sorted in the Array so that we may traverse them in order from furthest left to furthest right when moving the character.

We can do this via a function object or lambda object and pass this as a sorting predicate to `TargetArray`. If that is unclear to you, a function object is simply an object that is only responsible for one function and has no members, a lambda is the new C++11 syntax that allows us to write these on the fly. A predicate is simply a check that is used with sorting algorithms to determine the need for a sort. Add the following code to the `BeginPlay` function now:

```
auto SortPred = [](const AActor& A, const AActor& B)->bool
{
    return(A.GetActorLocation().Y < B.GetActorLocation().Y);
};

TargetArray.Sort(SortPred);
```

We are using a lambda (denoted by `[]`) to create a function that takes in two `const` `AActor` references and returns a `bool`. Within this lambda, we are simply checking that the Y value of the first `AActor` is less than the second. We then save this Lambda into a `SortPred` handle that is of type `auto`. This is another C++ 11 keyword that allows for the compile time type checking of the right-hand argument (right-hand side of the assignment operator), `auto` then automatically changes to that type during the assignment.

This predicate will be used when sorting the array where actor `A` will be one element of the `TArray` and actor `B` will be the very next. If the statement returns false, it means `B` needs to shift onto the other side of `A`; thus, a sort is needed. We then pass this predicate as a parameter to `Sort()`. We are able to use a predicate expecting `AActor` references here as `ATargetPoint` inherits from `AActor`.

The last thing we need to do is ensure that the character starts the game in the middle most lane. We can do this with some simple math. Add the following code underneath `TargertArray.Sort(SortPred)`:

```
CurrentLocation = ((TargetArray.Num() / 2) + (TargetArray.Num() % 2) -
1);
```

This will get the number of elements in the target array, divide that by two, and then add the result of the number of elements modulus 2. Meaning the remainder of that number is divided by 2. We then minus the result of this calculation by 1 to ensure that we shift the result to incorporate index 0. Because we are dealing with integer values truncation of decimal fractions is intended and means the logic is sound.

We are interacting with the member `CurrentLocation` that we declared in the `ABountyDashCharacter` class definition earlier. The purpose of this member is to indicate at which `ATargetPoint` in `TargetArray` the character is currently situated. As it is of type integer, this means that we are able to use it for `TArray` lookups via the subscript operator (`[int]`).

Setting up inputs in C++

Before we write our tick functionality, let's first look at binding inputs to the character. The first thing we need to do is create axis and action mappings in the editor like we always have. Navigate to **Edit | Project Settings** in the level editor and then navigate to the **Engine Input** section and add three action mappings **MoveRight**, **MoveLeft**, and **Jump**. Bind them to *D*, *A*, and *space bar*, respectively. Your input map should look as follows:

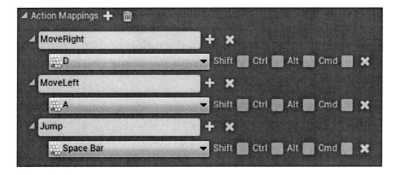

Binding actions

With the action mappings established, lets now bind these mappings to functions in the `ABountyDashCharacter` object. The `SetupPlayerInputComponent()` function provided by the `APawn` interface (which we have access to via inheritance) will be called by the engine to request bindings. A `UInputComponent` is parsed into the function, and it is with this component that we will bind the functionality. This is done in a very similar manner to binding functions to `OnOverlap` delegates. The following code shows you how to bind the `MoveRight` and `MoveLeft` functions we declared in the `ABountyDashCharacter` class definition. Add this code to `ABountyDa shCharacter::SetupPlayerInputComponent()` underneath the `Super` call now:

```
// Set up gameplay key bindings
check(InputComponent);
InputComponent->BindAction("Jump", IE_Pressed, this,
&ACharacter::Jump);

InputComponent->BindAction("Jump", IE_Released, this,
&ACharacter::StopJumping);

InputComponent->BindAction("MoveRight", IE_Pressed, this, &ABountyDash
Character::MoveRight);

InputComponent->BindAction("MoveLeft", IE_Pressed, this, &ABountyDashC
haracter::MoveLeft);
```

Again, we use `check(InputComponent)` to validate the parsed input component. Following that, we bind the `Jump` action when pressed to the `Jump` function found in the `ACharacter` parent class. We do this by passing the name of the action we wish to bind, the state of the action (`IE_PRESSED` or `IE_RELEASED`), the object that owns the function to bind, and a pointer to the function itself to `BindAction()`. As you can see we do this for the `MoveRight` and `MoveLeft` action mappings as well. You should also note that we bind the release event of `Jump` to the function `StopJumping()` found in the `AChracter` base class. This calls into the character movement component and stops any further lift being applied to the character. This allows for things such as short hops and quick jumps.

Next, we need to definite the functions we just bound with meaningful functionality. Add the following code to `BountyDashCharacter.cpp`:

```
void ABountyDashCharacter::MoveRight()
{
if ((Controller != nullptr))
{
    if (CurrentLocation < TargetArray.Num() - 1)
    {
```

```
        ++CurrentLocation;
    }
    else
    {
        // Do Nothing
    }
}
}

void ABountyDashCharacter::MoveLeft()
{
if ((Controller != nullptr))
{
    if (CurrentLocation > 0)
    {
    --CurrentLocation;
    }
    else
    {
        // Do Nothing
    }
}
}
```

These two functions are quite simple. We first check that this character is being controlled by something by checking the state of the `Controller` handle. This will be populated with a valid object if something is currently in possession of the character. As we possessed the character with the first player controller at begin play, this should never fail. We then check if the `CurrentLocation` member is within the maxims of the `TargetArray` bounds (either the number of elements in the array less one or greater than zero), and then either increment the current location if we want to move right or decrement the location if we want to move left. These two functions in combination will allow us to traverse the lanes that we set up. We also included checks to see if the player has reached the furthest right or furthest left target point. If so, and the player is still trying to move in that direction, we do nothing.

How our Character is going to Tick

Now, with everything established for our character, we can write the tick function that we are going to use for the character. The main thing `Tick()` will be responsible for is maintaining the characters position with regards to the current `ATargetPoint` we wish the character to occupy. We can do this using the `CurrentLocation` value to look up in `TargetArray`, which point is our target. We can then linearly interpolate or lerp between the character's current position and that of the target location. This will ensure that the character always maintains the correct place when traversing lanes.

Add the following code to `ABountyDashCharacter::Tick()`:

```
void ABountyDashCharacter::Tick(float DeltaSeconds)
{
Super::Tick(DeltaSeconds);

if(TargetArray.Num() > 0)
{
FVector targetLoc = TargetArray[CurrentLocation]-
    >GetActorLocation();
    targetLoc.Z = GetActorLocation().Z;
targetLoc.X = GetActorLocation().X;

if(targetLoc != GetActorLocation())
    {
SetActorLocation(FMath::Lerp(GetActorLocation(), targetLoc, CharSpeed
* DeltaSeconds));
    }
}

}
```

We called the parent tick function via `Super::Tick()`. We then check that our `TargetArray` has been populated with at least one target point. If so we get the location the of the current point. We merge this location with the X and Z value of the character's location, so we can allow jumping and pushing movement without affecting the `lerp`. We then set the actor location to the output form a `Lerp` function. This function takes in a current location, the location we wish to move too and a delta. This is how much should be interpolated this frame. For us, that is the delta time * the character's interpolation speed (`10.0f` by default).

Compile time

With all of that in place, it is nearly time to compile! First, we need to provide empty function definitions for the component overlap functions and `ScoreUp()`. We will be populating these function definitions with code soon! The following will suffice for now:

```
void ABountyDashCharacter::myOnComponentOverlap(AActor* OtherActor,
UPrimitiveComponent* OtherComp, int32 OtherBodyIndex, bool bFromSweep,
const FHitResult& SweepResult)
{
}
```

```
void ABountyDashCharacter::myOnComponentEndOverlap(AActor* OtherActor,
UPrimitiveComponent* OtherComp, int32 OtherBodyIndex)
{
}

void ABountyDashCharacter::ScoreUp()
{
}
```

Ok, now we can compile the code!

Creating the C++ world objects

With the character constructed, we can now start to build the level. We are going to be creating a block out for the lanes we will be using for the level. We can then use this block out to construct a mesh we can reference in code. Before we get into the level creation, we should ensure the functionality we implemented for the character works as intended. With the BountyDashMap open, navigate to the C++ classes folder of the content browser. Here, you will be able to see the BountyDashCharacter! Drag and drop the character into the game level onto the platform. Then, search for TargetPoint in the **Modes** panel. Drag and drop three of these target points into the game level, and you should be presented with the following:

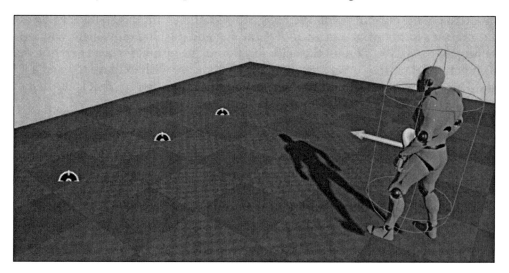

Now, press the **Play** button to enter the PIE mode (Play In Editor). The character should be automatically possessed and used for input! Also, ensure that when you press *A* or *D* the character moves to the next available target point!

Now that we have the base of the character implemented, we should start to build the level. We require three lanes for the player to run down and obstacles for the player to dodge. For now, we should focus on the lanes the player will be running on. Let's start by blocking out how the lanes will appear in the level. Drag a BSP box brush into the game world. You can find the Box brush in **Modes** panel under the **BSP** section under the name **Box**. Place the box at world location (0.0f, 0.0f, and -100.0f). This will place the box in the center of the world. Now, change the **X** property of the box under the **Brush settings** section of the **Details** panel to 10,000.

We require this lane to be long, so that later on we can hide the end using fog without obscuring the objects the player will need to dodge. Next, we need to click on and drag two more copies of this box. You can do this by holding *ALT* while moving an object via the transform widget. Position one box copy at world location (0.0f, -230.0f, and -100) and the next at (0.0f, 230, and -100). The last thing we need to do to finish blocking the level is place the **Target** points in the center of each lane. You should be presented with this when you are done!

Converting BSP brushes to a static mesh

The next thing we need to do is convert the lane brushes we made into one mesh so that we can reference it within our code base. Select all of the boxes in the scene. You can do this by holding *CTRL* while selecting the box brushes in the editor. With all of the brushes selected, address the **Details** panel. Ensure that the transform of your selection is positioned in the middle of the three brushes. If it is not, you can either reselect the brushes in a different order or group the brushes by pressing *CTRL-G* while the boxes are selected. This is important as the position of the transform widget shows what the origin of the generated mesh will be. With the grouping or boxes selected address the **Brush Settings** section in the **Details** panel, there is a small white expansion arrow at the bottom of the section, click on this now. You will then be presented with a **create static mesh** button, press this now. Name this mesh `Floor_Mesh_BountyDash` and save it under `Geometry/Meshes/` of the content folder.

Smoke and mirrors with C++ objects

We are going to be creating the illusion of movement within our level. You may have noticed that we have not included any facilities in our character to move forward in the game world. That is because our character will never advance past his X positon at 0. Instead, we are going to be moving the world toward and past him. This way we can create a very easy spawning and processing logic for the obstacles and game world without having to worry about continuously spawning objects the player can move past further and further down the x-axis.

We require some of the level assets to move through the world so we can establish the illusion of movement for the character. One of these moving objects will be the floor. This requires some logic that will reposition floor meshes as they reach a certain depth behind the character. We will be creating a swap chain of sorts that will work with three meshes. The meshes will be positioned in a contiguous line. As the meshes move underneath and behind the player, we need to move any mesh that is far enough behind the player's back, to the front of the swap chain. The effect is a never ending chain of floor meshes constantly flowing underneath the player. The following diagram may help to understand the concept:

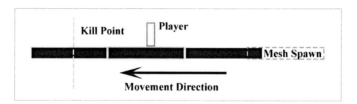

Obstacles and coin pickups will follow a similar logic. However, they will simply be destroyed upon reaching the Kill point in the preceding diagram.

Modifying the BountyDashGameMode

Before we start to create code classes that will feature in our world, we are going to modify BountyDashGameMode that was generated when the project was created. The game mode is going to responsible for all of the game state variables and rules. Later on, we are going to be using the game mode to determine how the player respawns and when the game is lost.

BountyDashGameMode class definition

The game mode is going to be fairly simple. We are going to a add a few member variables that will hold the current state of the game such as game speed, game level, and the number of coins needed to increase the game speed. Navigate to BountyDashGameMode.h and add the following code:

```
UCLASS(minimalapi)
class ABountyDashGameMode : public AGameMode
{
GENERATED_BODY()

UPROPERTY()
float gameSpeed;

UPROPERTY()
int32 gameLevel;
```

As you can see, we have two private member variables gameSpeed and gameLevel. These are private as we wish no other object to be able to modify the contents of these values. You will also note that the class has been specified with minimalapi. This specifier effectively informs the engine that other code modules will not need information from this object outside of the class type. This means that you will be able to cast to this class type but functions cannot be called within other modules. This is specified as a way to optimize compile times as no module outside of this project API will require interactions with our game mode.

Next, we declare the public functions and members we will be using within our game mode. Add the following code to the ABountyDashGameMode class definition:

```
public:
ABountyDashGameMode();

    void CharScoreUp(unsigned int charScore);

    UFUNCTION()
    float GetInvGameSpeed();

    UFUNCTION()
    float GetGameSpeed();

    UFUNCTION()
    int32 GetGameLevel();
```

The `CharScroreUp()` function takes in the player's current score (held by the player) and changes game values based on that score. This means we are able to make the game more difficult, as the player scores more points. The next three functions are simply the accessor methods we can use to get the private data of this class in other objects.

Next, we need to declare our protected members we exposed to be `EditAnywhere`, so we may adjust these from the editor for testing purposes.

```
protected:

UPROPERTY(EditAnywhere, BlueprintReadOnly)
int32 numCoinsForSpeedIncrease;

UPROPERTY(EditAnywhere, BlueprintReadWrite)
float gameSpeedIncrease;

};
```

The `numCoinsForSpeedIncrease` variable will determine how many coins it takes to increase the speed of the game and the `gameSpeedIncrease` value will determine how much faster the objects move when the `numCoinsForSpeedIncrease` value has been met.

BountyDashGameMode function definitions

Let's begin add some definitions to the `BountyDashGameMode` functions. They will be very simple at this point. Let's start by providing some default values for our member variables within the constructor and by assigning the class to be used for our default pawn. Add the definition for the `ABountyDashGameMode` constructor:

```
ABountyDashGameMode::ABountyDashGameMode()
{
    // set default pawn class to our ABountyDashCharacter
    DefaultPawnClass = ABountyDashCharacter::StaticClass();

    numCoinsForSpeedIncrease = 5;
    gameSpeed = 10.0f;
    gameSpeedIncrease = 5.0f;
    gameLevel = 1;
}
```

Here, we are setting the default pawn class by calling `StaticClass()` on `ABountyDashCharacter`. As we have just referenced the `ABountyDashCharacter` type, ensure that `#include "BountyDashCharacter.h"` is add to the `BountyDashGameMode.cpp` include list. The `StaticClass()` function is provided by default for all objects and returns the class type information of the object as a `UClass*`. We then establish some default values for member variables. The player will have to pick up five coins to increase level, the game speed is set to 10.0f (10m/s) and the game will speed up by 5.0f (5m/s) every time the coin quota is reached. Next, let's add a definition for the `CharScoreUp()` function:

```
void
ABountyDashGameMode::CharScoreUp(unsigned int charScore)
{
    if (charScore != 0 &&
        charScore % numCoinsForSpeedIncrease == 0)
    {
        gameSpeed += gameSpeedIncrease;
        gameLevel++;
    }
}
```

This function is quite self-explanatory. The character's current score is passed into the function. We then check that the character's score is not currently 0 and that if the remainder of our character score is 0 after being divided by the number of coins needed for a speed increase, that is, if it divided equally thus the quota has been reached. We then increase the game speed by the `gameSpeedIncrease` value and then increment the level.

The last thing we need to add is the accessor methods described earlier. They do not require too much explanation short of the `GetInvGameSpeed()` function. This function will be used by objects that wish to be pushed down the x-axis at the game speed:

```
float
ABountyDashGameMode::GetInvGameSpeed()
{
    return -gameSpeed;
}

float
ABountyDashGameMode::GetGameSpeed()
{
    return gameSpeed;
}
```

```
int32 ABountyDashGameMode::GetGameLevel()
{
    return gameLevel;
}
```

Getting our game mode via Template functions

The `ABountyDashGame` mode now contains information and functionality that will be required by most of the `BountyDash` objects we create going forward. We need to create a light-weight method to retrieve our custom game mode ensuring that the type of information is preserved. We can do this by creating a template function that will take in a world context and return the correct game mode handle. Traditionally, we could just use a direct cast to `ABountyDashGameMode`; however, this would require including `BountyDashGameMode.h` in `BountyDash.h`. As not all of our objects will require knowledge of the game mode, this is wasteful. Navigate to the `BoutyDash.h` file now. You will be presented with the following:

```
#pragma once

#include "Engine.h"
```

What currently exists in the file is very simple, `#pragma once` has again been used to ensure the compiler only builds and includes the file once. Then `Engine.h` has been included, so every other object in `BOUNTYDASH_API` (they include `BountyDash.h` by default) has access to the functions within `Engine.h`. This is a good place to include utility functions you wish all objects to have access to. In this file, include the following lines of code:

```
template<typename T>
T* GetCustomGameMode(UWorld* worldContext)
{
    return Cast<T>(worldContext->GetAuthGameMode());
}
```

This code, simply put, is a template function that takes in a game world handle. Get the game mode from this context via the `GetAuthGameMode()` function, then cast this game mode to the template type provided to the function. We must cast to the template type as the `GetAuthGameMode()` simply returns a `AGameMode` handle. Now, with that in place, let's begin coding our never ending floor!

Coding the floor

The construction of the floor will be quite simple in essence, as we only need a few variables and a tick function to achieve the functionality we need. Use the class wizard to create a class named **Floor** that inherits from AActor. We will start by modifying the class definition found in Floor.h navigate to this file now.

Floor class definition

The class definition for the floor is very basic. All we need is a Tick() function and some accessor methods, so we may provide some information about the floor to other objects. I have also removed the BeginPlay function provided by default by the class wizard as it is not needed. The following is what you will need to write for the AFloor class definition in its entirety. Replace what is present in Floor.h with this now (keeping the #include list intact):

```
UCLASS()
class BOUNTYDASH_API AFloor : public AActor
{
GENERATED_BODY()

public:
    // Sets default values for this actor's properties
    AFloor();

    // Called every frame
    virtual void Tick( float DeltaSeconds ) override;

    float GetKillPoint();
    float GetSpawnPoint();

protected:
    UPROPERTY(EditAnywhere)
    TArray<USceneComponent*> FloorMeshScenes;

    UPROPERTY(EditAnywhere)
    TArray<UStaticMeshComponent*> FloorMeshes;

    UPROPERTY(EditAnywhere)
    UBoxComponent* CollisionBox;

    int32 NumRepeatingMesh;
    float KillPoint;
    float SpawnPoint;
};
```

We have three UPROPERTY declared members. The first two being TArrays that will hold handles to the USceneComponent and UMeshComponent objects that will make up the floor. We require the TArray of scene components, as the USceneComponent objects provide us with a world transform that we can apply translations to so that we may update the position of the generated floor mesh pieces. The last UPROPERTY is a collision box that will be used for the actual player collisions to prevent the player from falling through the moving floor. The reason we are using a BoxComponent instead of the meshes for collision is that we do not want the player to translate with the moving meshes. Due to surface friction simulation, having the character collide with any of the moving meshes will cause the player to move with the mesh.

The last three members are protected and do not require any UPROPRTY specification. We are simply going to use the two float values, KillPoint and SpawnPoint, to save output calculations from the constructor so we may use them in the Tick() function. The integer value NumRepeatingMesh will be used to determine how many meshes we will have in the chain.

Floor function definitions

As always, we will start with the constructor of the floor. It is here that we will be performing the bulk of our calculations for this object. We will be creating USceneComponents and UMeshComponents that we are going to use to make up our moving floor. With dynamic programming in mind, we should establish the construction algorithm so that we can create any number of meshes in the moving line. Also as we will be getting the speed of the floors movement form the game mode, ensure that #include "BountyDashGameMode.h" is included in Floor.cpp.

AFloor::AFloor() constructor

Start by adding the following lines to the AFloor constructor AFloor::AFloor() found in Floor.cpp:

```
RootComponent =CreateDefaultSubobject<USceneComponent>(TEXT("Root"));

ConstructorHelpers::FObjectFinder<UStaticMesh>myMesh(TEXT(
"/Game/Barrel_Hopper/Geometry/Floor_Mesh_BountyDash.Floor_Mesh_
BountyDash"));

ConstructorHelpers::FObjectFinder<UMaterial>myMaterial(TEXT(
"/Game/StarterContent/Materials/M_Concrete_Tiles.M_Concrete_Tiles"));
```

To start with, we are simply using `FObjectFinders` to find the assets we require for the mesh. For the `myMesh` finder, ensure you parse the reference location of the static floor mesh we created earlier. We also create a scene component to be used as the root component for the floor object. Next, we are going to be checking the success of the mesh acquisition, and then establishing some variables for the mesh placement logic:

```
if (myMesh.Succeeded())
{
    NumRepeatingMesh = 3;

    FBoxSphereBounds myBounds = myMesh.Object->GetBounds();
    float XBounds = myBounds.BoxExtent.X * 2;
    float ScenePos = ((XBounds * (NumRepeatingMesh - 1)) / 2.0f) * -1;

    KillPoint = ScenePos - (XBounds * 0.5f);
    SpawnPoint = (ScenePos * -1) + (XBounds * 0.5f);
```

Note that we have just opened an `if` statement without closing the scope; from time to time, I will split segments of code within a scope across multiple pages. If you are ever lost as to the current scope, we are working from look for this comment; `<-- Closing If(MyMesh.Succed())` or in the future, a similarly named comment.

Firstly, we are initializing the `NumRepeatingMesh` value with three. We are using a variable here instead of a hard coded value so that we may update the number of meshes in the chain without having to refactor the remaining code base.

We then get the bounds of the mesh object using the `GetBounds()` function on the mesh asset we just retrieved. This returns a `FBoxSphereBounds` struct, which will provide you with all of the bounding information of a static mesh asset. We then use the X component of the member `BoxExtent` to initialize Xbounds. BoxExtent is a vector that holds the extent of the bounding box of this mesh. We save the X component of this vector, so we can use it for mesh chain placement logic. We have doubled this value as the `BoxExtent` vector that represents the extent of the box from origin to one corner of the mesh. Meaning if we wish for the total bounds of the mesh, we must double any of the `BoxExtent` components.

Next, we calculate the initial scene position of the first `USceneCompoennt` we will be attaching a mesh to and storing in the `ScenePos` array. We can determine this position by getting the total length of all of the meshes in the chain (`XBounds * (numRepeatingMesh - 1)`), then halve the resulting value so we can get the distance the first `SceneComponent` will be from the origin along the x-axis. We also multiply this value by `-1` to make it negative as we wish to start our mesh chain behind the character (at X position 0).

We then use `ScenePos` to specify our `killPoint`, which represents the point in space at which floor mesh pieces should get to before swapping back to the start of the chain. For the purposes the swap chain, whenever a scene component is half a mesh piece length behind the position of the first scene component in the chain, it should be moved to the other side of the chain. With all of our variables in place, we can now iterate through the number of meshes we desire (3) and create the appropriate components. Add the following code to the scope of the if statement we just opened:

```
for (int i = 0; i < NumRepeatingMesh; ++i)
{
// Initialize Scene
FString SceneName = "Scene" + FString::FromInt(i);
FName SceneID = FName(*SceneName);
USceneComponent* thisScene = CreateDefaultSubobject<USceneComponent>(
SceneID);
check(thisScene);

thisScene->AttachTo(RootComponent);
thisScene->SetRelativeLocation(FVector(ScenePos, 0.0f, 0.0f));
ScenePos += XBounds;

floorMeshScenes.Add(thisScene);
```

Firstly, we are creating a name for the scene component by appending `Scene` with the iteration value we are up too. We then convert this appended `FString` to an `FName`; then provide this to the `CreateDefaultSubobject` template function. With the resultant `USceneComponent` handle, we call `AttachTo()` to bind it to the root component. Then, we set the `RelativeLocation` of `USceneComponent`. Here, we are parsing in the `ScenePos` value we calculated earlier as the x component of the new relative location. The relative location of this component will always be based off the position of the root `SceneComponent` we created earlier.

With `USceneCompoennt` appropriately placed, we then increment the `ScenePos` value by that of the `XBounds` value. This will ensure that subsequent `USceneComponents` created in this loop will be placed in an entire mesh length away from the previous, forming a contiguous chain of meshes attached to scene components. Lastly, we add this new `USceneComponent` to `floorMeshScenes`, so we may later perform translations on the components. Next, we will construct the mesh components by adding the following code to the loop:

```
// Initialize Mesh
FString MeshName = "Mesh" + FString::FromInt(i);
UStaticMeshComponent* thisMesh = CreateDefaultSubobject<UStaticMeshCom
ponent>(FName(*MeshName));
check(thisMesh);
```

```
thisMesh->AttachTo(FloorMeshScenes[i]);
thisMesh->SetRelativeLocation(FVector(0.0f, 0.0f, 0.0f));
thisMesh->SetCollisionProfileName(TEXT("OverlapAllDynamic"));

if (myMaterial.Succeeded())
{
    thisMesh->SetStaticMesh(myMesh.Object);
    thisMesh->SetMaterial(0, myMaterial.Object);
}

FloorMeshes.Add(thisMesh);
} // <--Closing For(int i = 0; i < numReapeatingMesh; ++i)
```

As you can see, we performed a similar name creation process for `UMeshComponents` as we did for `USceneComponents`. The construction process following is quite simple. We attach the mesh to the scene component so the mesh will follow any translations we apply to the parent `USceneComponent`. We then ensure that the mesh's origin will be centered around `USceneComponent` by setting the Mesh's **relative** location to be (0.0f, 0.0f, and 0.0f). We then ensure that the meshes do not collide with anything in the game world, we do that with the `SetCollisionProfileName()` function.

If you remember when we used this function earlier, you provide a profile name you wish the object to use the collision properties from. In our case, we wish this mesh to overlap all dynamic objects; thus, we parse `OverlapAllDynamic`. Without this line of code, the character may collide with the moving floor meshes, and that will drag the player along at the same speed thus breaking the illusion of motion we are trying to create.

Lastly, we assign the static mesh object and material we obtained earlier with the `FObjectFinders`. We ensure that we add this new mesh object to the `FloorMeshes` array in case we need them later. We also close the loop scope we created earlier.

The next thing we are going to do is create the collision box that will be used for character collisions. With the box set to collide with everything and the meshes set to overlap everything, we will be able to collide on the stationary box while the meshes whip past under our feet. The following code will create the box collider:

```
collisionBox =CreateDefaultSubobject<UBoxComponent>(TEXT("CollsionB
ox"));
check(collisionBox);

collisionBox->AttachTo(RootComponent);
collisionBox->SetBoxExtent(FVector(spawnPoint, myBounds.BoxExtent.Y,
myBounds.BoxExtent.Z));
collisionBox->SetCollisionProfileName(TEXT("BlockAllDynamic"));

} // <-- Closing if(myMesh.Succeeded())
```

As you can see, we initialize `UBoxComponent` as we always initialize components. We then attach the box to the root component as we do not wish to move it. We also set the box extent to be that of the length of the entire swap chain by setting the `spawnPoint` value as the X bounds of the collider. We set the collision profile to `BlockAllDynamic`. This means that it will block any dynamic actors such as our Character! Note that we have also closed the scope of the if statement opened earlier. With the constructor definition finished, we might as well define the accessor methods for `spawnPoint` and `killPoint` before we move onto the `Tick()` function:

```
float AFloor::GetKillPoint()
{
    return KillPoint;
}


float AFloor::GetSpawnPoint()
{
    return SpawnPoint;
}
```

AFloor::Tick()

Now, it is time to write the function that will move the meshes and ensure they move back to the start of the chain when they reach `KillPoint`. Add the following code to the `Tick()` function found in `Floor.cpp`:

```
for (auto Scene : FloorMeshScenes)
{
Scene->AddLocalOffset(FVector(GetCustomGameMode
<ABountyDashGameMode>(GetWorld())->GetInvGameSpeed(), 0.0f, 0.0f));

if (Scene->GetComponentTransform().GetLocation().X <= KillPoint)
{
    Scene->SetRelativeLocation(FVector(SpawnPoint, 0.0f, 0.0f));
}
}
```

Here, we are using a C++ 11 range for loop. Meaning that for each element inside of `FloorMeshScenes`, it will populate the scene handle of type auto with a pointer to whatever type is contained by `FloorMeshScenes`, in this case `USceneComponent *`. For every scene component contained within `FloorMeshScenes`, we are adding a local offset to each frame. The amount we offset each frame is dependent on the current game speed.

We are getting the game speed from the game mode via the template function we wrote earlier. As you can see, we specified the template function to be of type `ABountyDashGameMode`, thus we will have access to the bounty dash game mode functionality. We have done this so that the floor will move faster under the player's feet as the speed of the game increases. The next thing we do is check the X value of the Scene components location. If this value is equal to or less than the value stored in `KillPoint`, we reposition the scene component back to the spawn point. As we attached the meshes to these `USceenComponents` earlier, the meshes will also translate with the scene components. Lastly, ensure that you have added #include nBountyDashGameMode.h" to the `.cppts` include list.

Placing the Floor in the level!

We are done making the floor! Compile the code and return to the level editor. We can now place this new floor object in the level! Delete the static mesh that would have replaced our earlier box brushes and drag and drop the **Floor** object into the scene. The floor object can be found under the `C++ classes` folder of the content browser. Select the `Floor` in the level and ensure that its location is set too (0.0f, 0.0f, and -100.f). This will place the floor just below the player's feet around origin. Also ensure the `ATargetPoints` we placed earlier are in the right positions above the lanes. With this all in place, you should be able to press play and observe the floor moving underneath the player indefinitely. You should see something similar to this:

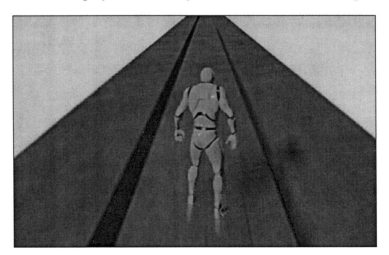

You will notice that as you move between the lanes by pressing *A* and *D* the player maintains the X Position of the target points but nicely travels to the center of each lane.

Creating the obstacles

The next step for this project is to create the obstacles that will come flying at the player. These obstacles are going to be very simple and contain only a few members and functions. These obstacles are to only serve as a blockade for the player and all of the collision with the obstacles will be handled by the player itself. Use the class wizard to create a new class named **Obstacle** and inherit this object from `AActor`. Once the class has been generated, modify the class definition found in `Obstacle.h`, so it appears as follows:

```
UCLASS(BlueprintType)
class BOUNTYDASH_API AObstacle: public AActor
{
GENERATED_BODY()

    float KillPoint;

public:
    // Sets default values for this actor's properties
    AObstacle ();

    // Called when the game starts or when spawned
    virtual void BeginPlay() override;

    // Called every frame
    virtual void Tick( float DeltaSeconds ) override;

void SetKillPoint(float point);
float GetKillPoint();

protected:
    UFUNCITON()
    virtual void MyOnActorOverlap(AActor* otherActor);

    UFUNCTION()
    virtual void MyOnActorEndOverlap(AActor* otherActor);

public:
UPROPERTY(EditAnywhere, BlueprintReadWrite)
    USphereComponent* Collider;

    UPROPERTY(EditAnywhere, BlueprintReadWrite)
    UStaticMeshComponent* Mesh;
};
```

You will note that the class has been declared with the `BlueprintType` specifier! This object is simple enough to justify extension into blueprint as there is no new learning to be found within this simple object, and we can use blueprint for convenience. For this class, we added a private member `KillPoint` that will be used to determine when the `AObstacle` should destroy itself. We also added the accessor methods for this private member. You will notice that we added the `MyActorBeginOverlap` and `MyActorEndOverlap` functions that we will be providing to the appropriate delegates, so we can provide custom collision response for this object. We also declared these functions as virtual; this is so we can override these collision functions in child classes of `AObstacle`.

The definitions of these functions are not too complicated either. Ensure that you have included `#include "BountyDashGameMode.h"` in the `Obstacle.cpp`. Then, we can begin filling out our function definitions. The following is code what we will use for the constructor:

```
AObstacle::AObstacle()
{
PrimaryActorTick.bCanEverTick = true;

Collider = CreateDefaultSubobject<USphereComponent>(TEXT("Collider"));
check(Collider);

RootComponent = Collider;
Collider ->SetCollisionProfileName("OverlapAllDynamic");

Mesh = CreateDefaultSubobject<UStaticMeshComponent>(TEXT("Mesh"));
check(Mesh);
Mesh ->AttachTo(Collider);
Mesh ->SetCollisionResponseToAllChannels(ECR_Ignore);
KillPoint = -20000.0f;

OnActorBeginOverlap.AddDynamic(this, &AObstacle::MyOnActorOverlap);
OnActorBeginOverlap.AddDynamic(this, &AObstacle::MyOnActorEndOverlap);
}
```

The only thing of note within this constructor is again we set the mesh of this object to ignore collision response to all channels meaning. The mesh will not affect collision in any way. We have also initialized kill point with a default value of `-20000.0f`. Following that we are binding the custom `MyOnActorOverlap` and `MyOnActorEndOverlap` function to the appropriate delegates.

The `Tick()` function of this object is responsible for translating the obstacle during play. Add the following code to the Tick function of `AObstacle`:

```
void AObstacle::Tick( float DeltaTime )
{
    Super::Tick( DeltaTime );
float gameSpeed = GetCustomGameMode<ABountyDashGameMode>(GetWorld())->
GetInvGameSpeed();

    AddActorLocalOffset(FVector(gameSpeed, 0.0f, 0.0f));

    if (GetActorLocation().X < KillPoint)
    {
        Destroy();
    }
}
```

As you can see, the tick function will add an offset to the `AObstacle` each frame along the x-axis via the `AddActorLocalOffset` function. The value of the offset is determined by the game speed set in the game mode. Again, we are using the template function we created earlier to get the game mode to call `GetInvGameSpeed()`. The `AObstacle` is also responsible for its own destruction, upon reaching a maximum bounds defined by `killPoint` the `AObstacle` will destroy itself.

The last thing we need to add is the function definitions for the `OnOverlap` functions and `KillPoint` accessors:

```
void AObstacle::MyOnActorOverlap(AActor* otherActor)
{

}
void AObstacle::MyOnActorEndOverlap(AActor* otherActor)
{

}

void AObstacle::SetKillPoint(float point)
{
    killPoint = point;
}

float AObstacle::GetKillPoint()
{
    return killPoint;
}
```

Now, let's abstract this class into blueprint. Compile the code and go back to the game editor. Within the content folder, create a new blueprint object that inherits form the `Obstacle` class we just made, name it `RockObstacleBP`. Within this blueprint, we need to make some adjustments. Select the **collider** component we created and expand the shape sections in **Details** panel. Change the **Sphere radius** property to `100.0f`. Next, select the mesh component and expand the **Static Mesh** section; from the provided drop down, choose the `SM_Rock` mesh. Next, expand the transform section of the `Mesh` component details panel and match these values:

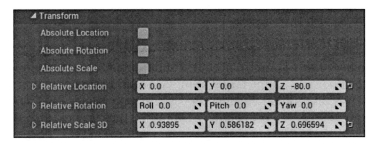

You should end up with an object that looks similar to this:

Spawning actors from C++!

Despite the Obstacles being fairly easy to implement from a C++ standpoint, the complication comes from the spawning system we will be using to create these objects in game. We will leverage a similar system to the player's movement by basing the spawn locations off of `ATargetPoints` that are already in the scene. We can then randomly select a spawn target when we require a new object to spawn. Open the class wizard now, and create a class that inherits from **Actor** and call it `ObstacleSpawner`. We inherit from `AActor` as even though this object does not have a physical presence in the scene, we still require the `ObstacleSpawner` to tick.

The first issue we are going to encounter is our current target points give us a good indication of the Y positon for our spawns but the X position is centered around origin. This is undesirable for the obstacle spawn point as we would like to spawn these objects a fair distance away from the player so we can do two things. One, obscure the **popping** of spawning the objects via fog and two, present the player with enough obstacle information so they may dodge them at high speeds. This means we are going to require some information from our floor object, we can use the `KillPoint` and `SpawnPoint` members of the floor to determine the spawn location and kill location of the Obstacles.

Obstacle Spawner class definition

This will be another fairly simple object. It will require a `BeginPlay` function, so we may find the floor and all the target points we require for spawning. We also require a `Tick` function so that we may process spawning logic on a per frame basis. Thankfully, both of these are provided by default by the class wizard. We created a protected `SpawnObstacle()` function, so we may group that functionality together. We are also going to require a few UPRORERTY declared members that can be edited from the level editor. We need a list of obstacle types to spawn; we can then randomly select one of the types each time we spawn an obstacle. We also require the spawn targets (though we will be populating these upon begin play). Finally, we will need a spawn time that we can set for the interval between obstacles spawning. To accommodate for all of this, navigate to `ObstacleSpawner.h` now and modify the class definition to match the following:

```
UCLASS()
class BOUNTYDASH_API AObstacleSpawner : public AActor
{
    GENERATED_BODY()

public:
    // Sets default values for this actor's properties
    AObstacleSpawner();

    // Called when the game starts or when spawned
    virtual void BeginPlay() override;

    // Called every frame
    virtual void Tick( float DeltaSeconds ) override;


protected:
```

```
    void SpawnObstacle();

public:
    UPROPERTY(EditAnywhere, BlueprintReadWrite)
    TArray<TSubclassof<class AObstacle*>> ObstaclesToSpawn;

    UPROPERTY()
    TArray<class ATargetPoint*>SpawnTargets;

    UPROPERTY(EditAnywhere, BlueprintReadWrite)
    float SpawnTimer;

    UPROPERTY()
    USceneComponent* scene;
private:
    float KillPoint;
    float SpawnPoint;
    float TimeSinceLastSpawn;
};
```

I have again used `TArray`s for our containers of obstacle objects and spawn targets. As you can see the obstacle list is of type `TSubclassof<class AObstacle>>`. This means that the objects in this `TArray` will be class types that inherit from `AObscatle`. This is very useful as not only will we be able to use these array elements for spawn information; the engine will also filter our search when adding object types to this array from the editor! With these class types, we will be able to spawn objects that inherit from `AObject` (including blueprints!) when required. We also included a scene object, so we can arbitrarily place `AObstacleSpawner` in the level somewhere and two private members that will hold the kill and spawn point of the objects. The last element is a `float` timer that will be used to gauge how much time has passed since the last obstacle spawn.

Obstacle Spawner function definitions

Okay, now we can create the body of the `AObstacleSpawner` object. Before we do, ensure the include list in `ObstacleSpawner.cpp` is as follows:

```
#include "BountyDash.h"
#include "BountyDashGameMode.h"
#include "Engine/TargetPoint.h"
#include "Floor.h"
#include "Obstacle.h"
#include "ObstacleSpawner.h"
```

Following this, we have a very simple constructor that establishes the root scene component:

```cpp
// Sets default values
AObstacleSpawner::AObstacleSpawner()
{
// Set this actor to call Tick() every frame.  You can turn this off
to improve performance if you don't need it.
PrimaryActorTick.bCanEverTick = true;

Scene = CreateDefaultSubobject<USceneComponent>(TEXT("Root"));
check(Scene);
RootComponent = scene;

SpawnTimer = 1.5f;
}
```

Following the constructor, we have `BeginPlay()`. Inside this function, we are going to do a few things. First, we are simply performing the same in level object retrieval we executed in `ABountyDashCarhacter` to get the location of `ATargetPoints`. However, this object also requires information from the floor object in the level. We are also going to get the `Floor` object the same way we did with the `ATargetPoints` by utilizing `TActorIterators`. We will then get the required kill and spawn point information. We will also set `TimeSinceLastSpawn` to `SpawnTimer`, so we begin spawning objects instantaneously:

```cpp
// Called when the game starts or when spawned
void AObstacleSpawner::BeginPlay()
{
    Super::BeginPlay();

for(TActorIterator<ATargetPoint> TargetIter(GetWorld()); TargetIter;
    ++TargetIter)
    {
        SpawnTargets.Add(*TargetIter);
    }

for (TActorIterator<AFloor> FloorIter(GetWorld()); FloorIter;
        ++FloorIter)
    {
        if (FloorIter->GetWorld() == GetWorld())
        {
            KillPoint = FloorIter->GetKillPoint();
            SpawnPoint = FloorIter->GetSpawnPoint();
        }
```

```
    }
    TimeSinceLastSpawn = SpawnTimer;
}
```

The next function we will detail is `Tick()`, which is responsible for the bulk of the `AObstacleSpawner` functionality. Within this function, we need to check if we require a new object to be spawned based on the amount of time that has passed since we last spawned an object. Add the following code to `AObstacleSpawner::Tick()` underneath `Super::Tick()` now:

```
TimeSinceLastSpawn += DeltaTime;

float trueSpawnTime = spawnTime / (float)GetCustomGameMode
<ABountyDashGameMode>(GetWorld())->GetGameLevel();

if (TimeSinceLastSpawn > trueSpawnTime)
{
    timeSinceLastSpawn = 0.0f;
    SpawnObstacle ();
}
```

Here, we are accumulating the delta time in `TimeSinceLastSpawn`, so we may gauge how much real time has passed since the last obstacle was spawned. We then calculate the `trueSpawnTime` of the `AObstacleSpawner`. This is based on a base `SpawnTime`, which is divided by the current game level retrieved from the game mode via the `GetCustomGamMode()` template function. This means that as the game level increases and the obstacles begin to move faster, the obstacle spawner will also spawn objects at a faster rate. If the accumulated `timeSinceLastSpawn` is greater than the calculated `trueSpawnTime` we need to call `SpawnObject()` and reset the `timeSinceLastSpawn` timer to `0.0f`.

Getting information from components in C++

Now, we need to write the spawn function. This spawn function is going to have to retrieve some information from the components of the object that is being spawned. As we allowed our `AObstacle` class to be extended into blueprint, we also exposed the object to a level of versatility we must compensate for in the codebase. With the ability to customize the mesh and bounds of the Sphere Collider that makes up any given obstacle, we must be sure we spawn the obstacle in the right place regardless of size!

To do this, we are going to need to obtain information form the components contained within the spawned `AObstacle` class. This can be done via `GetComponentByClass()`. It will take the `UClass*` of the component you wish to retrieve and will return a handle to the component if it has been found. We can then cast this handle to the appropriate type and retrieve the information we require! Let's begin detailing the spawn function by adding the following code to `ObstacleSpawner.cpp`:

```
void AObstacleSpawner::SpawnObstacle()
{
if (SpawnTargets.Num() > 0 && ObstaclesToSpawn.Num() > 0)
{
    short Spawner = FMath::Rand() % SpawnTargets.Num();
    short Obstical = FMath::Rand() % ObstaclesToSpawn.Num();
    float CapsuleOffset = 0.0f;
```

Here, we ensure that both of the arrays have been populated with at least one valid member. We then generate the random look up integers that we will use to access the `SpawnTargets` and `obstacleToSpawn` arrays. This means that every time we spawn an object, both the lane spawned in and the type of the object will be randomized. We do this by generating a random value with `FMath::Rand()` and then we find the remainder of that number divided by the number of elements in the corresponding array. The result will be a random number that exists between 0 and the number of objects in either array minus one, which is perfect for our needs. Continue by adding the following code:

```
FActorSpawnParameters SpawnInfo;

FTransform myTrans = SpawnTargets[Spawner]->GetTransform();
myTrans.SetLocation(FVector(SpawnPoint, myTrans.GetLocation().Y,
myTrans.GetLocation().Z));
```

Here, we are using a `struct` called `FActorSpawnParameters`. The default values of this `struct` are fine for our purposes. We will soon be parsing this `struct` to a function in our world context. After that, we create a transform that we will be providing to world context as well. The transform of the spawner will suffice apart from the X Component of the location. We need to adjust this so the x value of the spawn transform matches the spawn point we retrieved from the floor. We do this by setting the x component of the spawn transforms location to be the `spawnPoint` value we received earlier, and the other components of the location vector to be the Y and Z components of the current location.

The next thing we must do is actually spawn the object! We are going to utilize a template function called `SpawnActor()` that can be called form the `UWorld*` handle returned by `GetWorld()`. This function will spawn an object of a specified type in the game world at a specified location. The type of the object is determined by passing a `UClass*` handle that holds the object type we wish to spawn. The transform and spawn parameters of the object are also determined by the corresponding input parameters of `SpawnActor()`. The template type of the function will dictate the type of object that is spawned and the handle that is returned from the function. In our case, we require `AObstacle` to be spawned. Add the following code to the `SpawnObstacle` function:

```
AObstacle* newObs = GetWorld()-> SpawnActor<AObstacle>(obstacleToSpawn
[Obstical, myTrans, SpawnInfo);

if(newObs)
{
newObs->SetKillPoint(KillPoint);
```

As you can see, we are using `SpawnActor()` with a template type of `AObstacle`. We use the random look up integer we generated before to retrieve the class type from the `obstacleToSpawn` array. We also provide the transform and spawn parameters we created earlier to `SpawnActor()`. If the new `AObstacle` was created successfully, we then save the return of this function into an `AObstacle` handle that we will use to set the kill point of the obstacle via `SetKillPoint()`.

We must now adjust the height of this object. The object will more than likely spawn in the ground in its current state. We need to obtain access to the sphere component of the obstacle so that we may get the radius of this capsule and adjust the position of the obstacle, so it sits above the ground. We can use the capsule as a reliable resource as it is the root component of the obstacle, thus we can move the obstacle entirely out of the ground if we assume the base of the sphere will line up with the base of the mesh. Add the following code to the `SpawnObstacle()` function:

```
USphereComponent* obsSphere = Cast<USphereComponent>
(newObs->GetComponentByClass(USphereComponent::StaticClass()));

if (obsSphere)
{
newObs->AddActorLocalOffset(FVector(0.0f, 0.0f, obsSphere->
GetUnscaledSphereRadius()));
}
}//<-- Closing if(newObs)
}//<-- Closing if(SpawnTargets.Num() > 0 && obstacleToSpawn.Num() > 0)
```

Here, we are getting the sphere component out of the newObs handle we obtained from SpawnActor() via GetComponentByClass(), which was earlier mentioned. We pass the class type of a USphereComponent via the static function StaticClass() to the function. This will return a valid handle if the newObs contains USphereComponent (which we know it does). We then cast the result of this function to USphereComponent* and save it in the obsSphere handle. We ensure this handle is valid; if it is, we can then offset the actor we just spawned on the z-axis by the unscaled radius of the sphere component. This will result in all obstacles spawned be in line with the top of the floor!

Ensuring the Obstacle Spawner works

Okay, now it is time to bring the obstacle spawner into the scene. Be sure to compile the code then navigate to the **C++ classes** folder of the content browser. From here, drag and drop ObstacleSpawner into the scene. Select the new ObstacleSpawner via the **World Outlier** and address the **Details** panel. You will see the exposed members under the ObstacleSpawner section like so:

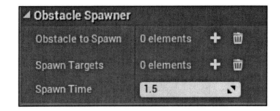

Now, add the RockObstacleBP we made earlier to the ObstacleToSpawn array. Press the small white plus next to the property in **Details** panel; this will add an element to the TArray that you will then be able to customize. Select the dropdown that currently says **None**. Within this drop down search for the RockObstacleBP and select it. If you wish to create and add more obstacle types to this array feel free. We do not need to add any members to the **Spawn Targets** property as that will happen automatically. Now, press **Play** and behold a legion of moving rocks!

Minting the coin object

We are nearly ready to start playing `BountyDash`! First, we need to create a coin system. Coins will function in a very similar way to obstacles, but they require other specific functionality that warrants their own class. What we can do, however, is create the coin as a child class of `AObstacle`! This means that we do not have to write duplicate functionality! Use the class wizard to create another class called `Coin`; however, this time be sure to make the parent class `AObstacle`.

Coin class definition

Once the class generation is complete, navigate to the `Coin.h` file. You will notice that we are given no default functionality and we must specify it all. Still much like the `AObstacle`, our class definition is going to be very minimal. Most of the functionality we require for the coin has already been included in the `AObstacle` base class. All we need to do here is override the `Tick()` and `MyOnActorOverlap()` functions, so we can add additional coin functionality.

The following is the class definition for the `ACoin` object:

```
UCLASS()
class BOUNTYDASH_API ACoin : public AObstacle
{
    GENERATED_BODY()

    ACoin();
```

```
    // Called every frame
    virtual void Tick(float DeltaSeconds) override;

    UFUNCTION()
    virtual void MyOnActorOverlap(AActor* otherActor) override;
};
```

Simple right? As you can see, we declared a `ACoin()` constructor and we are overriding the `virtual Tick` function. You will notice that we have also included the `UFUNCITON` macro above the `MyOnActorOverlap` function that we will be passing to the overlap delegate for this actor so that the delegate association succeeds.

Coin function definitons

Let's now define how the coin is going to work navigate to `coin.cpp` now. Start by adding the following to the include list if they are not already present:

```
#include "BountyDash.h"
#include "BountyDashCharacter.h"
#include "BountyDashGameMode.h"
#include "Coin.h"
```

Now, we are going to define our coin's constructor. `AObstacle` base class already constructs the mesh and collider objects, so we do not have to do that here. It also provides the `MyOnActorBeginOverlap` function to the `OnActorBeginOverlap` delegate. Because the `MyOnActorBeginOverlap` function was specified as virtual and we have overridden this function in `ACoin`, we do not need to re-bind the functions. We can define our constructor with no functionality as the following:

```
ACoin::ACoin()
{

}
```

Following that, we can define the `Tick()` function. This function is going to be used to rotate the mesh component of the object so it spins while moving toward the player. Add the following to `Tick()` within `Coin.cpp`:

```
void ACoin::Tick(float DeltaTime)
{
Super::Tick(DeltaTime);
    Mesh->AddLocalRotation(FRotator(5.0f, 0.0f, 0.0f));
}
```

Here, you can see we are calling `Super::Tick()`, so the functionality we implemented in `AObstacle` is executed. We then add a local rotation to the mesh component every frame via the `AddLocalRotation` function. We yaw the coin roughly at 5 degrees per frame.

Ok, now we can define our overridden `MyOnActorOverlap` functionality. We will be detailing the collisions between objects in more detail later in the chapter. For now, we will write code that will handle when a coin is spawned on top of an obstacle object. This may happen from time to time as they will be sharing spawning locations but not necessarily have exclusive spawn times. We need to detect if the coin is currently colliding with an obstacle. If so, we need to adjust the height of the coin object, we can do that with the following code:

```
void ACoin::MyOnActorOverlap(AActor* otherActor)
{
    if (otherActor->GetClass()->IsChildOf(AObstacle::StaticClass()))
    {
USphereComponent* thisSphere = Cast<USphereComponent>(GetComponentByCl
ass(USphereComponent::StaticClass()));

USphereComponent* otherSpehre = Cast<USphereComponent>(otherActor-> Ge
tComponentByClass(USphereComponent::StaticClass()));

        if (otherSpehre)
        {
AddActorLocalOffset(FVector(0.0f, 0.0f, (otherSpehre->
GetUnscaledSphereRadius() * 2.0f) + Collider->
GetUnscaledSphereRadius())));
        }
    }
}
```

The first thing we do is use the class type information of the `AActor` object to see if the offending actor is either a `AObstacle` or a child of `AObstacle`. We do this with the `IsChildOf()` function. This function can be called on any actor to determine if it is a child of a specific class type or of that type itself. For the input parameter, we parse the class type of `AObstacle` via `StaticClass()`. If this check succeeds, we need to get information from the sphere component of the other actor now proven to be of type `AObstacle`. We do this as we did previously using `GetComponentByClass()` and parsing the class information of the type of component we require. We then check that this function returned a valid handle. If so, we will add a local offset to the coin actor. We will only be adding an offset on the z-axis. We will offset by the `otherSphere` radius * 2 plus the radius of the coin sphere so that the coin will be placed on top of the obstacle mesh.

Making the coin Blueprint!

Let's create the blueprint that is going to extend from the coin object. Create a new `Blueprint` class somewhere in the content browser and inherit the blueprint from the `Coin` class we just made. Call this class `CoinBP`. We are going to assemble this blueprint in the same way we did `RockObstacleBP`. For the collider component, set the **Sphere Radius** property of the **Shape** section in the details panel to `60.0f`. Then, set the **Static Mesh** property of the **Static Mesh** section of the **mesh** component to `SM_AssetPlatform`. After that, add a member to the **Override Materials** list in the **Rendering** section of **Details** panel. Set this member to be the `M_Metal_Gold` material. Then, change the transform settings of this component so they match the following:

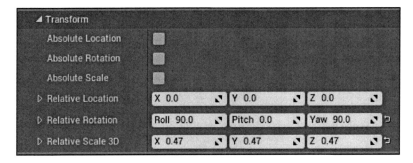

You will then be presented with a blueprint object that looks like this!

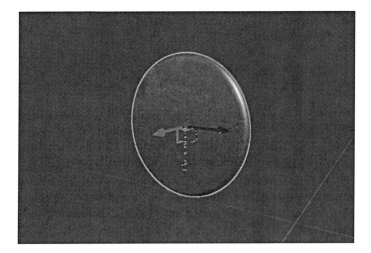

Making it rain coins, creating the coin spawner

We now need to create a system that will spawn the coins. This time, we cannot use the `AObstacleSpawner` we created previously as a base class. This is because the spawning logic for the coin spawner is much more involved. For the coins in `BountyDash`, we need to construct the system so the coins will spawn in sets of a random number. Also, within each set we need to ensure that the coins spawn far enough apart. The result will be periodically spawning streams of coins the player can pick up. Open the class wizard again and create a class that inherits from Actor; call it `CoinSpawner`. This class is going to be very minimal with regards to methods, but it will have quite a few properties.

Coin Spawner class Definition

We will be keeping most of the default functionality provided by the class wizard. The only function we will be removing is the `Tick()` method, as we are going to utilize the `FTimerManager` object to drive our spawning functionality. More on this later. Ensure that you remove the Tick function declaration and add the following publically declared member variables:

```
public:
    UPROPERTY(EditAnywhere)
    TSubclassOf<ACoin> CoinObject;

    UPROPERTY()
    TArray<class ATargetPoint*> SpawnTransforms;

    UPROPERTY()
    USceneComponent* Root;

    UPROPERTY(EditAnywhere)
    int32 MaxSetCoins;

    UPROPERTY(EditAnywhere)
    int32 MinSetCoins;

    UPROPERTY(EditAnywhere)
    float CoinSetTimeInterval;

    UPROPERTY(EditAnywhere)
    float CoinTimeInterval;

    UPROPERTY(EditAnywhere)
    float MovementTimeInterval;
```

Here, we have a TSubclassOf<class ACoin> handle called CoinObject. This has been declared as EditAnywhere, as we wish to edit this value from the editor much like the obstacle TArray of AObstacleSpawner. It will act as the class object that we use when spawning the coins. We included another TArray of ATargetpoints to be used for our coin spawn locations. Following that is another USceneComponent that will be used to arbitrarily position the spawner in the world. Underneath that, we have all of the properties that we are going to use to dictate the spawning logic for the coins. You will notice that they have all been declared with the UPROPERTY macro and specified, so we may edit the values from the editor. MaxSetCoins and MinSetCoins will be used to determine a random number of coins to spawn within a set between those two maxims. Next, we have all of the float timers that will dictate how long it takes between each major spawner action. We have one for each set of coins, each individual coin within a set, and a movement interval.

Following that, we have our protected members that will be used for internal logic and thus do not need to be exposed:

```
protected:
    void SpawnCoin();
    void SpawnCoinSet();
    void MoveSpawner();

    int32 NumCoinsToSpawn;

    float KillPoint;
    float SpawnPoint;
    int32 TargetLoc;

    FTimerHandle CoinSetTimerHandle;
    FTimerHandle CoinTimerHandle;
    FTimerHandle SpawnMoveTimerHandle;
```

We declared several spawning functions. These functions are going to be used to invoke the various spawning methods we require for our coins. We then declare a series of variables. The first NumCoinsToSpawn is an integer value that will hold the number of coins we need to spawn for any given set. We also have the two float values KillPoint and SpawnPoint that will be used for spawning logics. Following this, we have an int value that will be used to determine within which lane we are spawning coins.

Lastly, we have a new object type we have yet to interact with the `FTimerHandle` object. Unlike our obstacle spawner, we are not going to be using traditional float timers that are incremented within a `Tick()` function. We are instead going to be leveraging the `TimerManager` object that is present in our `GameWorld` (`UWorld`). Through the time manager, we are able to create timer objects that will invoke a provided function after a given time period. The three timer handles here will be used to initialize the various timers we require for this coin spawner.

Coin Spawner function definitions

With our member variables set up, we can now define how the coin spawner will function. As always, ensure the include list at the top of the `coinspawner.cpp` matches these:

```cpp
#include "BountyDash.h"
#include "Engine/TargetPoint.h"
#include "Coin.h"
#include "Floor.h"
#include "CoinSpawner.h"
```

The constructor for the coin spawner is very simple and does not require much of an explanation. The constructor simply initializes `USceneComponent` and assigns it as the root and establishes some default values for the coin spawn variables. Ensure that the `ACoinSpawner` constructor found in the `CoinSpawner.cpp` matches the following:

```cpp
// Sets default values
ACoinSpawner::ACoinSpawner()
{
// Set this actor to call Tick() every frame.  You can turn this off
to improve performance if you don't need it.
    PrimaryActorTick.bCanEverTick = true;

    Root = CreateDefaultSubobject<USceneComponent>(TEXT("Root"));
    RootComponent = Root;

MaxSetCoins = 5;
    MinSetCoins = 3;
    CoinSetTimeInterval = 4.0f;
    CoinTimeInterval = 0.5f;
    MovementTimeInterval = 1.0f;
}
```

We then need to define our `BeginPlay()` function. This function will be responsible for obtaining the information we require from our level as well as initialize the timers we spoke of earlier. Add the following definition for `ACoinSpawner::BeginPlay()` now:

```
// Called when the game starts or when spawned
void ACoinSpawner::BeginPlay()
{
    Super::BeginPlay();

    for (TActorIterator<ATargetPoint> TargetIter(GetWorld());
      TargetIter; ++TargetIter)
    {
        SpawnTransforms.Add(*TargetIter);
    }

    for (TActorIterator<AFloor> FloorIter(GetWorld()); FloorIter;
        ++FloorIter)
    {
        if (FloorIter->GetWorld() == GetWorld())
        {
            KillPoint = FloorIter->GetKillPoint();
            SpawnPoint = FloorIter->GetSpawnPoint();
        }
    }

    // Create Timers
    FTimerManager& worldTimeManager = GetWorld()->
      GetTimerManager();

worldTimeManager.SetTimer(CoinSetTimerHandle, this,
&ACoinSpawner::SpawnCoinSet, CoinSetTimeInterval, false);

worldTimeManager.SetTimer(SpawnMoveTimerHandle, this,
&ACoinSpawner::MoveSpawner, MovementTimeInterval, true);
}
```

As you can see, the first section of `BeginPlay()` is identical to that of the `AObstacleSpawner`. Following this, however, we are creating two of the timers we are using for the spawning logic. We first get a handle to the timer manager for this game world via `GetWorld()->GetTimeManager()`. With this `FTimeManager` handle, we are able to set two of the timers we require. We do this via `SetTimer()`. This method takes in an `FTimerHandle` to populate (we provide the handles we declared in the `ACoinSpawner` class definition), an object to call the provided function on, a handle to the function we wish executed upon timer completion, a timer rate (how long it will take for the timer to execute), and if we wish the timer to loop.

Here, we are setting two timers. The first is a coin set timer; this timer will invoke our `SpawnCoinSet` function after a provided time (4.0f by default). We specified that this method is to **not** loop as we will be resetting this timer ourselves. The second timer we are setting is the `Move` timer; this timer will invoke `MoveSpawner()` every second by default. This method will periodically shift the lane in which the coins spawn.

Next, we must define the various methods that will be invoked by our timers. Let's begin with the `SpawnCoinSet` function. Add the following code to `CoinSpawner.cpp` now:

```
void ACoinSpawner::SpawnCoinSet()
{
    NumCoinsToSpawn = FMath::RandRange(MinSetCoins, MaxSetCoins);

    FTimerManager& worldTimeManager = GetWorld()->
GetTimerManager();

    // Swap active timers
worldTimeManager.ClearTimer(CoinSetTimerHandle);

worldTimeManager.SetTimer(CoinTimerHandle, this,
&ACoinSpawner::SpawnCoin, CoinTimeInterval, true);
}
```

The first thing we do is generate the number of coins we will be spawning in this set by calling `FMath::RandRange` and providing the two maxims we declared earlier. As the `SpawnCoinSet()` method was invoked via a timer we now need to clear the coin set timer and active the per coin timer. This is so we can guarantee our spawn coin set timer will only reactivate once all individual coins for a given set have been spawned. We can do this by calling `ClearTimer()` on the `FTimerManager` handle, which will remove the timer from execution. We parse the handle of the timer we wish to clear to the manager (in this case `CoinSetTimerHandle`).

Following this, we set another timer via the `SetTimer` method we used earlier. This time we are setting the individual spawn coin timer. We have set this timer to loop as we wish the timer continue to spawn coins until all coins have been spawned. Following this, we can define the `MoveSpawner` function. This function is very simple and simply changes the `TargetLoc` integer we declared earlier. This integer will be used for a look up into the `SpawnTransforms` array. Add the following function definition to the `CoinSpawner.cpp`:

```
void ACoinSpawner::MoveSpawner()
{
    TargetLoc = FMath::Rand() % SpawnTransforms.Num();
}
```

We are nearly done with the coin spawner. The last thing we need to do is define the SpawnCoin() function. This function is very similar to AObstacleSpawn::SpawnObstacle(). It appears as follows:

```cpp
void ACoinSpawner::SpawnCoin()
{
    FActorSpawnParameters spawnParams;

    FTransform coinTransform = SpawnTransforms[TargetLoc]->
GetTransform();

coinTransform.SetLocation(FVector(SpawnPoint, coinTransform.
GetLocation().Y, coinTransform.GetLocation().Z));

ACoin* spawnedCoin = GetWorld()->SpawnActor<ACoin>(CoinObject,
coinTransform, spawnParams);

    if (spawnedCoin)
    {
USphereComponent* coinSphere = Cast<USphereComponent>(spawnedCoin->
GetComponentByClass(USphereComponent::StaticClass()));

        if (coinSphere)
        {
        float offset = coinSphere->
GetUnscaledSphereRadius();

spawnedCoin->AddActorLocalOffset(FVector(0.0f, 0.0f, offset));
        }

        NumCoinsToSpawn--;
    }

    if (NumCoinsToSpawn <= 0)
    {
        FTimerManager& worldTimeManager = GetWorld()->
GetTimerManager();

worldTimeManager.SetTimer(CoinSetTimerHandle, this,
&ACoinSpawner::SpawnCoinSet, CoinSetTimeInterval, false);

        worldTimeManager.ClearTimer(CoinTimerHandle);
    }
}
```

The first section of this function is exactly the same as the spawn method used in the `AObstacleSpawner`. The most noticeable difference is the inclusion of the timer swap logic and the end of the function. Each time a coin has spawned, we decremented the `NumCoinsToSpawn` variable. Once this value has reached 0 or lower, we swap our timers again. This swap is very similar to the one we performed in the `SpawnCoinSet()` method, yet this time we are clearing the individual coin timer and resetting the coin set timer.

Testing what we have so far!

Ok now that we have our floor, our coins, our obstacles, and our character set up, let's add the coin spawner to the level to complete the world object set! Do this by navigating back to the C++ classes folder of **Content** browser and dragging an `ACoinSpawner` object into the world. Select the new `CoinSpawner` in **World Outlier** and address the details panel. Within the details panel, set the **Coin Object** property under the **Coin Spawner** section to be `CoinBP`. With that in place, press **Play** and you will see rocks and coins hurtling at the player at 10 m/s!

Creating the interactions between the world objects

Finally, we have created the game world for `BountyDash`! Now, it is time to make it all interact with one another. We have already done this somewhat by having the coin adjust height when it is spawned on top of an obstacle object. We must scrutinize how we are going to interact with the player when it runs into the objects around him. First, let's detail how the player is going to be colliding with the obstacles.

Pushing the Character

When the player runs into a rock, we want the player avatar to be pushed back into the game world down the x-axis. This will be quite simple to implement; we can introduce the same offset backwards to the player that we do for all the other objects if he is currently colliding with a rock obstacle! This is very easily done. Navigate to the `BountyDashCharacter.cpp` in code; we are going to be defining the collision function.

ABountyDashCharacter Collision functions

The first collision function we will be defining is `MyOnComponentOverlap()`. The purpose of this function is to detect if the player has collided with an obstacle from a reasonably head on approach. We do this so that when the player is skipping between lanes there is a margin of allowance for moving over the back of an obstacle. If so, we are going to be enacting on the collision. Add the following code to `ABounty DashCharacter::myOnComponentOverlap`:

```
if (OtherActor->GetClass()->IsChildOf(AObstacle::StaticClass()))
{
FVector vecBetween = OtherActor->GetActorLocation() -
GetActorLocation();

float AngleBetween = FMath::Acos(FVector::DotProduct(vecBetween.
GetSafeNormal(), GetActorForwardVector().GetSafeNormal()));

    AngleBetween *= (180 / PI);

    if (AngleBetween < 60.0f)
    {
        bBeingPushed = true;
    }
}
```

We check that the offending actor is either of type `AObstacle` or a child of the class. If so, we get a vector between the character and the obstacle. We determine if the character is heading toward the obstacle within a margin by checking the angle between the direction of the vector between the two objects and the forward vector of the character. We do this by obtaining a dot product between the two vectors via the `FVector::DotProduct` function.

We then plug the result of this calculation into `FMath::Acos`. We do this as the dot product will return a ratio value that when parsed through an `arccos` function will return the angle between the two vectors in radians. To change this value to degrees, we multiply it by *(180 / PI)* as PI radians = 180 degrees. If the angle between vectors is less than `60.0f`, we can assume that the collision is fairly direct, so we then inform the character of a collision with the obstacle by setting the `bBeingPushed` Boolean to `true`. As we just referenced the `AObstacle` type, ensure you add `#include "Obstacle.h"` to the include list of this `.cpp`.

Next, we define the `MyOnActorEndOverlap()` function. This one is much less complicated, we will simply check that the leaving actor is of type `AObstacle`; and if so, we will enact on the end of the overlap, add the following code to `ABountyDashCharacter::myOnComponentEndOverlap`:

```
if (OtherActor->GetClass()->IsChildOf(AObstacle::StaticClass() ))
{
bBeingPushed = false;
}
```

As you can see, we set the `bBeingPushed` value to false when the obstacle leaves the bounds of the character f capsule component collider. Now, we must add some code to the `Tick()` function to ensure the character's position updates when he is being pushed by an obstacle.

Pushing the character back

In `ABountyDashCharacter::Tick()`, we are going to be checking if the `bBeingPushed` value is set to true; if so, we will be offsetting the character's location down the x-axis at the same speed as the obstacles. Add the following code to `ABountyDashCharacter::Tick()`:

```
if (bBeingPushed)
{
    float moveSpeed = GetCustomGameMode<ABountyDashGameMode>
      (GetWorld())->GetInvGameSpeed();
    AddActorLocalOffset(FVector(moveSpeed, 0.0f, 0.0f));
}
```

As you can see, if the character is currently being pushed we will add an offset to the character's position down the x-axis. The effect this will create is the player will feel as though the character has stopped moving! The idea is to then convince that a wall of death has caught up with them and it is game over. But, we will be programming the wall of invisible death in the next chapter.

Picking up coins

The next thing we have to implement is the collecting of coins! The collision functionality for this is much simpler than that defined for the obstacle collision. We will simply detect if the player has overlapped with a coin. If so, we will inform the player to score up. We will also have to properly define that function, so the player score increases and the game mode is informed of the new score!

Coin collision

Let's start with the coin collision functionality. Add the following code to `ACoin::MyOnActorOverlap()` found in `Coin.cpp`:

```
if (otherActor->GetClass()->IsChildOf(ABountyDashCharacter::StaticCla
ss()))
{
ABountyDashCharacter* myChar = Cast<ABountyDashCharacter>(otherActor);

myChar->ScoreUp();

GetWorld()->DestroyActor(this);
}
```

We are simply going to check if the offending actor is of type `ABountyDashCharacter`. If so, we are going to inform the character to score up. We then inform the game world to destroy the coin actor. Next, we have to define the functionality for `ABountyDashChara racter::ScoreUp()`. The purpose of this function is to increment the player's internal score count as well as informing the `Game Mode` of that increment. Add the following to code to `ABountyDashCharacter::ScoreUp()`:

```
Score++;
GetCustomGameMode<ABountyDashGameMode>(GetWorld())-
>CharScoreUp(Score);
```

This will increment the score then inform the game mode to score up thus invoking the functionality we previously implemented.

Summary

We implemented a rudimentary endless runner! Compile the changes we just made and run the game! You be pushed back by obstacles and you will be able to pick up coins! We will continue developing bounty dash in the next chapter as it is far from finished at the moment. We are yet to add in sound effects, fog, so we can't see our objects popping in, particle effects, respawning logic for the character and don't forget the invisible wall of death!

Congratulations on making it this far through the book. We are almost half way through our journey with Unreal Engine 4! In this chapter, we learned many important C++ techniques such as getting world data within objects and reading component data from objects. We wrote our very first C++ character, and in doing, so we learned how to tie the different layers of UE together with the use of polymorphism, UClasses, and template functions! We will be learning even more about Unreal and C++ in the next chapter when we finish Bounty Dash and add the layer of polish that brings the Unreal Factor!

6
Power Ups for Your Character, Power Ups for the User

Welcome to Chapter 6! During this chapter, we are going to finish and polish the Bounty Dash project. We are going to be looking into the Unreal Engine plugin system and how to create reuseable plugins we can share between projects! This chapter, much like the last, will be heavily based on C++. The purpose of this chapter is to complete your foundation knowledge of how to use C++ with Unreal Engine.

We are going to be writing our first C++ plugin as well as our first custom C++ HUD object. We will use the first to create a power-up system so we may collect power ups and have them result in a gameplay change for the character. The HUD class will be used so we may show gameplay information as screen text. During this chapter, we will also be polishing the Bounty Dash project. We are going to learn how to load and run sound cues from C++, how to load and play particle effects from C++, and how we can utilize the destructible Mesh functionality of Unreal Engine to create a power up that will let the player smash through any obstacles and finish the encroaching wall of death!

We will be covering the following topics:

- Creating a plugin for Unreal Engine using C++
- Working with plugins from within our project codebase
- Loading and playing assets such as sounds and particle effects from C++
- Creating a HUD class using C++
- Working with destructible meshes in UE and C++
- Adjusting object hierarchies from within C++

Cleaning up shop and object hierarchies

We are going to start this chapter off by preparing our codebase. During the course of this chapter we are going to be adding new objects to the game scene, such as power ups, particle effects, and destructible objects that we need to behave much in the same way as obstacles and coins currently do. As our current class hierarchy has our `ACoin` object inheriting from `AObstacle`, we have begun an inheritance chain that will lead to many development headaches. Now is a good time for us to right this with a quick fix, and construct a much smarter and cleaner object hierarchy.

When creating object hierarchies, we should ask ourselves, what functionality will be shared among all objects in the hierarchy? Any functionality you can think of that would adhere to this question should be included in the base object. Currently, most of our base functionality is present in the `AObstacle` object. This process will be removing a large amount of functionality from this object and placing it in a generic base class object.

BountyDashObject

Let's begin by creating a new base object called `BountyDashObject` (through the C++ class wizard) that inherits from `AActor`. This object is going to act as our base class for our object hierarchy. We will be migrating most of the functionality out of `AObstacle` into this object. Once the object has been generated, address the `BountyDashObject.h` file, and amend this file so that it appears as follows:

```
UCLASS()
class BOUNTYDASH_API ABountyDashObject : public AActor
{
    GENERATED_BODY()

    float KillPoint;

public:
    // Sets default values for this actor's properties
    ABountyDashObject();

    // Called when the game starts or when spawned
    virtual void BeginPlay() override;

    // Called every frame
    virtual void Tick(float DeltaSeconds) override;
```

```
        void SetKillPoint(float point);
        float GetKillPoint();

    protected:
        UFUNCTION()
        virtual void MyOnActorOverlap(AActor* otherActor);

        UFUNCTION()
        virtual void MyOnActorEndOverlap(AActor* otherActor);

        UPROPERTY(EditAnywhere)
        USphereComponent* Collider;
    };
```

As you can see, this currently looks very similar to that of the AObstacle object definition; don't worry about that for now, we will tidy that up soon. First off, let's quickly break down this object.

It contains two members; one is a private float value called KillPoint that will be used for despawn logic. The second is a protected USphereComponent handle that will be used to store the sphere collider, which will be included in all objects that inherit from this class. This sphere collider will act as the root component. This object also contains the standard BeginPlay() and Tick() functions that we expect in a class that inherits from AActor. We have also included the two collision functions, MyOnActorOverlap() and MyOnActorEndOverlap(), as most of the objects that will inherit from this class will require collision in some way. Getter and Setter methods have also been provided for the killPoint float variable.

Based on this class definition, we can assume that every object that inherits from this class will need to tick on a per-frame basis, collide with things through the USphereComponent, and despawn through the killPoint variable. That seems like a good start for our base functionality. Let's now work with the BountyDashObject. cpp file to define the base functionality. Open the generated .cpp file and add the following code to the constructor:

```
    ABountyDashObject::ABountyDashObject()
    {
        // Set this actor to call Tick() every frame.  You can turn this
        off to improve performance if you don't need it.
        PrimaryActorTick.bCanEverTick = true;

        Collider
        = CreateDefaultSubobject<USphereComponent>(TEXT("Collider"));
        check(Collider)
```

```
        RootComponent = Collider;
        Collider->SetCollisionProfileName("OverlapAllDynamic");

        OnActorBeginOverlap.AddDynamic(this,
        &ABountyDashObject::MyOnActorOverlap);

        OnActorBeginOverlap.AddDynamic(this,
        &ABountyDashObject::MyOnActorEndOverlap);
}
```

This will ensure that any object that inherits from this class will have a properly initialized USphereComponent as its root. This constructor also ensures that every inherited object has the two collision functions bound to the correct overlap delegates. As we saw in *Chapter 5, Upgrade Activated – Making Bounty Dash with C++*, objects that inherit from this class may override these functions virtually without having to rebind the function to the delegate.

Next we can define the BeginPlay() and Tick() functions. These have already been described many times in *Chapter 5, Upgrade Activated – Making Bounty Dash with C++* so we do not need an explanation:

```
// Called when the game starts or when spawned
void ABountyDashObject::BeginPlay()
{
    Super::BeginPlay();

}


// Called every frame
void ABountyDashObject::Tick(float DeltaTime)
{
    Super::Tick(DeltaTime);

float gameSpeed = GetCustomGameMode<ABountyDashGameMode>(GetWorld())->
GetInvGameSpeed();

    AddActorLocalOffset(FVector(gameSpeed, 0.0f, 0.0f));

    if (GetActorLocation().X < KillPoint)
    {
        Destroy();
    }
}
```

It is important to note that the `Tick()` function definition will cause any object that inherits from `ABountyDashObject` to translate down the game field until the specified `KillPoint`, much like coins and obstacles do now. Also we just referenced our Bounty Dash game mode, ensure to add `#include BountyDashGameMode.h` to the include list for this `.cpp`.

Lastly, we must include empty bodies for our bound collision functions. These have been left empty, we do not wish to specify any generic functionality as almost every inherited object will require unique functionality for collision. We are also going to define the getter and setter methods for the `KillPoint` member variable:

```
void ABountyDashObject::MyOnActorOverlap(AActor* otherActor)
{

}

void ABountyDashObject::MyOnActorEndOverlap(AActor* otherActor)
{

}

void ABountyDashObject::SetKillPoint(float point)
{
    KillPoint = point;
}

float ABountyDashObject::GetKillPoint()
{
    return KillPoint;
}
```

Now that we have defined our base functionality, we can re-write the `AObstalce` and `ACoin` objects.

Modifying existing objects

We need to remove the duplicate functionality from `AObstacle` then re-parent it to `ABountyDashObject`. The changes to `ACoin` will be much less drastic as this object was already created with most of the inheritance in place already in mind. Let's start with `Obstacle.h`. Change the code within so it matches the following:

```
#include "BountyDashObject.h"
#include "Obstacle.generated.h"
```

```
UCLASS(BlueprintType)
class BOUNTYDASH_API AObstacle : public ABountyDashObject
{
    GENERATED_BODY()

public:
    // Sets default values for this actor's properties
    AObstacle();

public:
    UPROPERTY(EditAnywhere, BlueprintReadWrite)
    UStaticMeshComponent* Mesh;
};
```

What we have done here is remove all of the functionality that was defined in `ABountyDashObject`, then re-parented `AObstalce` to `ABountyDashObject` so that the functionality will be inherited instead. Now change `Obstacle.cpp` to match the following:

```
// Sets default values
AObstacle::AObstacle()
{
    // Set this actor to call Tick() every frame.  You can turn this
off
    to improve performance if you don't need it.
    PrimaryActorTick.bCanEverTick = true;

Mesh = CreateDefaultSubobject<UStaticMeshComponent>(TEXT("Mesh"));
    check(Mesh);

    Mesh->AttachTo(Collider);
    Mesh->SetCollisionResponseToAllChannels(ECR_Ignore);
}
```

As the rest of the functionality is included in `ABountyDashObject`, we can remove the `BeginPlay()`, `Tick()`, `KillPoint`, `getter` and `setter` methods, and `collision` functions from this `.cpp`.

Now we can work with the `ACoin` object. When working with `Coin.h`, all we have to do is re-parent the class to `ABountyDashObject` and add a `UStaticMeshComponent` handle. The code should appear as follows:

```
#include "BountyDashObject.h"
#include "Coin.generated.h"

UCLASS()
class BOUNTYDASH_API ACoin : public ABountyDashObject
```

```
{
    GENERATED_BODY()

    ACoin();

    // Called every frame
    virtual void Tick(float DeltaSeconds) override;

    UFUNCTION()
    virtual void MyOnActorOverlap(AActor* otherActor) override;

protected:
    UPROPERTY(EditAnywhere, BlueprintReadWrite)
    UStaticMeshComponent* Mesh;

};
```

As we have changed the parent class, we must also change `#include "Obstacle.h"` to `#include "BountyDashObject.h"`. Then, in `coin.cpp`, ensure the constructor appears as follows:

```
ACoin::ACoin()
{
Mesh = CreateDefaultSubobject<UStaticMeshComponent>(TEXT("Mesh"));

    check(Mesh);
    Mesh->AttachTo(RootComponent);
    Mesh->SetCollisionProfileName("OverlapAllDynamic");
}
```

Also ensure you add `#include "Obstacle.h"` to the include list as we have removed it from the header, and reference `AObstacle` in the `ACoin::MyOnActorOverlap` override.

Great work! We are now done modifying the existing codebase to support our new generic hierarchy. Ensure the code compiles and the project still functions as it did at the end of *Chapter 5, Upgrade Activated – Making Bounty Dash with C++*.

The next thing we are going to do is create our very own C++ plugin!

Creating a Plug-in with C++

Now it is time for us to create your very first plugin, with which we can provide our codebase with a power-up object. The plugin itself will be very simple, as the purpose of this exercise is to teach you how to include plugins within your own Unreal Engine project. The following section of this chapter will break down how to create a new C++ plugin from scratch with the help of the Unreal plugin wizard. Refer to the following screenshot:

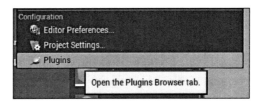

Begin by opening the `Bounty Dash` project. From the **Level Editor**, select the **Edit selection** from the dropdown menu at the top of the screen, from here select **Plugins**. This will open the plugin wizard. You will be presented with a list of already installed and available plugins. We are not concerned with these just yet. What we need to do is create a new plugin; we can do this by selecting the **New plugin** button in the bottom right-hand corner of the plugin wizard window:

Selecting this button will present you with a list of plugin template types. From this list, select **Blank** (it should be the first option). Be sure to specify the name of this plugin to be `PowerUpPlugin`. With the **Blank** category selected and the name specified, press the **Create Plugin** button. This will create a new blank plugin called `PowerUpPlugin` that contains minimal code and is a great starting point for our custom plugin.

Modules and code files

Before we embark on our journey with plugins, it is important to bring up a new semantic that will help with understanding how plugins and Unreal Engine 4 work. Unreal Engine 4 is made up of a collection of various modules. A module is a grouping of code that is responsible for a specific set of functionality featured in Unreal Engine. It is important to understand that each module is responsible for a section of the Unreal Engine codebase. For example, the Core module is responsible for the core engine-programming environment, and the Engine module is responsible for defining actors and components, and implements the game framework.

If you want a complete list of all of the Engine modules, they can be found here:

`https://docs.unrealengine.com/latest/INT/API/`

You will probably find yourself referencing the online API documentation more and more as you dive deeper into C++ and Unreal Engine, as the API will inform you which module a given object is part of. For example, the `AActor` object is part of the Engine module, as can be seen at the bottom of this page:

`https://docs.unrealengine.com/latest/INT/API/Runtime/`
`Engine/GameFramework/AActor/index.html.`

In the same sense, plugins are also made up of modules. Each module is responsible for a certain set of functionality within the plugin. Simple plugins will usually only contain one module, however, as a plugin's complexity increases, so does that of its module count. It is also important to note that plugin modules do not know about all of the Unreal Engine modules by default. You must specify which modules the plugin needs to know about to gain access to the objects contained within those modules. How this is done will be detailed in the following sections of this chapter.

The anatomy of a plugin

Before we begin working with our new blank plugin, we will first look into the different code files that make up a plugin and how a plugin is saved within a project folder. Each plugin will be accompanied by the following files:

- `*.uplugin`: This file type is used as a descriptor file for the plugin and informs the engine how the plugin should be interpreted and when it should be loaded. The `*.uplugin` file is where you specify most of the information about the plugin, such as name, version, type, engine version, and so on. It is also here where you will specify how many code modules will be present within the plugin and the settings for those modules.

- `*.Build.cs`: This file is used to inform the engine where to find the given source for this plugin and what modules of the engine this plugin will be concerned with. It is here where you will specify whether the plugin will need to access functionality from the `CoreUObject` module or the `Renderer` module, and so forth. Also, it should be noted that plugins can contain multiple modules and each plugin module will be accompanied by a `*.Build.cs` file.

- `PCH.h`: A `PCH.h` file is a precompiled header file. This file will be used to include files that are needed across a plugin module. If you specify in the `.Build.cs` that you need access to the `CoreUObject` module, it is in the `PCH` file that you will add the `#include`, which includes the desired code file from that module. So, if you wish to have your plugin include or inherit from `UObject`, you will need to add `#include "CoreUObject.h"` to the `PCH`. It is also here you will include any of the module's private headers that will be needed in most of the module's other source files.

- `Source`: Every plugin will have source files associated with the plugin. These files will be used to both load the plugin and create the functionality the plugin will add to the engine/project.

- `Content`: Plugins may or may not include content. This content will be physical assets such as sounds files, image files, meshes, and so on. It is also here the icon used for the plugin can be specified.

Every plugin created will be located under the `Plugins` folder of the `project` directory. In our case, the `PowerUpPlugin` can be found under `BountyDash/ Plugins/PowerUpPlugin`. Within this file, you will find the `.uplugin` file mentioned previously, along with a resources folder used to hold the content of the plugin, and a source folder. If you open the `resources` folder now, you will note that the wizard has automatically populated the plugin with an icon file `icon128.png`. You may replace this file with an image of the same name and dimensions if you wish. We will not be adding any further content to the `PowerUpPlugin`.

Now, open the aforementioned source folder and you will find that it contains another folder titled `PowerUpPlugin`. Why the duplicate folder name? This is because plugins, much like the engine, can be made up of multiple code modules with the default module named after the plugin itself. Within the scope of this chapter, our plugin will only contain one module; however, it is important to note the ability to add more modules if needed.

Now, address the Visual Studio project and you will find that the plugin directory has been added to the solution explorer, meaning we can edit all of the plugin files directly from Visual Studio! Open the `PowerUpPlugin.uplugin` file now.

Describing a plugin

With the `.uplugin` file open, you will be presented with a file format that looks very similar to JSON. In this file, we have a series of categories followed by a value. Each of these categories describes something about the plugin. There are more categories that can be specified than included by default in the `PowerUpPlugin.uplugin` file.

The most relevant are detailed as follows:

- `FileVersion`: The version of the `.uplugin` descriptor format itself. This is used primarily for backwards compatibility. In our case, this version has been set to 3 as that is the most recent file format version for a `.uplugin` file. If we wish to create a plugin that utilizes an older `.uplugin` format, we can specify a different number here. However, this is not recommended.

- `Version`: This is the version number of the plugin itself. This is so you can keep track of which version of your plugin you are working with. This number is not generally shown to the end user and is more for the plugin creator's benefit.

- `VersionName`: This is simply the version of the plugin displayed in the editor UI. This is not used for any version checks and can be any format you wish. A `Major.minor` format is suggested. For example, plugin version 1.0, 1.1, 2.0, and so on.

- `EngineVersion`: Allows you to specify the minimum engine version that has to be used for this plugin to load. This is useful when accessing engine code modules that are only present in later versions of the engine, and the plugin may be distributed to users with an earlier version of the engine.

- `FriendlyName`: The name of the plugin that will be displayed in editor. This name will default to the `.uplugin` file name.

- `Description`: A paragraph of text that describes what the plugin is used for.

- `Category`: This is a special dot-seperated path string that lets you specify which category your plugin will feature within the editor UI. For example, `BountyDash.PowerUps` will have the plugin feature under `BountyDash|PowerUps` within the plugin wizard.

- `CreateBy`: The individual or company name that created the plugin.

- `URL`: Each of the categories ending in URL can be used to specify hyperlinks for each of the categories.

- `Modules`: This is where you specify the code modules the plugin contains, and essential details about each module that will dictate how the module is loaded and when it can be accessed by developers. This will be covered in more detail in the next section.

PowerUpPlugin.uplugin

Make sure the .uplugin file for the PowerUpPlugin appears as follows:

```
{
    "FileVersion": 3,
    "Version": 1,
    "VersionName": "1.0",
    "FriendlyName": "PowerUpPlugin",
    "Description": "",
    "Category": "Other",
    "CreatedBy": "",
    "CreatedByURL": "",
    "DocsURL": "",
    "MarketplaceURL": "",
    "SupportURL": "",
    "Modules": [
        {
            "Name": "PowerUpPlugin",
            "Type": "Runtime",
            "LoadingPhase": "Default"
        }
        ],
    "EnabledByDefault": true,
    "CanContainContent": false,
    "IsBetaVersion": false,
    "Installed": false
}
```

Translated in short. This plugin uses file version 3 of the .uplugin format. It is the first version of this plugin and will be referenced as PowerUpPlugin under the Other category within the Editor UI. It contains one code module that is named PowerUpPlugin and is of type developer that will use the default loading phase and is enabled by default. What this means will be described now.

Each code module is described with the following categories:

- Name: The unique name of this plugin module that will be loaded with the plugin. The engine will use this name to locate similarly named binaries for this plugin at runtime. Each uniquely named module that has a source directory requires a matching .Build.cs file.

- `Type`: This category determines when the plugin will be loaded based on the application type the plugin will be used for. This is because you may wish to create a plugin that is only used within the editor (a plugin that assists with object placement perhaps). This plugin should not be loaded when building a shipping version of the product. The valid options for the type category are `Runtime`, `RuntimeNoCommandlet`, `Developer`, `Editor`, `EditorNoCommandlet`, and `Program`. Runtime modules will be loaded in all cases, even in shipped games. Developer modules will only be loaded in development, runtime, or editor builds but never in shipping builds, and Editor modules will only be loaded when the editor is starting up.

- `LoadingPhase`: If specified, this category controls when the plugin is loaded at startup. This option is advanced and is not required by default.

The descriptor file can be used to exercise multiple loading options for the plugin itself. As we have only one module for our `PowerUpPlugin`, the `.uplugin` file will remain mostly unchanged from the provided default. However, we do need to modify the `Module` category slightly. As we are creating a plugin that we wish to reference within our game code at runtime in all builds of the application, we need to change the `Type` of the `PowerUpPlugin` module to `Runtime`. Leaving it as developer will cause issues when we build the project to a binary format.

It should be noted that plugins can serve many different purposes. As mentioned previously, they can be used to augment how you interact with the engine at an editor level, meaning that the plugin is completely detached from your game code. Plugins may also be used to include pre-made functionality you wish to include in your project code; this can be done to include things such as artificial intelligence packages or inventory systems. The latter, however, creates a static link between the plugin and the project code, as once a plugin of this type is included in the project code, your project cannot run without the plugin being installed or enabled. This may be undesirable and does limit the flexibility of a plugin somewhat. This is why we are able to specify the type for each code module included in a plugin.

The `module` category should appear as follows:

```
"Modules": [
    {
        "Name": "PowerUpPlugin",
        "Type": "Runtime",
        "LoadingPhase": "Default"
    }
],
```

Working with our first plugin module

Now that we have described our plugin and its module, we can begin to specify what our only code module within the plugin is going to do. The purpose of the `PowerUpPlugin` is to create a power-up type we can include in a game code object that will be constructed with a random power-up type. We can then identify this type from within the game code and enact functionality based on that type. As we are going to be creating a type that needs to be identified by the engine, we will need to inherit our type from `UObject`. This means our plugin is going to need access to the `CoreUObject` module provided by the engine. This also means that our plugin module will need to be publically exposed to our project codebase so we may include the plugin type. This is creating the aforementioned static link between the plugin and the project codebase.

PowerUpPlugin.Build.cs

We can create these associations by modifying the `.Build.cs` file. You will notice that the `Build.cs` file contains a class named after the module that inherits from the `ModuleRules` object. It is within the constructor of this C# object that you can specify the different include paths and dependencies of the module. These include paths and dependencies are found in the form of arrays that contain string literals indicating either an include path or a module dependency. The first element range modified in the generated `*.Build.cs` file is `PublicIncludePaths`. It is with this element that you may specify a range of public include paths through the `AddRange()` function. This function takes in a string array of include paths. By default, `"PowerUpPlugin/Public"` is specified as follows:

```
PublicIncludePaths.AddRange(
new string[] {
        "PowerUpPlugin/Public"
        // ... add public include paths required here
    }
    );
```

Adding this include path means that any source located in the `Public` folder under `PowerUpPlugin/Source/PowerUpPlugin/Public` will be included publically within our project codebase. Because of this, any plugin API code within files we include in this Public folder will be exported publically when the plugin is loaded. This will create a direct dependency between the plugin's API set and game code. As we are creating a game content plugin, this is OK.

We then specify the private include paths within the *.Build.cs file. Refer to the following code:

```
PrivateIncludePaths.AddRange(
    new string[]{
        "PowerUpPlugin/Private",
        //      add other private include paths required here
    }
    );
```

Private dependencies within a plugin are ok as they will be hidden away from Unreal Engine or game code, and any code files stored within the Private folder will only be referenceable by code objects declared within the plugin module itself.

The next section within the module build file specifies which dependencies the plugin has with engine modules. This is where we begin to associate which engine objects our plugin will need to include. In the case of the PowerUpPlugin, we simply need public access to the CoreUObject module as we will be inheriting our power-up type from UObject. Do this now by ensuring the range added to PublicDependencyModuleNames is as follows:

```
PublicDependencyModuleNames.AddRange(
    new string[] {
        "Core",
        "CoreUObject",
        // ... add other public dependencies that you statically
        link with here ...
    }
    );
```

This will ensure that the PowerUpPlugin module has public access to the CoreUObject and Core modules. We can leave the private dependency range as is; we do not require any more exposed functionality. The next range DynamicallyLoadedModuleNames would be used to specify any engine modules that you would need dynamically loaded by the plugin module.

Declaring the PowerUpPlugin code module

By default, the plugin wizard will have provided you with three source files. One in the public source folder PowerUpPlugin.h, and two in the private source folder PowerUpPlugin.cpp and PowerUpPluginPrivatePCH.h. It is within these three files you will begin to construct the makeup of your plugin module.

Let's first address `PowerUpPlugin.h`:

```
#pragma once

#include "ModuleManager.h"

class FPowerUpPluginModule : public IModuleInterface
{
public:

    /** IModuleInterface implementation */
    virtual void StartupModule() override;
    virtual void ShutdownModule() override;
};
```

Each `module` has a lifetime, a lifetime that begins when `StartupModule()` is called, and ends when `ShutdownModule()` is called. The first will be called when the `module` is loaded into memory at the phase described in the `*.uplugin` file (loading phase). The second is called when the `module` is shut down and can be used to clean up your `module` upon shutdown if need be.

As you can see, the `FPowerUpPluginModule` inherits from the `IModuleInterface`. This interface is the same one that is used by all engine modules and it is through this interface that the module is loaded with regard to the description specified in the `*.uplugin` file. As you can see, the `StartupModule()` and `ShutdownModule()` functions have been overridden, as they are present in the interface. We do not need to add anything to this file as our `PowerUpPlugin` is very simple in nature. Let's now address the `PowerUpPlugin.cpp`:

```
// Copyright 1998-2015 Epic Games, Inc. All Rights Reserved.

#include "PowerUpPluginPrivatePCH.h"

#define LOCTEXT_NAMESPACE "FPowerUpPluginModule"

void FPowerUpPluginModule::StartupModule()
{
}

void FPowerUpPluginModule::ShutdownModule()
{
}

#undef LOCTEXT_NAMESPACE

IMPLEMENT_MODULE(FPowerUpPluginModule, PowerUpPlugin)
```

As you can see, the PCH has been included here as it will be for all .cpp source files included in the module. We then see two empty definitions for StartupModule() and ShutdownModule(). We do not need to change these as we will not be performing any post-load or pre-shutdown operations on this code module.

There are two important things to note in this .cpp file. The first is the unique #define LOCTEXT_NAMESPACE "FPowerUpPluginModule". This acts as a guard, ensuring that this module is not implemented again somewhere else in the plugin codebase. The second is the line IMPLEMENT_MODULE(FPowerUpPluginModule, PowerUpPlugin). It is this line of code that preps the module for loading, and informs that this module must be implanted with regards to the details specified in the Modules section of the *.uplugin file. This is why the module name as declared in the *.uplugin file can be found as the second parameter of the macro.

The next thing we need to do is prepare the PCH file for use within the plugin. By default, the PCH file will only contain the following:

```
// Copyright 1998-2015 Epic Games, Inc. All Rights Reserved.

#include "PowerUpPlugin.h"

// You should place include statements to your module's private header
files here. You only need to
// add includes for headers that are used in most of your module's
source files though.
```

All we need to do is add an include to the engine module we will be interfacing with, the CoreUObject module. Add the following line to the PCH above #include "PowerUpPlugin":

```
#include "CoreUObject.h"
```

Adding the PowerUp object

Now that we have established the basic codebase for the module, we can now add the code object we are going to be including in our game code. Start by adding a header file to PowerUpPlugin/Source/PowerUpPlugin/Public and call it PowerUpObject.h. Open this code file now.

Within this code file, we need to define an enum type that will hold all of the possible power-up types that we are going to need. We are also going to have to define the power-up class that we will be including in our game code. This object will need to have a member variable of the enum type variable we declare, as well as an accessor method for that variable.

Let's start by defining the enum type. Add the following lines of code to PowerUpObject.h:

```
#pragma once
#include "PowerUpObject.generated.h"

enum class EPowerUp : uint8
{
    SPEED = 1 UMETA(DisplayName="Speed"),
    SMASH = 2 UMETA(DisplayName="Smash"),
    MAGNET = 3 UMETA(DisplayName="Magnet")
};
```

Here, we have specified we wish this code file to only be compiled once through the pre-processor directive #pragma once, we have also included the generated header file that will be created for this object. Next, we have defined our strongly typed enum class EPowerUp. This enum class has been strongly typed to uint8 as we will not need more the 256 unique enum values. Inside of this enum, we have declared three types: speed, smash, and magnet. These will be the power-up types that are used in our game code.

It should be noted that the functionality that we are including in this plugin is heavily linked to that of our game code. Usually, this would not be a plugin and simply additional game code files. Normally, plugin code is very generic and transportable between multiple game projects. If you wish to maintain a generic approach, you may call these power ups POWERUP_1, POWERUP_2, POWERUP_3, or something along those lines.

Next, we must define the object itself. Do this by adding the following lines to the plugin:

```
UCLASS()
class POWERUPPLUGIN_API UPowerUpObject : public UObject
{
    GENERATED_UCLASS_BODY()
public:

    EPowerUp GetType();
```

```
private:
    EPowerUp Type;
};
```

Here, we have declared a UCLASS UPowerUpObject that inherits from UObject.
You will also note that this class has been declared with the POWERUPPLUGIN_API
macro, meaning this object will be exposed to other modules. As we have contained
this code file within the public source folder, it will be exposed publicly to engine
modules and game code. Within this class, we have a very simple implementation.
A getter method GetType() that will retrieve the enum type variable saved within
this object, and the private EPowerUp type. Now add another source file to the plugin
module, this time to the private folder, and call it PowerUpObject.cpp. Within this
file, add the following code:

```
#include "PowerUpPluginPrivatePCH.h"
#include "PowerUpObject.h"

UPowerUpObject::UPowerUpObject(const FObjectInitializer&
ObjectInitializer)
    : Super(ObjectInitializer)
{
    int iType = FMath::Rand() % 3;

    switch (iType)
    {
    case 0:
    {
        Type = EPowerUp::SPEED;
        break;
    }
    case 1:
    {
        Type = EPowerUp::SMASH;
        break;
    }
    case 2:
    {
        Type = EPowerUp::MAGNET;
        break;
    }
    default:
        break;
    }
}
```

```
EPowerUp UPowerUpObject::GetType()
{
    return Type;
}
```

As you can see, the object definition is quite simple. Within the constructor, we are generating a random number from 0 to 2 inclusive. We then assign the appropriate `enum` type based off of the result of this random number through a `switch` case. We have also defined the `getter` method for `Type`. We are now done writing code for our plugin! Admittedly, this is a very simple plugin; however, the knowledge covered thus far in this chapter provides you with the ability to create larger and more complex plugin implementations. If you wish to learn more about plugins in Unreal Engine 4, information can be found at `https://docs.unrealengine.com/latest/CHN/Programming/Plugins/index.html`.

Using our plugin in engine

There is one last thing we have to do before our plugin can be used by our codebase, and that is modifying the `build.cs` file for our project so that we may complete the link between the publically exposed API content of the `PowerUpPlugin` module and the project code. We do this by opening the `BountyDash.Build.cs` under `BountyDash\Source\BountyDash`. Within this file, we need to add another value to the `PublicDependencyModuleNames` range so that it appears as follows:

```
PublicDependencyModuleNames.AddRange(new string[]
{ "Core", "CoreUObject", "Engine", "InputCore", "PowerUpPlugin" });
```

This will add the `PowerUpPlugin` module as a public dependency of the project and we will be able to include the `PowerUpObject.h` we just created in our game code. Any time you wish to publically expose functionality from within a plugin module, you must add the module to this public dependency list, otherwise the exposed API will not be linked to the project.

Now that we have this in place, compile the code! If everything has gone according to plan, the code should compile and build. If not, re-address the previous code.

Creating the BountyDashPowerUp object

Now that we have publically linked our plugin module, we can include the `PowerUpObject` in our game code files! Let's do this now. First, create a new class called `BountyDashPowerUp` through the C++ class `wizard` within the Editor. Ensure that this class inherits from `ABountyDashObject` as it will be part of the generic object hierarchy.

Modify the `ABountyDashPowerUp` class definition found in `BountyDashPowerUp.h` so it appears as follows:

```
#include "BountyDashObject.h"
#include "BountyDashPowerUp.generated.h"

UCLASS()
class BOUNTYDASH_API ABountyDashPowerUp : public ABountyDashObject
{
    GENERATED_BODY()

public:
    // Sets default values for this actor's properties
    ABountyDashPowerUp();

    UFUNCTION()
    virtual void MyOnActorOverlap(AActor* otherActor) override;

protected:
    UPROPERTY(EditAnywhere)
    UStaticMeshComponent* Mesh;

private:
    class UPowerUpObject* PowerUp;
};
```

We are overriding the `MyOnActorOverlap()` function provided in the `ABountyDashObject` base class as this object will require custom overlap functionality. We have included a `UStaticMeshComponent` handle to be used to hold the mesh for this object. We have also included a handle to the `UPowerUpObject` defined in our plugin module. This power-up object will be used to determine which of the three powers the object will be.

Open `BountyDashPowerUp.cpp` now. First, add `#include "PowerUpObject.h"` to the include list for this file so we can match the forward declaration of `UPowerUpObject` found in the class definition. Then add the following code to the constructor of the object:

```
// Sets default values
ABountyDashPowerUp::ABountyDashPowerUp()
{
    // Set this actor to call Tick() every frame.  You can turn
    this off to improve performance if you don't need it.
    PrimaryActorTick.bCanEverTick = true;
```

```
thisPowerUp = CreateDefaultSubobject<UPowerUpObject>(TEXT(
"PowerUp"));
check(thisPowerUp);

mesh = CreateDefaultSubobject<UStaticMeshComponent>(TEXT("Mesh"));
check(mesh);

mesh->AttachTo(RootComponent);
mesh->SetCollisionProfileName("OverlapAllDynamic");
```

Here, we are populating the handle to the UPowerUpObject type we included from the PowerUpPlugin module we made earlier. As we have publically linked the plugin module type to the project code, we have gained full use of the construction and initialization functions provided by the engine. Populating this handle is done in exactly the same way as member components. We have used the CreateDefaultSubobject template function to create a new UPowerUpObject, then we have saved a handle to this object into the PowerUp handle. The next thing we are doing is creating a static mesh component and saving that into the provided handle as well.

Now we are going to be loading a mesh based off of the EPowerUp Type member of the UPowerUpObject. There are three different enum values that the UPowerUpObject could hold. Because of this, we need to load the mesh we want to use in a slightly different way. Add the following code to the constructor:

```
FString AssetName;
switch (thisPowerUp->GetType())
{
case EPowerUp::SPEED:
AssetName = "/Game/StarterContent/Shapes/Shape_QuadPyramid.Shape_
QuadPyramid";
    break;

case EPowerUp::SMASH:
AssetName = "/Game/StarterContent/Shapes/Shape_WideCapsule.Shape_
WideCapsule";
    break;

case EPowerUp::MAGNET:
AssetName = "/Game/StarterContent/Shapes/Shape_Pipe_180.Shape_
Pipe_180";
    break;

default:
    break;
```

```
}

ConstructorHelpers::FObjectFinder<UStaticMesh> myMesh(&AssetName.
GetCharArray()[0]);

if (myMesh.Succeeded())
{
    mesh->SetStaticMesh(myMesh.Object);
}
} // <- closing ABountyDashPowerUp::ABountyDashPowerUp()
```

Here, we have declared a local `FString` variable `AssetName`; this variable will hold the asset path we are going to use to load the mesh we desire. To determine which path we populate this `FString` with, we have used a switch case with the `EPowerUp Type` member of `UPowerUpObject` as the target via the `GetType()` method. As this `UPowerUpObject` has already been constructed, we can guarantee that a randomly generated power-up type has already been assigned.

We then parse this populated `FString` variable through to the `FObjectFinder` constructor helper so that our mesh object may be found and loaded from the Content browser, as we have done many times before. However, the constructor of an `FObjectFinder` expects a `const TChar*` as an input parameter. So, this time, we are passing the address of the first element of the char array that makes up the `FString` through `&AssetName.GetCharArray()[0]`.

The last thing we need to do is add a blank definition for the `MyOnActorOverlap` method we overrode in the class definition. Do this now by adding the following code to `BountyDashPowerUp.cpp`:

```
void ABountyDashPowerUp::MyOnActorOverlap(AActor* otherActor)
{

}
```

We will be populating this method with the appropriate functionality soon.

Incorporating power-ups into Bounty Dash

We have successfully created and integrated a power-up plugin and plugin module into our game project. Now we can utilize the functionality of this plugin to incorporate power ups in the `Bounty Dash` project. We are going to have to create a way for the power ups to spawn, collide, and affect the game state of the `Bounty Dash` character. Let's start by spawning the power ups.

Modifying the Coin Spawner

Instead of creating a whole new `spawner` object for power ups, we can augment one of our previously created objects to incorporate power-up spawns. As our coin `spawner` already provides most of the functionality we require, we can modify this class. We are going to adjust this class so that every time a coin would be spawned, there is a chance that a random power up will be spawned in its place. We will start by modifying the class definition. Under the public section of the `ACoinSpawner` class definition found in `CoinSpawner.h`, add the following properties:

```
UPROPERTY(EditAnywhere)
TSubclassOf<class ABountyDashPowerUp> PowerUpObject;

UPROPERTY(EditAnywhere, meta = (ClampMin = "0.0", ClampMax = "100.0",
UIMin = "0.0", UIMax = "100.0"))
int32 PowerUpChance;
```

The first is simply a `TSubclassOf<class ABountyDashPowerUp>` that will hold the type of `ABountyDashPowerUp` we created earlier. We are using this instead of `ABountyDashPowerUp::StaticClass()` to spawn our power ups in case we wish to extend `ABountyDashPowerUp` into different blueprint objects at some point.

The next property, `PowerUpChance`, is simply an int32 that will hold the percentage chance that any given coin to be spawned will be a power up instead. The interesting thing about this property is the meta data we have added to the `UPROPERTY` macro. First, we have exposed this value with `EditAnywhere` so that we may adjust this value from the editor. Second, we also included some new meta data that you will be unfamiliar with. Under the element meta, we have specified four values: `ClampMin`, `ClampMax`, `UIMin`, and `UIMax`.

These values represent the limits of the value when edited from the level editor. The `Clamp` values are used to set physical clamp limitations so that the user may not adjust the value of `powerUpChance` past `100` or below `0`. The `UIMin` and `UIMax` values are used to restrict the value that is presented when adjusting the variable from the editor. If your `UIMin` or `UIMax` values are outside the bounds of your `Clamp` values, it will appear to the user that they may set greater or smaller values than allowed; however, in the backend, the value will still be clamped. The result of adding this meta data is that, instead of a textbox field presented to edit the value, we are given a slider! A slider that can be adjusted from `0` to `100`.

Next, we need to add a function we can use to spawn power ups. Under the protected section of the class definition, add the follow function declaration:

```
void SpawnPowerUp();
```

We are simply going to use this to group and separate the power-up spawn functionality from that of the coin spawn functionality. Navigate to `CoinSpawner.cpp` now. The first thing we need to do is add `#include "BountyDashPowerUp.h"` to the include list at the top of `CoinSpawner.cpp`. Next, we must make a small edit to the `SpawnCoin()` function so that we can check whether a random number generated between 0 and 99 inclusive is less than the `powerUpChance` value. If so, we must spawn a power up instead of a coin.

Now, modify the code of `ACoinSpawner::SpawnCoin()` to match the following:

```
if (FMath::Rand() % 100 < PowerUpChance)
    {
        SpawnPowerUp();
        NumCoinsToSpawn--;
    }
    else
    {
        FActorSpawnParameters spawnParams;

        FTransform coinTransform = SpawnTransforms[TargetLoc]->
        GetTransform();

        coinTransform.SetLocation(FVector(SpawnPoint, coinTransform.
        GetLocation().Y, coinTransform.GetLocation().Z));


        ACoin* spawnedCoin = GetWorld()->
        SpawnActor<ACoin>(CoinObject, coinTransform, spawnParams);

        if (spawnedCoin)
        {
            spawnedCoin->SetKillPoint(KillPoint);

            USphereComponent* coinSphere = Cast<USphereComponent>(spa
            wnedCoin->
            GetComponentByClass(USphereComponent::StaticClass()));

            if (coinSphere)
            {
                float offset = coinSphere->
                GetUnscaledSphereRadius();

                spawnedCoin->
                AddActorLocalOffset(FVector(0.0f, 0.0f, offset));
            }
```

```
                NumCoinsToSpawn--;
            }
    }

    if (NumCoinsToSpawn <= 0)
    {
        FTimerManager& worldTimeManager = GetWorld()->
         GetTimerManager();

        worldTimeManager.SetTimer(CoinSetTimerHandle, this,
         &ACoinSpawner::SpawnCoinSet, CoinSetTimeInterval, false);

        worldTimeManager.ClearTimer(CoinTimerHandle);
    }
```

As you can see, we have made adjustments so that every time a coin would be spawned, a quick check is carried out (`FMath::Rand() % 100 < powerUpChance`). This checks whether the mod 100 of a random number is less than `powerUpChance`. This will push the value generated between a range of 0 and 99. If this is resolved to true (and the generated number is within our generation percentage chance), we need to call `SpawnPowerUp()`.

Next, we need to define the `SpawnPowerUp()` method. This function will be similar to the other spawn functions we have created thus far. Add the following code to `CoinSpawner.cpp`:

```
void ACoinSpawner::SpawnPowerUp()
{
    FActorSpawnParameters SpawnInfo;

    FTransform myTrans = SpawnTransforms[TargetLoc]->
    GetTransform();

    myTrans.SetLocation(FVector(SpawnPoint,
    myTrans.GetLocation().Y, myTrans.GetLocation().Z));

    ABountyDashPowerUp* newObs = GetWorld()->
    SpawnActor<ABountyDashPowerUp>(PowerUpObject, myTrans,
    SpawnInfo);

    if (newObs)
    {
        newObs->SetKillPoint(KillPoint);
```

```
USphereComponent* powerUpSphere = Cast<USphereComponent>(newObs->
GetComponentByClass(USphereComponent::StaticClass()));

        if (powerUpSphere)
        {
            float offset = powerUpSphere->
GetUnscaledSphereRadius();

            newObs->AddActorLocalOffset(FVector(0.0f, 0.0f,
offset));
        }
    }
}
```

Build, run, and test!

Now we can compile this code and build the project again. Before we play the project, we need to make some edits to the **Coin Spawner** that exists in the level. Select the **Coin Spawner** from the **World Outlier** and navigate to the **Details** panel found on the right-hand side of the level editor. Ensure that the details under the **Coin Spawner** section of the panel match the following:

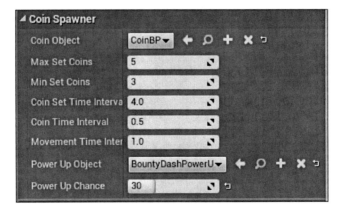

As you can see, we have set the `PowerUpObject` property to `BountyDashPowerUp` and we have set the `PowerUpChance` to `30` using the slider we included through the `UPROPERTY` macro. This power-up chance is very high and should be reduced to 10, but we will leave it high for now so we can test that the power ups will actually spawn.

Now we can run the game! What I would suggest doing is pausing the play session as soon as you can by selecting the **Pause** button in the **Toolbar Panel**, then eject from the character by pressing the **Eject** button in the same panel. Move your now free `camera` to the end of the track where the power ups will be spawning, and watch as power ups begin to spawn and travel down the map!

Colliding with power ups

Now that our power ups are spawning and traveling down the game field, we can add the collision functionality that we require for the power ups. The first thing we need to do is add a short function to the `ABountyDashCharacter` class definition. Navigate to the `BountyDashCharacter.h` and add the following line to the public section of the class definition:

```
void PowerUp(EPowerUp Type);
```

As we are referencing the `enum` type in our plugin, we must also add `#include "PowerUpObject.h"` to the include list of `BountyDashCharacter.h`.

Then navigate to `BountyDashCharacter.cpp` and add a blank definition for this function, as follows:

```
void ABountyDashCharacter::PowerUp(EPowerUp Type)
{

}
```

We have added this now as we will be calling this function from the `MyOnActorOverlap` function found within `ABountyDashPowerUp`. Let's finish the definition for that function now. Navigate to `BountyDashPowerUp.cpp` and add the following code to the `MyOnActorOverlap` definition:

```
if (otherActor->GetClass()->IsChildOf(AObstacle::StaticClass()))
{
```

```
USphereComponent* otherSpehre = Cast<USphereComponent>(otherAct
or->
GetComponentByClass(USphereComponent::StaticClass()));

if (otherSpehre)
{
    AddActorLocalOffset(FVector(0.0f, 0.0f, (otherSpehre->
    GetUnscaledSphereRadius()) + Collider->
    GetUnscaledSphereRadius() * 2));
}
}
```

Here, we are simply performing the same obstacle collision check we perform on the ACoin object to ensure that no power ups are spawned clipping into a spawned obstacle. Next, we need to add the code to this function that will detect collisions with the ABountyDashCharacter. If this happens, we need to inform the character of this collision and pass the correct power-up type to the characters so that we may change the state of that character appropriately. Add the following code to the function now:

```
if (otherActor->GetClass()->
    IsChildOf(ABountyDashCharacter::StaticClass()))
    {
        ABountyDashCharacter* thisChar = Cast<ABountyDashCharacter>(o
        therActor);

        if (thisChar)
        {
            thisChar->PowerUp(PowerUp->GetType());
            GetWorld()->DestroyActor(this);
        }
    } // <- closing ABountyDashPowerUp::MyOnActorOverlap()
```

Here, we are simply checking whether the offending overlapping actor is a child of ABountyDashCharacter (or is of that type). If so, we are going to inform the offending character that they just collided with a power up by passing the type of the UPowerUpObject contained within ABountyDashPowerUp to the PowerUp() method we created earlier. We then destroy this power up as it is no longer needed in the game world. Along with this code, also add #include"Obstacle.h" and #include BountyDashCharacter.h to the include list for BountyDashPowerUp.cpp. Now we can write the code that will power up our character!

Powering up the character

We need to augment the `ABountyDashCharacter` to support power ups. There are three different types of power up that we have listed in the `EPowerUp` enum class— `SPEED`, `SMASH`, and `MAGNET`. We need to create three different sets of functionality that can accommodate for these three power-up types:

- `SPEED`: The game speed will reduce so that the player may balance out game speed as they pick up coins. The game speed cannot slow down past the speed that is set at the beginning of the game.

- `SMASH`: The character will be able to literally smash through any of the obstacles set in their path. We will be leveraging the **Destructible Mesh** capabilities of Unreal Engine to create this effect.

- `MAGNET`: Coins in all lanes will attract the character so that the player no longer has to manually collide with the coins to pick them up.

The last two power ups should only last for a certain amount of time so that the game does not become too easy. Let's start by modifying the class definition to accommodate for this new power-up functionality. Add the following properties to the protected section of the `ABountyDashCharacter` class definition:

```
// Smash Time
    UPROPERTY(EditAnywhere, Category = PowerUps)
    float SmashTime;

    // Magnet Time
    UPROPERTY(EditAnywhere, Category = PowerUps)
    float MagnetTime;

    UPROPERTY(EditAnywhere, Category = PowerUps)
    float MagnetReach;
```

We have exposed all of these properties to the editor so that we may tweak the values of these power-up properties in the editor. The first two will dictate how long the smash and magnet power ups last. The last property will dictate the radius around the player within which coins will attract. Next we need to add the Boolean flags that we can check against to see which power ups are active. Add the following private members to the `ABountyDashCharacter` class definition now:

```
// Power up properties
bool CanSmash;
bool CanMagnet;
```

Finally, we need to add two short functions that we will call via two new timers. Add the following protected functions to the `ABountyDashCharacter` class definition now:

```
UFUNCTION()
void StopSmash();

UFUNCTION()
void StopMagnet();
```

Reducing the game speed

Let's start with the simplest power up, reducing the game speed. This power up will reduce the game speed by the same amount it is increased by when the coin limit is reached. To accommodate for this power up, we have to add a short function to the `ABountyDashGameMode`. Navigate to `BountyDashGameMode.h` now. Under the public section of the class definition, add the following function:

```
void ReduceGameSpeed();
```

Then navigate to `BountyDashGameMode.cpp`. We are going to be adding a definition for this function with the following:

```
void
ABountyDashGameMode::ReduceGameSpeed()
{
    if (gameSpeed > 10.0f)
    {
        gameSpeed -= gameSpeedIncrease;
        gameLevel--;
    }
}
```

This function simply ensures that the game speed is currently greater than that of the game speed at game start (10m/s). If so, we will reduce the game speed by `gameSpeedIncrease`. This means that the player will be able to balance these power ups with the amount of coins picked up to mediate the game speed. We also reduce the `gameLevel` variable for later use in animation.

With this small method in place, we can now flesh out the `PowerUp()` function we created in the character earlier. Navigate to `BountyDashCharacter.cpp` and find the empty `ABountyDashCharacter::PowerUp()` function definition. Modify this function definition so it appears as follows:

```
void ABountyDashCharacter::PowerUp(EPowerUp Type)
{
    switch (Type)
```

```
        {
        case EPowerUp::SPEED:
        {
            GetCustomGameMode<ABountyDashGameMode>(GetWorld())->
            ReduceGameSpeed();
            break;
        }
        case EPowerUp::SMASH:
        {
            CanSmash = true;

            FTimerHandle newTimer;
            GetWorld()->GetTimerManager().SetTimer(newTimer, this,
            &ABountyDashCharacter::StopSmash, SmashTime, false);

            break;
        }
        case EPowerUp::MAGNET:
        {
            CanMagnet = true;

            FTimerHandle newTimer;
            GetWorld()->GetTimerManager().SetTimer(newTimer, this,
            &ABountyDashCharacter::StopMagnet, MagnetTime, false);

            break;
        }
        default:
            break;
        }
    }
```

Here, we have implemented a switch case based off of the type of power up that has been collided with. As you can see, if the power up is of type SPEED then we will call the function we just created in the ABountyDashGameMode through the GetCustomGameMode() function. If the power up is of time SMASH or MAGNET, we simply set the CanMagnet or CanSmash Booleans to true, and set a timer that will execute our stop functions after the given time period. Now add the following function definitions to BountyDashCharacter.cpp:

```
void ABountyDashCharacter::StopMagnet()
{
    CanMagnet = false;
}
```

```
void ABountyDashCharacter::StopSmash()
{
    CanSmash = false;
}
```

All we need to do now is check on these logical values during the characters `Tick()`
and enact the appropriate power-up functionality.

Making the coin magnet

To make the coin magnet, we are going to have to check every frame that we should
still be pulling coins towards the character. If so, we need to iterate through all of the
coins and interpolate the coin position towards that of the player. Start by adding the
following function declaration to the `ABountyDashCharacter` class definition under
the protected section:

```
// Power up functions
void CoinMagnet();
```

We also need to add a new member to the `ACoin` object class definition. Navigate to
`Coin.h` now and add the following member to the class definition:

```
public:
bool BeingPulled;
```

This flag is going to be used when checking for coin collisions with obstacles, as we
do not wish for the coin to adjust position when being pulled. Therefore, we must
also modify the `MyOnActorOverlap()` function in `Coin.cpp`. Modify the first if
statement in `ACoin::MyOnActorOverlap` so that it matches the following:

```
void ACoin::MyOnActorOverlap(AActor* otherActor)
{
    if (otherActor->GetClass()->
    IsChildOf(AObstacle::StaticClass()) && !BeingPulled)
    {
```

With these changes in place, we can finish our modifications to
`ABountyDashCharacter`. Navigate to `BountyDashCharacter.cpp` and add the
following code to `ABountyDashCharacter::Tick()`:

```
        if (CanMagnet)
        {
        CoinMagnet();
        }
```

This will simply check against the Boolean flag we declared earlier and execute the `CoinMagnet` functionality if it resolves to `true`. Now we must define the `CoinMagnet()` function. Add the following to `ABountyDashCharacter.cpp`:

```
void ABountyDashCharacter::CoinMagnet()
{
    for (TActorIterator<ACoin> coinIter(GetWorld()); coinIter;
        ++coinIter)
    {
        FVector between = GetActorLocation() - coinIter->
        GetActorLocation();

        if (FMath::Abs(between.Size()) < magnetReach)
        {
            FVector CoinPos = FMath::Lerp((*coinIter)->
            GetActorLocation(), GetActorLocation(), 0.2f);

            (*coinIter)->SetActorLocation(CoinPos);
            (*coinIter)->BeingPulled = true;
        }
    }
}
```

This function iterates through all of the active coins within the current level through a `TActorIterator` of type `ACoin`. We will increment this iterator with each iteration of the for loop. This will traverse across all active `ACoin`s until the iterator becomes invalid. For each `ACoin` found, we check whether the `ACoin` is within the magnet pull radius of the character. If so, we then interpolate the `ACoin` position towards the character through `FMath::Lerp()`. We then set the position of the `ACoin` by de-referencing the `ACoin` iterator, thus exposing the actual `ACoin` handle, then using `SetActorLocation()`, passing the interpolated coin position as the input. We then set the `BeingPulled` flag we created earlier to true. As we just referenced the `ACoin` object, be sure to add `#include "Coin.h"` to the include list of the `BountyDashCharacter.cpp`.

Before we go on to create the smash power-up functionality, now is a good time to compile and run the new code we just implemented!

How to create, load and smash Destructible Meshes

The next power-up type, SMASH, is going to require a new Unreal Engine feature we have yet to work with and that is the Destructible Mesh feature supported by the PhyX integration featured in UE4. We are also going to have to adjust the `AObstacle` object to accommodate for a Destructible Mesh instead of a standard static mesh. Let's start by creating our very own Destructible Mesh!

In the UE4 level editor, use the **Content** browser to navigate to the location of the obstacle Mesh. It will be located under `Content/StarterContent/Props/SM_Rock` or simply search for `SM_Rock`. You will be presented with the following asset:

Right-click this thumbnail in the content browser and select **Create Destructible Mesh**:

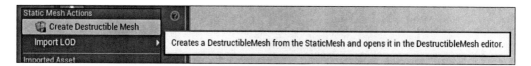

This will create a new Destructible Mesh `SM_Rock_DM` and open up the Destructible Mesh editor. This is fairly simple and does not require much of an explanation, and appears as follows:

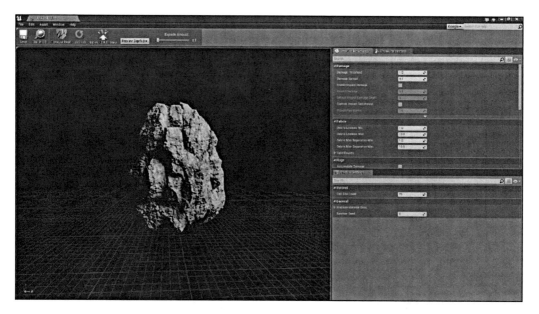

As you can see, it boasts a **Viewport** to preview the state of the Destructible Mesh, and a **Toolbar** with options that allows you to perform actions on the Destructible Mesh. On the right-hand side of the editor, you are presented with the Destructible Mesh Settings panel. It is here where you can set the various properties of the Destructible Mesh such as **Damage Threshold**, **Damage Spread,** and, if you are to, **Enable Impact Damage**. Underneath this panel, we have the **Fracture Setting Panel**. This panel is used to determine how many pieces the Destructible Mesh will smash into and how the material of the Mesh will apply to the split chunks.

For our Mesh, we need a few of these settings to be changed from the default. First, ensure that the **Damage** section of the **Destructible Setting Panel** matches the following (for the key differences, look for the small arrows):

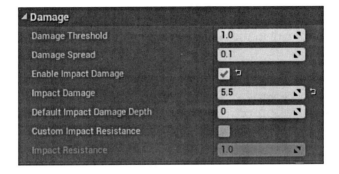

The previous settings will ensure that when the Mesh receives a damage value greater than 1, it will shatter. We have also enabled impact damage, meaning if the Mesh is hit by something with force, it will suffer impact damage. We have then set the **Impact Damage** value to 5.5. These two settings are important as we can only shatter a Destructible Mesh by applying damage to the Mesh. We then need to ensure the Mesh will fracture properly by adjusting the **Fracture Settings** panel to the following:

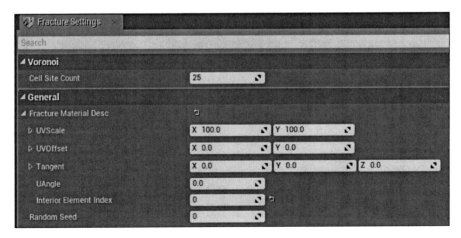

This arrangement of settings will have the Mesh split into 25 different chunks. We then want these chunks to use the first material index for their interior material, as can be seen by the property **Interior Element Index**, which is set to 0. Test these settings all work, and address the **Toolbar** at the top of the editor. Press the **Fracture Mesh** button now. This will create the appropriate fracturing for the Mesh. You are able to preview the Mesh fracture by adjusting the **Explode Amount** slider, also featured in the toolbar. When you are done, you should see something similar to the following:

Congratulations! You just created your first destructible Mesh in UE4! We can now modify our AObstacle class. Because we abstracted all of the base functionality out of AObstacle earlier, we are able to make drastic changes to this object without worrying about the flow-on effects it will have on other objects. Navigate to the Obstacle.h file now. We are going to be replacing the UStaticMeshComponent handle for a UDestructibleComponent handle, and adding a get method for this destructible component. Modify for the class definition of AObstacle now so it matches the following:

```
UCLASS(BlueprintType)
class BOUNTYDASH_API AObstacle : public ABountyDashObject
{
    GENERATED_BODY()
public:
    // Sets default values for this actor's properties
    AObstacle();

    UDestructibleComponent* GetDestructable();
```

```
protected:
    UPROPERTY(EditAnywhere)
    UDestructibleComponent* Mesh;
};
```

We then need to modify the `AObstacle` constructor slightly to accommodate this change. Navigate to `Obstacle.cpp` and adjust `AObstacle::AObstacle()` to match the following:

```
// Sets default values
AObstacle::AObstacle()
{
    // Set this actor to call Tick() every frame.
    You can turn this off to improve performance if you don't need it.
    PrimaryActorTick.bCanEverTick = true;

    Mesh = CreateDefaultSubobject<UDestructibleComponent>(TEXT("Me
sh"));
    check(Mesh);

    Mesh ->AttachTo(Collider);
    Mesh ->SetCollisionResponseToAllChannels(ECR_Ignore);
}
```

As you can see, we initialize the `UDestructibleComponent` in exactly the same way as other components. We also need to add a definition for the `getter` method we have declared for the `UDesctructibleComponent`:

```
UDestructibleComponent* AObstacle::GetDestructable()
{
    return Mesh;
}
```

The last thing we need to do to finish our adjustment of the `AObstacle` object is modifying the `RockObstacleBP` we created earlier and setting the destructible component to `SM_Rock_DM`. Do this now by navigating to and opening `RockObstacleBP`. In the **Components Panel**, select the **Mesh(inherited)** element, then address the **Details Panel**. Navigate to **Mesh | DestructibleComponent**, adjust the Destructible Mesh property so that it is populated with `SM_Rock_DM`, like so:

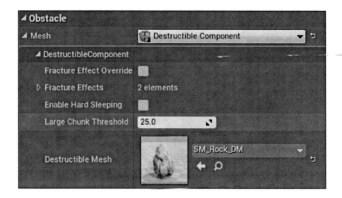

Ensure that the new Destructible Mesh is positioned correctly within the **Viewport** so that it assumes the same position and scale as the old static `Mesh`. I used the following transform settings:

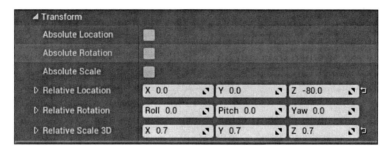

We are now done modifying our `AObstacle`! The next thing we need to do is add the functionality to `ABountyDashCharacter` to shatter the Destructible Mesh upon impact!

To actually shatter the destructible mesh, we need to modify `ABountyDashCharacter::myOnComponentOverlap`. We will still perform the same angle of impact check we were doing previously; however, if it resolves to true, we also need to check whether the character can currently smash. If so, destroy the `Mesh` of the obstacle we just encountered; if not, simply set `bBeingPushed` to `true`. Modify the appropriate section of `ABountyDashCharacter::myOnComponentOverlap()` to match the following:

```
if (AngleBetween < 60.0f)
    {
        AObstacle* pObs = Cast<AObstacle>(OtherActor);

        if (pObs && CanSmash)
        {
```

```
pObs->GetDestructable()->ApplyRadiusDamage(10000, GetActorLocation(),
10000, 10000, true);
        }
        else
        {
            bBeingPushed = true;
        }
    }
```

Here, you can see that if the other offending actor is successfully cast to an `AObstacle`, we also check whether the character can smash. If so, we get the destructible component from the offending `AObstacle` through the getter method `GetDestructible()`. With this reference, we then call `ApplyRadiusDamage()` on it. This function takes in a base damage value, a damage origin, a damage radius, an impulse force amount, and whether the full damage will be received. We have set all the damage parameters to large values to ensure a shattering of the mesh takes place. For the location of the damage, we have simply provided the location of the `ABountyDashCharacter`. This function will apply damage to the destructible mesh with the parameters provided. The resultant effect will be the obstacle exploding around the character when they run through it!

Now it is time to test that this works! You may either play `Bounty Dash` until a smash power up spawns to test the functionality, or temporarily remove the `canSmash` check so that the Destructible Mesh is always shattered. I prefer the second option. Build and run the code now, then play the game. You should have an effect that is similar to this:

We are done implementing our power ups! Awesome work! Take a quick break and enjoy playing around with power-up spawn frequencies and timers to fine-tune the gameplay of BountyDash. The next thing we are going to be doing is creating our very own HUD class!

Creating HUDs using C++

Now that we have almost all of the gameplay finished for BountyDash, we need to be able to report the current game state to the player. We are going to do this in a similar way to that of Barrel Hopper; however, this time we will be creating our HUD object entirely in C++ code. HUD objects in UE4 utilize something called a Canvas. A Canvas is simply a draw area within the screen that we can use to do things such as draw text, images, and other HUD-related imagery. On our HUD object, we will be displaying the player's current runtime and the player's current score.

ABountyDashHUD

Let's start by creating a new HUD object via the C++ class wizard found within the editor. Create a new class that inherits from HUD and call it BountyDashHUD. Once the code has been generated, open the BountyDashHUD.h file. Ensure the class definition matches the following:

```
UCLASS()
class BOUNTYDASH_API ABountyDashHUD : public AHUD
{
    GENERATED_BODY()
    ABountyDashHUD();

    UPROPERTY()
    UFont* HUDFont;

    virtual void DrawHUD() override;
};
```

In ABountyDashHUD, we have included a constructor, a UFont handle that we will use to save the font we wish to use for onscreen text, and we have overridden the DrawHUD() method. This will allow us to specify custom HUD drawing functionality so we may draw our text to the screen.

Before we begin to define this object, we need to create a font object that we can use for our screen text. In the content browser of the editor, create a font object that is exactly the same as the one we created in Barrel Hopper; however, this time call it BountyDashFont. The settings for the font should appear as follows:

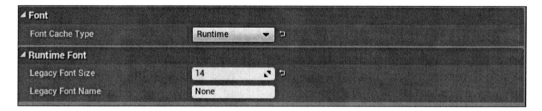

Now navigate to BountyDashHUD.cpp and add the following code for the HUD constructor:

```
ABountyDashHUD::ABountyDashHUD()
{
    static ConstructorHelpers::FObjectFinder<UFont>OurHudFont
    (TEXT("/ Game/BountyDashFont.BountyDashFont"));

    HUDFont = OurHudFont.Object;
}
```

This constructor simply initializes the HUDfont handle we declared earlier to that of the custom font we just created. Next, add an empty definition for DrawHUD(). We will come back to this shortly:

```
void ABountyDashHUD::DrawHUD()
{
}
```

Getting information from our objects

Before we define the DrawHUD() method, we are going to require some information from the ABountyDashCharacter and ABountyDashGameMode objects. We require the score from ABountyDashCharacter and the runtime from ABountyDashGameMode.

Let's start by modifying the ABountyDashCharacter so that we may get the score. Navigate to BountyDashCharacter.h and, in the class definition, add the following method under public:

```
int GetScore();
```

This `accessor` method will be used to retrieve the player score. Now we can navigate to `BountyDashCharacter.cpp`.

Add a function definition for the method we just declared:

```
int ABountyDashCharacter::GetScore()
{
    return Score;
}
```

Now we must add a runtime clock to the game mode. This is a very simple process. We simply have to add a float member to `ABountyDashGameMode` and increment that float value every frame by the delta tick to accumulate the time passed during a game run. Navigate to `BountyDashGameMode.h` now and add the following protected member:

```
UPROPERTY()
float RunTime;
```

We also need an `accessor` method for this member and, if we have not already, to override the `Tick()` function so we may have our game mode tick. Add the following public methods to the `ABountyDashGameMode` class definition:

```
float GetRunTime();
UFUNCTION()
virtual void Tick(float DeltaSeconds) override;
```

Now navigate to `BountyDashGameMode.cpp`. We are going to write the defines for the `Tick()` and `accessor` methods. Add the following code to `BountyDashGameMode.cpp`:

```
void ABountyDashGameMode::Tick(float DeltaSeconds)
{
    RunTime += DeltaSeconds;
}

float ABountyDashGameMode::GetRunTime()
{
    return RunTime;
}
```

Setting the HUD class in the game mode

While we are working with the ABountyDashGameMode, we should add code to the constructor of this object so that our new custom BountyDashHUD is set as the default HUD class for this game mode. Within ABountyDashGameMode::ABountyDashGameMode(), add the following code:

```
HUDClass = ABountyDashHUD::StaticClass();
```

HUDClass is a member found in the AGameMode base class that is used to identify which object type we wish to use as the game HUD. In our case, that is the UClass type returned by the StaticClass() method found in ABountyDashHUD. Also ensure you add the appropriate include for ABountyDashHUD to the include list of the BountyDashGameMode.cpp.

Implementing a custom DrawHUD function

Now that we have the means to access all of the information we require, we can write our DrawHUD() function. Navigate back to BountyDashHUD.cpp and add the following to the include list at the top of the .cpp:

```
#include "BountyDashCharacter.h"
#include "BountyDashGameMode.h"
```

Now we are going to add code to the empty DrawHUD() function definition. Begin by adding the following:

```
Super::DrawHUD();

FVector2D ScreenDimensions = FVector2D(Canvas->SizeX, Canvas->SizeY);

ABountyDashCharacter* DashCharacter =
Cast<ABountyDashCharacter>(UGameplayStatics::GetPlayerPawn(
GetWorld(), 0));

ABountyDashGameMode* DashGameMode =
GetCustomGameMode<ABountyDashGameMode>(GetWorld());
```

Here, we are calling DrawHUD on the super class so that we do not lose out on any of the base DrawHUD functionality found in the AHUD parent class. We are then getting the screen dimensions from the Canvas object mentioned previously. If you cannot remember what a Canvas is, it is simply an object that represents the draw area we have access to when drawing content to the HUD. It is from and through the Canvas object we can perform actions such as getting screen dimensions, drawing images, and drawing text. The default Canvas object is the entire screen space available and will be the object we use.

We are saving the screen dimensions in a FVector2D. Next, we are attaining a handle to both the game mode and the character. We are going to be using these handles to retrieve the information we specified previously. Next, we are going to generate the FString that will hold the text we are drawing to the screen. Add the following code:

```
FString HUDString = FString::Printf(TEXT("Score: %d Runtime: %.4f"),
DashCharacter->GetScore(), DashGameMode->GetRunTime());
```

Here, we are utilizing the printf functionality of the FString object to generate a text string. As you can see, the %d character will be replaced with the game score retrieved from the DashCharacter handle we retrieved earlier. We then use %.4f so that printf will only pull four decimal places from the floating point value we are using to hold the game time. If you are unfamiliar with printf semantics, I strongly suggest looking up the stl::printf functionality set so you may use the similar FString::printf effectively.

Now that we have the string we will be drawing to screen, we need to inform the HUD to draw this text. We can do this with a very simple function. Add the following code to DrawHUD():

```
DrawText(HUDString, FColor::Yellow, 50, 50, HUDFont);
```

This function takes in an FString to use for screen text, a color value to color the text, screen position co-ordinates (in this case, 50 on the X and 50 on the Y), and a font object to use. This will draw our generated text to the screen. Compile and build the project then run the game. You should see the following in the top left-hand side of the screen:

Score: 0 Runtime: 16.5932

Completing the Bounty Dash game loop!

With our HUD in place, we can now implement the functionality to finish the Bounty Dash game loop. We need to be able to end the game when the player reaches the same kill point that destroys the objects that are moving down the game field. Upon reaching this kill point, we should pause the game and present the player with game over text. Upon game over, the player should also be able to press *R* to reset the game. To achieve this, we are going to have to make edits to the ABountyDashGameMode class to support game over and pause functionality, to the ABountyDashCharacter class to support restarting, and to the ABountyDashHUD class so that we can draw the game over text.

The beginning of the end and pausing the game

Instead of having the game suddenly pause when the player reaches the kill point, it would be more user-friendly to have the character fall for a short while before we pause the game and report that the game is over. To do this, we are going to have to set up a timer within the `ABountyDashGameMode` class and a few Boolean flags we can use to represent the different game over states. Navigate to `BountyDashGameMode.h` and add the following public functions to the class definition now:

```
UFUNCTION()
bool GetGameOver();

UFUNCTION()
void GameOver();
UFUNCTION()
void SetGamePaused(bool gamePaused);
```

The first will be used to query whether the game is in fact over, and the second will be called when the character detects that it has reached the kill point. This will start the game over timer. Once the timer has reached a specified time, we will set a game over flag to true. The last one will be used to pause the game once the game over timer has run its course. We now need to add a few protected members to the class definition:

```
UPROPERTY()
bool bGameOver;

UPROPERTY()
bool startGameOverCount;

UPROPERTY()
float timeTillGameOver;

UPROPERTY()
float gameOverTimer;
```

The first is a Boolean flag that represents if the game is in fact over. The next Boolean flag is used to gauge when to start the game over timer. The next two floating point values are used for the timer itself. The first will be used to hold how long it will take between the character reaching the `KillPoint` and the game over screen being shown. The second is the accumulated time since `startGameOverCount` was set to true.

Navigate to `BountyDashGameMode.cpp` now. We need to add some default values for the new protected members we just created; let's do that now by adding the following code to the constructor:

```
RunTime = 0.0f;
bGameOver = false;
startGameOverCount = false;
timeTillGameOver = 2.0f;
gameOverTimer = 0.0f;
```

The game over timer will run for two seconds before we pause the game. We have also added some safe defaults for the Boolean flags and the `RunTime` counter we made earlier.

Next, we need to adjust the tick function so that it includes the new game over timer. Modify `ABountyDashGameMode::Tick()` so that it appears as follows:

```
if (!startGameOverCount)
{
    RunTime += DeltaSeconds;
}
else
    {
    gameOverTimer += DeltaSeconds;

    if (gameOverTimer >= timeTillGameOver)

            bGameOver = true;
        }
    }
```

Here, we are checking whether we have begun the game over timer. If not, we need to increment the runtime as the game is still in progress. Otherwise, we need to increment the game over timer until it is greater than or equal to `timeTillGameOver`. If so, we will change the `bGameOver` flag to true. Next, we need to add the following simple functions to the `.cpp`:

```
bool ABountyDashGameMode::GetGameOver()
{
    return bGameOver;
}

void ABountyDashGameMode::GameOver()
{
    startGameOverCount = true;
}
```

The first simply returns the `bGameOver` flag and the second is used to start the game over timer.

Pausing the Game

Now we can write our pause function. Pausing a game from C++ is very easy; all we need is a handle to a player controller. In our case, this will be the first player controller. We can then call `SetPause` on this controller to pause the game. Define the `ABountyDashGameMode::SetGamePaused` method as follows:

```cpp
void ABountyDashGameMode::SetGamePaused(bool gamePaused)
{
    APlayerController* myPlayer = GetWorld()->
    GetFirstPlayerController();

    if (myPlayer != nullptr)
    {
        myPlayer->SetPause(gamePaused);
    }
}
```

Here, we are simply getting the first player controller from the world context, ensuring the controller is valid, and then calling `SetPause` on the controller.

Restarting the game

We now need to allow the player to restart the game somehow while the game is paused. We can do this by binding another input action to the `ABountyDashCharacter`. We are then going to inform that action to be allowed to execute even when the game is paused. The first thing we need to do is create a new action mapping in the editor. Do this now. Navigate to `Edit->ProjectSettings->Engine->`Input and add the following action mapping:

We need to bind this mapping to a new function in `ABountyDashCharacter`. Navigate to `BountyDashCharacter.h` and add the following protected method to the class definition:

```cpp
UFUNCTION()
void Reset();
```

This function will be bound to the input event and defined so that the game level is reset. Navigate to `ABountyDashCharacter::SetupPlayerInputComponent()` in `BountyDashCharacter.cpp`. We need to add one more binding to the definition of this function. Add the following line of code:

```
InputComponent->BindAction("Reset", IE_Pressed, this,
&ABountyDashCharacter::Reset).bExecuteWhenPaused = true;
```

What we are doing here is binding the `Reset()` method we just created to the Reset input action mapping pressed state. The `BindAction` function returns a reference to a newly created `FInputActionBinding`. We are then setting the `bExecutWhenPaused` member of this new binding to true. Whenever you want an input action to be carried out, even when a game state is paused, you must set this flag appropriately.

Now we can define the `Reset()` method. Add the following code to the `.cpp` now:

```
void ABountyDashCharacter::Reset()
{
    UGameplayStatics::OpenLevel(GetWorld(),
    TEXT("BountyDashMap"));
}
```

This code utilizes the `UGameplayStatics` namespace function `OpenLevel`. This function will open the level specified, given a game world context. Reloading this level will perform the same action as resetting the level.

We need to do one last thing before we are done editing `ABountyDashCharacter`. We need to add some code to the `Tick` function so that when the player reaches the `killPoint` of the floor object, the game mode will be informed to start the game over counter.

First, we need to retrieve and save the kill point somewhere. Add the following protected member to the `ABountyDashCharacter` class definition:

```
// Kill Point
float Killpoint;

Now modify ABountyDashCharacter::BeginPlay in BountyDashCharacter.cpp
to include the following code:
for (TActorIterator<AFloor> TargetIter(GetWorld()); TargetIter;
++TargetIter)
{
    Killpoint = TargetIter->GetKillPoint();
    }
```

This code will retrieve the floor actor in the level and save the `killPoint` into the value we just declared. As we just reference `AFloor` in this `.cpp`, ensure to add the appropriate include to the include list. Finally, we can add the following code to `ABountyDashCharacter::Tick()`:

```
if (GetActorLocation().X < Killpoint)
{
    GetCustomGameMode<ABountyDashGameMode>(GetWorld())->
    GameOver();
}
```

Simply, if the character reaches the `killPoint`, we need to inform the game to start the game over counter.

Drawing the game over text

We are nearly done! All we need to do now is draw the game over text within the HUD when `ABountyDashGameMode::bGameOver` has been set to true. Navigate to `ABountyDashHUD::DrawHUD()` in `BountyDashHUD.cpp` and add the following code:

```
if (DashGameMode->GetGameOver())
{
    FVector2D GameOverSize;
    GetTextSize(TEXT("GAME OVER!!! Press R to Restart!"),
    GameOverSize.X, GameOverSize.Y, HUDFont);

    DrawText(TEXT("GAME OVER!!! Press R to Restart!"),
    FColor::Yellow, (ScreenDimensions.X - GameOverSize.X) / 2.0f,
    (ScreenDimensions.Y - GameOverSize.Y) / 2.0f, HUDFont);

    DashGameMode->SetGamePaused(true);
}
```

This section of code is checking whether the game is over. If so, we need to draw `GAME OVER!!! Press R to Restart!` in the middle of the screen. We can do this by using the same draw text function we created earlier; however, this time, instead of parsing hard-coded values (such as 50), we are simply calculating the position of the text. We have used the `GetTextSize()` method to retrieve how much space the previous sentence will take up in screen space when using the font we made earlier. We are then using these text size dimensions to place the game over text in the middle of the screen. We do this by subtracting the appropriate text dimension from the corresponding screen dimension, then dividing the resulting value by `2.0f`. This will place the text in the middle of the screen while compensating for screen text size. Then, finally, we have set the game to pause!

Great! We are now done with the Bounty Dash game loop! Compile, build, and run the code. Let the player be pushed off the back of the floor object, wait two seconds and you should be presented with this:

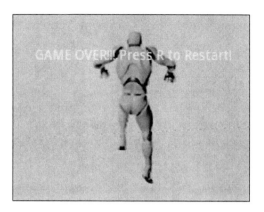

Now when you press *R*, the game will restart and you can try beating your previous score!

Finishing the wall of death and polishing the project

We are so nearly finished with BountyDash. The only things we have yet to do are to add the soundscape, add the particle effects, make the character run, and create the illusion of a wall of death! These small feature additions will add to the overall polish of the project and add that Unreal Factor that separates Unreal projects from others. We can leave the sound and particle effects till last as they will require less work than the wall of death.

Making the wall of death

We can finally make our invisible wall of death! In a way, we have been working with it this whole time. The killPoint variable we have been using to destroy objects and end the game has been our wall thus far. What we are going to do is utilize the same logic with the Destructible Mesh feature of UE4 and our AFloor object. We are going to be modifying the floor so that instead of having three long floor pieces constantly moving and swapping out, we are going to have numerous smaller pieces, around 80 or so. We are still going to use the same swap chain logic.

This time, however, when we swap a piece back to the front of the queue, we are going to spawn a destructible mesh version of that floor piece in its place and shatter it instantly, creating the illusion of an invisible wall that destroys all! This is going to require a new class, `ADestroyedFloorPiece`, a new floor mesh that we will make in a very similar manner to the first, and some modifications to our existing `AFloor` object.

Making the new floor mesh

The new floor mesh piece will be very similar to the first, we will simply be keeping all X, Y, and Z dimensions at an equal value. We are doing this so we may destroy more pieces at a faster rate without having the floor immediately under the character's feet disappear.

To create the new piece, simply drag a new **BSP Box Brush** into the level from the **Modes Panel** within the level editor. Ensure that this box is positioned at X: 0, Y: 0, Z: -100. Once in place, duplicate this box twice and place these new brushes at X: 0, Y: 230, Z:-100, and X:0, Y: -230, Z:-100, respectively. Select all of these brushes at once, ensuring that the transform widget is found within the center-most brush (this should be the last brush selected).

If you are using the current level to do this (without the existing floor object), you will see something like this:

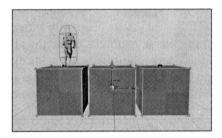

Again, all we need to do is navigate to the **Brush Settings** section of the **Details Panel**, hit the small white expansion arrow at the bottom of the section, then select the **Create Static Mesh** button. Refer to the following screenshot:

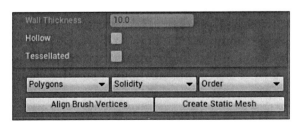

Save this new `Mesh` as `Destroyable_Mesh`. Now all you need to do is create a destructible mesh version of this asset. Use the following settings for the Destructible Mesh and name it `Destroyable_Mesh_DM`:

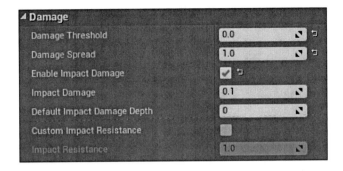

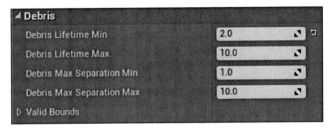

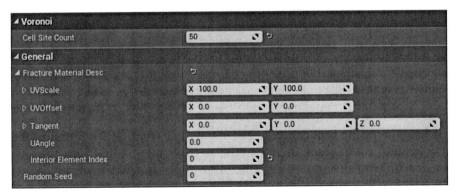

We are done with creating the new `mesh` assets!

ADestroyedFloorPiece

Now we need to make the code object that we will be spawning in when a floor piece is moved back to the front of the queue. Create a new C++ class using the class wizard that inherits from `AActor` and call it `DestroyedFloorPiece`. This new object will be responsible for two things. The first is the Destructible Mesh we just created, the second is the destruction of the object itself after a period of time. We need this object to despawn after a given time limit. To do this, we are going to be using a timer. Navigate to `ADestroyedFloorPiece` in `DestroyedFloorPiece.h` and modify it to match the following:

```
UCLASS()
class BOUNTYDASH_API ADestroyedFloorPiece : public AActor
{
    GENERATED_BODY()

public:
    // Sets default values for this actor's properties
    ADestroyedFloorPiece();

    void Death();

    UPROPERTY()
    UDestructibleComponent* Destructable;
};
```

We have removed the `Tick()` function and we have added a `UDestructibleComponent` handle and a `Death()` function we will call from a timer. Now navigate to `ADestroyedFloorPiece::ADestroyedFloorPiece()` in the `DestroyedFloorPiece.cpp`.

We need to initialize the root component with a scene component, initialize the Destructible Mesh component, then load the asset we just created so we can assign it to the Destructible Mesh component. The following code will perform these actions:

```
// Sets default values
ADestroyedFloorPiece::ADestroyedFloorPiece()
{
    // Set this actor to call Tick() every frame.  You can turn this
    // off to improve performance if you don't need it.
    PrimaryActorTick.bCanEverTick = true;

RootComponent = CreateDefaultSubobject<USceneComponent>(TEXT("Root"));
    check(RootComponent);
```

```
Destructable =
CreateDefaultSubobject<UDestructibleComponent>
(TEXT("Destructable"));
check(Destructable);

Destructable->AttachTo(RootComponent);
Destructable->SetCollisionProfileName("OverlapAllDynamic");

ConstructorHelpers::FObjectFinder <UDestructibleMesh>
myDestMesh(TEXT("/Game/Geometry/Meshes/
Destroyable_Mesh_DM.Destroyable_Mesh_DM"));

if (myDestMesh.Succeeded())
{
    destructable->SetDestructibleMesh(myDestMesh.Object);
}
}
```

Great! Now we simply need to define the `Death()` and `BeginPlay()` functions:

```
void ADestroyedFloorPiece::BeginPlay()
{
    Super::BeginPlay();

    FTimerHandle thisTimer;
    GetWorld()->GetTimerManager().SetTimer(thisTimer, this,
    &ADestroyedFloorPiece::Death, 4.0f, false);
}

void ADestroyedFloorPiece::Death()
{
    GetWorld()->DestroyActor(this);
}
```

In `BeginPlay()` we start the timer that will call `Death()`. `Death()` itself as a simple function, which will simply inform the world to destroy this floor piece.

Modifying the AFloor object

Thankfully, due to our futureproof implementation of the `AFloor` constructor, we do not need to make many changes to the codebase of `AFloor` to achieve our new functionality set. Navigate to `AFloor::AFloor()` now. All we need to do is change the look-up name we are using when loading the `UStaticMesh` for the `UStaticMeshComponent` and change the number of repeating meshes to `80`.

We can do that with the following code:

```
RootComponent = CreateDefaultSubobject<USceneComponent>(TEXT("Root"));
ConstructorHelpers::FObjectFinder<UStaticMesh>myMesh(TEXT("/Game/
Geometry/Meshes/Destroyable_Mesh.Destroyable_Mesh"));

ConstructorHelpers::FObjectFinder<UMaterial>myMaterial(TEXT("/Game/
StarterContent/Materials/M_Concrete_Tiles.M_Concrete_Tiles"));

if (myMesh.Succeeded())
{
    numRepeatingMesh = 80;
```

Lastly, we need to ensure that we spawn the new `ADestroyedFloorPiece` object when a floor piece is relocated at the front of the queue. First, ensure you add `#include "DestroyedFloorPiece.h"` to the include list at the top of the `.cpp`. Navigate to `AFloor::Tick()` and add the following code, where we are resetting a floor piece after it travels past the calculated kill point:

```
if (floorMeshScenes[i]->GetComponentTransform().GetLocation().X <=
    KillPoint)
{
    // spawn destructible mesh and destroy
    ADestroyedFloorPiece* thisPiece = GetWorld()->SpawnActor <ADestroy
    edFloorPiece>(ADestroyedFloorPiece::StaticClass(),
    floorMeshScenes[i]->GetComponentTransform());

    if (thisPiece)
    {
        thisPiece->Destructable->ApplyDamage(100000, thisPiece->
        GetActorLocation(),
        FVector(-FMath::RandRange(-10, 10),
            -FMath::RandRange(-10, 10),
            -FMath::RandRange(-10, 10)), 10000);
    }

    floorMeshScenes[i]->SetRelativeLocation(FVector(spawnPoint, 0.0f,
    0.0f));
}
```

Here, we are spawning an `ADestroyedFloorPiece` object at the location of the floor mesh piece we are about to move. We then apply damage to the destructible mesh component of this new object instantly, thus shattering the mesh. This time, when providing a direction for this damage, we use a `FVector` with randomized values between a range of `-10` and `10`. This is so the destruction of the meshes will have the shattered pieces always move in different directions. Try removing the randomization after we are finished to see how it looks without it. Once this damage has been applied, we then update the position of the floor mesh piece we were about to move. Ok! That's it. Build and run this new code. Once the game has built, play the project then detach the camera and navigate it to the `killPoint` of the floor and you will see this:

If required, you can reduce the **Cell Site Count** of the `Destroyed_Mesh_DM` asset to improve performance.

Bells, whistles and explosions

Now that our technical feature set is complete, we can add the final layers of polish to this project before we say goodbye and move on. We need to play sound from the player, create explosions from the coins, and modify the `Animation Blueprint` we imported to get the character running.

Playing sound from C++

The first thing we need to do is add sound to our game. Import the `Ding.wav` and `Grunt.wav` sound files provided with this book and create a `DingCue` for one and `GruntCue` for the other. If you need refreshment on how to create sound cues, refer to *Chapter 3, Advanced Blueprint, Animation, and Sound.*

We are going to be loading these cues into the `UAudioComponent` handles we added to the `ABountyDashCharacter` in *Chapter 5, Upgrade Activated – Making Bounty Dash with C++.* Navigate to `ABountyDashCharacter.cpp` now. We need to add the following code to the constructor:

```
// Create Sound
HitObstacleSound=
CreateDefaultSubobject<UAudioComponent>(TEXT("HitSound"));
HitObstacleSound->bAutoActivate = false;
HitObstacleSound->AttachTo(RootComponent);

ConstructorHelpers::FObjectFinder<USoundCue> mySoundCue(TEXT("/Game/
GruntCue.GruntCue"));

if (mySoundCue.Succeeded())
{
    HitObstacleSound->SetSound(mySoundCue.Object);
}
```

Here, we are initializing an `UAudioComponent` named `HitObstacleSound`. We are then setting the `bAutoActivate` flag to false so that the sound does not play at game startup. We then attach this new audio component to the root. Loading sound cues is done in exactly the same way as other content browser assets, by using the `ConstructorHelpers FObjectFinder`. We then associate the `GruntCue` with this audio component. The following code will do the same for the `DingCue`:

```
DingSound= CreateDefaultSubobject<UAudioComponent>(TEXT("Ding"));
DingSound->bAutoActivate = false;
DingSound->AttachTo(RootComponent);

ConstructorHelpers::FObjectFinder<USoundCue> myCue(TEXT("/Game/
DingCue.DingCue"));

if (myCue.Succeeded())
{
    DingSound->SetSound(myCue.Object);
}
```

Next, we need to inform these `UAudioComponents` when to play. Navigate to `ABountyDashCharacter::myOnComponentOverlap()`. When the player detects successful collision with an obstacle, we need to play the sound. To ensure the sound is only played once when being pushed by an object, we will only play the sound when the character is not already being pushed. To do this, add the following code to `ABountyDashCharacter::myOnComponentOverlap()`:

```
if (AngleBetween < 60.0f)
{
    AObstacle* pObs = Cast<AObstacle>(OtherActor);

    if (!bBeingPushed)
    {
        HitObstacleSound->Play();
    }
}
```

Next, we need to play the `DingCue`. Navigate to `ABountyDashCharacter::ScoreUp()` and add `DingSound->Play();` to the function definition.

Alright, nice work! We are done implementing sounds for this project. Now we need to make our coins explode!

Playing particles from C++

We are about to make our last object for the `Bounty Dash` title! We need to create a particle system of an explosion when a player picks up a coin. To maintain visual believability, we need this particle effect to translate down the game field while it is playing. Otherwise we will have explosions floating next to the player as he runs forward. To do this, we can create a new object that inherits from `ABountyDashObject`. This time, it will be called `BountyDashParticle`. Do this now via the C++ class wizard. Once the class is created, navigate to `BountyDashParticle.h` and ensure it matches the following:

```
UCLASS()
class BOUNTYDASH_API ABountyDashParticle : public ABountyDashObject
{
    GENERATED_BODY()

public:

    ABountyDashParticle();

    UPROPERTY()
    UParticleSystemComponent* particleSystem;

};
```

As you can see, this object is very basic, with only a `UParticleSystemComponent` handle we will be initializing with the appropriate system to play. This handle is exposed publically as we will need to access it from `ACoin`. Now add a definition for the constructor of this object. Navigate to `BountyDashParticle.cpp` and add the following code:

```
ABountyDashParticle::ABountyDashParticle()
{
    particleSystem = CreateDefaultSubobject<UParticleSystemComponent>(
    TEXT("Explosion"));
    check(particleSystem);

    ConstructorHelpers::FObjectFinder<UParticleSystem> thisSys(TEXT("/
    Game/StarterContent/Particles/P_Explosion.P_Explosion"));

    if (thisSys.Succeeded())
    {
        particleSystem->SetTemplate(thisSys.Object);
    }

    particleSystem->AttachTo(RootComponent);
}
```

This code will initialize a `UParticleSystemComponent`, then, using an `FObjectFinder`, will load the appropriate system. I have chosen the explosion template provided within the starter content for our explosion. Alright, we are done! We have again benefited from the generic object hierarchy we created earlier in the chapter. This particle system will still translate down the game field and destroy itself upon reaching the `killPoint` at the end of the level.

Now all we need to do is spawn one of these when a player picks up a coin. Navigate to `ACoin::MyOnActorOverlap()` now. Before we start, add `#include BountyDashParticle.h` to the include list at the top of the `.cpp`. Then add the following code to the collision function for the coin when it detects a collision with an `ABountyDashCharacter`:

```
if (otherActor->GetClass()->
    IsChildOf(ABountyDashCharacter::StaticClass()))
{
    ABountyDashParticle* particleSys = GetWorld()->SpawnActor
    <ABountyDashParticle>(ABountyDashParticle::StaticClass(),
    GetTransform());

    particleSys->SetKillPoint(GetKillPoint());
```

Ensure you add the include for `ABountyDashParticle` to the `Coin.cpp` as well. Now the coins will explode when the player picks them up!

Getting the character to run

Phew! That has been a lot of C++! Well, now we get to quickly dive back into the world of blueprints. We need to modify the `AnimBlueprint` that was imported to this project when we imported the skeletal mesh. It is called `BH_Character_AnimBP`. We want to change two things about this `AnimBlueprint`. The first is we always want the character to run. The second is we want the play rate for the animation to increase as the game level increases. First, navigate to the Event Graph for this `Animation Blueprint`. At the end of the execution path, you will see a `Speed` variable set node; the input for this node is the length of a vector that is returned from a `GetVelocity` node. We need to disconnect this input and replace it with a hard-coded value of `600`, like so:

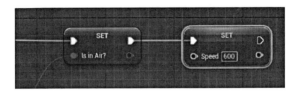

We then need to navigate to the **Idle State** node of the **Character_Locomotion** state machine found within the **AnimGraph** of this `Animation Blueprint`. If you cannot remember what this is, refer to *Chapter 3, Advanced Blueprint, Animation, and Sound*. Within this state node we need to modify the values we are passing into the `BH_Idle_Run_BS`. In this case we need to modify the play rate input. We need to get the game mode, cast it to `ABountyDashGameMode`, get the game level variable, and divide it by two (so that we only increase the `anim` speed when the game level is an even number). We then need to clamp this value between `1` and `7`, then parse this to the `BH_Idle_Run_BS`. The following node arrangement shows how this can be done:

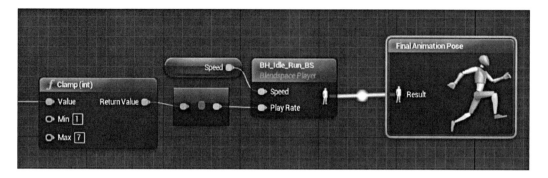

Note that the select node acts in a similar way to a branch node; if the cast of the game mode to `ABountyDashGameMode` fails, it will choose a default play rate of one instead of the calculated value.

The last bit of concealer

Ok, we are nearly done! The very last thing we need to do is add some fog to the level so that we can conceal the popping of meshes into the game scene. This is done very easily. Within the **Modes Panel** of the editor, search for an object called **Exponential Height Fog Component**. This fog allows you to create variable fog that *thickens* based on the values you provide. Click and drag this object into the scene. With **Exponential Height Fog Component** selected, address the **Details Panel**. Under the **Exponential Height Fog Component** change the settings to match the following:

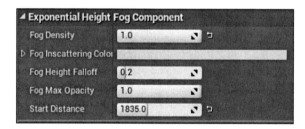

This will add a fog that covers the end of the floor where the objects spawn, yet leaves enough visible room for the player to see obstacles so they may dodge them in time. I would encourage tweaking these values so you can get an understanding of what each one does to the fog.

With all of the combined polish, we just made the game scene look like the following screenshot:

Summary

We are finally done polishing the project! `Bounty Dash` is officially done. Unless, of course, you wish to expand the project to greater heights. We have learnt so much throughout this project; in this chapter alone, we have learnt about generic hierarchies, plugins, power ups, HUDs in C++, polishing a project, making a wall of death, and some C++ practices to ensure the game does not crash.

In the next chapter, we are going to be learning about the UE4 AI system and use it to create a boss AI. I look forward to taking you through that project soon and congratulations on making it this far!

7

Boss Mode Activated –
Unreal Robots

So far we have conquered the basics of UE. We have learnt how to navigate
and utilize the engine's extensive editor set. We have used Blueprint to create
a platforming mini-game complete with particle effects, sound, and hilarious
ragdoll effects. We have thrown down with C++, making an endless runner purely
implemented with our own custom C++ objects, while utilizing destructible meshes
and the UE4 plugin system. Now it is time to step it up a notch and embark on
our journey with Unreal's AI and Rendering systems. These systems personify
the harmony between the UE4 editors and a user-created C++ backend. We will
be leveraging the knowledge gained in previous chapters to fully utilize this very
powerful system so we may create our third game project, **Boss Mode**!

During this chapter we are going to be establishing the core functionality and
creating the base objects for Boss Mode. We will be creating an AI-controlled
character that will represent our boss! Eventually, this boss will boast three AI
states, each with their own associated behavior. The AI will be created using UE4's
AI toolset. Then, in the next chapter, we will create custom UE4 materials using the
Material Editor to give the boss a sci-fi sinister look. Boss Mode will boast a first-
person perspective where you, as the player, will fire homing projectiles at the boss.
We will be creating a C++ first-person character that will be controlled by the user,
as well as the projectile object the player will fire. Through this chapter we will
cover the following learning objectives:

- Creating a first-person character using UE4 and C++
- Working with projectiles and projectile movement components
- Utilization of the UE4 AI toolsets (blackboard, behavior trees, AI controllers)
- Communication between animation assets and C++ objects

- Utilization of pathfinding objects such as `NavMesh` and `NavAgent` properties
- Creation of custom AI assets using both Blueprint and C++
- Working with and creating custom collision channels in UE4

Setting up the project

As always, the first thing we need to do is create the project itself. Using the Epic Games Launcher, run UE 4.10. This will navigate you to the Unreal project browser. From here we are going to be creating a new project based on the Basic Code C++ template. This can all be found under the **New Project | C++ | Basic Code**.

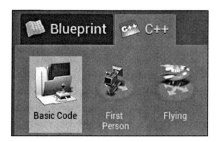

Call this new project `Boss Mode`. Now we can work with our project from the ground up!

The first-person character

The character we aim to create is going to require the ability to move, jump, turn, and shoot a gun. The visual presence of a **first-person character** (FPC) is very different to that of a third. For one, instead of an entire character mesh being used, we only need the *hands* and *gun* model. Instead of having the camera set back and detached from this character model, we need the arms and gun to rotate with the camera as the FPC turns and moves. The character we are going to create requires some imported assets from another UE4 template. We do this, instead of using the template objects directly so we can emphasize the workings of the objects provided in these templates, by creating them ourselves.

Importing what we need

Again, this is going to require the migration of a few assets. Open UE 4.10 again and navigate to the Unreal project browser. This time create a new Blueprint template from the First Person Template as follows:

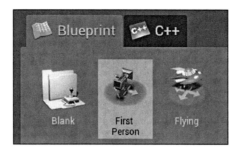

Call this project `Temp`. We are going to be migrating all of the content from the `First Person` folder within the `Content` Browser.

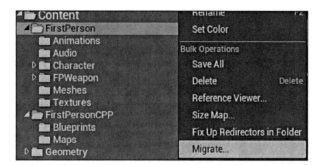

When the migration requests a destination folder, navigate to the `content` folder of the recently created `BossMode` project. This will migrate all of the media assets required for the first-person character. Now let's get to writing some code! During the course of this chapter we will be bouncing from C++ code to blueprint implementations. This development process is a cornerstone of UE 4's experience. If you wish you may now delete the `Temp` project from your hard drive as it will no longer be needed.

Beginning the FPC

Let's add our first code class to the `BossMode` project. Open the C++ wizard and create a new class that inherits from a character called `BMCharacter` (BM standing for `BossMode`). This object is going to represent our player character in the game. We will be creating input controls for this character so that the player may aim via the mouse or right analogue stick, and move via the keyboard or left analogue stick. We will later be adding a gun and projectiles that the character can shoot.

Establishing a FPC aim/movement

We can begin by writing the class definition for BMCharacter. Let's start with the private members, navigate to BMCharacter.h and add the following code to the class definition underneath GENERATED_BODY():

```
// Pawn Mesh, will only be seen by self
UPROPERTY(VisibleDefaultsOnly, Category = Mesh)
class USkeletalMeshComponent* FPMesh;

// Gun Mesh, will only be seen by self
UPROPERTY(VisibleDefaultsOnly, Category = Mesh)
class USkeletalMeshComponent* FPGunMesh;

// First person camera
UPROPERTY(VisibleAnywhere, BlueprintReadOnly, Category = Camera,
meta = (AllowPrivateAccess = "true"))
class UCameraComponent* FPCameraComponent;
```

Here we have created two skeletal mesh components, one for the arms of the pawn and one for the gun the arms will be holding. Each of these meshes will only be visible to the owning pawn. This is because, if we were to ever have other players, cameras, or reflective objects view our character, we would want them to see something similar to the mesh we have been using in our third-person projects thus far. The final component is a camera component that will be used for the first person camera. We have specified that this component is VisibleAnywhere and can be read from blueprint.

We have also used the meta specifier again. The meta specifier allows you to specify more nuanced settings for the property. Last time we used this specifier it was to establish slider settings for an exposed property. In this case we have specified that this camera component can be accessed privately with meta = (AllowPrivateAccess = "true"). This is so that we may expose this object to blueprint for reading, however the object itself remains *privately* protected within the codebase.

Now, let's move onto our public members. We are going to require some members that will control how the character feels when adjusting the aim with a controller. Add the following code to the class definition under the public encapsulation section and the class constructor declaration:

```
public:
// Sets default values for this character's properties
ABMCharacter();

// Base Turn Rate in deg/sec
```

```
UPROPERTY(VisibleAnywhere, BlueprintReadOnly, Category = Camera)
float BaseTurnRate;

// Base Lookup/Down rate in deg/sec
UPROPERTY(VisibleAnywhere, BlueprintReadOnly, Category = Camera)
float BaseLookUpRate;

// Called when the game starts or when spawned
virtual void BeginPlay() override;

// APawn interface
virtual void SetupPlayerInputComponent(class UInputComponent*
InputComponent) override;
// End of APawn interface

virtual void Tick(float DeltaSeconds) override;
```

The two `float` values will be utilized when we receive an input command from the engine to gauge how much the character will turn when the aim analogue stick is moved. We then override the `SetupPlayerInputComponent()` method so that we may provide custom bindings to the `UInputComponent`, the `Tick()` method so we can provide custom per-frame functionality, and the `BeginPlay()` method so we design some start-up functionality for the `BMCharacter`.

Next we need to add some `protected` methods that we will use to drive the character's movement and aim. Add the following code to the class definition:

```
protected:


// Handles forwards and backwards movement
void MoveForward(float Val);

// Handles left and right strafing movement
void MoveRight(float Val);

/**
* Will be called via input axis mapping
* @param Rate this is the normalized rate, 1.0 means full turn rate
*/
void TurnAtRate(float Rate);

/**
* Called via input to turn look up/down at a given rate.
```

```
 * @param Rate this is the normalized rate, 1.0 means full turn rate
 */
void LookUpAtRate(float Rate);
```

Each of these functions will be bound to an axis mapping via the
`SetupPlayerInputComponent()` method that we override from the `APawn` interface.

Awesome, that will do for now. Let's define the functions we just declared.

Defining the FPC constructor

As always, we will start with the default constructor
`ABMCharacter::ABMCharacter()`, we are going to start by initializing the camera
and capsule components:

```
ABMCharacter::ABMCharacter()
{
    // Set this character to call Tick() every frame.  You can turn
    this off to improve performance if you don't need it.
    PrimaryActorTick.bCanEverTick = true;

    // Set size for collision capsule
    GetCapsuleComponent()->InitCapsuleSize(42.0f, 96.0f);

    // Set the character turn rates
    BaseTurnRate = 45.0f;
    BaseLookUpRate = 45.0f;

    // Create a CameraComponent
    FPCameraComponent =
    CreateDefaultSubobject<UCameraComponent>
    (TEXT("FirstPersonCamera"));
    FPCameraComponent->AttachParent = GetCapsuleComponent();

    // Position the camera
    FPCameraComponent->RelativeLocation = FVector(0, 0, 64.f);
    FPCameraComponent->bUsePawnControlRotation = true;
```

Here we have defined the capsule size and set the base turn/lookup rates to be 45
degrees per second. We then use `CreateDefaultSubobject()` to create the camera
component. We attach the camera to the capsule as we wish the camera to update
with the capsule. You will notice that we position the camera so that it sits 64 units
up the Z axis. This will position the camera two-thirds up the capsule (as we set the
capsule height to 96), resulting in a chest-high perspective for the character. This
works perfectly for a first person character as usually you do not assume the view
from the eyes of the character but the position of the chest or gun when it is at rest.

Lastly we set the `bUsePawnControlRotation` to `true`. This is very important as it allows us to apply input rotations to the pawn and have it affect the first person camera. This will result in the type of aim behavior we expect from a first person character. If you wish to experiment, once we have established the first person character properly, change this variable to false and see how the character behaves.

Next we must initialize the skeletal mesh components we created earlier. Add the following code to the default constructor:

```
// Create a mesh component that will only be viewed by the controlling
pawn
FPMesh = CreateDefaultSubobject<USkeletalMeshComponent>(TEXT
("CharacterMesh1P"));

FPMesh->SetOnlyOwnerSee(true);
FPMesh->AttachParent = FPCameraComponent;
FPMesh->bCastDynamicShadow = false;
FPMesh->CastShadow = false;
```

Here we are initializing the first person mesh. This will appear as a pair of arms in the game. We have set the mesh component so that it will only be visible to the owning object via `FPMesh->SetOnlyOwnerSee(true)`. This is important as we only wish the `FPCameraComponent` to see this mesh. Otherwise other players or game cameras will see a pair of floating arms! We also don't want this mesh to cast a shadow. If the player saw the shadow of just two arms on a wall it would completely break the illusion they are controlling a fully fleshed character. We do this by setting `bCastShadow` and `bCastDynamicShadow` to `false`. We then attach the mesh to the camera so the mesh position will update relative to the camera. Next we add similar code for the gun mesh:

```
FPGunMesh = CreateDefaultSubobject<USkeletalMeshComponent>(TEXT("FP_
Gun"));
FPGunMesh->SetOnlyOwnerSee(true);// only the owning player will see
mesh

FPGunMesh->bCastDynamicShadow = false;
FPGunMesh->CastShadow = false;

FPGunMesh->AttachTo(FPMesh, TEXT("GripPoint"), EAttachLocation::SnapTo
TargetIncludingScale, true);
```

Again we are initializing the gun mesh so that only the owning player can see the mesh, as well as preventing it from casting any kind of shadow. Next we are attaching the mesh in a new way. We are attaching the mesh to a socket that is present in the FPMesh. This is so that the gun mesh will be positioned properly in the FPMesh hands. This will also ensure that when FPMesh updates in position and rotation, so does the FPGunMesh.

We are doing this by using an overloaded version of the AttachTo() method. This one takes in a pointer to the skeletal mesh that will own the socket we are attaching the mesh to, the name of the target socket, an attach type (we have used SnapToTargetIncludingScale as this will snap the FPGunMesh to the socket location even if we scale the FPMesh), and a boolean flag determining whether we wish these bodies to be wielded under a physics simulation. Note that if the provided socket name does not exist within the skeletal mesh assigned to FPMesh, the function will assume a default relative position of 0,0,0.

> Note that we have not associated these skeletal mesh components with any assets. That is because we are going to be making these asset associations in the **Blueprint abstraction** of this object. Going forward, this is the preferred method when using UE4. This means it is much easier for us to swap out assets on a code object. Your game designers will thank you!

Defining the FPC move and aim functions

Next we can add definitions for the move and aim functions we declared earlier. Add the following code to the BMCharacter.cpp:

```
void ABMCharacter::MoveForward(floatValue)
{

    if (Value != 0.0f)
    {

        // add movement in that direction
        AddMovementInput(GetActorForwardVector(), Value);

    }

}
```

This function simply takes in a value from the axis mapping, we then call `AddMovementInput()` and pass in the character's forward vector as well as the movement value. This method will utilize the settings stored within the `UCharacterMovementComponent` such as move speed and walking capabilities to drive the movement of the character. We only need to specify one function for forwards and backwards movement as `Value` will range from -1 to 1. If the value is negative, we will move backwards along the character's forward vector:

```
void ABMCharacter::MoveRight(float Val)
{
    if (Value != 0.0f)
    {
        // add movement in that direction
        AddMovementInput(GetActorRightVector(), Val);
    }
}
```

This method works in much the same way as the previous yet, this time, we pass the character's right vector. The two functions together provide the user lateral control of the character.

Next we are going to define the `TurnAtRate()` and `LookUpAtRate()` methods. These methods are going be used so we can support controllers in `BossMode`:

```
void ABMCharacter::TurnAtRate(floatRate)
{
    // calculate delta for this frame from the rate information
    AddControllerYawInput(Rate * BaseTurnRate *
    GetWorld()->GetDeltaSeconds());
}
```

Here we are calling the `AddControllerYawInput()` method. Again this method will utilize the settings specified in the `UCharacterMovementComponent`. We are passing the `Rate` value passed in (which will range from -1 to 1), we then multiply this value by `BaseTurnRate` (we specified as 45), and then multiply that by the delta tick. This will ensure that the character rotates at the appropriate per second rate regardless of frame rate:

```
void ABMCharacter::LookUpAtRate(floatRate)
{
    // calculate delta for this frame from the rate information
    AddControllerPitchInput(Rate * BaseLookUpRate *
    GetWorld()->GetDeltaSeconds());
}
```

Again this function is very similar to the first however, this time, we are calling `AddControllerPitchInput()`. We only need to define functionality for the controller input specifically as we are expecting a variable `Rate` from that input device. The rate value will range between `-1` and `1` based on how tilted a given analogue stick is. This is different to mouse input as the mouse input will provide us with a fixed delta value we can directly use for turn rate. Such a method is defined in the pawn class for us.

Alright! Compile and run this code now, we must set up our input mappings before we can continue working with the `ABMCharacter`.

Creating the input bindings

This will be the third time we establish input bindings so this time I will keep it brief. Once the code has compiled and the project is running, navigate to **Project Settings | Input** and set up the following **Axis Mappings**:

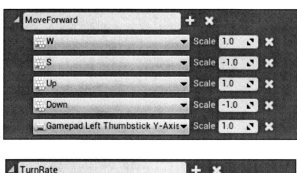

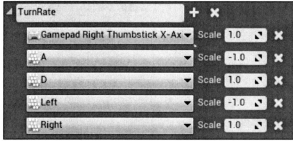

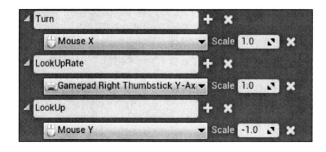

The previous mappings will allow use of both keyboard/mouse and controller when moving/aiming the ABMCharacter. While we are here we should also set up some **Action Mappings** we are going to require later on in the project:

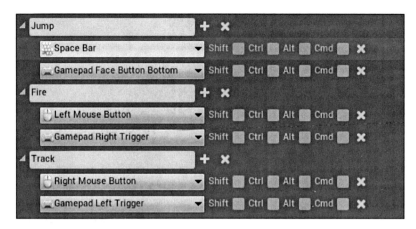

We will use these mappings to get the character to jump, fire the gun, and track. Tracking will be described in the next chapter.

Binding the inputs

Navigate back to the BMCharacter.cpp and add the following code to the SetupPlayerInputComponent() method definition:

```cpp
// Called to bind functionality to input
void ABMCharacter::SetupPlayerInputComponent(class UInputComponent*
InputComponent)
{
    Super::SetupPlayerInputComponent(InputComponent);

    check(InputComponent);

    InputComponent->BindAction("Jump", IE_Pressed, this,
    &ACharacter::Jump);
    InputComponent->BindAction("Jump", IE_Released, this,
    &ACharacter::StopJumping);
    InputComponent->BindAxis("MoveForward", this,
    &ABMCharacter::MoveForward);
    InputComponent->BindAxis("MoveRight", this,
    &ABMCharacter::MoveRight);
```

Here we are simply binding the action mapping `Jump` and the axis mappings `MoveForward` and `MoveRight` to the appropriate functions found in the `ABMCharacter` object. Underneath this code, add the following:

```
InputComponent->BindAxis("Turn", this,
&APawn::AddControllerYawInput);
InputComponent->BindAxis("TurnRate",
this, &ABMCharacter::TurnAtRate);
InputComponent->BindAxis("LookUp", this,
&APawn::AddControllerPitchInput);
InputComponent->BindAxis("LookUpRate", this,
&ABMCharacter::LookUpAtRate);
} // <-- closing SetupPlayerInputComponent()
```

It is important to note that the axis mappings that are expecting input from the mouse have been bound directly to `AddControllerYawInput()` and not the `TurnAtRate()` functions we created earlier. That is because we can expect an absolute delta from our mouse input. Meaning that the value that is returned from the drivers for the mouse can be directly parsed to the `AddControllerYaw()` method. The reason we have made our own `TurnAtRate()` is to handle input from the variable axis input we can expect from an analogue stick, as mentioned previously.

Abstracting a BM character into Blueprint

Ok, now we can compile the code we just wrote and run the project. We are now going to be creating a new Blueprint based from the `ABMCharacter` object. Within your **Content** browser create a new Blueprint now (again, the folder setup and tidiness of your project is up to you), you can do this by right-clicking within the **Content** browser and selecting **Blueprints | Blueprint Class**. This will open the **Blueprint Wizard**, search for our **BMCharacter** in the list of base classes available. Call this Blueprint `FPCharacter`.

We are not going to do much within the blueprint itself, simply associate and position some of the assets we defined in the `ABMCharacter` base class. With the Blueprint editor open, navigate to the **Viewport** panel. Under the **Components** panel on the left-hand side of the editor window you will see the `FPMesh` and `FPGunMesh` skeletal mesh components. We need to provide references to the correct assets for each of these components.

With the `FPMesh` component selected, address the **Details** panel on the right-hand side of the editor. Under the **Animation** section, change the **Anim Blueprint Generated Class** property to `FirstPersonAnimBP` from the provided dropdown. Next, change the **Skeletal Mesh** property under the **Mesh** section to `SK_Mannequin_Arms`. Then change the Z component of the **Location** property under the Transform section to **-155.0cm**.

Then select the FPGunMesh and address the **Details** panel again. Change the **Skeletal**
Mesh property under the Mesh section to SK_FPGun. You will notice that the FPGunMesh
will automatically be placed in the hands of the FPMesh thanks to our AttachTo() call
we made in the base class. You should currently see something like this:

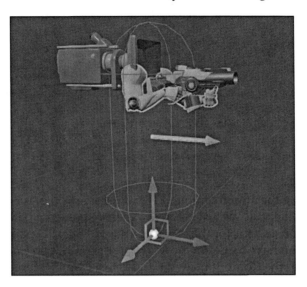

Setting a Blueprint object as the default pawn in a C++ game mode

Ok, now we need to set this Blueprint we just created as the default pawn within
the game mode. Upon creation of this C++ project, a default C++ game mode was
provided, we will modify this to support the FPCharacter as the default pawn class.
We can do this by utilizing another construction helper. So far we have used the
ObjectFinder construction helper. There is another that is very useful for this given
situation. We can leverage the capabilities of the FClassFinder , which is also part
of the ConstructHelpers namespace. This object will find the generated class for
any blueprint asset, given the correct path to the asset location within the content
folder. Let's do this now by modifying the ABossModeGameMode that will have been
generated upon creating the project. Navigate to BossModeGameMode.h now and add
the following code to the class definition:

```
UCLASS()
Class ABossModeGameMode : public AGameMode
{
    GENERATED_BODY()

public:
```

```
    ABossModeGameMode();
};
```

All we have done here is declare a default constructor that we can use to make the default pawn association. Navigate to the `BossModeGameMode.cpp` now and add the following code:

```
ABossModeGameMode::ABossModeGameMode()
    : Super()
{
    // set default pawn class to our Blueprinted character
    Static ConstructorHelpers::FClassFinder<APawn>
    PlayerPawnClassFinder(TEXT("/Game/FPCharacter"));

    DefaultPawnClass = PlayerPawnClassFinder.Class;
}
```

Here we are utilizing the aforementioned `FClassFinder` object of type `APawn` to find our `FPCharacter` Blueprint we just created. We have parsed a path to the class object as an input to the constructor for the `FClassFinderObject`. Be sure to use your own path here. If you have forgotten how to find the path, you can right-click on the **FPCharacter** asset in the **Content** browser and select **Copy Reference**. You can then paste the reference path into the code file. Be sure to remove the object type from the path as well as anything past the '.' Character, for example— `Blueprint'/Game/FPCharacter.FPCharacter'` should be `'/Game/FPCharacter'`.

Testing what we have!

Ok, now compile and run the project and we will test the movement/aim inputs we just created! Press the play button and you will see something similar to this:

We have finished creating the basics for our `FPCharacter`. You will be able to move the character around the level freely as well as aim with the mouse!

Adding a custom HUD and drawing a cross hair

No first person character perspective is complete without a small cross hair to denote the center of the screen. Let's create one now by making a custom code HUD. Using the C++ class wizard, create a code object that inherits from HUD called BMHUD.

BMHUD class definition

Now, navigate to BMHUD.h. All we need to do here is override thc DrawHUD() method so we can define custom HUD functionality, define a default constructor, and add a UTexture2D handle to hold the crosshair image we are going to use. This can be done with the following code:

```
UCLASS()
class BOSSMODE_API ABMHUD : public AHUD
{
    GENERATED_BODY()

public:
    ABMHUD();

    /** Primary draw call for the HUD */
    virtual void DrawHUD() override;

private:
    /** Crosshair asset pointer */
    class UTexture2D* CrosshairTex;
};
```

Defining the BMHUD

First off, we need to populate the UTexture2D handle with an appropriate asset. We will do this in the default constructor. Add the following code to BMHUD.cpp:

```
ABMHUD::ABMHUD()
{
    // Set the crosshair texture
    staticConstructorHelpers::FObjectFinder<UTexture2D>
    CrosshiarTexObj(TEXT("/Game/FirstPerson/Textures/
    FirstPersonCrosshair"));

    CrosshairTex = CrosshiarTexObj.Object;
}
```

Here we are again utilizing a `ConstructHelper` to find the crosshair asset that was imported with the `FirstPerson` folder. Remember, if this was a blueprint object we would always prefer to make this asset association there instead of the codebase.

We are going to be utilizing the `Canvas` to draw this crosshair image to the screen and we are going to do that by using a new object, `FCanvasTileItem`. This object will allow us to draw an image to the screen. The image will be bound within a tile or rectangle. This means that, for each image we draw to the screen, we require unique `FCanvasTileItem` objects that simply hold information on how each tile will be drawn to the `Canvas` area.

Before we draw the cross hair we require two screen points of data. The first will be the center of the screen. The second is where we need to draw the `FCanvasTileItem` so that the crosshair appears in the very center. To do this we need to subtract half of the image dimensions from the center of the screen, as all tile items are positioned based on the top left-hand corner of the image. To do this we add the following code to `BMHUD.cpp`:

```
voidABMHUD::DrawHUD()
{
    Super::DrawHUD();

    // find center of the Canvas
    const FVector2D Center(Canvas->ClipX * 0.5f, Canvas->ClipY *
    0.5f);

    // offset by half the texture's dimensions so that the center of
    the texture aligns with the center of the Canvas
    const FVector2D CrosshairDrawPosition(
    (Center.X - (CrosshairTex->GetSurfaceWidth() * 0.5)),
    (Center.Y - (CrosshairTex->GetSurfaceHeight() * 0.5f)));
```

Here we are obtaining the center of the screen from the `Canvas` member of AHUD by halving the dimensions of the screen. We then subtract the x and y components of this 2D position by half of the x and y dimensions of the cross hair texture image. This will find a location that ensures the image is placed in the center of the screen. The next thing we need to do is create the `FCanvasTileItem` and draw it. We can do that with the following code:

```
    // draw the crosshair
    FCanvasTileItem TileItem(CrosshairDrawPosition,
    rosshairTex->Resource,
    FLinearColor::White);

    TileItem.BlendMode = SE_BLEND_Translucent;
```

```
        Canvas->DrawItem(TileItem);
}
```

Here we have created a FCanvasTileItem by parsing a draw position, a resource (being the texture resource pointed to by the UTexture2D handle), and a linear color for the tile item to the constructor of the object. This color is used as a default if image data cannot be found. We then set the BlendMode for this tile item to be SE_BLEND_Translucent. This means that, where there is *alpha* present in the crosshair image, the on-screen tile will be *translucent*. Lastly we call on the Canvas to draw the tile item.

Before we can see this come into effect we must set the default HUD class in our game mode. Navigate to BossModeGameMode.cpp and add the code #include"BMHUD.h" to the includes list and HUDClass = ABMHUD::StaticClass(); to the ABossModeGameMode constructor.

Compile and run the code now and you should see something similar to this:

Creating the projectile

Now we have a player character and we have a cross hair, all we need now is something to shoot! We need to create an object that can be fired forward and act the same way a weighted projectile would under the effects of gravity, similar to a grenade or small cannon ball. We can do this by utilizing another movement-based component. This one is called a ProjectileMovementComponent and can be used alongside the physics engine to dictate how a projectile will move through space. Using the C++ class wizard create a class that inherits from Actor called BMProjectile.

Defining the Projectile

Let's start by defining the ABMProjectile class. We can begin with the private members of the class, navigate to BMProjectile.h and add the following code to the class definition under GENERATED_BODY():

```
/** Sphere collision component */
UPROPERTY(VisibleDefaultsOnly, Category = Projectile)
class USphereComponent* ProjCollision;

UPROPERTY(BlueprintReadWrite, EditAnywhere, Category = Projectile,
meta = (AllowPrivateAccess = "true"))
class UParticleSystemComponent* ProjParticle;

UPROPERTY(BlueprintReadWrite, EditAnywhere, Category = Projectile,
meta = (AllowPrivateAccess = "true"))
class UStaticMeshComponent* ProjMesh;

/** Projectile movement component */
UPROPERTY(VisibleAnywhere, BlueprintReadOnly, Category = Movement,
meta = (AllowPrivateAccess = "true"))
class UProjectileMovementComponent* ProjMovement;
```

Here we have added a sphere component we will use for projectile collision, a particle system component we will play when the projectile hits something, a static mesh component so we can display the projectile, and a projectile movement component that we will be using to define how the projectile moves.

As you can see, we have again declared that the particle system, static mesh, and projectile movement components allow private access. This is so we can have these components read from or accessed via the editor and blueprint, but remain *encapsulated* within the codebase.

Next we can add our public methods to the class definition with the following:

```
// Sets default values for this actor's properties
ABMProjectile();

    /** called when projectile hits something */
    UFUNCTION()
    void OnHit(AActor* OtherActor,
    UPrimitiveComponent* OtherComp, FVector
     NormalImpulse, const FHitResult& Hit);

UFUNCTION()
void OnDestoyedProjectile();
```

Here we have defined a default constructor, an OnHit() method we will use for custom collision functionality, and an OnDestroyedProjectile() method that we will call when the projectile is destroyed.

Initializing the Projectile

Ok, now we can begin to set up how this projectile is going to behave. Let's begin by defining the default constructor add the following code to BMProjectile.cpp:

```cpp
// Sets default values
ABMProjectile::ABMProjectile()
{
    // Use a sphere as a simple collision representation
    ProjCollision = CreateDefaultSubobject
    <USphereComponent>(TEXT("SphereComp"));

    ProjCollision->InitSphereRadius(10.0f);
    ProjCollision->
    BodyInstance.SetCollisionProfileName("BlockAll");

    ProjCollision->OnComponentHit.AddDynamic(this,
    &ABMProjectile::OnHit);

    OnDestroyed.AddDynamic(this, &ABMProjectile::OnDestoyedProjecti
le);
```

Here we are initializing the sphere component and setting its initial radius to be 10.0f. We then set the collision profile name to BlockAll. We will be changing this later to a custom collision profile so we do specific checks on projectiles. We then ensure that the OnComponentHit and OnDestroyed delegates are bound to the methods we declared earlier. We then add the following code to ensure the player cannot walk on these projectiles:

```cpp
    ProjCollision->
    SetWalkableSlopeOverride(FWalkableSlopeOverride(
    WalkableSlope_Unwalkable, 0.f));

    ProjCollision->CanCharacterStepUpOn =ECB_No;

        RootComponent = ProjCollision;
```

We do this so that, if there are any projectiles that have not been destroyed lying on the ground, the player will not be able to set up onto these projectiles, resulting in unreasonable movement behavior and camera jitter. We also set this collision component to be the root component for this object.

Next we must initialize the mesh and particle components:

```
ProjMesh = CreateDefaultSubobject <UStaticMeshComponent>(TEXT
("MeshComp"));

ProjMesh->AttachTo(ProjCollision);
ProjMesh->SetCollisionProfileName(TEXT("NoCollision"));

ProjParticle = CreateDefaultSubobject
<UParticleSystemComponent>(TEXT("ParticleComp"));

ProjParticle->bAutoActivate = false;
ProjParticle->AttachTo(ProjCollision);
```

Here we ensure that no collisions are carried out on the mesh and that the particle component will not auto activate. If we did not specify this, the particle effect would play immediately when we spawn the projectile. Note that we are not associating any assets with these components as we will be doing that from an abstracted blueprint.

Now we can finally begin to work with our `ProjectileMovementComponent`. As stated before, this component will control how the projectile moves upon being spawned. Add the following code to the constructor:

```
// Use a ProjectileMovementComponent to govern this projectile's
movement
ProjMovement =
CreateDefaultSubobject<UProjectileMovementComponent>
(TEXT("Projectile
Comp"));

ProjMovement->UpdatedComponent = ProjCollision;
ProjMovement->InitialSpeed = 3000.f;
ProjMovement->MaxSpeed = 3000.f;
ProjMovement->bRotationFollowsVelocity = true;
```

We initialize the component as we always do with `CreateDefaultSubobject()`. We then bind the sphere collision component as the `UpdatedComponent`. This means the `ProjectileMovementComponent` will update the transform of the sphere component, thus all attached child components as well. We have set the collision component as our root therefore all other components will update appropriately.
We then specify that at spawn we wish this projectile to be moving at 3000 cm/s. We do this via the `InitialSpeed` property of the projectile movement component. This will dictate the launch velocity of the projectile upon spawn. We then say that this is also the maximum speed this projectile can reach via `MaxSpeed`. We then state that the projectile's rotation should follow the velocity, meaning that if we were to use an arrow mesh for the projectile, the arrow will always point in the direction of the projectile movement.

We also need to set the life span of the actor so that if it exists for too long, it will delete itself automatically. The member `InitialLifeSpan` can do this for us. This member is part of the `AActor` base class:

```
// Die after 3 seconds by default
InitialLifeSpan = 3.0f;
```

Colliding with the Projectile

Now we can add a simple function definition to the `OnHit` method so we can have some meaningful response when the projectile hits something. We wish for the particle component to play, the mesh to stop drawing, and the projectile to cease collision with other objects. We need to ensure we detach the particle component from the object as well, otherwise the particle effect will continue to move with the invisible projectile! The following code can achieve this:

```
void ABMProjectile::OnHit(AActor* OtherActor, UPrimitiveComponent*
OtherComp, FVector NormalImpulse, const FHitResult& Hit)
{
    if (!OtherActor->GetClass()->IsChildOf(this->StaticClass()))
    {
        ProjCollision->
        SetCollisionProfileName(TEXT("NoCollision"));
        ProjCollision->bGenerateOverlapEvents = false;
        ProjMesh->SetVisibility(false);

        ProjParticle->Activate();
        ProjParticle->DetachFromParent(true);
    }
}
```

We first ensure that we are not colliding with an object of our own type (meaning projectiles will not collide with each other) via an `if` statement based on the result of the `ISChildOf()` method. We then stop drawing the mesh of the projectile and set its collision profile to `NoCollision`. This effectively renders the projectile useless and invisible until it is de-spawned after three seconds.

We then activate the particle component and detach it from the parent. We will be coming back to this function in the next chapter. We will be modifying it so we may detect collisions with the Boss object and deal damage using UE4's damage system!

Finally, all we need to do is add an empty definition for the `OnDestroyedProjectile()` method we created earlier:

```
void ABMProjectile::OnDestoyedProjectile()
{

}
```

Subclass templates and firing the projectile

Before we can fire our projectile we need to add the projectile class to the `BMCharacter` we made earlier. Instead of using a naked `UClass*` pointer like we have been previously, we are going to utilize a more secure type of class association. We are going to use the `TSubclascOf` template object. This object allows us to define a class type that is bound within the hierarchy of the provided template type. In other words, when we declare this template with a class type of `ABMProjectile`, only `ABMProjectiles` and other objects that inherit from `ABMProjectile` may be assigned to the member.

Modifying BMCharacter accommodate for the projectile

We need to add two public members to the `BMCharacter`, the first is the aforementioned `TSubclassOf` template object and the second is a `USceneComponent` we will use to act as a location when spawning the projectile objects. Add the following public members to the `ABMCharacter` class definition:

```
// Projectile class to use
UPROPERTY(EditDefaultsOnly, Category = Projectile)
TSubclassOf<ABMProjectile> ProjectileClass;
// Projectile Spawn
UPROPERTY(BlueprintReadWrite, EditAnywhere, Category = Projectile)

class USceneComponent* ProjSpawn;
```

As you can see, we have declared the `TSubclassOf projectileClass` member to be of type `ABMProjectile`. We have used the `UPROPERTY()` specifier `EditDefaultsOnly` so we may set the class this member holds from the Blueprint abstraction `FPCharacter` so we can avoid asset associations in code. Unfortunately we are unable to forward declare the `ABMProjectile` class type as we are referencing it via a whole type as opposed to a pointer type. Add `#include "BMProjectile.h"` to the include list of `BMCharacter.h` now.

The next thing we need to do is add a method we can bind to the **Fire** action mapping we created earlier. Add a protected method to the ABMCharacter class definition called OnFire() that returns void:

```
protected:
    /** Fires a projectile. */
    void OnFire();
```

With all of this in place, let's modify our method definitions to accommodate for spawning the projectiles. Add the following lines of code to the end of the ABMCharacter default constructor:

```
ProjSpawn =
CreateDefaultSubobject<USceneComponent>(TEXT("ProjectileSpawn"));
ProjSpawn->AttachTo(FPGunMesh);
```

This will initialize the scene component that will act as the projectile spawn location and rotation. We attach this location to the gun mesh as we want the position to remain relative to the gun as it moves about the level. We will be defining the position of this scene component in Blueprint. Now add a new input binding to the SetupPlayerInputComponent() method definition:

```
InputComponent->BindAction("Fire", IE_Pressed, this,
&ABMCharacter::OnFire);
```

This will call the new OnFire() method when either the left mouse button is pressed or the left trigger of a game pad is pressed.

Now we can define the on fire function as follows:

```
void ABMCharacter::OnFire()
{
    // Attempt to fire Projectile
    if (ProjectileClass != nullptr)
    {
        if (GetWorld() != nullptr)
        {
            GetWorld()->SpawnActor<ABMProjectile>(ProjectileClass,
            ProjSpawn->GetComponentLocation(),
            ProjSpawn->GetComponentRotation());
        }
    }
}
```

Here we are ensuring that a projectile class has been set. We then simply spawn a new projectile by passing the `ProjectileClass` member and the transform details of the `ProjSpawn` scene component to `SpawnActor()`. The result will be a projectile that is of the type that we specify in blueprint at the location of the `ProjSpawn` scene component.

We do not need to do any more than this, as the moment we spawn the projectile, the projectile movement component will come into effect. Our projectile will launch off along its forward vector at 3,000 cm/s. If this projectile collides with anything, particle effect will play and the rest of the projectile will disappear.

Creating the FPProjectile Blueprint

Now we simply need to abstract our base class into blueprint and ensure we assign it in the `FPCharacter` **Details** panel as the `ProjectileClass` member we created earlier.

Let's begin by making the Blueprint. Navigate to your **Content** browser and create a new blueprint class that inherits from `BMProjectile`. Call this `FPProjectile`. We need to make some asset associations so that our projectile appears as we desire. First, select the `ProjMesh` component and under the **Details** panel change the `StaticMesh` property of the `StaticMesh` section to be `FirstPersonProjectileMesh`. Then set the `RelativeScale3D` property of the **Transform** section to 0.06 on all axis.

Once that is done we can then assign the particle effect to `ProjParticle`. Select the `ProjParticle` component and under the **Particles** section in the **Details** panel set the `Template` property to `P_Explosion`. You should now see something similar to this:

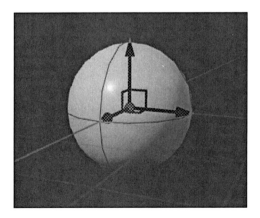

Modifying FPCharacter

The last things we have to do are assign the projectile class in the FPCharacter Blueprint and position the ProjSpawn scene component so the projectiles will spawn in the correct place. First off, select the **FPCharacter (Self)** reference in the **Components Panel**, under the **Projectile** section of the **Details** panel change the **Projectile Class** property to the FPProjectile Blueprint we made earlier. As you can see, only objects that inherit from BMProjectile are shown.

Next, select the new **ProjSpawn** scene component in the **Components** panel then position this component so that it sits inside the barrel of the gun mesh, as follows:

With all that in place, run the project! We can now fire our projectile and watch it detonate on the ground.

Unreal Robots

Alright, now we need a hovering and tracking AI boss character! It's time for us to dive into the UE AI layer. The UE4 AI implementation is robust and covers everything you will need to create intelligent, well-functioning AI. Much like everything else in UE4, the AI interface can be expanded and modified using C++ objects that inherit from the UE4-provided base classes. The next section of this chapter will run you through the basics of the AI system.

AI breakdown

The AI toolset present in UE4 is made up of many different asset types and objects. Each object is responsible for a certain subset of the AI's functionality. The following list provides a brief description of the major elements that go into creating an AI in UE4:

- **AI Characters**: AI character objects and normal character objects do not differ at all. In fact, they can derive from the same `UCharacter` base class. An AI character is simply controlled by an `AIController` instead of a `PlayerController`. In this sense any character can be an AI character or a player character.

- **Behavior Trees**: Behavior trees are the visual representation of the decision-making structure of your AI. It is within these trees that you will plot all of the logic flow for the AI and the resulting decisions of this logic. Behavior trees are made up of seven unique node types — Decorators, Services, Tasks, Selectors, Sequences, Simple Parallel, and a root node. These seven elements will be described in detail later in the chapter.

- **AI Controllers**: AI controllers are responsible for the movement of the AI character after all navigation calculations have been made. In other words, it is through this controller that the character is controlled by the governing AI, via the execution of various methods (`Move To`, for example). You may create your own AI controllers within which you can create your own movement functions to better articulate your AI during runtime. AI controllers will still use the movement properties of a character's `CharacterMovementComponent`.

- **Blackboard**: Blackboard is a very key feature of the AI system. It allows you to create variables that can be retrieved and assigned by ALL AI elements within a given system. This means we are able to set a flag in a blackboard from an AI controller that will dictate a logic-making decision in a behavior tree as long as both have reference to the same blackboard asset.

- **Navigational Meshes**: `NavMesh` for short, are a way we can identify an area for an AI to move within, which accommodates for obstacle avoidance, pathing, and patrolling. `NavMesh` will handle the pathing generation for any specified AI movement agents within the area covered by a `NavMesh` volume. This asset is not directly referenced by the others mentioned previously but is a core component of the AI system within UE4.

During the rest of this chapter we are going to be making our own abstractions of some of these objects. Thanks to the dependence of these assets within themselves, we are able to create an efficient bi-directional network of objects. Through this network we are able to easily create any AI behavior we can conceive.

Preparing your project for AI intergration

Over the course of the next two chapters we are going to be referencing and including a new series of objects and functions that are part of UE4's AI module. To ensure that we have no linking or `#include` problems going forward, it is a good idea to explicitly add this module as a public dependency to our project's `build. cs`. Navigate to the `BossMode.Build.cs` and ensure that the public dependency modules name list matches the following:

```
PublicDependencyModuleNames.AddRange(new string[] { "Core",
"CoreUObject", "Engine", "InputCore", "AIModule" });
```

As you can see, we have included `AIModule` to the list, this will ensure that all of the objects contained within this module are linked publically to our project. With this in place we begin to work the backend for our boss character. We will start by creating a basic AI character that is based in C++.

Creating the AI character base class

Much like our standard player characters, we require an object that will represent our boss character. AI characters are created in much the same manner as standard player characters, however they are not possessed by player controllers but AI controllers instead. Start by creating a new C++ class using the wizard. The base class for this new object is to be **Character**. Call this new object `BMBossCharacter`. This abstraction of the `UCharacter` base class is going to be very simple. We are going to be including a handle to a **Behavior Tree** asset that can be assigned from the editor.

Navigate to `BMBossCharacter.h` now and simply modify the contents of the definition to match the following:

```
UCLASS()
class BOSSMODE_API ABMBossCharacter : public ACharacter
{
    GENERATED_BODY()

public:
    // Sets default values for this character's properties
    ABMBossCharacter();

    virtual float TakeDamage(float Damage, struct FDamageEvent const&
    DamageEvent, AController* EventInstigator, AActor* DamageCauser)
    override;

    UFUNCTION(BlueprintCallable, BlueprintPure, Category = AI)
    const float GetHealth();

    UPROPERTY(EditAnywhere, Category = Pawn)
    class UBehaviorTree* BehaviorTree;

private:

    UPROPERTY()
    float Health;
};
```

As you can see, we have removed the `Tick()`, `Begin Play()`, and `SetupPlayerInputComponent()` methods as they will not be used by our AI-controlled character. Ensure you delete the corresponding methods from the `BMBossCharacter.cpp` otherwise the project will not compile. We have also added some methods. As you can see, we have overridden the `TakeDamage()` method. This method takes in the various parameters that make up a damage event in UE4. We will describe this in more detail later. Following this we have added a standard accessor method for the `Health` of this character (a private member declared below).

The last thing to note is that we have added a handle to a `UBehaviorTree`. As this is not a `UBehaviorTreeComponent` we do not need to initialize the handle with anything, we will simply be assigning the correct `UBehaviorTree` asset from the **Details** panel in editor. Now we will define these functions, so navigate to `BMBossCharacter.cpp`.

```
Define the constructor for this object as follows:
// Sets default values
```

```
ABMBossCharacter::ABMBossCharacter()
{
    // Set this character to call Tick() every frame.  You can turn
    this off to improve performance if you don't need it.
    PrimaryActorTick.bCanEverTick = true;

    Health = 100.0f;

    GetMovementComponent()->NavAgentProps.AgentHeight = 320.0f;
    GetMovementComponent()->NavAgentProps.AgentRadius = 160.0f;
}
```

Here we are simply flagging that this character is to `tick`, setting the health of this character to `100.0f`, and establishing some of the parameters for this AI-controlled character's navigation agent properties. These navigation agent properties are used by the navigation system to accurately plot pathing points when generating path-following behavior for AI characters—More on this later. Next, define the `TakeDamage()` method as follows:

```
float ABMBossCharacter::TakeDamage(float Damage, struct FDamageEvent
const& DamageEvent, AController* EventInstigator, AActor*
DamageCauser)
{
    Super::TakeDamage(Damage, DamageEvent, EventInstigator,
    DamageCauser);

    Health -= Damage;

    return Damage;
}
```

This method simply subtracts the damage value parsed from the `Health` property. We will be using this value later to influence the decision making of this AI character. Finally, we need to define the `GetHealth()` accessor method as follows:

```
const float ABMBossCharacter::GetHealth()
{
    return Health;
}
```

Now we can create the AI controller that will drive the movement of our boss!

Creating your first AI controller

Much like that of the ABMBossCharacter, this controller will be a very basic abstraction and provide us with a common place to store handles to the various AI assets we will eventually create and use for the boss AI character. Don't worry, these assets will receive their own detailed explanation shortly. Start by creating a new class using the C++ wizard. This class is to inherit from the AIController class provided by UE4 and call it BMAIController. Navigate to BMAIController.h now. Modify the class definition to match the following:

```
UCLASS()
class BOSSMODE_API ABMAIController : public AAIController
{
    GENERATED_BODY()

public:
    ABMAIController();
    virtual void Possess(APawn* InPawn) override;

    UBlackboardComponent* GetBlackboard();

protected:
    UPROPERTY(BlueprintReadWrite, Category = Behavior)
    class UBlackboardComponent* BlackboardComp;

    UPROPERTY(BlueprintReadWrite, Category = Behavior)
    class UBehaviorTreeComponent* BehaviorTreeComp;
};
```

Here we are simply providing the object with a default constructor, overriding the Possess() method (which is part of the AAIController interface), and declaring handles to the blackboard and behavior tree components that will be used by our AI. We have also included a public accessor method for the UBlackboardComponent called GetBlackboard(). It is with the creation of this object that we begin to see the network of our AI assets form. Now navigate to the BMAIController.cpp.

Firstly, we need to update the include list of this object to accommodate the UBlackboardComponent and UBehaviorTreeComponent types as well as the ABMBossCharacter type we just created. Do this by adding the following #includes:

```
#include "BMBossCharacter.h"
#include "BehaviorTree/BlackboardComponent.h"
#include "BehaviorTree/BehaviorTree.h"
```

Next we are to define the constructor for this object. Within the constructor we are simply going to initialize the two components via `CreateDefaultSubobject`:

```
ABMAIController::ABMAIController()
{
    BlackboardComp = CreateDefaultSubobject<UBlackboardComponent>
    (TEXT("BlackboardComp"));
    check(BlackboardComp);
    BehaviorTreeComp = CreateDefaultSubobject
    <UBehaviorTreeComponent>(TEXT("BehaviorTreeComp"));
    check(BehaviorTreeComp);
}
```

Following this we must define the override for the `Possess()` method we declared earlier. The `Possess()` method is responsible for providing control of a character to a given controller. We can also utilize this function to retrieve the blackboard and behavior tree assets from the possessed pawn. As not every pawn has a behavior tree and corresponding blackboard asset, we need to ensure that the pawn to be possessed is of type `ABMBossCharacter`. We can do this with the following code:

```
Void ABMAIController::Possess(APawn* InPawn)
{
    Super::Possess(InPawn);

ABMBossCharacter* possessedPawn = Cast<ABMBossCharacter>(InPawn);
    if (InPawn != nullptr)
    {
        BlackboardComp->InitializeBlackboard(*(possessedPawn->
        BehaviorTree->BlackboardAsset));

        BehaviorTreeComp->StartTree(*(possessedPawn->
        BehaviorTree));

    }<-- closing if(InPawn != nullptr)
}<-- closing ABMAIController::Possess()
```

This code will attempt to cast the parsed `APawn` to an `ABMBossCharacter` object. If the cast succeeds, the `possessedPawn` pointer will be populated and the following `if` statement will pass. Within the scope of this `if`, check we get access to the `UBehaviorTree` handle we declared in the `ABMBossCharacter` earlier. With this handle we can initialize the `UBlackboardComponent BlackboardComp` via passing a `const` reference to the blackboard asset associated with the behavior tree to the `InitailzeBlackboard` method. This will ensure that any queries made to `BlackboardComp` about variable states will retrieve information from the blackboard asset assigned to the behavior tree we set in the `ABMBossCharacter`.

Next, we start the behavior tree by parsing a `const` reference to the behavior tree to the `StartTree()` method of the `BehaviorTreeComponent`. This will ensure that the tree that has been assigned to this pawn starts upon possession and the implemented AI behavior will take place.

The last thing we need to add is a definition for the `GetBlackboard()` accessor method we declared earlier:

```
UBlackboardComponent* ABMAIController::GetBlackboard()
{
    return BlackboardComp;
}
```

Behavior tree breakdown and logic flow

Much like a Blueprint, a behavior tree is a grouping of connected nodes that, when fired, will perform some kind of functionality. Unlike Blueprints, we have advanced control over the flow of our behavior tree and the order in which the nodes execute. Node execution in behavior trees is dictated by the way the nodes are connected, and if the previous nodes have either succeeded or failed. Success or failure of a node is gauged by the node's ability to perform its given action. When a node fails its parent node, the previous node in the logic flow will be informed of the failure. This may result in the entire tree failing or simply a single branch of the tree failing, resulting in the logic flow of the tree to shift.

Before we go ahead and begin to make behavior trees of our own, it is important to understand the basic components that make up a behavior tree. As stated previously, there are several important pieces to behavior trees and they are described as follows:

- **Root Node**: Simply the entry point for the behavior tree, all BT's (behavior trees) will have a root node and provide us with a clear entry point for the tree. If a tree ever fails (a command is hit that cannot be carried out or is aborted), the tree will reset from the root node.

- **Task Nodes**: Tasks are operations that the AI can perform. Tasks are things such as `Move To`, `Rotate`, and `Wait`. Tasks can also be created from scratch by either creating a blueprint that inherits from the task base class, or a C++ object that does the same.

- **Service Nodes**: Service nodes are things that can perform at a certain frequency, for example every 0.5 seconds. It is with services that we can get our AI to perform ticking actions or ticking checks. For example, a good use of a service is to check every 0.3 seconds whether an enemy is close enough to the AI for the AI to engage with that enemy. Much like tasks, these can be created from scratch via C++ or blueprint.

- **Selector Nodes**: Selector nodes are utilized in the flow control of the behavior tree. You can have multiple child nodes connected to a selector node. The selector node will parse the logic flow to its child nodes from left to right until one succeeds (meaning child nodes of that child also succeed, and so forth). This means we are able to create behavior trees that execute a given branch based on the success or failure of other branches. It is important to note that if all children of a selector node fail, the selector node itself fails.

- **Sequence Nodes**: Sequence nodes are also utilized in the flow control of the behavior tree, but differ from selector nodes. Sequence nodes will execute all children from right to left until one child fails. This means we can create a series of steps that must execute in order. If one of the steps fails, the order is stopped and the tree is reset. If all of the child nodes succeed, the sequence succeeds!

- **Simple Parallel Nodes**: Simple parallel nodes can boast two children: One a task node and the other can be a complete subtree if desired. This allows us to perform one task while having other behaviors running in the background. The task child must be of a single task with optional decorators.

- **Decorator Nodes**: Decorators are attached to the aforementioned node types (apart from Root) and act as conditional checks for the nodes to execute. For example, you can have a decorator that checks whether the AI is close enough to a desired location. If this decorator passes, the attached node can execute. If not, the attached node fails and the following nodes will not be executed. This is a great way to control logic flow within your behavior tree. For example, you may have a selector node that has three children, each with their own decorator. If child 1's decorator fails, then child 2 will be checked, if this fails then child 3, and so forth.

What are blackboards?

As described previously, blackboards provide us with a way to create a set of values that we can write to and read from within any of the associated AI assets or objects. This is done through blackboard keys. Blackboard keys are identifiers that allow us to obtain any given value (or variable) within a Blackboard asset. For example, we can have a key saved in our blackboard called `HomeLocation` that is of type vector. We can now retrieve this vector from our blackboard by specifying we wish to retrieve the value `HomeLocation` from the blackboard asset as a vector type. The use of keys provides us with the ability to retrieve and set data types held in our blackboard from anywhere within our AI network.

Creating a basic behavior tree and black-board!

Ok, now that we have a rough idea of the workings of a behavior tree, let's work with one directly so we can solidify that knowledge and understanding. The purpose of this tree is to provide AI behavior to our boss character. We can start by simply getting our boss to identify the player as a target and track to the player. If the player runs far away from the boss or is occluded by blocking geometry, the AI will begin to path between a home location and last location the player was seen.

Setting up the blackboard

Start by creating a new behavior tree asset by right-clicking in the **Content** browser and selecting **Behavior Tree** from the **Artificial Intelligence** section of the provided list, as follows:

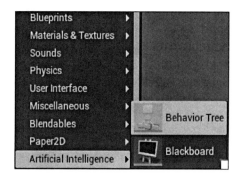

Call this new behavior tree BossBT. Then create a new **Blackboard** asset from the same category. Call this BossBB. We will start by adding the blackboard keys we are going to be utilizing in BossBT. Open the BossBB asset we just created and you will be presented with the blackboard editor.

The blackboard editor is quite simple; it contains two panels, the first is **Blackboard**. Through this panel you can manage your existing keys by selecting them from a drop-down list or adding new keys by pressing the large **New Key** button located at the top of the panel. The second is **Blackboard Details**. It is through this panel that you will be able to change the details of each blackboard key. You will be able to modify things such as **Key Name**, **Key Type**, and whether the key is synced across all instances of the blackboard asset.

Start by adding three new keys. The first two are going to be of type vector and named HomeLocation and TargetLocation. We will use these keys to hold the location our AI was at when it found the target, and the location of the target the AI is going to track to. The third key is to be of type Object and called TargetToFollow. This key will be used as a direct reference to the player object the AI will be following.

You add keys to the blackboard by selecting the **Add Key** button then choosing the appropriate type from the provided dropdown. If you ever need to make adjustments to a key, you can select it from the **Blackboard Panel** and modify it within the **Blackboard Details** panel. Once you have added the three keys, your blackboard should appear as follows:

With our blackboard keys in place we can begin to craft the behavior tree for the AI. Open BossBT now.

The behavior tree Editor

We are now presented with another GUI editor. As you can see, the behavior tree editor is quite simple. It consists of four panels and they are responsible for the following:

- **Toolbar**: This panel is used to house the control buttons for the BT. Here we are able to create new services, tasks, and decorators on the fly. Selecting one of the new buttons will create a blueprint of the corresponding type and open up the blueprint editor. We will be using these buttons ourselves shortly.

- **Behavior Tree**: Within this panel is the node graph you will be working with to create the main node structure of a behavior tree. Navigation of this graph is very similar to that of the Blueprint editor.

- **Details**: The details panel will provide you with access to any exposed properties of a selected BT node or object. This allows us to tweak the default values of our tasks, services, and decorators easily.

- **Blackboard**: This panel will show the state of any keys we have created in the associated blackboard asset. This is very useful as we are able to debug the state of the given blackboard's variables at runtime.

Setting up the behavior Tree

The first thing we need to do is create an association between `BossBT` and `BossBB`. We can do this by clicking in any blank area of the BT node graph. This will update the **Details** panel with one property, `BlackBoard Asset`. Via the dropdown of this property found within the **Details** panel, select `BossBB`. You will notice this updates the **Blackboard** panel with the keys we created earlier.

Currently our BT graph only contains a root node. As described earlier, the root node is simply the entry point to the behavior tree. The first thing we are going to do is create a selector node. This node will be used to choose between branches of the tree based on decorators that will check the state of one of our blackboard keys. Simply put, the AI will do one thing if there is an available target, and another if there is not.

We can create a selector node by right-clicking in the BT graph, expanding the **Composites** section within the provided dropdown, and selecting **Selector**. Nodes such as selectors, sequences, and simple parallels are all grouped under the **Composites** section. Once you have created your selector node you can connect the **Root** node and **Selector** node together by clicking and dragging from the dark section of the root node, to the dark section of the selector node as follows:

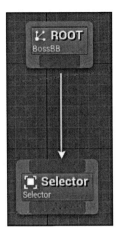

 Alternatively, you can drag and release an arrow from any node to bring up a context sensitive search. The Composite nodes will be present by default.

The white arrow denotes the *flow of logic* between the two nodes. The **Selector** node is now a child of the root node (as all nodes will be). From this selector node, we are going to be adding two children. One will be another selector node and the other a sequence node. This will effectively create a branch in the tree. The parent selector node will have to choose between either of its children based on any attached decorator nodes. Begin by creating and parenting the selector and sequence nodes to the previous selector node. Your graph should appear as follows:

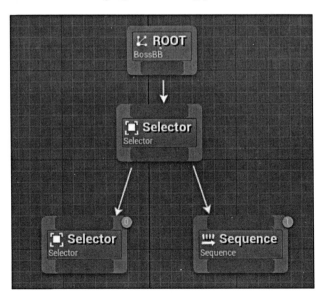

You may have noticed small grey circles containing a number have appeared on these nodes. This number is the child ID of that node and represents the **order** in which the nodes will be executed. As the parent is a selector, it will check whether child 0 is available for execution before it checks child 1. If child 0 succeeds in execution, child 1 will not be executed.

Currently, our parent selector node has no way of determining which of the two children to execute so it will always execute child 0. To remedy this, we are going to be adding decorators to the child selector and sequence nodes. As stated previously, decorators perform a check that can resolve to either `true` or `false`. If a decorator resolves to be `false`, the node will fail. For example, if child 0 had an attached decorator that resolved to `false`, the parent selector node would then attempt to run child 1 instead, much like an if statement in C++.

We wish the behavior tree to cause the AI to move towards a tracked player if there is a valid target. Otherwise patrol between the location the AI was situated when it found the target and the last known target location. The first action is a single task that will be executed if a target is found, therefore this should be appended to the selector child node.

The second will be a series of events that need to take place in order, thus we will attach that functionality to the sequence node. The child order now becomes very important as we do not wish for the patrolling functionality to take place if there is a valid target. This is why the selector is at child index 0 and the sequence node is at child index 1.

Ok, enough talk, let's attach these decorators! To attach a decorator right-click on the node you wish to execute if the decorator passes. In our case, right-click the selector node at child index 0. This will open a dropdown menu of all of the available actions we can perform on this node. From this dropdown, hover over **Add Decorator...** this will provide you with a list of available decorators and a search bar for this list.

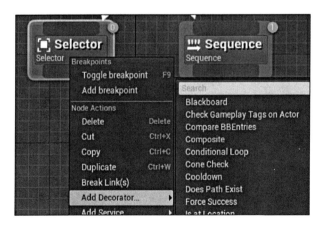

From this list of decorators, select **Blackboard**. This decorator type allows us to query the state of a blackboard key. This will make the node appear like this:

The decorator is represented as another section to the node. As you can see, the subtext of the decorator states **Blackboard: HomeLocation is Set**. That means if the `HomeLocation` key is set, the decorator will pass and the node will execute. We need to modify this so that, instead, it checks whether `TargetToFollow` is set. We can do this by adjusting the decorator properties in the **Details** panel. Each element of a single node can be selected, do this now by clicking on the blue part of the node. The selection is denoted by a thin red border around the selected node element.

With the decorator selected, address the **Details** panel and modify the settings so they appear as follows:

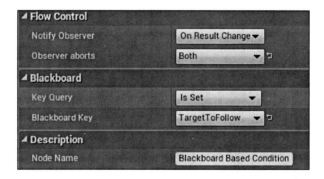

Here we have changed the **Blackboard Key** property to be `TargetToFollow`. It is important to note the other properties that can be seen here. Firstly, the **Key Query** property can be changed to adjust what check we are performing on the variable. If the key in question is of type `float`, the **Key Query** list will update to include options such as **Is Greater than** or **Is Equal To**. This again provides us with more power to dictate how the AI will behave.

Another important property set is the **Flow Control** section. Here we have stated that we wish this decorator observer (the selector node) to be notified when the result of this decorator changes. This is only meaningful when we address the second property of the **Flow Control** section **Observer Aborts**. This property can be set to three different states. **Self, Lower Priority,** and **Both**. Setting this property to **Self** will result in the node the decorator is attached to abort when the state of the decorator changes. This abort will cause the selector to fail (thus all of its children to fail as well). **Lower Priority** will result in all BT nodes with a greater child index to abort. For example, if a decorator on a node at child index three with this state set changes, all child nodes of the BT with an index greater than three will abort.

The last state **Both** is self-explanatory, as both the node and all lesser nodes will abort. With this tool we are able to abort an AI task based off of the result of a decorator. This is very useful as some tasks will halt tree execution until the task is complete. In our case, if the decorator result is changed, we wish to abort both this node and any lower priority nodes (which will be the sequence node and children). Do this now by setting the **Observer aborts** property of the new decorator node to **Both**.

Next we can add a similar decorator to the sequence node that checks whether the `TargetToFollow` key is not set. Do this now by adding a new decorator to the sequence node and adjusting the properties in the **Details** panel accordingly. This ensures that either branch will only execute if the desired state of `TargetToFollow` is met. Your graph should currently look like this:

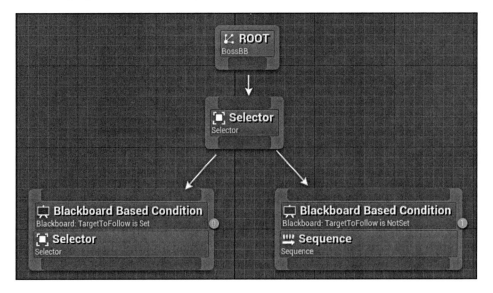

Now we can add tasks to the sequence node. These tasks will be in the form of child nodes. Task nodes cannot have any children; thus we require a sequence node to execute a series of tasks. From the sequence nodes bottom bar, click and drag an arrow; upon releasing an arrow you will be presented with a search menu for any available actions. Within this action, search for the task `MoveTo`.

Simply put, this will move the AI towards a specified location via the AI controller. Select this new `MoveTo` node and address the **Details** panel. Here we can set some properties for this task. Under the **Node** section of the **Details** panel we are presented with the ability to dictate when the node will stop executing via the `Acceptable Radius` and `Stop on Overlap` properties. We need to set the **Blackboard Key** property of the **Blackboard** section to `TargetLocation` as this is where we wish the AI to move to. You will notice that the subtext of the move to node created will also update when these properties are changed.

The sequence of tasks we wish to execute should result in the AI patrolling between two points. We can do this by adding two more child tasks to the sequence node. The first is a **Wait** node, which will simply wait a specified time before registering a success, the second is another **MoveTo** node. Select the **Wait** node and, via the **Details** panel, set the **WaitTime** under the **Wait** section to be `2.5`. Next, ensure the **Blackboard Key** for the second **Move To** node is set to **HomeLocation** (it should be set to this by default). When you are finished, your tree should look similar to this:

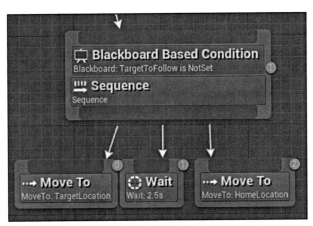

We aren't done yet though, this previous node arrangement could be prone to bugs and undesirable behavior. We need additional decorators for the sequence node before we can safely execute the tasks. We have specified that the AI needs to move to `TargetLocation`, therefore we should ensure that a value for this location has been set. Add another blackboard decorator to the sequence node and adjust the details so that it queries whether the target location is indeed set.

Creating a custom task via blueprint

Ok, now that we have one of the tree branches completed, let's work on the other. We need the child of the first selector node to execute functionality that will cause the AI to track towards the object set at `TargetToFollow`. We cannot use a standard `MoveTo` task for this, as we require the AI to move towards an object not a `vector` location. This means we will need to create our own custom task that will be carried out by the AI. Tasks, services, and decorators have all been designed so that we may create our own using either blueprint or C++ abstractions. We will be creating a task that allows the AI to move towards the target object found at the `TargetToFollow` blackboard key.

We can create new blueprint versions of these nodes by selecting the appropriate button in the BT editor. Navigate to the `BossBT` editor now and press the **New Task** button. This will bring up the task Blueprint editor. This editor is very similar to that of the blueprint editor we are used to. However, this one is lacking a **Components Panel** and any form of viewport as they are not required for Tasks. This new task will come with a generated name that is undesirable, rename the task by locating it in your **Content Browser** (it will be in the same folder as the `BossBT` asset) and rename it to `BMMoveTo`. You can also change the **Node Name** in the **Class Defaults** to `BMMoveTo` if you wish.

To create meaningful functionality for this task we need to intercept when the task has been informed to execute. We can do that by spawning an overridable function node. Address the **My Blueprint** panel, you will see that under the **Functions** category there is some grey text stating **(6 overridable)**.

If you hover your mouse over this category, you will notice that a small dropdown titled **Override** appears. If you open this dropdown you will see a list of the functions that we can override to create our own functionality for this task.

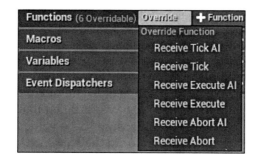

The function we wish to override is **Receive Execute**. This is the function that is called when the task is informed to execute by the parent. This will place an Event `ReceiveExecute` node in the **Blueprint Graph**. Before we begin working with the graph we should add the variables we require for the logic of this task. Add two new variables. The first is to be called `AI_Controller` and is to be of type `BMAIController` reference. The second is to be called `TargetToFollow` and be of type `BlackboardKeySelector`.

We will not be setting a default value for these variables, however ensure `TargetToFollow` is editable by clicking the small eye icon on the right-hand side of the `TargetToFollow` variable entry in the **MyBlueprint** panel.

This will mean we can set the value of this variable from the BT editor (much like we have with the **MoveTo** blackboard key locations).

Ok, now we can work with the graph! The first thing we are going to do is check whether we have populated the `AI_Controller` variable with a valid reference. If not, we will cast the `Owner Actor` input pin provided by the `Event ReceiveExecute` node to a `BMAIController`, which we will then assign into the `AI_Controller` variable. This check is purely for optimization so that we are not performing an expensive cast every time the event is executed. The nodes can be arranged as follows:

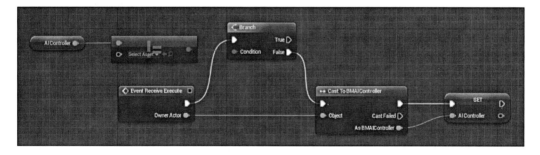

Following this we wish to call the method `AIMoveTo`. This can be found by right-clicking anywhere in the graph and using the context sensitive search. This will bring up a node that takes in a pawn to move, a destination for the pawn to move to, a target actor, an `AcceptanceRadius`, and whether the move should stop on overlap. For the pawn input reference, we are going to be getting the pawn from our `BMAIController` by using the `GetControlledPawn` method of the `BMAIController`. We will not be setting a destination vector as we want the AI to move towards an actor.

For the `Target Actor` input pin, we are going to be parsing the value located at the blackboard key identified by the `BlackboardKeySelector` variable `TargetToFollow`.

To get the value located at this key we are going to call the `GetBlackboardValueAsActor` method of the `BlackboardKeySelector`. This will return whatever value is present at that key in the blackboard as an actor. Set the `AcceptanceRadius` to `200` as we wish the AI to stop moving if it encroaches within `200` units of the target actor. Ensure to connect the execution paths from both the set `AI_Controller` node and the `True` execution path of the previous `branch` node to the `AI MoveTo` node. The arrangement may appear as follows:

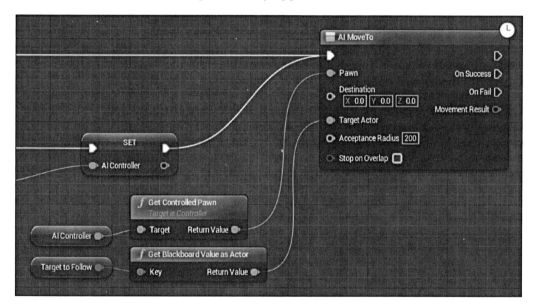

The last thing we need to do within this task is report whether the task executed successfully or failed. We can do this by calling the FinishExecute method found within the Task object itself. Do this now by right-clicking anywhere in the graph and using the search to find this node. Connect this node to the OnSuccess execution output of the AIMoveTo node and ensure that you tick the success bool input pin. This means that when AIMoveTo successfully finishes, this task node will flag success and the parent nodes will be informed. Do the same for the OnFail path but do not tick the success input pin. Your final node arrangement should appear as follows:

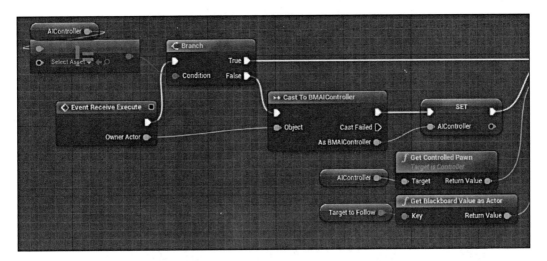

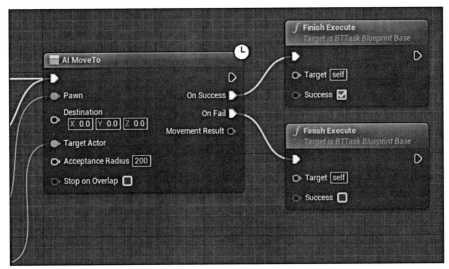

Summoning our new task in the BT graph is very easy, we simply have to search for the BMMoveTo task as we would any other. Do this now and summon the node into the graph. Attach this node as a child to the selector node. Select the BMMoveTo node and change the TargetToFollow variable to the TargetToFollow blackboard key via the **Details** panel. Your branch should look like this:

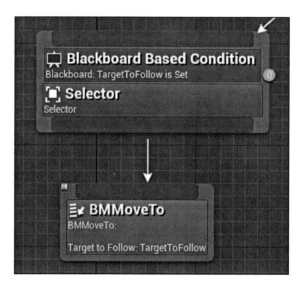

Creating a custom decorator using blueprint

We should add one more decorator to the parent selector node before we continue. Even though there is an acceptance radius that we specified on the AIMoveTo node within the BMMoveTo task, we should add a decorator that will only call this event if the AI is outside a certain range to the player. Unfortunately, this check does not already exist so we have to again create our own. We can do this by clicking the **New Decorator** button in the BT editor. This will generate a blueprint decorator and open the blueprint editor. Be sure to rename this decorator to BMCloseEnough.

The editor for tasks, services, and decorators is all the same. However, this time we are going to be overriding a different function. This time we need to override PerformConditionCheck. Unlike EventReceiveExecute, this function has a return type. As all decorators need to report success or failure, this function returns a boolean that represents just that.

The purpose of this decorator is to check whether the actor stored at the
`TargetToFollow` blackboard key is within a certain range to the player. We
should start by adding the variables we are going to need for this graph. The
first is another reference to a `BMAIController` object `AI_Controller`, the second
is a blackboard key selector titled `TargetToFollow`, and the last is a float value
`AcceptableDistance` that will be used as the range value for this graph. Ensure
`TargetToFollow` and `AcceptableDistance` are editable, as we would like to set
both of these values from the BT editor.

Within the graph we are simply going to check the distance between the
`TargetToFollows` location and the location of the pawn the AI controller is
controlling. As always, the first thing we need to do is check whether we have
assigned a valid reference to `AI_Controller`. If we have, we will be performing
the distance check, if not, we need to perform the cast as we did in the `BMMoveTo`
task, then perform the distance check.

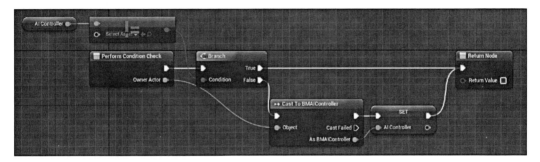

Now we need to generate a meaningful input for the `Return Value` input pin. To do
this we are again going to be getting the controlled pawn from the `AI_Controller`
reference and the actor from the `TargetToFollow BlackboardKeySelector`
via `GetBlackboardValueAsActor`. We are going to find a vector between these
two objects, if the length of the vector is greater than or equal to the value stored
at `Acceptable Distance` we wish the decorator to pass. The following node
arrangement will do this:

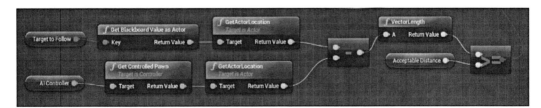

Plug the resulting `boolean` value into the `return value` input pin of the `Return` node and we are done! Now navigate back to `BossBT` and add the decorator we just created to the `BMMoveTo` node, ensure the `TargetToFollow` blackboard key is set to `TargetToFollow`, and the **Acceptable Radius** property is set to `500`.

Creating a custom service using C++

Now that we have finished creating the behavior tree for our AI, it is about time we go about setting the blackboard keys that a large amount of our logic is based on. We are going to do this with a service. As stated previously, a service is something that will take place at a certain frequency or tick. Services act as a way to update AI information and states during runtime from the behavior tree. We have created enough BT assets using blueprint, so it is time we create one in C++! The purpose of this service is to check an area around the AI for an `ABMCharacter`, if one is found, set it as the target for the AI to follow.

Start by creating a new C++ class via the wizard, this time the class will inherit from `BTService`. Ensure you do not inherit from `BTService_BlueprintBase` as that abstraction is to only be used by blueprints. Call this new class `BMAgroCheck`. Once the engine has generated the new code files, navigate to `BMAgroCheck.h`.

Defining the BMArgoCheck class

As this new class is part of the AI network we are creating, we are going to need to include some members that will act as handles to important AI objects. We also need to override the function required for our custom service functionality. Modify the `UBMAgroCheck` class definition to match the following:

```cpp
UCLASS()
class BOSSMODE_API UBMAgroCheck : public UBTService
{
    GENERATED_BODY()

protected:
    virtual void TickNode(UBehaviorTreeComponent& OwnerComp, uint8*
    NodeMemory, float DeltaSeconds) override;

private:
    UBehaviorTree* ThisTree;
    class ABMAIController* ThisController;
    class ABMBossCharacter* ThisAICharacter;
};
```

Here we are overriding the `TickNode()` method of the `UBTService` base class so that we may include custom tick functionality. As you can see, this function takes in a reference to a `UBehaviorTreeComponent`, through this reference we will be able to get a handle to the AI controller that is currently being processed. We have also included handles to the AI assets that will be required during the service check functionality. Remember, when a member or input parameter is declared with the class keyword, this makes the declaration a prototype. Meaning we will have to include the appropriate code files in the `.cpp` to complete the partial type.

Advanced collision in UE4

Before we define the functionality for our new service, let's quickly talk about collision in UE4. Collision in UE4 uses a channel system. Collision channels are effectively flags we can set on each collidable object to inform how the object should behave in any given collision situation. You may have noticed when we set up the collidable component of an object we set the collision profile name or collision type to either `NoCollision`, `OverlapAllDyanmic`, `Pawn`, and so forth. These profiles not only set the collision type of the object but also how that object will react to different collision channels.

Most of our interactions with UE4's collision system have appeared as follows:

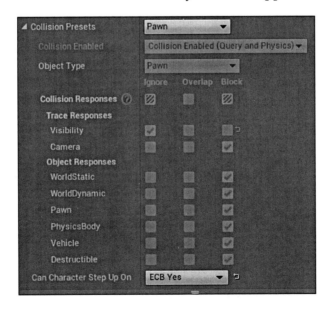

The important elements to note here are the `Object Type` property and the `CollisionResponses` matrix. In the previous example we are stating that this object is of type `Pawn`. Meaning that any time something detects a collision with this object, it will be considered part of the `Pawn` channel. Within the `CollisionResponses` matrix, we are informing the engine how this object is going to react to other trace and object channels during the event of a collision. In the previous example, this object will block *ALL* collision queries apart from that with a trace channel type of Visibility.

This is a very powerful tool as we could create a custom arrangement of these settings so that a given object collides with all pawns but ignores vehicles completely as they are two different collision channels.

For example, imagine if object A was to collide with another object B, and A is of type `Pawn` and B is of type `Vehicle`. If we have stated in the `CollisionResponses` matrix of A to block `Vehicle` channel collisions, and in the collision response grid of B to block `Pawn` channel collisions, then this clash will result in the objects successfully colliding. However, if either of the objects have set to ignore the opposing collision channel then this collision will not take place. This is very useful for setting up collision queries where we would have an object pass through some object types, yet be blocked by others.

The Object A in the previous example where a collision does not take place with `Vehicle` types would have collision properties that look like this:

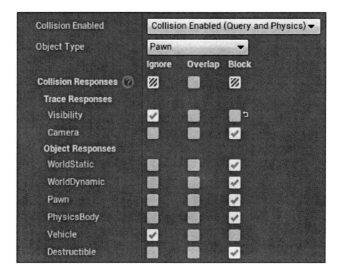

UE4 also allows us to define up to 18 custom collision channels via the project settings. During the course of this chapter and the next, we will be using some of these channels. These custom channels can also be used in code collision queries, however we must use previously defined enumerated types that will resolve to the correct collision channel during compilation.

Alright, let's finish defining our new C++ service!

Defining the service tick

Navigate to the BMAgroCheck.cpp now and modify the #include list at the top of the file to match the following:

```
#include "BossMode.h"
#include "BMAIController.h"
#include "BehaviorTree/BlackboardComponent.h"
#include "BehaviorTree/Blackboard/BlackboardKeyAllTypes.h"
#include "BehaviorTree/BehaviorTree.h"
#include "BMBossCharacter.h"
#include "DrawDebugHelpers.h"
#include "BMAgroCheck.h"
```

The previous include list will ensure that we have included all required code types for the following functionality. Let's start by performing an assignment check similar to that of the AI_Controller check that took place in our custom blueprint AI assets.

Within the TickNode() method we are going to be performing a sphere sweep check for any players within a certain radius of the AI character that is currently being controlled by the parsed UBehaviorTreeComponent. That means we need access to the BMAIController, the BMBossCharacter, and the behavior tree.

Add the following code to TickNode():

```
void UBMAgroCheck::TickNode(UBehaviorTreeComponent&OwnerComp, uint8*
NodeMemory, floatDeltaSeconds)
{
    Super::TickNode(OwnerComp, NodeMemory, DeltaSeconds);

if (ThisTree == nullptr || ThisController == nullptr ||
        ThisAICharacter == nullptr)
    {
        ThisTree = OwnerComp.GetCurrentTree();

        ThisController =
        Cast<ABMAIController>(OwnerComp.GetAIOwner());

        ThisAICharacter = Cast<ABMBossCharacter>
```

```
                    (ThisController->GetPawn());

          if (ThisTree == nullptr || ThisController == nullptr||
          ThisAICharacter == nullptr))
                 {
                         UE_LOG(LogTemp, Warning,
                         TEXT("Warning Agro Service
                         performed on invalid AI"));
                         return;
                 }
          }
}
```

The previous code checks whether any of the handles we declared in the class definition are invalid. If so, we need to repopulate all of our handles with the appropriate values. We can get the behavior tree asset from the parsed `UBehaviorTreeComponent OwnerComp` via the method `GetCurrentTree()`. We get a handle to the AI controller by casting the return from the `GetAIOwner()` method of `OwnerComp` to a `ABMAIController`. We then get a handle to the AI character via casting the result of the `GetPawn()` method of the `ABMAIController` to a `ABMBossCharacter`. If any of these fail, we use the `UE_LOG` macro to log a warning, stating that the service is trying to perform on an invalid AI and we return out of the function.

To perform the actual sweep check we are going to require the use of a few new objects. One is `FCollisionQueryParams`. This object is a `struct` that acts as an input parameter to most collision query functions. It is with this `struct` we are able to define most of the options for the sweep check. We can specify whether we are to use complex checking, what actors to ignore, and the name of the sweep check. We are also going to use `FCollisionObjectQueryParams`. It is with this `struct` we will define which objects we are going to be checking for via the object collision channels mentioned before. The final `struct` we are going to be using is `FHitResult`. This struct is used to populate the return information from a collision query function. It is with this `struct` we can get relevant collision data such as the offending actor and penetration details.

Add the following code to the `TickNode()` method:

```
// Initialize a sweep params struct with trace complex set to true
FCollisionQueryParams SphereSweepParams(FName(TEXT("AgroCheckSweep")),
true, ThisAICharacter);

FCollisionObjectQueryParams ObjectQuery(ECC_GameTraceChannel1);

// Initialize Hit Result
FHitResult HitOut(ForceInit);
```

Here we are creating a `FCollisionQueryParam` object called `SphereSweepParams`. We are using the constructor to initialize this `struct` with the name of the sweep (`AgroCheckSweep`) to trace complex (higher accuracy), and we are passing the `ABMBossCharacter` handle to the constructor as an actor to ignore so that the sweep check does not detect the `ABMBossCharacter` itself.

We then initialize a `FCollisionObjectQueryParams` struct with the enum variable `ECC_GameTraceChannel1`. This enum represents one of the custom collision channels mentioned previously. Once we have completed this object we will add the custom collision channel via the editor and assign it as a collision type to the player character.

The next thing we are going to do is draw a debug sphere so we have a visual representation of the sweep check we are about perform. Add the following code to the `TickNode()` method:

```
// Draw debug sphere to check we are sweeping the right area
DrawDebugSphere(ThisAICharacter->GetWorld(),
ThisAICharacter->GetActorLocation(),
1500, 12, FColor::Red, false, 4.0f);
```

The previous code will draw a sphere via the `DrawDebugSphere` method that is part of `DrawDebugHelpers.h`, which we added to our include list earlier. The first parameter is the world context to draw the sphere in, the second is the location to draw the sphere, the third is sphere radius, the fourth is the number of segments that will make up the sphere (higher number, higher sphere fidelity), the fifth is the color, the sixth is a boolean representing whether the lines are to be persistent after drawing, and the last is the lifetime the sphere will be visible. The previous function call will draw a red sphere with a 1500 unit radius at the location of the AI character for 4 seconds.

Now we can finally perform the sweep test! A sweep test simply sweeps a sphere along a path. If any objects collide with the sphere along the sweep, a collision will be registered. Add the following code to the `TickNode()` method:

```
// Perform the sweep and check boolean return, we will only be
checking for BMCharacter objects
bool bResult = ThisAICharacter->GetWorld()->
SweepSingleByObjectType(HitOut,
        ThisAICharacter->GetActorLocation(),
        ThisAICharacter->GetActorLocation() +FVector(0.0f, 0.0f,
        10.0f),
        FQuat(),
        ObjectQuery,
        FCollisionShape::MakeSphere(1500),
        SphereSweepParams);
```

The previous code is using the `SweepSingleByObjectType` method of the `UWorld` object. This function will perform a sphere sweep and return a hit upon the first positive collision. The function takes in a `FHitResult` struct to populate with return data, an origin location for the sweep, a destination location for the sweep, the rotation of the sweep, the `FCollisionObjectQueryParams` struct for information on the type of objects to seek collisions with, a shape to perform the sweep with (in our case a sphere with a 1500 radius) and, finally, a `FCollisionQueryParams` struct used to detail the information about the query itself. The `SweepSingleByObjectType` returns a `bool` that represents the success of the sweep, `true` if there was a collision, `false` if there was not.

The previous function call will sweep for objects that are of type `ECC_GameTraceChannel1` or in our case the first custom collision channel we create. The sweep will be performed from the `ABMBossCharacters` location to 10 units up on the Z axis. It is important to provide different locations for the sweep origin and sweep end as, if they are the same, the sweep will fail. This sweep query will use the details we outlined earlier within the `SphereSweepParams` struct.

Finally, we have to check whether the sweep returned a positive hit. If so, we need to set those blackboard keys we did all this work for! Add the following code to the `TickNode()` method:

```
if (bResult)
{
    ThisController->GetBlackboard()->
    SetValueAsObject(TEXT("TargetToFollow"), HitOut.GetActor());

    ThisController->GetBlackboard()->
    SetValueAsVector(TEXT("HomeLocation"), ThisAICharacter->
    GetActorLocation());

    ThisController->GetBlackboard()->
    SetValueAsVector(TEXT("TargetLocation"), HitOut.GetActor()->
    GetActorLocation());

}
else
{
    ThisController->GetBlackboard()->
    SetValueAsObject(TEXT("TargetToFollow"), nullptr);
}

} // <-- closing TickNode()
```

The previous code will check whether the result of the sphere sweep was successful. If so, we are to set the blackboard keys `TargetToFollow`, `HomeLocation`, and `TargetLocaiton` respectively. We are doing this via the `UBlackboardComponent` of the `ABMAIController` reference we retrieved earlier. If the hit result fails, we wish to set the `TargetToFollow` key to `nullptr` as we do not wish for the AI to have a target.

Adding the C++ service to the BossBT

Now compile the code and re-run the project. We are about to include the service in our `BossBT`. Once the project has compiled, open the `BossBT` again. Within the tree, select the first selector node we created. Right-click within the node and hover over **Add Service...**. From the provided dropdown, select `BMAgroCheck`. Your final behavior tree should appear as follows:

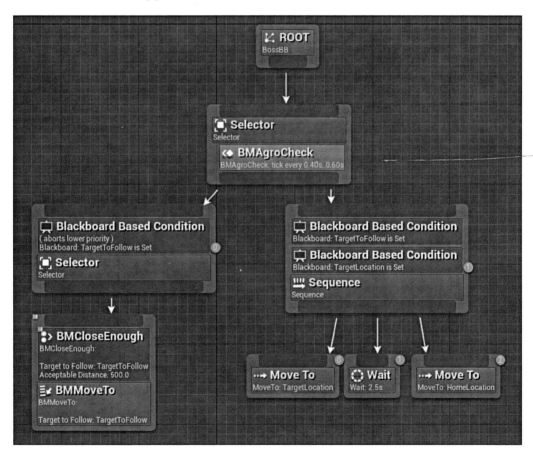

Before we are done with this tree, we need to change one property of the
`BMAgroCheck` service. Select the service and address the details panel. Under the
Service section, click the down expansion arrow and then tick the **Call Tick on
Search Start** property. This will ensure the service is called from the beginning of
the behavior tree logic search. The details panel will appear as follows:

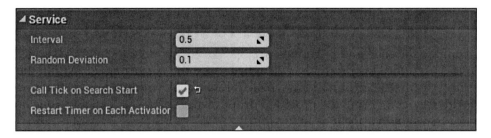

Integrating the AI Character

Now with all of this in place we can finally create the boss AI character! The first
thing you will need to do is import the mesh that the boss will be using. Import the
provided `BossMesh.fbx` by right-clicking in your content browser and selecting
`Import To /Game....` Navigate to the `BossMesh.fbx` that was provided with the
resources for this book. Once selected to import, ensure you check `Import as`
`Skeletal` as we desire the imported mesh to be used for a character. The other
import settings appear as follows:

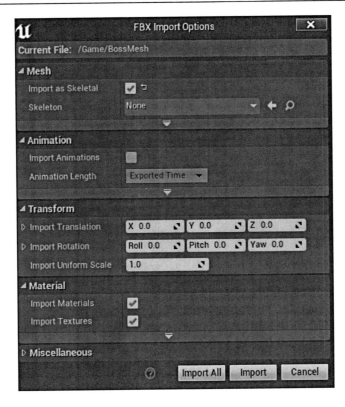

With the mesh imported we can now create a new blueprint class that inherits from ABMBossCharacter. Do this now and call it FPBossCharacter. We need to set some of the asset associations in the character and adjust some settings before it is good to go. Start by opening the new blueprint, selecting the **FPBossCharacter(self) Component**, and address the **Details** panel.

To ensure that this character is always possessed by our BMAIController, we need to adjust some properties in the **Pawn** category. First off we can set the BehaviorTree asset we declared in the BMBossCharacter base class. Do this by setting the BehaviorTree property to BossBT. Then we need to adjust the AutoPossessAI property so that it states **Placed in World or Spawned**. This will ensure that, regardless of how the FPBossCharacter comes into the game world, it will be possessed by the BMAIController.

The last property we have to change here is the **AI Controller class**, ensure this is set to BMAIController. The **Pawn** section of the **Details Panel** should appear as follows:

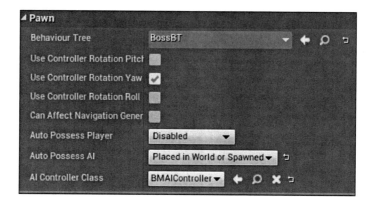

Next we need to adjust some properties in **CapsuleComponent(Inherited)**. The boss AI we are creating will be a large ball of sorts that appears to hover on the spot. Because of this we need to slightly oversize our colliding capsule. Set the **Capsule Half Height** and **Capsule Radius** properties under the **Shape** section of the **Details** panel so that they equal 160.

The next thing we need to do is adjust the move speed of our FPBossCharacter so that our player can run away from the boss and have the TargetToFollow blackboard key unset and the patrolling behavior take place. Select the CharacterMovementComponent and set the **Max Walk Speed** property under the **Character Movement: Walking** section to 200.

Finally, we can add our Boss Mesh. Select the **Mesh(Inherited)** component and set the **Skeletal Mesh** property of the **Mesh** category to BossMesh! You will now see something similar to this:

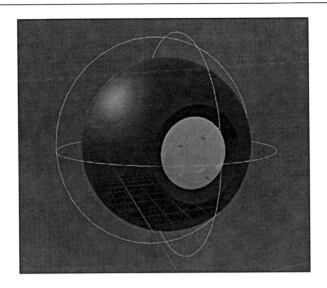

Creating a custom object collision channel

We are nearly ready to place all of our pieces in the game world. Before we do that we need to create the aforementioned custom collision channel. We can do this via **Project Settings**. Navigate to **Edit | Project Settings**. Once there, navigate to **Engine | Collision**. This will present you with a settings menu with two categories `ObjectChannels` and `TraceChannels`. We are going to be adding a new object channel. This can be done by pressing the `NewObjectChannel` button, which will present you with this wizard:

With this wizard create a new channel called `BMCharacter` with a default response of **Block**. This channel is the one we are going to be setting as the collision type on our `FPCharacter`. As this is the first custom channel we have created, the `ECC_GameTraceChannel1` enum will resolve to this channel and our sweep test will only pick up collisions with objects that have set `BMCharacter` to be their collision type.

Open the `FPCharacter` blueprint now and select the **Capsule** component from within the **Components** panel. Within the **Details** panel navigate to the **Collision** section and expand the **Collision Presets** category, ensure it matches the following:

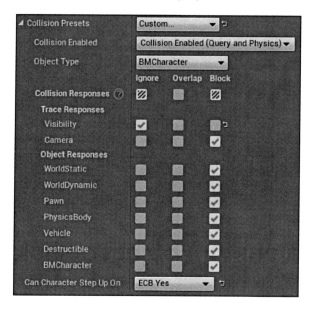

Here we have stated that we wish to use a **Custom...** collision preset. We have set the object type to be our new BMCharacter (which would have been added to the list of available options, if it didn't, ensure you added the custom collision object channel correctly). We have then set the collision response grid to replicate that of a pawn so the character will still function as intended within the game world. Now we can finally modify our level to show off our AI!

Modifying the level to support AI

Alright! Now we can place all the puzzle pieces together by modifying our level to support our AI character. That means we have to adjust the size of the floor (as it is too small for both the player character and the AI character at this point) and place a `NavMesh` in the scene.

Let's start by adjusting the floor size. Within the world outliner, select the **Floor** `StaticMeshActor`. Address the **Details** panel and change the **Scale** property of the **Transform** section so that each axis is set to 8. This will give us a large enough area to run around in. Now we need to generate a navigation mesh for our floor so our AI can `pathfind` properly.

What is a navigation mesh

A navigation mesh is a generated mesh that acts as an area (defined by the polygons of the navigation mesh) for the AI to path within. Navigation meshes, or `NavMeshes` for short, are generated within the bounds of a Navigation Mesh volume. They can support slopes, obstacles, rough terrain, and much more. The idea is the generated mesh will conform and contour to any regions the AI can path to, we can then query this generated navigation mesh for pathing points the AI will follow.

When generating a `NavMesh`, the engine will take into account the size of the AI that will be maneuvering the mesh. This is because as an AI agent's size increases, the regions within which they can path will decrease proportionally. We need to be able to inform the engine of the size of our AI agents beforehand so the `NavMesh` is generated appropriately.

Adjusting the NavMesh generation settings

As our AI is quite large we are going to have to place a `NavMesh` into the scene that supports the size of the AI character's collider. To do this we are again going to have to change some project settings. Navigate to **Edit | Project Settings**. Once here, navigate to **Engine | NavigationMesh**. As our character has a capsule radius of 160 and a capsule height of 320, we need to allow navigation mesh generation to support this capsule size. Under the **Generation** section of the `NavigationMesh` settings page, change the `AgentRadius` property to 160, the `AgentHeight` property to 320, and the `AgentMaxHeight` property to 340. This will ensure the navigation mesh will be able to generate a mesh that supports these values. The settings should appear as follows:

We are not done yet as we need to still add our Boss AI capsule dimensions to a list of supported agents to the navigation system, so that the correct navigation paths will be generated for our boss AI. Within the project settings, navigate to **Engine | Navigation System**. Within this settings page we need to add an element to the **Supported Agents** array under the **Agents** category. You can do this by clicking the small `white plus`. Once an element has been added to the array you can expand the settings by clicking the small `arrow` on the left-hand side of the property. Then do the same for the entry `0`. Within these settings, change the **Name** property to **Boss**, the `NavAgentRadius` property to `160`, and the `NavAgentHeight` property to `320`. The settings will appear as follows:

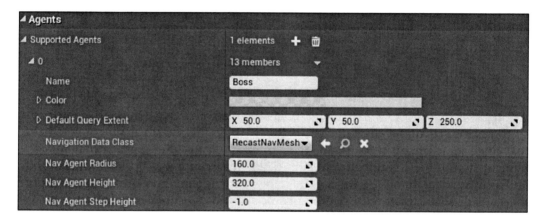

Placing a NavMesh in the scene

Now that we have adjusted the `NavMesh` generation properties we need to generate a `NavMesh` in the scene. We will do this with a `NavMeshBoundsVolume` object. This object defines a volume within which the engine will generate a navigation mesh for each supported agent listed in the **Supported Agents** property of the **Navigation System Settings** page. These generated `NavMesh` are called `RecastNavMeshs`. Navigate to the level editor and, within the **Modes** panel, search for a `NavMeshBoundVolume` and drag this volume into the now by selecting and dragging the Modes Panel entry.

Select this new `NavMeshBoundsVolume` entry in the `WorldOutlier` and ensure that it is situated around origin. Then scale the volume so that it encompasses the entire floor mesh and scale the height of the `NavMesh` so that it encompasses a large vertical area. The transform for my `NavMeshBoundsVolume` appears as follows:

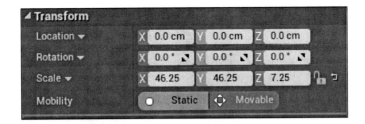

With the `NavMesh` in the scene you will see another entry in the **WorldOutiler**, **RecastNavMesh-Boss**. This is the actual navigation mesh that has been generated within the `NavMeshBoundsVolume`. This one has been generated specifically for the Boss agent entry we added to the **Supported Agents** list earlier. If there were more **SupportedAgents** there would be more `RecastNavMesh` objects in the level. To see the generated `NavMesh`, simply press the *P* key. Everywhere that is green is where our AI will be able to path to. Anywhere that is red is blocked or still generating, and anywhere without color is where the AI cannot path to. Feel free to add some obstacles to the scene by dragging in **Cube** objects from the `ModesPanel`. I chose to drag in a couple and scale them like so:

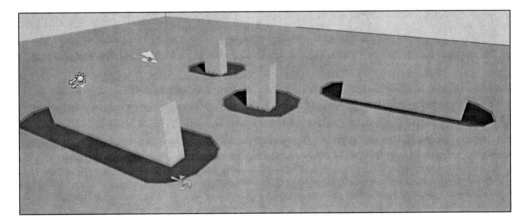

As you can see, the `NavMesh` has updated so that the areas closest to these obstacles cannot be pathed to, this will avoid any unwanted collisions during AI pathing.

Placing the AI in the level and testing

OK! We are done! Now all we have to do is place the AI in the level and test that everything we have done works! Ensure you place the AI at least 1500 units away from the player so that it does not automatically detect the player's location. With the AI in level, press **play** and you will see something similar to this:

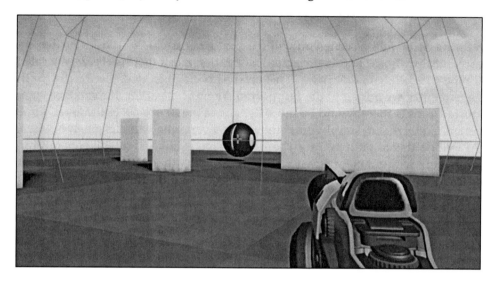

The red lines we are seeing is the debug sphere that is drawn during the sphere check. If you move within these lines, the AI will start to move towards you while pathing around the obstacles thanks to the NavMesh! Once the AI has targeted you, try running outside the bounds of the detection sphere and wait. The AI will stop chasing you and begin to path between the home location and the last known target location.

Summary

Great job working through all of that! We are not done with our Boss AI yet though. During this chapter, we learnt the fundamentals of the AI system within Unreal Engine 4 and created our own C++ first person character to boot! In the next chapter, we are going to add some advanced AI functionality to the character so that it will shoot at our player and take damage. The more damage the boss takes the more aggressive it will become. We will also be learning about Unreal's Epic Rendering system in the next chapter. See you there!

Advanced AI and Unreal Rendering

Great job on creating the beginnings of your boss AI and the first person character in Chapter 7! In this chapter we will be utilizing advanced concepts of the AI and projectile systems to expand both of these objects to match the feature set we described in the previous chapter. The other purpose of this chapter is to expose you to the rendering systems found within UE4. We will be learning how to create custom material for our boss character that utilizes some of the advanced properties of the UE4 rendering system.

We will also cover some basic graphics programming theory that will assist in understanding what's happening under the hood. When working with any graphics system it is always important to have a firm understanding of the theory within which the system will operate. In short, we will be learning the following topics:

- Homing projectile implementations
- C++ implementation of a task within a behavior tree
- Advanced AI controller interaction
- C++ `enum` and how to use them in blackboard
- State-based decision making in UE4 behavior trees
- UE materials
- Physically based rendering
- Material creation
- Texture channel theory
- Texture UVs

Expanded AI and tracking projectiles

Before we break into the rendering portions of UE4, we first need to finish looking into projectiles and AI in UE4. We are going to be modifying our `ABMCharacter` to enable the projectiles to track to a given target. We are then going to be arming our boss with the same projectiles, as well as expanding on the AI behavior tree so that we can effect AI behavior based on a given AI state. Let's begin by modifying our `ABMCharacter`.

Tracking projectiles and you

Tracking projectiles are very easy to set up in UE4. We must simply provide the projectile movement component with information on how much the tracking will affect the projectiles during flight, and a target to track to. The first is simple, as I will be providing you with good starting values for any tracking behavior. The latter, on the other hand, will require that we create another custom collision channel and perform something called a line trace.

Creating the line trace

Let's first acquire the target we wish the projectiles to track to. We can do this by creating another object collision channel specifically for boss objects, we will then perform a line trace looking for objects that are part of this collision channel. If the line trace returns a successful collision, we have found a target for our projectiles.

We are going to have to add a couple more members to the `ABMCharacter` object as well. Navigate to `BMCharacter.h` now and add the following code to the class definition:

```
protected:
USceneComponent* TrackingSceneComponent;
```

This `USceneComponent` will act as the tracking target for our projectile. Thankfully the `ABMBossCharacter` contains one via inheritance from the `AActor` interface. Now we must simply perform our trace and, upon successful collision, obtain a reference to the `USceneComponent`. Add the following `protected` method to the `ABMCharacter` class definition:

```
void OnTrack();
```

The purpose of this function will be to perform a line trace that begins from the center of the screen and extends outwards into the game world to some specified length. If a boss is found somewhere along this trace, we will use it as the tracking target. Navigate to `BMCharacter.cpp`, we are going to be defining this function via the following code:

```
void ABMCharacter::OnTrack()
{
    FVector MousePos;
    FVector MouseDir;
    FHitResult Hit;
    FCollisionObjectQueryParams ObjectQueryParams;
    ObjectQueryParams.AddObjectTypesToQuery(ECC_GameTraceChannel2);

    APlayerController* playerController =
    Cast<APlayerController>(GetController());
```

Here we are simply declaring the variables we will be using for the trace logic. The line trace call we will be making is very similar to that of the sphere sweep test we performed in the previous chapter during the agro check C++ service. We have declared two vectors, `MousePos` and `MouseDir`, to hold the origin and direction of the line trace in world space. We have also declared the `FHitResult Hit` to save the output of the line trace function.

The final object we declared is a `FCollisionObjectQueryParams` object that will be used to specify the collision query details of this line trace. Via the constructor for this object we specify to look for objects that are of type `ECC_GameTraceChannel2`. As we are using an additional custom object channel, we must look for `ECC_GameTraceChannel2` instead of the `ECC_GameTraceChannel1` we used in the previous chapter. The last thing we do is get a handle to our player controller so that we may call functions that project screen space positions into world space.

Beneath this code, add the following:

```
    if (GEngine->GameViewport != nullptr && playerController !=
    nullptr)
    {
        FVector2D ScreenPos = GEngine->GameViewport->Viewport-
        >GetSizeXY();

        playerController->DeprojectScreenPositionToWorld(ScreenPos.X /
        2.0f,
                            ScreenPos.Y / 2.0f,
        MousePos,
```

```
MouseDir);
    MouseDir *= 100000.0f;

    GetWorld()->LineTraceSingleByObjectType(Hit, MousePos, MouseDir,
    ObjectQueryParams);
```

Here we are ensuring that a valid game viewport has been set and that the player controller handle we populated earlier is valid. With these handles we are going to be populating the `MouseDir` and `MousePos` vectors.

We use the `GameViewport` handle to get the current screen dimensions and assign them to the `ScreenPos` 2D vector. We can then use the player controller to de-project this 2D screen space position to provide us with a world space point and direction. This is done via the `DeprojectScreenPositionToWorld()` method. This method takes in an `X` and `Y` value to use for the screen space point, and references to vectors that are to be populated with the 3D point and direction.

Here we have passed `mousePos` and `mouseDir` to the function to be populated. For the screen space position values, we have provided the halved components of the `ScreenPos` `FVector2D` we populated earlier. This will project the center of the screen into world space with regards to the current position and angle of the game camera.

This function will return `false` if the point could not be determined. It would be good practice to check the result of this de-projection but I have omitted this check for code brevity. We then scale the `mouseDir` vector by a very large amount to ensure that the line trace we perform reaches far into the game scene.

Next we perform the actual line trace via `LineTraceSingleByObjectType()`. This method takes in a `FHitResult` struct to save the results of the trace, a start position and direction for the trace, and a `FCollisionObjectQueryParams` to specify the parameters of the trace. We pass `Hit` to this function to be populated with the results of the trace, `MousePos` and `MouseDir` as the start and direction of the trace, and `ObjectQueryParams` to ensure we only search for objects that are part of `ECC_GameTraceChannel2`. Underneath this, add the following code:

```
if (Hit.bBlockingHit)
{
    UE_LOG(LogTemp, Warning, TEXT("TRACE HIT WITH %s"), *(Hit.
    GetActor()->GetName()));

    TrackingSceneComponent = Cast<USceneComponent>(Hit.GetActor()->
    GetComponentByClass(USceneComponent::StaticClass()));

}
else
```

```
{
UE_LOG(LogTemp, Warning, TEXT("No Trace"));
TrackingSceneComponent = nullptr;
}
} <-- closing If(GEngine->GameViewport != nullptr...)
} <-- closing OnTrack()
```

Here we are checking the result of the trace. If a blocking hit was found, it means our trace has successfully picked up a boss! Here I am logging that our trace succeeded via the UE_LOG macro, this macro can be used to log to the output window from anywhere. I then retrieve the USceneComponent from the hit actor and assign it to TrackingSceneComponent. If the trace fails, I log that no trace was found and set TrackingSceneComponent to nullptr. This means we can also untrack by purposefully missing a track.

Before we get on to preparing the projectile, let's make sure we bind the Track input action we created in the previous chapter to the OnTrack() method we just made by adding the following code to the SetupPlayerInputComponent() method:

```
InputComponent->BindAction("Track", IE_Pressed, this,
&ABMCharacter::OnTrack);
```

Preparing the projectile

Ok, now that we have our scene component to track to, let's set up the projectile so that it is ready to act as a homing missile. Let's start by exposing the ProjectileMovementComponent via adding the following code to the BMProjectile class definition found in BMProjectile.h:

```
FORCEINLINE class UProjectileMovementComponent*
GetProjectileMovement() const { return ProjMovement; }
```

This function acts as a quick accessor method for the ProjectileMovementComponent. This function has been specified with the FORCELINE macro to ensure that this function is inlined regardless of compiler heuristics. Now we can add a couple of settings to the constructor for this object so that the projectile movement component acts as a tracking projectile. Add the following code to ABMProjectile::ABMProjectile() where we are setting up the ProjMovement component:

```
ProjMovement->bIsHomingProjectile = true;
ProjMovement->HomingAccelerationMagnitude = 10000.0f;
```

This simply sets the projectile to act as a homing projectile and ensures that the tracking acceleration is very large to ensure the projectile tracks drastically within a short flight time. Feel free to adjust that value to your liking. With these settings in place, all we need to do is assign the scene component we want the projectile to track to. Navigate back to `BMCharacter.cpp` and add the following code to the `OnFire()` method:

```
ABMProjectile* ThisProjectile = GetWorld()->
  SpawnActor<ABMProjectile>(ProjectileClass, ProjSpawn->
  GetComponentLocation(), GetControlRotation());


ThisProjectile->GetProjectileMovement()->HomingTargetComponent =
TrackingSceneComponent;
```

This simply modifies our previous functionality to obtain a handle to the created projectile so we can assign `TrackingSceneComponent` as the `HomingTargetComponent` via the `GetProjectileMovement()` accessor we made earlier. Ensure this new code has replaced the old spawn logic.

Creating the custom channel and testing the tracking!

The last thing we need to do is create the custom object collision channel and assign it to our boss object. Do this now by navigating to the **Collision section** of the **Project Settings** and adding another Object channel via the **New Object Channel...** button. This time call it `BMBoss`. You should see something similar to this:

Name	Default Response
BMCharacter	Block
BMBoss	Block

Now navigate to the `FPBossCharacter` Blueprint and select the **Capsule Component** from the components panel. With this selected, address the **Details** panel under the collision section, set the **Collision Presets** to **Custom...**, and ensure the setting matches the following:

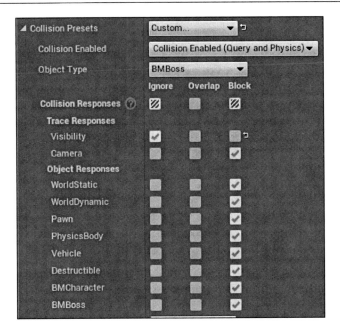

We are done! That was easy. Now all you need to do is compile the code and right-click when the boss is in the center of the screen, and then let some projectiles fly! You should see the following output upon a successful trace:

```
[2016.03.16-10.05.00:007][309]LogTemp:Warning: TRACE HIT WITH
FPBossCharacter_3
```

You will also see that, with the boss tracked, the projectiles will home towards it no matter where you are looking!

Expanded AI

Ok, now it is time to retrofit the AI on our boss so that we update the behavior. We need the boss to exist in three states. The first will be the state we have already created for it, idle and tracking. The next will have the boss stop tracking the player and begin to act like a turret, looking at the FPCharacter the whole time while firing a salvo of tracking projectiles. The last state will have the boss randomly path around the player within the NavMesh area, also while firing projectiles.

To do this we are going to have to do the following:

- Add Health to BMBossCharacter and explore UE4's damage system so the player projectiles do damage to the boss
- Add an EBossState enum so that we may gauge what AI state the boss is in based on its current hit points
- Modify the ABMAIController to include functionality for looking at the player and firing missiles at the player
- Update the BossBT to support the three behaviors mentioned previously

Damage in UE4

Let's start by explaining the health and the ability to take damage to ABMBossCharacter. Remember how we modified the ABMBossCharacter class definition to match the following:

```
public:
    // Sets default values for this character's properties
    ABMBossCharacter();

    virtual float TakeDamage(float Damage, struct FDamageEvent const&
    DamageEvent, AController* EventInstigator, AActor* DamageCauser)
    override;

    UFUNCTION(BlueprintPure, Category = AI)
    const float GetHealth();

    UPROPERTY(EditAnywhere, Category = Pawn)
    class UBehaviorTree* BehaviourTree;

private:

    UPROPERTY()
    float Health;

};
```

Here we have added a virtual `TakeDamage()` method that is inherited from the `AActor` interface. This function takes in a damage amount, a `FDamageEvent struct` that details the damage event, a Controller object that will be the instigator of the damage event, and a handle to the actor that caused the damage. It is with this function we will be transferring damage from collided bullets to the boss. We also added a private `Health` property and an accessor method for the health. The accessor method `GetHealth()` has been specified as `BlueprintPure` so we may retrieve the variable in blueprint without having to provide an execution path to the function.

Now navigate to the `BMBossCharacter.cpp` and add the following code to the constructor:

```
Health = 100.0f;
```

This simply ensures the boss always starts with 100 health. Now add the following definition for the `TakeDamage()` method:

```
float ABMBossCharacter::TakeDamage(float Damage, struct FDamageEvent
const& DamageEvent, AController* EventInstigator, AActor*
DamageCauser)
{
    Super::TakeDamage(Damage, DamageEvent, EventInstigator,
    DamageCauser);

    Health -= Damage;

    return Damage;
}
```

This function is very simple, all it does is take the damage amount that is parsed to the function and subtracts that from the health pool. The last thing we need to do is add the accessor method for the health:

```
const float ABMBossCharacter::GetHealth()
{
    return Health;
}
```

Alright! Now we can send some damage to our boss's character. Let's do this via the collision function we created in the `BMProjectile` in the last chapter. Navigate to the `BMProjectile.cpp` and add the following code to the `OnHit()` method above our previous functionality:

```
if (OtherActor->GetClass()->
    IsChildOf(ABMBossCharacter::StaticClass()))
{
    FDamageEvent DamageEvent(UDamageType::StaticClass());
```

```
        OtherActor->TakeDamage(10.0f, DamageEvent, GetWorld()->
        GetFirstPlayerController(), this);
    }
```

You will need to add `#include "BMBossCharacter.h"` to the include list as well.

Here we check that the object the bullet has collided with is a child of `ABMBossCharacter`. If so, we then create a damage event that is based off of the `UDamageType` class. We then call `TakeDamage` on the other actor. Given that we just overrode that function in `ABMBossCharacter`, we can guarantee that our custom `TakeDamage()` functionality will be called. To this method we pass 10.0f as the damage amount, the damage event we just created, the first player controller as the instigator, and a handle to the projectile itself as the damage causer. I would strongly suggest looking at the parameters of the `FDamageEvent` struct so that you may familiarize yourself with the amount of information you can parse within a damage event.

Ok, now our boss will be taking damage! The next thing we need to do is create an `enum` that will represent the boss's current state and update that `enum` depending on the boss's current health. We do this so we can make decisions in the `BossBT` based off of the value of the `enum`.

Boss state and enums in blackboard!

Now we can create the `enum` that we will use to gauge the state of our boss from blackboard. Navigate to `BMAIController.h` now. Above the class definition, add the following code:

```
UENUM(BlueprintType)
enum class EBossState : uint8
{
    BS_FOLLOW = 0 UMETA(DisplayName = "Follow"),
    BS_TURRET = 1 UMETA(DisplayName = "Turret"),
    BS_FINAL = 2 UMETA(DisplayName = "Final")
};
```

This is creating a strongly typed `enum` class. A typed `enum` class simply means that the `enum` can only occupy the size specified by the type, in this case 8bits. We have used the `UENUM` macro to specify this `enum` as a `BlueprintType`, meaning that this `enum` will be picked up by the UBT and usable in our blueprints. We have created three states here, `BS_FOLLOW`, `BS_TURRET`, and `BS_FINAL`. We have used the `UMETA` macro to specify the display name for each of these states. The display name will be how we see the `enum` values in Blueprint.

Next we need to add a few things to the BMAIController class definition. First, add the following public method:

```
virtual void Tick(float DeltaTime) override;
```

We will use this to specify our own custom tick functionality. Next, add the following private members:

```
class ABMBossCharacter* ControlledChar;
FBlackboard::FKey BossStateBlackboardKey;
```

The first is a reference to the boss's character that is being controlled by this AI controller. The second is an object we can use to hold blackboard key IDs so we may access blackboard keys from C++.

Now we can add code to the .cpp that will update the blackboard key with the right state. First though, we need to add the following to the .h include list:

```
#include "BehaviorTree/Blackboard/BlackboardKeyAllTypes.h"
```

The object information contained within this header file will let us set the key value properly. Navigate to BMAIController.cpp now. Modify the OnPosses() function definition to match the following:

```
ControlledChar = Cast<ABMBossCharacter>(InPawn);

if (InPawn != nullptr)
{
    BlackboardComp->InitializeBlackboard(*(ControlledChar->
    BehaviourTree->BlackboardAsset));

    BehaviourTreeComp->StartTree(*(ControlledChar-
    >BehaviourTree));

    BossStateBlackboardKey = BlackboardComp-
    >GetKeyID("BossState");
}
```

Here we are populating the ControlledChar handle we made earlier and then populating the blackboard key ID we just declared using the GetKeyID method of the blackboard component. This method takes in a string name of the key we wish to retrieve the ID from. Here we have passed BossState, which is a key name we have yet to create. We will later populate a blackboard key of the appropriate type with this name. Next we define the Tick method as follows:

```
void ABMAIController::Tick(float DeltaTime)
{
```

```
        EBossState bossState;

        if (ControlledChar->GetHealth() > 66.0f)
        {
            bossState = EBossState::BS_FOLLOW;
        }
        else if (ControlledChar->GetHealth() > 33.0f)
        {
            bossState = EBossState::BS_TURRET;
        }
        else
        {
            bossState = EBossState::BS_FINAL;
        }

    BlackboardComp-> SetValue<UBlackboardKeyType_
    Enum>(BossStateBlackboardKey, (uint8)bossState)
    }
```

For now, all our tick function is doing is checking the current health value of the controlled boss's character and then ensuring that we set the boss state blackboard key to the correct enumerated value. As you can see, we are using the blackboard key we created earlier and casting the `bossState` variable to a `uint8` and setting it via the `SetValue` template function. We can make this conversion safely as we typed the `EBossState` class `enum` to be of `uint8`. We are using `UBlackboardKeyType_Enum` as the type for the template, this ensures that the value is set appropriately. This method of setting and getting variables from blackboard with C++ is a more efficient alternative than the string method we used in the `BMAgroCheck` service in the previous chapter.

Interpreting our C++ enum in Blackboard

Now that we have implemented our damage and boss state logic in C++, we now need to prepare our Behavior Tree and Blackboard to utilize the `EBossState` enum. Unfortunately, our blackboard will not know of our C++ side `enum` type. Thankfully one of the properties exposed to use for blackboard keys that are of the enum type can handle this for us.

Open `BossBB` and press `NewKey`. Call this key `BossState` and set its type to be `enum`, then address the **Blackboard Details** panel. We need to change the type of this `enum` to be that of the `EBossState`. We can do this by typing the code side name of our enum into the **Enum** name property. Set this to `EBossState` now. The panel should appear as follows:

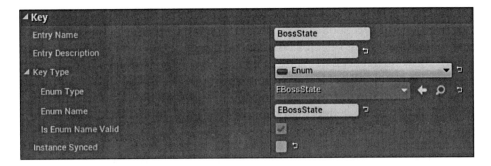

With this in place, the code we wrote in ABMAIController, which set the value of this blackboard key to be that of the appropriate EBossState, will function as intended and we will be able to affect behavior tree decisions.

Modifying the BossBT to support Boss States

Now that we have our boss state enum established, let's work with the BossBT to begin creating the framework for our different boss behaviors. Open the BossBT now. We are going to modifying our tree so that the first node in the tree, after the root, is a selector node. This node will act as the gate that will determine which set of BT functionality is executed based off of the current BossState value. From this node, connect one path to the selector we made in the last chapter for following and patrolling. Then create two more selector nodes and connect those to the first selector node. You should see something similar to this:

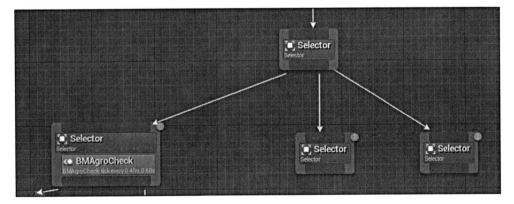

Each of the child selectors will be used to drive the behavior for the three AI states. First we need to add Blackboard type decorators to the child selectors so that we can ensure that the parent selector will choose the right behavior set. Blackboard decorators allow us to check the state of a blackboard key to determine whether a node will succeed, and thus be chosen for execution. Do this by right-clicking a node, selecting **Add Decorator...** from the dropdown, and searching for/selecting the **Blackboard** option. Ensure that the properties for these three blackboard decorators appears as follows:

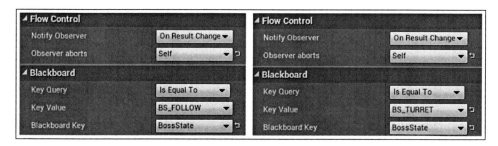

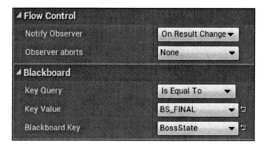

The selectors in your graph should appear as follows:

As you can see, we are starting to form the BT structure for our boss state-based behavior. With the current setup, the tracking and patrolling behavior will only happen if the blackboard key `BossState` is set to `BS_FOLLOW`, the middle behavior when the `BossState` is `BS_TURRET`, and the right-hand behavior when `BossState` is `BS_FINAL`. Before we begin to create the functionality and nodes for our next two behaviors, let's quickly ensure that our current setup will work by debugging our `BossBT`!

Debugging BossBT to check Blackboard values

With the `BossBT` open in one window and the level editor open in another. Run the project by pressing the **Play** button. While the game is running, navigate back to the `BossBT` window and address the **Toolbar** panel. There will be a dropdown button that reads **No Debug Object Selected**. It is with this dropdown you can select an in-game AI controller to debug so that you may see the current state of that controller's behavior tree and blackboard variables. From this dropdown select `BMAIController_0` (it may be `BMAIController_#` where # is the number of times you have run the project since compilation).

Now run into the boss's area of detection with the `BossBT` editor window in sight and you will see certain nodes in the behavior tree go yellow and their connecting paths pulse! This shows the nodes that are currently firing within the tree. You will see something similar to this:

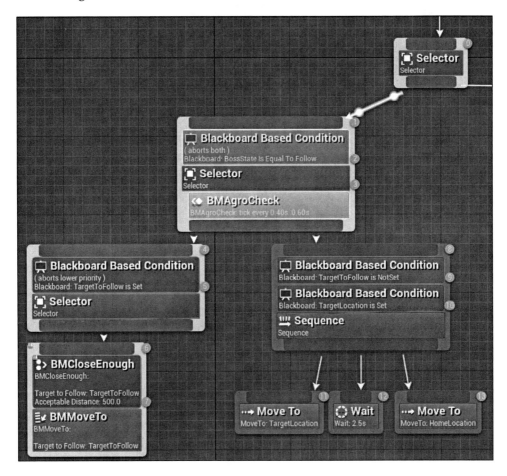

You will also notice that the blackboard panel has also updated with the current variable states of each key. This is a very powerful feature for AI debugging. While looking at this panel, shoot the boss multiple times and, as the boss's health decreases, the state of `BossState` will change! The blackboard panel should appear as follows after you have shot the boss four times:

Upgrading the ABMIController

We can now finish implementing `ABMAIController`. We are going to be adding functionality that will rotate the boss to always look towards its current target and provide the ability to fire salvos of missiles at the player. We could create these as services or tasks to be used in behavior trees but this functionality will be very specific to the `BossAI`, therefore we are including it in the `ABMAIController`.

Tracking to the player

Navigate to `BMAIController.h` now. We are going to be adding two new methods for tracking and two new members that will be used during the tracking logic. Add the following `public` methods to the class definition:

```
UFUNCTION(BlueprintCallable, Category = Behaviour)
void TrackToTarget();

UFUNCTION(BlueprintCallable, Category = Behaviour)
void StopTrack();
```

The previous methods have both been declared as `BlueprintCallable` so that we can call them from blueprint-based tasks. Now add the following `private` members:

```
FBlackboard::FKey TargetBlackboardKey;
class ABMCharacter* Target;
bool bIsTracking;
```

Here we have declared a blackboard key ID that we will use to retrieve the `TargetToFollow` blackboard variable. We also declared an `ABMCharacter` handle that we will use to save the tracking target, and a Boolean flag that we will be checking against to see whether we wish the boss to rotate towards the target.

These variables will be utilized so that we can inform the ABMAIController to start tracking and it will handle all tracking logic internally via its own tick method. This saves us from having to call a service at a given frequency from the BossBT. Now navigate to BMAIController.cpp. As we just prototyped the ABMCharacter object, add #include "BMCharacter.h" to the include list at the top of the .cpp.

The first thing we need to do is retrieve the key ID for our target. Add the following to the Possess() method underneath where we retrieve the BossState key:

```
TargetBlackboardKey = BlackboardComp->GetKeyID("TargetToFollow");
```

Next we need to modify the Tick() method so that it supports tracking. Underneath where we determine and set the boss state, add the following code:

```
if (bIsTracking && Target != nullptr)
{
    FVector CharLoc = ControlledChar->GetActorLocation();

    FVector dirToTarget = Target->GetActorLocation() - CharLoc;
    FRotator rotToTarget = dirToTarget.Rotation();

    ControlledChar->SetActorRotation(FMath::Lerp(ControlledChar->
    GetActorRotation(), rotToTarget, DeltaTime * 5));
}
```

Here we are simply checking that we both have a target to track and that we wish the AI to track. We then get a vector between the boss and the target, then based off of this vector we create a rotator. We then use FMath::Lerp() to interpolate between this desired rotator and that of the current rotator of the ControlledChar. FMath::Lerp() takes in a current FRotator, a desired FRotator, and an interpolation value. For the lerp value we have specified five times the delta tick. You may have noticed that this is an override of the lerp function that we used in Bounty Dash. Lastly, we need to provide definitions for the TrackToTarget() and StopTrack() methods, they appear as follows:

```
void ABMAIController::TrackToTarget()
{
    Target = Cast<ABMCharacter>(BlackboardComp->
    GetValue<UBlackboardKeyType_Object>(TargetBlackboardKey));

    if (Target != nullptr)
    {
        bIsTracking = true;
    }
```

```
    }

    void ABMAIController::StopTrack()
    {
        bIsTracking = false;
        Target = nullptr;
    }
```

In the `TrackToTarget()` method we are retrieving the `Target` via the templated `GetValue()` method. Unlike earlier when we set the boss state key, we are using `UBlackboardKeyType_Object` as the template type, this ensures that the `GetValue()` method returns the appropriate type. We then cast the return of this function to an `ABMCharacter` handle so we can use it for tracking. We do a quick sanity check to ensure the target is valid then set the `bIsTracking` flag to `true`. `StopTrack()` simply sets the flag to false and the target handle to `nullptr`.

Before we can test this functionality we have to inform the AI controller when to start and stop tracking. We can do this in the `BMAgroCheck` C++ service we created in the previous chapter. Navigate to `BMAgroCheck.cpp` now and the find the code where we assign values to the blackboard if the sweep test was successful. Once there, add `ThisController->TrackToTarget();` to the true scope of `if(bResult)`, and `ThisController->StopTrack();` to the false/else scope.

Testing what we have so far

Ok, now let's test what have put in so far. Upon entering the boss's agro check radius, the AI should start to follow the player and constantly look towards the player's location. If we leave the agro radius it should start its patrolling and stop looking towards the player. Alternatively, because of the adjustments we made to the `BossBT` with regards to boss state, if we are to damage the boss to the point that its state swaps into `BS_TURRET`, it will stop tracking to the player but it will continue to look at the player. Compile the code and run the project now to ensure this is the case. If everything goes well, the boss should be staring right at you!

Arming the boss

Now that we have our tracking functionality in place, we can arm the boss with a salvo of missiles. We will be using the same projectile objects that we use for our player. But this time we don't want just one rocket to fire, we want five rockets to fire. We wish for each of the five rockets to spawn above the boss, like so:

To do this we are going to have to do some quick sphere mathematics to figure out the launch position of each bullet. Navigate to the BMAIController.h and add the following public method to the class definition:

```
UFUNCTION(BlueprintCallable, Category = Behaviour)
void FireMissles();
```

We will call this method from a blueprint side service when it is time for the boss to fire missiles. Navigate to the `BMAIController.cpp` now, we are going add the following code as the definition for this method:

```
void ABMAIController::FireMissles()
{
    if(Target)
    {
        // Find Launch points (5)
        for (int i = 1; i <= 5; ++i)
        {
            float fAngle = 16 + i * 26;
            FVector circlePoint;
            circlePoint.Y = (FMath::Cos(PI / 2) *
            FMath::Sin((fAngle * PI / 180.0f)));

            circlePoint.Z = (FMath::Sin(PI / 2) *
            FMath::Sin((fAngle * PI / 180.0f)));

            circlePoint.X = (FMath::Cos((fAngle * PI / 180.0f)));
```

Here we find five launch points. We do this by setting up a for loop as an iteration structure that will iterate five times. Each iteration we are finding a point on a unit sphere by utilizing the basic formula:

- $x = r * cos(s) * sin(t)$
- $y = r * sin(s) * sin(t)$
- $z = r * cos(t)$

Where r is the *radius* of the sphere, s is the *angle*, and t is the *height angle* measured down from the z axis. These angles all have to be in radians, thus we have done so by multiplying our angle in degrees by *PI / 180.0f*. For our angle, we have specified for it to be *16 + i * 26*. This is so that our missiles are spaced *26* degrees apart, starting 16 degrees off axis. The result will be five unique points that are of unit length (as we have not specified a radius, thus assuming a radius of 1.0f) from origin. This is important as it means we can translate and scale these points according to the current world position and rotation of the controlled AI character. Underneath this code, add the following:

```
FRotator charRot = ControlledChar->GetActorRotation();
charRot.Yaw = charRot.Yaw + 90.0f;
circlePoint = charRot.RotateVector(circlePoint);
```

This ensures the unit vector we have found is rotated so that the fan of all five points will be so that they are facing the player, as seen in the previous image of the boss firing. Following this, add:

```
FVector SpawnLoc = ControlledChar->GetActorLocation() + circlePoint *
180.0f;
ABMProjectile* pThisProj = GetWorld()->
        SpawnActor<ABMProjectile>(Target->
ProjectileClass,
SpawnLoc,
ControlledChar->GetActorRotation());

pThisProj->GetProjectileMovement()->HomingTargetComponent =
Cast<USceneComponent>(Target->
GetComponentByClass(USceneComponent::StaticClass()));
} <-- closing if(Target)
} <-- closing for(int i = 1; i < 5; ++i)
} <-- closing FireMissles()
```

The first line simply translates and scales the unit vector we found via our point on sphere calculation, so that the final 3D spawn location of the projectile is updated with that of our boss. Next we spawn a boss mode projectile at this location and then we set the tracking target of the projectile to be that of `Target` inherits `USceneComponent`.

Adding the Turret boss state

Navigate back to the project content browser and open the `BossBT` we are going to be adding the nodes for our second boss state. Start by creating a new task by clicking the **New Task** button. Choose `BTTask_BlueprintBase` from the dropdown as the base class. Be sure to rename this task in the content browser to `FireMissiles`. Add the following nodes to the event graph of this task:

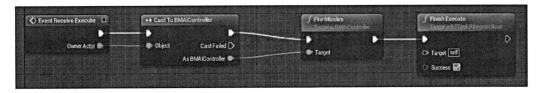

Here we have summoned the Event `ReceiveExecute` node in the same way we did in the previous chapter. We then cast the input from this node to be of type `BMAIController` from this cast, we then call the `FireMissiles()` method we made earlier. We finish the node graph by calling `FinishExectute()` and reporting a successful execution.

With this task in place we can now create the node structure for the Turret boss state. Navigate back to the BossBT. Under the child selector we created with the Blackboard decorator waiting for BS_TURRET, summon two task nodes, the first is FireMissiles the blueprint task we just created, and the second is **Move To**. Ensure the **Move To** target is set to be the HomeLocation blackboard key. The first will call the FireMissiles method we just created, the second will ensure that the boss stops any previous move commands. To finish this behavior, we need to add a Cooldown decorator to the FireMissiles task. Do this now by right-clicking the FireMissiles node and selecting **Cooldown** from the decorator list. In the **Details** panel for this decorator, set the **Cool Down Time** property to be three seconds. Cooldown decorators only allow a node to succeeded once the cooldown time has passed since last execution. This will ensure that the boss only fires missiles every three seconds. Once you are done, this node section should appear as follows:

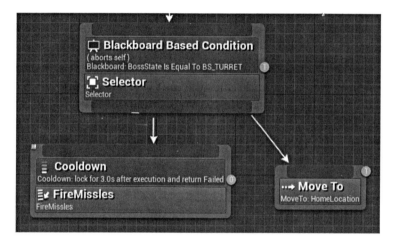

Nice! We are done adding the functionality for this behavior state. Run the project and damage the boss until it enters the BS_TURRET state. You will notice that the boss will stop moving towards you and will immediately start firing projectiles at you!

The Final Behaviour State

We are nearly done with the BossBT! We have one more state to add, the final state. This state will see the boss's fire rate increase as well as have the boss randomly patrol around the navigation area while firing continuously at the target. This will take some simple nodes and a new task that we can create, this time in C++!

BMRandomMoveTo

We will start by creating the C++ BT Task. The purpose of this task is to have the AI path to a random point within the `NavMesh` area constrained to a given radius. Open the class wizard and create a new class called `BMRandomMoveTo` that inherits from `BTTaskNode`. Once the code generation is finished, navigate to `BMRandomMoveTo.h` and modify the class definition to match this:

```
UCLASS()
class BOSSMODE_API UBMRandomMoveTo : public UBTTaskNode
{
    GENERATED_BODY()

    virtual EBTNodeResult::Type ExecuteTask(UBehaviorTreeComponent&
    OwnerComp, uint8* NodeMemory);

private:
    UBehaviorTree* ThisTree;
    class ABMAIController* ThisController;

};
```

This definition is very simple, we are virtually overriding the `ExecuteTask()` method that takes in a `UBehaviorTreeComponent` reference and `unit8` pointer to the node memory. It is important to note that the return type for this method is `EBTNodeResult`. It is with this return type that we will report the success or failure of the task. You will also note that we have added two `private` members, one is a handle to the behavior tree and the other is a handle to the AI controller. Now navigate to `BMRandomMoveTo.cpp` and add the following definition for the `ExecuteTask()` function we are overriding:

```
EBTNodeResult::Type
UBMRandomMoveTo::ExecuteTask(UBehaviorTreeComponent& OwnerComp, uint8*
NodeMemory)
{
    if (ThisTree == nullptr || ThisController == nullptr)
    {
        ThisTree = OwnerComp.GetCurrentTree();

        ThisController =
        Cast<ABMAIController>(OwnerComp.GetAIOwner());

            if (ThisTree == nullptr || ThisController == nullptr)
        {
```

```
                        UE_LOG(LogTemp, Warning, TEXT("Task assigned to
                        incorrect AI type"));

                            return EBTNodeResult::Failed;
                    }
            }
```

Here we are simply checking the states of our handles and populating them with the relevant objects. If the handles are unable to be retrieved, it means this task was included in a behavior tree that is owned by the wrong type of AI controller. If this is the case, we log a warning and return a failed node result status from the function. Next add:

```
            FNavLocation RandomPoint;
            if (GetWorld()->GetNavigationSystem()->
                GetRandomPointInNavigableRadius(ThisController->GetPawn()->
                GetActorLocation(), 5000.0f, RandomPoint))
            {
                ThisController->MoveTo(RandomPoint.Location);
                return EBTNodeResult::Succeeded;
            }

            return EBTNodeResult::Failed;
        }
```

Here we are querying the navigation system for a random point within a radius within the NavMesh area. We are doing this by calling GetRandomPointInNavigableRadius(). This function takes in an origin location, a radius to search within, and a FNavLocation object that will be populated with the results of the function. We have parsed the location of the boss a radius of 5000 and a temporary FNavLocation object we created previously. If a point is successfully obtained, the function will return true. We check the result of this function, if it resolves to be true, we tell the AI to move to the generated point and report a success. If not, we report a failure.

As we prototyped the ABMAIController class in the .h file for this object, ensure you add #include "BMAIController.h" to include list of .cpp at the top of the file.

Finishing the BossBT

We are so close to finishing the boss AI, all we have to do now is create the node setup for the BS_FINAL state. Open the BossBT now. Under the last childless selector node, summon the FireMissiles task and the BMRandomMoveTo task we just created. Add Cooldown decorators to both. To the FireMissiles decorator, set the cooldown time to be 1.5 seconds and, for the BMRandomMoveTo, set it to 3 seconds. This will double the rate of fire for the boss and have it patrol around the map. This means the player will have to keep up with the boss while dodging its bullets and firing back all at the same time! This section of BossBT should appear as follows:

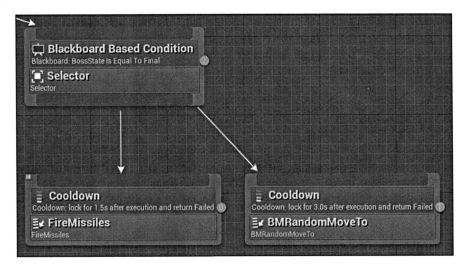

AI Complete

Nice! We are done with the boss AI! Going forward, feel free to tweak the various values in the CharacterMovementComponent of the FPBossCharacter Blueprint to manipulate how the AI moves. You don't have to stop here though! You can keep growing the boss into a complicated compelling boss fight. However, I think it is time we put down AI and start talking about rendering!

Rendering in UE4

Rendering when used in video games terms means the drawing of the various elements within a scene to produce a final image that is the game in its current visual state. We do this every frame, hopefully at 60 frames per second, to create smooth and immersive game worlds within which players can engage and explore. Unreal Engine 4 features one of the most robust and modern rendering engines that can be found in today's game development platforms. The rendering system is an all-new, DirectX 11 pipeline that includes deferred shading, global illumination, and many more interesting features.

It is with this rendering engine that you can tap into the powerhouse of Unreal and create game titles with visuals at the highest end of quality and technology. The next section of this chapter will detail how we can tap into the Unreal Engine rendering systems with ease and usability via the UE4 material system.

UE4 Materials

Alright! Let's start exploring the `visual material system` provided in UE4 that affords us the ability to create amazing and interesting rendering techniques without writing a **single line of code**! By the end of this chapter we will have created two materials that we will apply to the boss so that it looks like a sinister robotic powerhouse.

What are materials

UE4 materials are a visual node-based scripting system that is used to create rendering techniques to be applied to object surfaces. This system massively simplifies the process of developing visually impressive and complex shaders by removing the barrier to entry that is low-level shader programming! However if you wish to add to the systems vast feature set and shader library, the system is also extensible by allowing developers to write their own material expressions via shaders if need be.

Each node in a material graph represents a piece of shading code in some manner, they are known as material expressions. This means that as you increase the number of nodes in a material, the number of shaders required for compilation increases. Therefore, when creating materials in UE4 you have balance efficiency and visual output.

We are going to be leveraging this system to create two materials. One for the boss's outer shell and one for the boss's inner shell. By the end of this chapter you will be comfortable creating basic and intermediate-level materials. We will be working with masks, emissive coloring, color animation as a function of time, and normal maps.

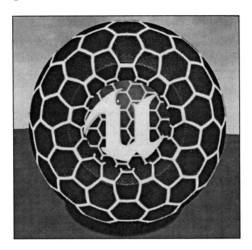

Physically Based Rendering

UE4 materials support **Physically Based Rendering** (PBR) for short. This is a new rendering technique within the games industry. Traditionally, when rendering objects, you would describe the lighting detail of the object specifically, per object. As in, this object is this color, this texture, and has this light affecting it. This is a very costly way to render complicated techniques. PBR is a technique where instead of describing the materials lighting and texture properties in detail, we will instead describe the material in a physical sense. If this confuses you, think of it this way. We are now informing the rendering system of how this material appears without any consideration of light or environment.

For example, if I were to describe concrete, I would say it is a rough, matt material that is not shiny at all. So if I were to create an object that requires a concrete material, I would inform the engine of the same information. Unreal Engine's rendering system is set up so that we can describe materials in this way, and its robust deferred shading model will handle rendering the material given different lighting and environmental factors.

The Material editor

Ok, let's create our first material and have a look at the material editor! This editor is fairly unique as there is still a graph within which you can plot and connect nodes, but this time there is no execution path. There is simply a large node that takes in multiple inputs for each element of the surface's properties. For every connected element to this final material node, there will be a series of nodes that must be compiled. Navigate to the content browser of your level editor and create a new material by right-clicking and selecting **Material** from the **Basic Assets** list or **Materials & Textures | Material**.

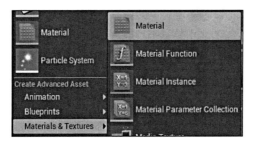

Call this material BossOuterMaterial. This will be the material we use to render the outer shell of the BossMesh. This editor features 6 panels. They are Toolbar, Graph, Viewport, Details, Stats, and Palette.

The Toolbar

The **Toolbar** panel of the material editor boasts 12 buttons that we can use to help with our material development pipeline. They are as follows:

- **Save**: Let's you save the current material.
- **Find in CB:** Allows you to find any texture or asset referenced in the material from within the **Content Browser**.
- **Apply**: Allows you to apply the changes you just made to the current material without saving, this allows you to preview in editor and in viewport, material changes without saving those changes.
- **Search**: Search within the graph for a given node or comment.
- **Home**: Shifts the graph view back to the main material node.
- **Clean Up**: Cleans any unused material expressions from within the graph.
- **Connectors**: Toggleable option that will show or hide any unused connectors (lines between pins).

- **Live Preview**: Toggleable option that when on, will update the viewport with any material changes as they happen. Having this on will enact a runtime cost when adding nodes to the graph, potentially slowing usability of the material editor.

- **Live Nodes**: Toggleable option that when on, will update node previews as the graph is edited, same cost as detailed previously.

- **Live Update**: Toggleable option that sets all nodes to live update as edits are made, same cost as detailed previously.

- **Stats**: Shows the runtime statistics of the material in the **Stats** panel.

- **Mobile Stats**: Shows the runtime statistics of the material if it were run on a mobile in the **Stats** panel.

The Viewport

The **Viewport** in the material editor is used to preview the material that is being created when applied to a preview mesh. The viewport boasts some toggleable options that affect the preview of the material. They appear as follows:

- **Dropdown**: Provides options that show stats such as frame per second and allow adjustments to field of view.

- **Perspective**: Lets you select which perspective you would like to view the preview mesh with.

- **Lit**: Lets you change which channel of the deferred rendering system is being used for the preview. This functions in the same way as the option provided in the **Level Editor** viewport.

- **Show**: Provides toggable options for showing things such as statistics, background, and grid.

The viewport also allows you to change which mesh is being used to preview the material via the following buttons:

The buttons from left to right will change the preview mesh to a cylinder, sphere, plane, box, and custom mesh. The button highlighted is the custom mesh button. To use this option, you must first have a mesh selected in the **Content** browser. Do this now by selecting BossMesh from within the **Content** browser and pressing the teapot button. This will change the Viewport preview mesh to match this:

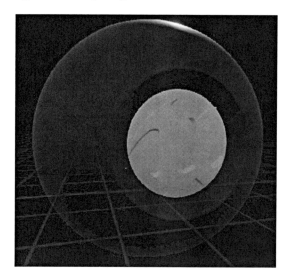

This is very useful for us, as it means we can preview how the material will look when already applied to the boss mesh!

The Graph and Base material node

The **Graph** panel for the material editor is the canvas with which you will create all of your materials. The nodes that we create in this graph are known as material expressions. They are instructions that will be carried out during material execution (usually at runtime). It is with these expressions that we can instruct how the material will behave and drive the output of the technique.

Every material will have some version of the following expression by default, as follows:

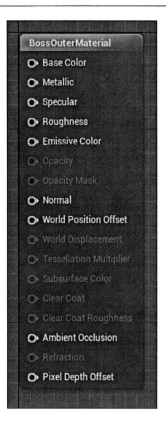

This is the main material expression. It is with this expression that we provide all color/material calculations that drive the material's final appearance. It is important to note that when we provide inputs to this expression, what we are effectively saying is for each pixel of this surface to be drawn, I want these calculations to take place. This means we can have explicit control over each pixel's physical appearance of a given surface, this also means that we can make our materials very expensive, very quickly. Usually these per-pixel calculations require in-depth logics to determine how to color each pixel based off of the inputs we provide. Thankfully the material system automates this process by doing much of the per-pixel calculations automatically behind the scenes for us. All we have to do is provide the correct textures, normal maps, and masks.

Pins within this expression will be disabled and enabled depending on the type of material that we are working with and the blend/shader properties specified in the **Details** panel for this expression. The previous arrangement is for a surface material type with default properties, which is perfect for us as we are trying to render an object surface. As UE4 boasts a PBR-supported material system, each pin provided is an element of the surface's physical properties. The pins are responsible for the following:

- **Basic Color**: The unedited base color of the surface. This is what was known as the diffuse channel for an object. The color provided to this pin should be the color of the surface before lighting and surface properties are considered

- **Metallic**: This parameter effects how metallic the surface will appear when lit. The more metallic a material looks, the more the surface color and reflection will be modified to look more metal-like, imagine a slightly old copper pot. Non-metals have a metallic value of 0 where metals have a metallic value of 1.

- **Specular**: This parameter affects how intensely reflections will shine, however this parameter is considered deprecated and it is recommended to use **roughness** instead and leave this as a default value of 0.5.

- **Roughness**: This parameter literally effects how rough a surface appears. A rougher material will scatter reflected light in more directions than a smooth material. This affects how blurry or sharp a surface's reflection is. Completely smooth is a value of zero where fully mat is a value of one.

- **Emissive Color**: This parameter drives any surface color values that you wish to glow as they will be emitting light. Ideally you would create this effect with a mask texture, the result is a clear glow area. Note that emissive color does not cast light on other objects, nor will shadows be generated.

- **Opacity**: Opacity is used when using a translucent blend mode. This allows you to specify a value that affects how transparent the surface is. Zero being fully transparent and one being fully opaque.

- **Opacity Mask**: Similar to Opacity however an opacity mask does not support any values between zero and one. This means a surface can either be fully transparent or fully opaque. You can set the threshold at which point the material will swap from opaque to transparent, for example 0.6 in the **Details** panel.

- **Normal**: A surface normal is a directional vector that can be used to calculate how any given pixel will be lit based off of the nearest normal. A normal is made up of three floats, therefore a normal can be represented by a color value. Because of this, specialized textures can be made to represent the normal of an object. This is known as a normal map. With this pin you can provide the surface normal map for the object.

- **World Position Offset**: This pin allows you to provide physical offsets for the vertices in world space. This allows us to create techniques that morph and adjust the shape of a rendered mesh.

- **World Displacement**: Works in the same way as world position offset but utilizes tessellation as opposed to the base vertices of the mesh. This allows for more detailed displacements.

- **Tessellation Multiplier**: Controls the amount of tessellation along a surface, allowing more detail to be added when needed. For this and world displacement to work, the tessellation property must be something other than none.

- **Subsurface Color**: This input allows you to add a color to your material to simulate shifts in color when light passes through the surface. Much like when light passes through a human character's ear or nose. For this input to be enabled, the subsurface shading model must be enabled in the material properties via the **Details** panel.

- **Ambient Occlusion**: This pin helps simulate self-shadowing within the crevices of a surface. Generally, this will be connected to a pre-baked AO map.

- **Refraction**: This input takes in a texture or value that simulates the index of refraction of the surface. This is useful for things such as glass and water, which refract light that passes through them.

- **Clear Coat**: The clear coat shading model can be used to simulate multilayer materials that have a thin translucent layer of film over the surface of the material. This is very effective for rendering materials such as acrylic, multi-tone car paint, and oils. Again this setting must be enabled within the properties of the material. Zero will use no clear coat coloring, one will use the full clear coat value.

The Details panel

The **Details** panel that is featured in the material editor is where we can find all of the properties for any given material expression. It is also here that you will be able to select the material properties such as shading, blending, and tessellation models for the material as a whole, if no expression or the main expression node is selected. The default properties for this material are as follows:

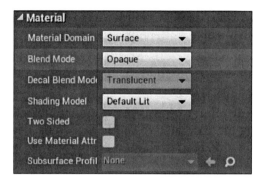

Here we have specified that this is a **Surface** type material using the **Opaque** blend mode with the **Default Lit** Shading Model. If you were to change any of these settings, you would see various pins enable and disable in the main material expression node.

The stats panel

It is with this panel that you can see any diagnostic output for the material. Here we can get output information about the material's current calculation cost, instruction count, and number of texture samples.

The Palette

The palette is one of the most important panels in the material editor, it is here where you can find all of the material expressions that can be used within the graph. The palette functions in the same way as the palette featured in blueprint and allows for the keyword searching of different expressions.

Starting the Boss outer material

Ok, let's start working with the material editor by creating our boss's outer shell! At first we are going to try to achieve something that looks similar to this:

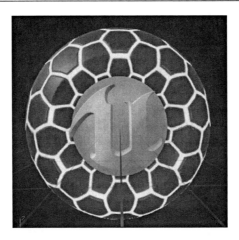

This is simply a material that has a hexagonal emissive pattern, an applied normal map, and a default base color. We will continue to develop this material so that we can achieve the look in the previous picture of the boss. Let's start by summoning our first material expression.

Your first material expression and color channels

Right-click in a blank area of the material graph or use the palette search for the expression `VectorParameter`. This will summon the following node:

This `VectorParameter` expression allows us to create a four float RGBA value that we can use as a color sample within the material. As you can see, there are five available pins. The top-most pin is the output four floats, or the color value as a whole. The other four pins are the different color channels. These pins represent the *Red*, *Green*, *Blue*, and **Alpha** channels in that order. Color channels are a very core concept of rendering theory as we can split maps and masks up into their individual color components. We do this so we can pack more data into one color map. This will become readily apparent when we start to work with masks and other texture types.

With this expression selected, address the **Details** panel. The panel will have updated with the properties of this material expression. Here we can set the default value for the vector parameter, which appears in the form of a color bar. Clicking on this color bar lets us use the Unreal color picker to choose a color for the parameter. Underneath this we have the expressions **Name** and **Group**. These do two things for us. The first is they provide us with a unique and hopefully contextual name we can use for the expression. The second is they allow us to get access to this parameter from blueprint and code. This process will be detailed in the next chapter.

Name this node `BaseColor` now and change the base color to pure white by double-clicking on the `Color Bar` and setting the picker to these values:

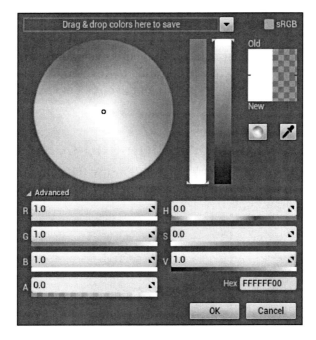

We will be changing this color later so that it looks more visually appropriate, but for now I have chosen white to demonstrate a drastic change from the default base color value of the main material expression node. Now drag a connection from the top-most pin on the `BaseColor` node and connect it to the `BossOuterMaterial` expression, like so:

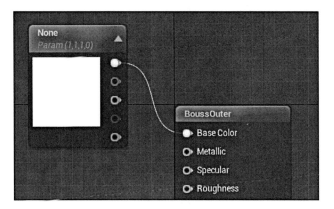

You will have noticed that the preview mesh within the viewport will have updated to appear as follows:

Applying a Normal Map and the texture viewer

With our temporary base color applied we can add a normal map to the material. As stated previously, normal maps provide a cheap way to add high amounts of detail to an object's surface. Thankfully all of the maps we will be using in this chapter are provided with the starter content that we created the project with. Summon our next material expression **Texture Sample**. This will summon the following node:

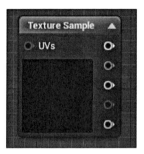

As you can see, this expression looks very similar to that of the **Vector Parameter** expression we created earlier. This expression still boasts the five output pins, one for the whole texture, the other for the channels of the texture, however this node also takes an input pin called **UVs**. UVs are a way for us to inform the material what part of the texture we would like to apply to this given vertex or mesh pixel. UVs are a two float vector, one parameter specifies the x value of the texture and the other the y. Combined, they will point to a specific point within a texture that we will sample for pixel calculations. This will be described in more detail soon, for now, select this node and address the **Details** panel.

Here we can see properties that let us modify the literal sample states for the texture and we can also see it is here where we can specify the texture we wish to use. Click on the dropdown next to the `Texture` property, search for and apply the `T_Tech_Hex_Tile_N` map. This is the normal map we are going to use. With this texture applied, the details panel will update to appear as follows:

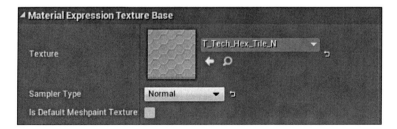

If you double-click on the texture thumbnail it will take you to the UE4 texture editor. This editor lets us edit the various properties of the texture as well as view each channel (RGBA) of the texture independently. We will expand on this later. Navigate back to the material editor. We are about to connect our normal map to the main expression. Connect the top-most output pin of the **Texture Sample** node to the **Normal** input pin of the main material expression, like so:

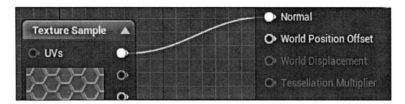

This now means that, for every pixel of the surface, this material expression will provide normal information so that the pixels can be lit properly. This results in a more detailed surface as can be seen in the preview window once the material updates.

Emissive color and masks

Ok, now that we have our base color and our normal map detail, let's work on the glowing hexagonal pattern. Summon another **Texture Sample** node but this time assign the `T_Tech_Hex_Tile_M` texture and open it in the Texture Editor by double-clicking the **Thumbnail**. The texture should appear like this:

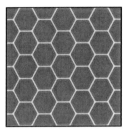

You will also notice a small **View** button in the top left-hand side of the **Viewport** panel of this editor. Clicking this button will show you the various view options available for this texture, like so:

As you can see, all of the color channels are currently ticked. These are toggleable options that allow us to view the various channels in the texture, alone or combined. Each channel for this texture appears as so:

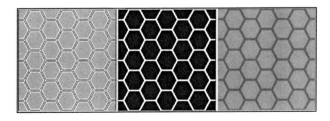

With the Red channel on the left, the Green channel in the middle, and the Blue channel on the right, as you can see, the green channel provides us with a white and black texture, where the regions within the hexagons will have a value of zero and the borders of the hexagons will have a value of one. This is very important, as this channel of this texture will act as the mask for our emissive glow!

In short, what we are going to do is take the color value of this mask and multiply that by a default emissive color. As the value from this mask will either be zero or one, the result of the multiplication will be a full emissive color or no emissive color. When we plug the result of this calculation into the emissive color pin of the main material expression, we will have an emissive glow on the object surface in the form of the pattern shown in the **Green** channel of this mask.

Before we continue, it is important to note that in this texture editor we can change some of the color properties of the mask and texture via the details panel. We can also see some statistics for the texture such as **Size**, **Format**, and **number of mips**. We will not be changing any of these values within the scope of this chapter. Let's set up the expressions for this now. Navigate back to the material editor.

Underneath the **Texture Sample** expression we just created, summon another `VectorParameter`. This time, set the name to be **Emissive Color 01** and set the color picker to these values:

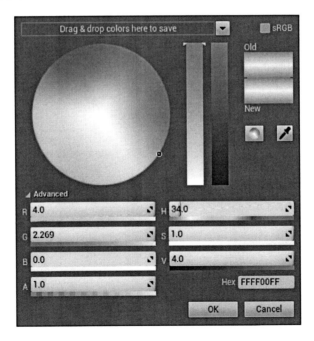

Next, summon a **Multiply** expression. This is a simple node that takes in two pins and outputs one. Plug the Green channel of the `TextureSample` Mask into the **A** pin and the output pin of **Emissive Color 01** node into the **B** pin. Plug the output pin of the multiply node into the **Emissive Color** pin of the final material expression. This will appear like so:

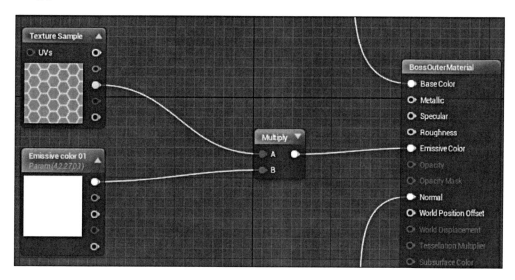

The last thing we need to do is set our `BaseColor` value back to black so that our emissive color really pops. Do this now. Your final graph should look similar to this:

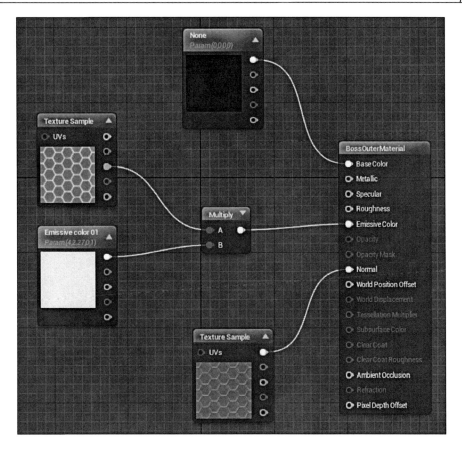

And your material preview should look similar to this (right is with a white base color, left is with black):

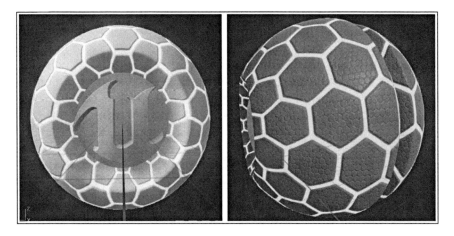

Adding more detail and advanced material use

Now that we have our basic material coloring set up, we can now add detail to the material. We are going to be adding sub detail within each of the hexagons and making our emissive glow pulse as if there was some unknown power contained within our boss. The output we are looking for will appear like this:

As you can see, we have added more detail to the interior of the hexagons. In the previous image I changed the base color to a lighter value so the details would be more obvious.

Texture UV's and adding normals

Ok, to achieve the detail we want, we are going to have to work with our normal maps some more. As mentioned previously, UVs drive how a given pixel is mapped to a mesh. Because of this we can adjust a UV property called **UV tiling**, which will affect how many times that texture repeats on a given surface. For example, with this normal map in question, the image on the left is a map with **UV tiling** set to 1 for both U and V, and the image on the right is a map with **UV tiling** set to **4**, in other words the map on the right will repeat four times in the space, the first will only repeat once:

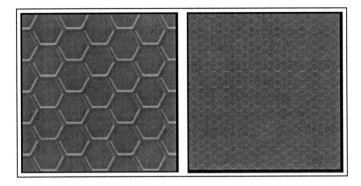

UVs are known by another name as well. Texture coordinates. This is because a UV is also the XY location to look at on a texture. If a UV scale is 1, U (0.5) and V (0.5) will give you the pixel in the very middle of the texture, whereas, U and V values of zero or one will give you the top left-hand and bottom right-hand corners respectively. This means we are able to index any location on a texture via UVs.

What we are going to be doing is taking normals from two different **Texture Samples** of the same normal map, but each with their own UV tiling. We are then going to be blending these together to create the detail effect we desire. The first thing we need to do is disable the emissive glow so we can better see our detail. Do this now so the material appears as so in the preview (note I have rotated the preview mesh for clarity):

Now, navigate to the area of the graph where we sample our normal map. Underneath this, create another **Texture Sample** expression with the same `T_Tech_Hex_Tile_N` texture applied. We are now going to be plugging something into the **UV** pin of this node. Summon a new expression called `TextureCoordinate`. This will summon a small red node called `TexCoord`. With this node selected, address the **Details** panel where you will see the properties of this texture coordinate node. Change the `UTiling` and `VTiling` properties to 8. Then plug the output of this `TexCoord` node into the input pin of the second Texture Sample we just created. So far everything should look like this:

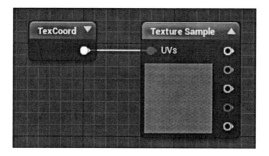

Now, before we blend our two normal maps together, we need to do some more masking operations. That is because if we were to blend our normal maps together now, we would get detail in the areas of our surface where the emissive glow is supposed to be. This would appear like so:

This could lead to some undesirable effects. Unfortunately, unlike our emissive mask, we cannot perform a straight multiply with the zero value of the mask. When working with normal maps (0, 0, 0) is not the color value of flat. We need to use (0, 0, 1) or 1, or on the Blue channel. This is because the RGB values of a color are converted to the XYZ values of a vector. Thus, with 1 in the B channel, we have a normal that is of 1 length in only the Z component, therefore the normal is pointing straight up and no detail will be added. We need to instead interpolate between our desired normal detail and this flat blue value based off of the value held in the mask. This will mean that when the mask value returns zero (inside the hexagon), we will use the full detail normal map, and when it returns 1 (inside the borders), we will use flat blue.

Underneath the **Texture Sample** we just created, summon a new expression. This one is called a `Constant3Vector`. This functions in a very similar way to that of our `VectorParameter` expressions, however these constants are not editable or modifiable from outside of the material editor, thus the name constant. We are also unable to provide these expressions with unique names. Set the color values of this constant in the color picker to appear as follows:

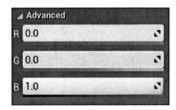

Underneath the `Constant3Vector`, summon another **TextureSample** expression and set the texture to be the mask we used earlier (`T_Tech_Hex_Tile_M`). Then summon another material expression called **Linear Interpolate**. We have used Lerps before in code and blueprint so I will not explain how this node works. However, we will plug the output of the UV tiled **Texture Sample** into **A**, the output of the `Constant3Vector` into **B**, and the Green channel of the mask into **Alpha**. All together it should appear as follows:

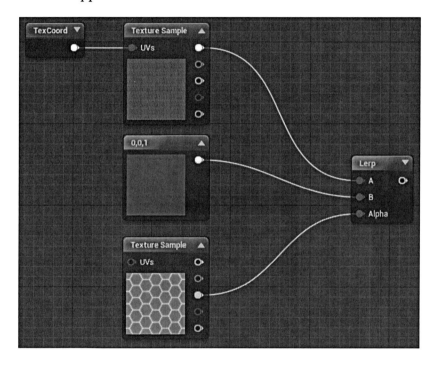

We now need to plug this output value into a special material expression that lets us blend normals together, it is called `BlendAngleCorrectedNormals`. Summon the expression now. This expression corrects the direction of normals that are blended on top of other normal maps. You can see the description of this expression by hovering your mouse over the node in the editor. We are going to be plugging our original untiled normal map sample into **BaseNormal(V3)** and our interpolated normal result into **AdditionalNormal(V3)**. We will then take the output of this node and plug it into the **Normal** input of the main material expression node. All together it will appear as follows:

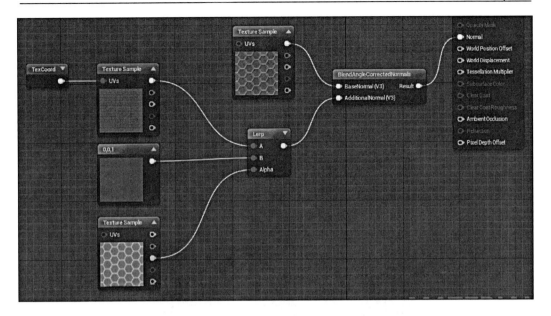

The output of this node arrangement will look like this:

Yay! Nice clean detail regions. Now we can add our emissive color value back in!

Functions of time within materials and pulsing glow

Instead of adding our emissive glow back in as it was before, we are going to be modifying the calculation so that the color pulses as a function of time. We are going to be interpolating between two emissive colors based off a sine ratio of real time! To do this we need to summon another `VectorParameter` expression, call this one **Emissive Color 02**. Set the color values of this vector parameter via the color picker to the following:

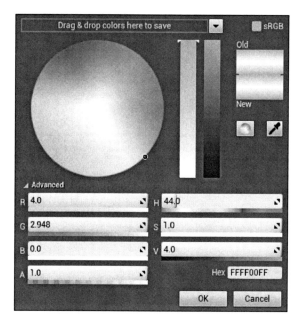

This is a slightly lighter color than **Emissive Color 01**. The next two expressions we need to summon are **Time** and **Sine**. **Time** is a simple expression that outputs the amount of real time that has passed since the application began. Sine is a simple expression that takes in a single float and outputs a sine ratio based on that value. As time increases, the sin ratio that is output will oscillate from -1 to 1. We can use this output to interpolate between our two emissive colors. We then need to pass the output of this interpolation to the mask calculation we were doing previously.

We can do this by summoning the **Time** and **Sine** expressions and a **Linear Interpolate** expression. Plug the value of **Time** into the **Sine** node, and the output of the **Sine** node into the **Alpha** parameter of the **Lerp** node. Plug **Emissive Color 01** into the **A** input of the **Lerp** node, and **Emissive Color 02** into the **B** input. Take the output of this Lerp node and plug it into the **B** input of the multiply node connected to our Mask **Texture Sample**. All together it will look like this:

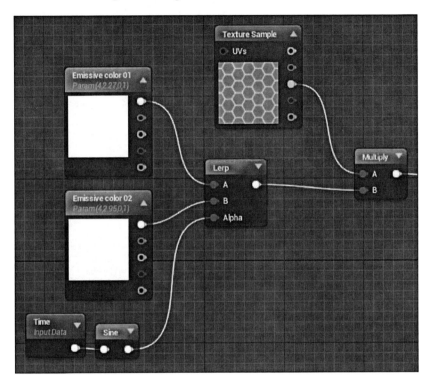

We can then plug the output of these calculations into the **Emissive Color** input of the final material node expression and we have our pulsing emissive glow! The last thing we need to do to our boss material is darken the base color and give it more of a metallic shine. We can do this by changing the base color vector parameter to 0 in each channel. For the metallic shine, create a **Constant** expression node, which is simply a single float value. Set this value to **0.4** and plug it into the **Metallic** and **Roughness** pins of the `BossOutMaterial` expression node.

Your final graph should look similar to this:

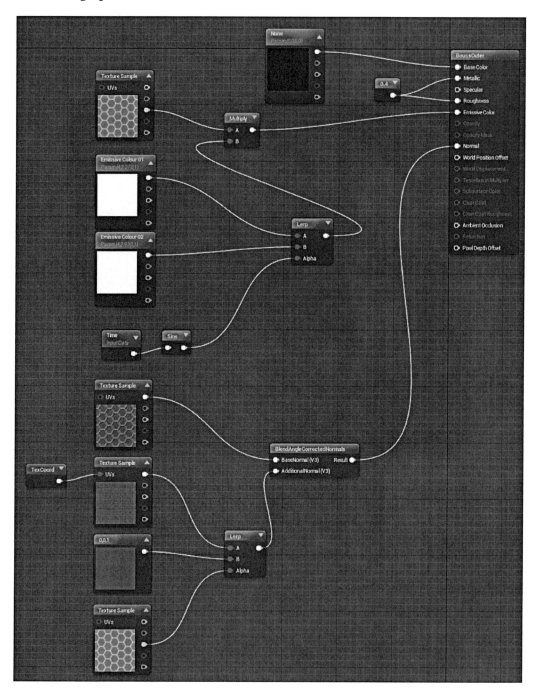

Making the Boss inner material

Now that we have made the exterior shell of the boss glow a sinister yellow, it is now time to make the inner component of the boss mesh glow blue, with the Unreal U logo nice and bright. To do this we are not only going to have to perform similar masking and time-based calculations, but we are also going to have to mask out a section of the mesh based on texture coordinates so that we can separate the U logo part of the mesh from the rest. Create a new material called `BossInnerMaterial` and open it. The desired output from this material is something like this:

Setting up what we know

Ok, let's start by recreating the stuff we already know. Summon a **Texture Sample** expression and assign the `T_Tile_Hex_Tile_M` texture to it. Summon two `VectorParameters`, call them **Emissive Color 01** and **Emissive Color 02** respectively and ensure the color values of each match the following:

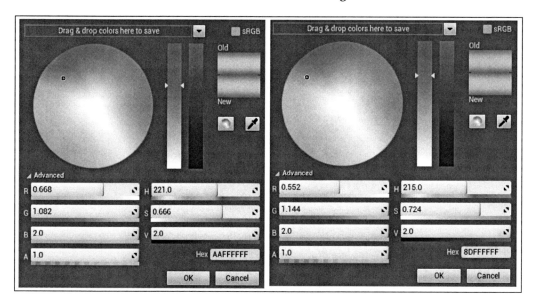

The left is for **Emissive Color 01** and the right for **Emissive Color 02**. Next, summon a **Time** expression, a **Sign** expression, and a **Liner Interpolation** expression, and connect the nodes as we did for the previous material. Summon a Multiply node and connect the green channel of the **Texture Sample** to the **A** pin, and the output of the linear interpolation to the **B** pin. By the way, if you expand the **Multiply** node, you will be presented with a preview of the output of that calculation. Your node setup should appear as follows:

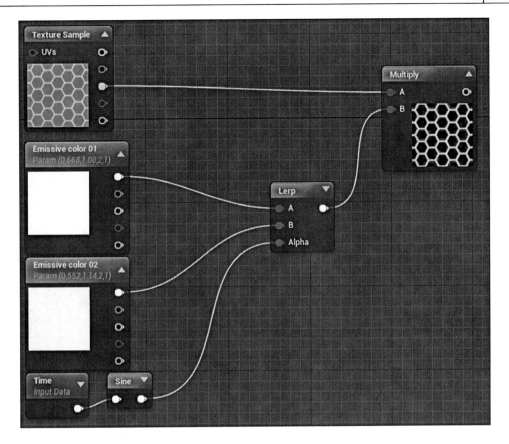

Now that we have done that, let's also recreate the normal map technique we used in the previous material as well. Summon two **Texture Samples**, both with `T_Tech_Hext_Tile_N` assigned to them as the texture, a **Constant3Vector** set to (0, 0, 1), and another **Texture Sample**, but this time with the `T_Tile_Hex_Tile_M` assigned. Summon a `TextureCoordinate` expression and set the U and V tiling to 8. Plug the output of this expression into one of the normal map texture samples (probably the second one). Then summon the `LinearInterpolate` and `BlendAngleCorrectedNormals` expressions. Plug the tiled texture sample into the **A** pin of the Lerp node, plug the `constant3Vector` into the **B** pin of the lerp node, and the green channel of the mask texture sample into the alpha input. Plug the result of this **Lerp** node into the `AdditionalNormal` input of the `BlendAngleCorrectedNormals` node, and plug the untiled texture sample of the normal map into the `BaseNormal` pin.

With all this in place, it should appear as follows:

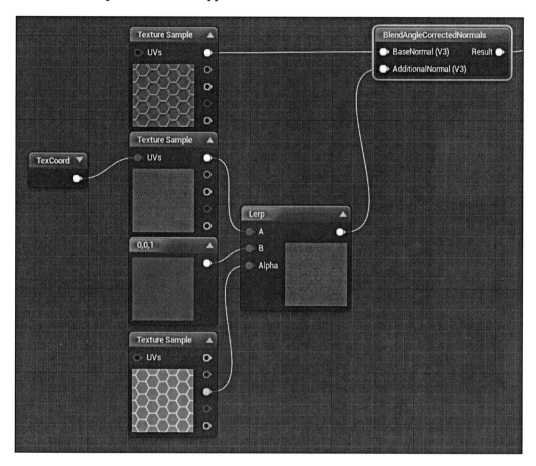

Masking values based on UV

Ok, now that we have our two node clusters that we know work in our previous material, we can adjust how these calculations work based on UV co-ordinates. The way artists project 2D textures to 3D meshes is via UV maps. Effectively, these maps are what the mesh would look like when the mesh is splayed out into 2D, much like if you were to make a cube out of paper and you have the cut-out in front of you before folding. This affords artists the ability to compose their textures so that they color specific areas of the mesh with the right details. I know that the UVs for the Unreal logo part of the BossMesh can be found in the lower half of the UV map (V values greater than 0.5). This means that any color changes that happen in the lower half of a texture are likely to only affect the Unreal logo. With this information in mind, we can make the Unreal U glow bright blue!

We need to create a calculation that will change any color value that has a texture co-ordinate with a V value greater than 0.5 to be our emissive color. To make things difficult we should also make sure that any normals found past a V co-ordinate of 0.5 are also set to be flat (0, 0, 1). We can do this by receiving a texture coordinate via the `TextureCoordinate` expression. Then by applying a mask to the output of the `TexCoord` node, so we are only working with the **V** channel, we can perform lerp and clamping calculations that will provide us with a 0 to 1 range value. Let's try this out.

Summon a `TextureCoordinate` expression and then summon a new expression called **Mask**. This expression allows us to provide it with any format of value, a single float, a float2, a float3, and so on. Based on the properties set within the **Details** panel of this expression, it will return the appropriate data type with a given data set masked out. In our case we will be parsing it a UV float 2, asking it to only pass through the V channel masking U out.

We do this by selecting the Mask node and addressing the **Details Panel**. Under the **Material Expression Component Mask** section, toggle the **G** property to true. As this expression can be used for datatypes up to a float 4, the standard RGBA format is used here. As V is the second element in a float 2 and G is the second element in the float 4, this property configuration will work. What we have told this node to do is mask out all other components apart from G (element 2). So what this node will output for us is just the *V* value of the texture coordinate with U being masked out.

Summon a `LinearInterpolate` expression and plug the output of the **Mask(G)** node into the **Alpha** pin of the lerp node. We are going to be interpolating between a constant value of -20 and positive value of 20. Do this by selecting the **Lerp** node we just created and address the **Details** panel. Under the **Material Expression Linear Interpolate** section, set the `ConstA` property to -20 and the `ConstB` property to 20. So far, your node setup will look like this:

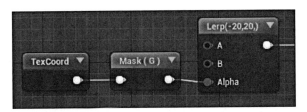

What we are going to do next is Clamp the value output from the **Lerp** node to be between 0 and 1. This is for two reasons. Firstly, we require a value of 0 to 1 to perform effective interpolation calculations. Secondly, as we just compressed a wide range of values (-20, to 20) to a short range of values (0.0 to 1.0), the rate in change of zero to 1 will be much more extreme. This will give us a clean mask of any V values past 0.5. If you wish to make the mask more vague, reduce the -20 to 20 range; if you want to make it sharper, increase the -20 to 20 range (to something like -100 to 100).

Summon a **Clamp** expression. By default, the clamp values are set to 0 and 1 respectively so all we have to do is plug the output of the **Lerp** node into this one. Following the clamp node, we need to create two **Lerp** expressions. Both of these expressions will have the clamped value we just created as their **Alpha** component. It is with these **Lerps** that we are doing the actual masking.

For the first **Lerp** we want to plug the output of the emissive-mask multiplication into the A pin, and the output of the emissive color calculation into the **B** pin. This means that anything past 0.5 V will receive our full emissive color without any normal mapping. As we know that our Unreal logo is located in the lower half of the UV map, this will guarantee the logo glows bright blue!

For the other **Lerp** we want to plug the result of our normal map addition calculation into the **A** pin, and into the **B** pin we want to plug a **Constant3Vector** with the value of (0, 0, 1). With all of this in place, the end of your material graph will appear as follows:

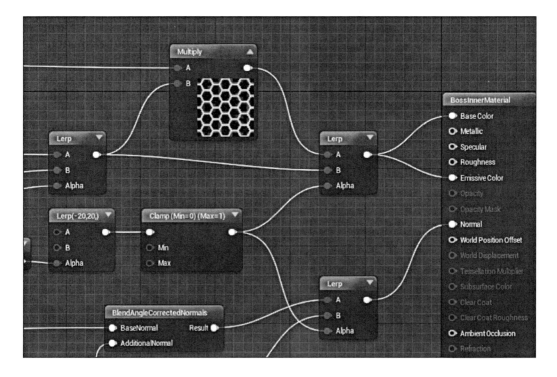

And the preview mesh (when set to a sphere mesh primitive) will look like this:

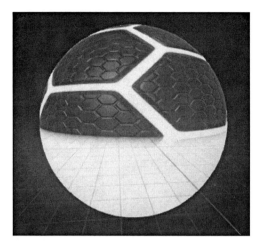

As you can see, anything in the lower half of the sphere is set to our emissive color! The result when applied to our boss mesh is that the Unreal U will glow bright blue!

Applying the material to the Boss

Navigate back to the content browser and open the FPBossCharacter Blueprint. With the **Mesh(Inherited)** component selected, address the **Details** panel and adjust the **Material** section so it matches the following:

Now when we run the game, our boss will look like this:

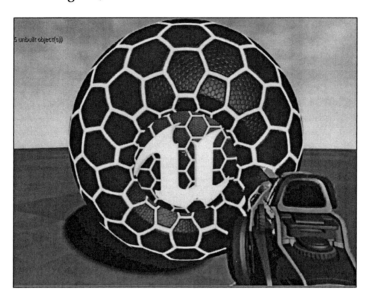

Summary

Awesome! We are done with the `BossMode` project! We won't be adding an end game state or restart functionality to this project as we have already covered those in previous chapters. What we have achieved, however, is a boss character that is controlled by AI that we created ourselves and rendered with our own materials. Over this chapter you learnt how to make `enumerations` in C++ that can be used for behavior tree logics via blackboard. You created your own BT Task in C++, as well modified our AI Controller to arm the boss with a salvo of missiles. We expanded our AI tree to incorporate two new AI states with their own associated behavior. We peaked into the vast depth that is the Unreal rendering system and created our own materials. It is now time to finally utilize all of the skills we have learnt in the book thus far and take it to the next level. In the next chapter we will be creating our own networked first-person shooter! See you there!

9
Creating a Networked Shooter

Welcome to the final chapters of *Unreal Engine 4 By Example*! Congratulations on making it to this point. We have covered a lot since you started this book and now we are going to be utilizing all of that knowledge to dig into the last major UE4 feature covered in this book. That feature is Unreal Networking! I have left this feature till last as it will require the knowledge and skills you have been working on throughout this book. We are going to be exploring this feature by creating our very own multiplayer FPS shooter, with which you will be able to play with your friends over LAN! To fully understand how UE4's networking is done, we will be covering some basic networking concepts, how UE4 leverages these concepts to create its networking layer, and most of the important objects that you will need to interact with. In short, we will be covering the following:

- Networking theory
- Client/server protocols
- Peer 2 Peer protocols
- Remote Procedure Calls
- The UE4 networking layer
- Variable and actor replication
- Network roles
- Game and player states
- UE4 network object persistence

Creating the project

We will be expanding the FPS C++ template provided to us by the engine. We have covered how to do this many times in this book; if you need a refresher go, to *Chapter 5, Upgrade Activated – Making Bounty Dash with C++*, otherwise create a new FPS C++ template project and call it **NS** (**Network Shooter**).

Adding a marketplace package

Before we begin working with the template, we must first add some additional assets to the project. Instead of migrating assets as we have done before, we will be adding a marketplace package to the project.

If you haven't already, open the Unreal Engine Launcher and navigate to the **Marketplace** tab:

You will see a grid-like storefront with packages denoted by image tiles and prices. In the top right-hand corner of this window you will see a search bar that states **Search Content....** Within this search field, look for **Animation Starter Pack**. This is a free animation pack that we will use to animate our character. The tile image for the animation pack looks as follows:

You may have noticed that the animation pack provides third-person animation assets even though we are creating a FPS. We will get to this later. Click on this tile and you will be presented with a window listing the details of this package. There will be a large yellow button that states either **Sign in to Buy** or **Download**:

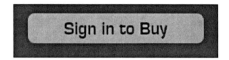

Press this button now and download the package (if you are required to sign in, do so). Once this package has been downloaded, it will be transferred to the **Vault** section of the **Library** tab within the Engine Launcher. Navigate to this section now and you will see the following:

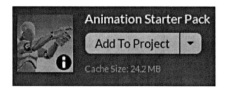

Press the **Add To Project** button and then search for the **NS** project we just created. This will add the animation assets to our project. Yay!

We will also have to modify the objects that have been given to us by default in the FPS template to get everything ready for development, but first, we will cover some networking theory.

Network multiplayer theory

What is networked multiplayer and why do we use it? Very simply, networked multiplayer is when *multiple* computers are sharing information with each other over a network so that they may all have a common game state. Everybody who is part of the multiplayer network can see each other and what is happening in the game world at (roughly) the same time. The uses of networked multiplayer are numerous; however, the two main uses are that we are able to create a game experience that people can interact with and enjoy from different parts of the world outside of a local network, and we are able to have many more people partake in the same game experience than would be possible on one machine.

However, this multiplayer network requires a series of rules to dictate how this information is shared and whose information within the network is *authoritative*. This set of rules is known as a protocol or pattern. In the next section, we will be covering two of the main networking patterns.

Networking patterns

It is important to note that, when working with networked games, there is *no longer only one version of an object*. If an object is to be part of the network, meaning it can be seen by all connected players, there will be multiple versions of that object. One that exists on the owning computer, and any number of other versions that exist on the connected computers or servers. This is because, even though the other computers might not control or own an object, they will still need to see and interact with this object. This now raises the question, if there are multiple versions of an object, which one has the correct information? Well, that is where networking patterns come in.

The two main design patterns you may have come across with regards to networked multiplayer are client/server and **Peer to Peer (P2P)**. First, we will briefly cover P2P as it is the one that UE4 does not support natively and is easier to understand. Before I dive into these patterns, I should mention that I will be throwing around words such as authoritative and net owner. This simply means who is in charge of a certain networked object and who can make changes to this object so that those changes are updated to all other connected clients.

Peer to Peer (P2P)

Very simply, a P2P pattern dictates that each connected computer is authoritative of its own information and that every peer shares its information with each other. This can be described with the following diagram:

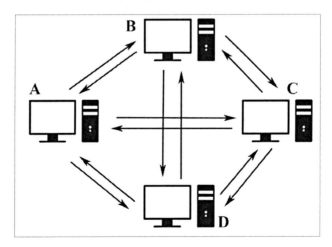

This form of networking pattern excels when there are only two computers communicating with each other. However, as the number of connected computers increases, the complexity of this networking pattern grows *exponentially* as well. As you can see, each computer must send its information to every other computer in the network. This means that as the number of connected peers increases, the number of times information has to be broadcast around the network increases. This will add more network load to each connected peer in a large network.

As an example, let's say computer A instructs its character to jump. On a non-networked game, we would simply execute a function on the character object that causes it to jump. However, within this P2P network, we must also now send information to all of the connected peers to instruct their versions of computer A's character to also jump. This leads to another problem; if there are connectivity issues between computer A and computer D, computer D's version of the computer A character will jump after everyone else's. Now we have disparaging information. Computer A says its character is in one place and computer D says it's in another. This can lead to all sorts of problems and only gets worse when you add varying latency between all of the connected clients!

This is where network authority comes into play. In the previous situation, computer A has authority over its own character (as is common with a P2P network). This means that if computer D were to interact in some way with computer A's character (say a collision or ray trace), then the visual position of its version of Character A on computer D would be invalid and instead would need to query computer A for the true position. This kind of communication needs to take place constantly between all connected peers.

All of this makes using P2P networks for large game networks very complicated and costly for the connected peers. However, P2P does have its benefits. When working with a reduced number of connected peers (two or three), it can become beneficial to utilize a P2P network as you may not require the inclusion of a server, and a P2P network can be easier to design for.

Client/server

The client/server networking pattern is supported natively by UE4 and is a much more robust solution when it comes to creating gameplay experiences that will feature multiple connected players. The client/server pattern differs from P2P in that each connected computer (called client from now on) only sends information to and receives information from one place, the server. The server is also completely authoritative of all objects and information that is being shared within a network.

The following diagram describes this networking pattern:

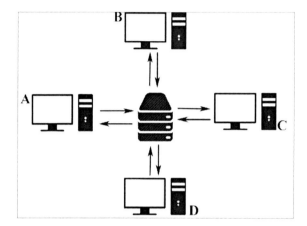

As you can see, each client is only dealing with one connection, to and from the server. This means that as the network complexity increases, the workload is distributed to the server instead of the connected clients. This is very important when working with multiplayer networks as we try to remove as much of the networking load from the clients as possible. This also means that all game-critical information (player positions, player states, and so on) is located in one place. This makes for much easier game logic code when it comes to character interactions. For example, if we are checking whether a collision between computer *A's* character and computer *D's* character takes place, we can simply ask the server.

However, there are still some hurdles when it comes to client/server networking patterns. Namely networking authority. As the server usually has authority over all network objects, this means we must change how our player/computer moves its character. Let's take jumping as an example. If computer *A* wishes for its character to jump, it can no longer call jump itself. *A's* information is only shared between the server and other clients; this would result in character *A* only jumping on computer *A*. Instead, computer A would send a message to the server requesting a jump action. Upon receiving this request, the server will jump the character and then send out the updated jumping position and state to all connected clients (including computer *A*).

With high latency, this can lead to very undesirable gameplay issues. If the game that is using the client/server pattern is fast paced or action based (like an FPS), then it would feel horrible to have to wait for your message to reach the server, for it to then execute the jump action, and then send the updated position back to your computer. To fix this, game developers have utilized a thing called network interpolation and prediction. These are simply generic terms for systems that smooth out information coming from the server in combination with the predicted movement of the client objects.

This means that the client will predict how the character will move before the server returns the positional updates associated with the jump, and move the client in anticipation. If there are any positional discrepancies after the positional values have been returned from the server, the differences will be interpolated over until the client position matches that of the server. As a predicted simulation has taken place on the client, any remaining discrepancies will be much smaller and less noticeable when corrected.

UE4 Networking

As stated previously, UE4 boasts a networking layer that closely matches a client/server pattern with its own solutions and adaptions to make it a great and robust networking layer, which we will use to create our first-person shooter! Thankfully, because of this layer, we do not have to implement our own connection/ interpolation code, we can leave that all up to the engine. All we have to do is write our gameplay code with networking in mind. It is also important to note that this game will be designed to take place over LAN. There are some key UE4 networking concepts we must cover first.

Dedicated or listen servers

When working with UE4, we can choose to run a dedicated or listen server. The main difference between the two is that on a dedicated server, the server does not own its own character. On a **listen server**, the server will have its own character that it can control. This means we are able to have a server with its own controlled character interacting with the game world and other players. Sometimes this is commonly referred to as the host in any multiplayer match, and these players will have a distinct advantage over connected players (no latency).

A dedicated server, on the other hand, has no such thing and is usually a non-visual version of the game world and is purely used for maintaining and updating the game world. When deciding which of the two to use, you must do so early on as they require very different coding methodologies. For the purposes of this chapter, we will be designing a listen server for ease of use.

UE4 replication

As stated previously in Networking Theory section, there will be networked objects whose information will be shared among all connected clients and the server. These objects are known as replicated objects. Within the UE4 hierarchy, anything that inherits from AActor can be replicated. This can be done by setting the AActor member bReplicates to true. This will flag the actor for replication and will be considered when the game performs a net update. A net update is the stage in which the engine will update all networking-related entities and objects.

Replicated objects can also specify which of their internal members are to be replicated via the UPROPERTY() macro and the Replicated property specifier. For example, if you wished to have a float value replicated that represents a character's health, you would declare the variable as such:

```
UPROPERTY(Replicated)
float CharacterHealth;
```

This would then register the variable for replication and, as long as the owning object is also replicated, it will be updated to all connected clients through the network. Any member that does not have this flag specified will not replicate. It is important to remember this. When the Unreal Build Tool/Unreal Header Tool encounters a replicated specifier in a header file, it will automatically add the following function declaration to the class definition at code generation time:

```
virtual void AYourActor::GetLifetimeReplicatedProps(TArray<FLifetimePr
operty>& OutLifetimeProps) const
```

We must then define this function in the .cpp of any replicated objects that contain replicated members. For the previous example, the definition would appear as follows:

```
{
    Super::GetLifetimeReplicatedProps(OutLifetimeProps);
    DOREPLIFETIME(AYourActor, CurrentHealth);
}
```

Within this definition, we have included a call to the super classes implementation of the function, then used the macro DOREPLIFETIME. This macro takes in the class type that the variable is owned by and the variable itself. This will replicate the CurrentHealth variable whenever it is changed over its lifetime. DOREPLIFETIME is optimized to only send a network update when the variable is changed. There are also multiple conditions that we can set when replicating variables. This is done using the DOREPLIFETIME_CONDITION macro. We will not be covering this facet of the UE4 networking layer but more information can be found at https://docs. unrealengine.com/latest/INT/Gameplay/Networking/Actors/Properties/ Conditions/index.html.

Network role

Now that we have replicated actors, we need to cover network roles. For every replicated actor, there are three roles that can be assumed—`Role_Authority`, `Role_AutonomousProxy`, and `Role_SimulatedProxy`. Which role a replicated actor assumes is very important:

- `Role_Authority`: It will always be the role of the version of a replicated actor that exists on the server. This is very important as it means that only the server has authority over the variables and states of this actor.

- `Role_AutonomousProxy`: It is assumed by the version of an actor that exists on the owning client. This means that the client can do things such as move the character around, send and receive direct RPCs to/from the server, and the player's input will have an effect on the server's interpolation of the actor position.

- `Role_SimulatedProxy`: It is assumed by the version of an actor that exists on all other clients; this is purely a simulation and will have no power over the state of the actor.

For example, referencing the client/server diagram used earlier, computer *A* requests the server to spawn a first-person character that it will control called Character *A*. The role of Character *A* on the owning client is `Role_AutonomousProxy`. The owning client being the one that created/requested the controlled character in the first place. The role of Character *A* that is created on the server is `Role_Authority`, and the role of Character *A* that is created on all other clients that can't control the character (computers *B* through D) is `Role_SimulatedProxy`.

The thing that these roles mostly represent is network ownership. For any replicated actor, there will always be a server owner actor (`Role_Authority`). There may or may not be a client owner of that actor (`Role_AutonomousProxy`) and there may or may not be a non-owning client with an instance of that actor (`Role_SimulatedProxy`).

Remote Procedure Calls (RPCs)

RPCs are the way in which we instruct the server or client versions of an object to execute functionality across a network. They are called locally but are executed remotely on another machine's object instance. For example, if we were to receive an `OnFire()` input command on a client, the RPCs would appear as follows:

- `OnFire()` **executed locally on client**: Begin local animation and effects, inform server of a fire

- **RPC rom client to server**: `FireMyWeapon()`

- **Fire My Weapon received on server**: Perform ray-trace to see whether anything was hit and inform clients to play `PlayerFired` visuals
- **RPC From Server To All connected Clients**: `PlayerFiredVisuals()`
- **PlayerFiredVisuals Received on all connected Clients**: Spawn and play particle emitters for gunshot and sounds for gunshot

Previously, we have an owning-client instance of a character receiving an `OnFire()` event (the player pressed the shoot button). The client will play local animation and effects that will not be seen by other players (first-person effects), then informs the server instance of the character to fire its weapon via an RPC. Note that as this is the owing client of the character, it is able to send this RPC to the server instance of this object.

This RPC will instruct the server instance of the character to perform the ray-trace calculations. As all of the characters found on the server are authority instances, we can assume that the positional information of these characters is correct. Also, upon receiving this `FireMyWeapon()`, RPC calls the server instance and informs all connected clients to play the third-person visual effects. This is important, as the other connected clients must witness the `Role_Simulated` Proxy version of the character fire its weapon. As we wish these effects to play on all client instances of a character, we must not use a direct client RPC (as that would only execute on a `Role_AutonomousProxy` client).

Types of RPC

Within the Unreal Networking layer, RPCs are declared via the `UFUNCTION` macro. There are three types of RPC and they are declared as follows:

```
UFUNCTION( Client )
void ClientRPCFunction();

UFUNCTION( Server )
void ServerRPCFunction();

UFUNCTION( NetMulticast )
void MulticastRPCFunction();
```

First, I will describe the traditional uses of these three RPCs then describe what will happen if they are called from an actor with the incorrect network role/ownership:

- **Client**: A client RPC should be called from the server and will be executed on the owning client (client instance with `Role_AutonomousProxy`). If a client RPC is invoked on a client or non-owning client, the function will only be called locally.

- **Server**: A server RPC should be called from the owning client. If so, the RPC will execute on the server. If it is invoked from a non-owning client (client instance with `Role_SimulatedProxy`), the function will be dropped and not executed.

- **NetMultiCast**: This is an interesting RPC as, if it is invoked from a server, it will be executed on both the server and all connected clients, even those with `Role_SimulatedProxy`. This is useful for functions you wish to execute on every instance of a replicated actor. If a `NetMultiCast` RPC is called from a client, non-owning or owning, it will only execute locally.

RPCs are unreliable by default and we must also specify `Reliable` in the `UFUNCTION` macro. If we want a validation check on an RPC before it is executed, we can include `WithValidation` to the `UFUNCTION` macro as well.

Defining RPCs

When the UBT/UHT encounters a function with the any of the RPC specifiers in the `UFUNCTION` macro, it will automatically replace that function declaration with generated versions depending on the contents of the `UFUNCTION` macro. Let's take `ClientRPCFunction` as an example. It would be replaced with the following:

```
void ClientRPCFunction_Implementation();
```

If we were to specify `WithValidation` as well, the following would also be added:

```
bool ClientRPCFunction_Validate();
```

Therefore, when we define our RPCs, we must do so with the previous function declarations in mind, otherwise we will receive linker errors when we try to build the project. With the previous example, the definitions in the `.cpp` would appear as follows:

```
void ClientRPCFunciton_Implementation()
{
    // Do something on the client
}

Bool ClientRPCFunction_Validate()
{
    bool bSomeCheck = SomeCheck();
    return bSomeCheck;
}
```

Net ownership, player controllers and game modes

We have briefly described network ownership through the use of network roles, but now it is time to be more specific. The main difference between an owning client and a non-owning client is the existence of a player controller. Player controllers are only created on the owning-client and that player controller is the channel through which all communication with the server takes place.

For example, computer A has the `PlayerController` for character A. All other versions of Character A on computers B through D do not have a `PlayerController` for Character A. Intern computer A does not have a `PlayerController` for any of the other computers either. This is a very important concept to understand as a connection to a server is done through the `PlayerController`. Each controller is replicated between the server and owning client.

In the same vein, the `GameMode` is only created on the network authority. In our case, that is the server. That is why when we have tried to get the `GameMode` from the game world, thus far we have called `GetAuthGameMode()`, or in long form, `GetAuthorityGameMode`. In a networked project, that function will return null on all clients.

The way that we then communicate game and player information between all clients and servers is via `GameState` and `PlayerState` objects. These two objects are replicated to all connected clients. It is also important to separate `PlayerState` from character state. A player state is information pertaining to the player that is connected to the server, not the character it is controlling. The same thing is said for the `GameState`; if we wish to parse game information to the connected clients, we must do so through a custom `GameState` object.

To summarize the idea of ownership in more clear terms, for every client that is connected to a server session, there will now be a series of new instances of the character object. Computer A will have the owning-client version of its own character, Character A. Computers B through D will now also have an instance of Character A; however, these will be non-owning versions (`Role_SimulatedProxy`). There is a final version of Character A; this one exists on the server and is the authority instance of the character. Meaning that if any changes are made to the authority, it will be replicated to all other connected client versions of Character A, including the owning-client instance. And, as stated previously, this will be the same for all of the other player characters added by computers B through D.

For each connected computer or player, there will also be a unique player state that is replicated to all connected network entities (servers and clients). For each multiplayer game session, there will be one game state that is also replicated to all network entities.

Starting the networked First Person Shooter

Ok, now that we have covered the basics, let's put this information to use and begin work on our network shooter project!

Preparing the NS project

The first thing we need to do is remove a few things that have been provided to us by default in the   project. We are going to be removing code from a few of the objects and adding some of our own. I will run through this very quickly, as any significant code changes will be described later in the project. First, navigate to NS.h and change #include "EngineMinimal.h" to #include "Engine.h".

Next, navigate to NSGameMode.h and add the following enum above the ANSGameMode class definition:

```
UENUM(BlueprintType)
enum class ETeam : uint8
{
    BLUE_TEAM,
    RED_TEAM
};
```

Here we have a classed enum that will represent the two teams that feature in the NS project. The enum has been classed to be of type uint8. Now that we have this in place, let's work with our ANSCharacter object. We are going to be removing quite a bit of code from this object as we do not need a lot of the generated code. Remove the following code from NSCharacter.h:

```
/** Projectile class to spawn */
UPROPERTY(EditDefaultsOnly, Category=Projectile)
TSubclassOf<class ANSProjectile> ProjectileClass;

struct TouchData
{
```

```
            TouchData()
            {
                bIsPressed = false;
                Location=FVector::ZeroVector; }
            bool bIsPressed;
            ETouchIndex::Type FingerIndex;
            FVector Location;
            bool bMoved;
        };
        void BeginTouch(const ETouchIndex::Type FingerIndex, const
        FVector
        Location);
        void EndTouch(const ETouchIndex::Type FingerIndex, const
         FVector
        Location);
        void TouchUpdate(const ETouchIndex::Type
        FingerIndex, const FVector Location);
        TouchData TouchItem;
        bool EnableTouchscreenMovement(UInputComponent* InputComponent);
```

Ensure that when you remove any function declarations from the class definition
that you remove the corresponding function definition in NSCharacter.cpp,
otherwise there will be compiler errors. You must also ensure that you remove the
code associated with the ProjectileClass member from ANSCharacter::OnFire()
and the if check surrounding the BindAction() method that is used to bind the
Fire action mapping to the OnFire() method within the SetupInputComponent()
method. Both methods should now appear as follows:

```
    void ANSCharacter::OnFire()
    {
        // try and play the sound if specified
        if (FireSound != NULL)
            {
    UGameplayStatics::PlaySoundAtLocation(this, FireSound,
    GetActorLocation());
        }
        // cont...
    void ANSCharacter::SetupPlayerInputComponent(class UInputComponent*
    InputComponent)
    {
        // set up gameplay key bindings
        check(InputComponent);

            InputComponent->BindAction("Jump", IE_Pressed, this,
            &ACharacter::Jump);
            InputComponent->BindAction("Jump", IE_Released, this,
            &ACharacter::StopJumping);
```

```
InputComponent->BindAction("Fire", IE_Pressed, this,
&ANSCharacter::OnFire);
// cont...
```

If you wish, you may also remove `NSProjectile.h` and `.cpp` entirely from the project as we will not be using a standard projectile object for this project. Be sure to remove any references to removed variables as well.

With those changes in place, build the project and ensure there are no compiler errors or warnings. Upon running a PIE session, you will be presented with a simple first person character that can run, jump, and look around with either a controller, or mouse and keyboard.

Making a networked player character

Alright, now we can finally begin adding code to this template project! Let's start by writing the code for our first-person character. Navigate to `NSCharacter.h` now. In the next section, we will be modifying this class definition to include all of the function declarations and variables we will need for this project.

NSCharacter visual and audio assets

As we are creating an object that is going to be replicated across the network and visually represented on all connected clients, we need to design the visual asset configuration of our `ANSCharacter` so that it can be viewed properly from two different perspectives. We need to add assets that will appear correctly when viewing the character from a first-person perspective, as will be seen by the owning-client of a character. We must also add assets that will appear correctly when viewing the character from a third-person perspective, as will be seen by all other non-owning clients and server. We also have to figure out a way to have only the first-person assets draw on the owning-client and only the third-person assets draw on the non-owning clients.

Thankfully, this functionality is supported by the `USkeletalMeshComponent` object. We will cover how to set this up when we start to modify `NSCharacter.cpp`. For now, add the following to the class definition of `ANSCharacter`:

```
/** Pawn mesh: 1st person view (arms; seen only by self) */
UPROPERTY(VisibleDefaultsOnly, Category=Mesh)
class USkeletalMeshComponent* FP_Mesh;

/** Gun mesh: 1st person view (seen only by self) */
UPROPERTY(VisibleDefaultsOnly, Category = Mesh)
class USkeletalMeshComponent* FP_Gun;
```

```
/** Gun mesh: 3rd person view (seen only by others) */
UPROPERTY(VisibleDefaultsOnly, Category = Mesh)
class USkeletalMeshComponent* TP_Gun;
```

Here we have renamed `Mesh1P` to `FP_Mesh`. Make sure that whenever you change a variable name, you also update any references to that variable. I would suggest using find and replace. Then we added a new `USkeletalMeshComponent` handle for a third-person gun mesh (`TP_Gun`). We have not added a `TP_Mesh` for the character here as we will use the default mesh handle included in `ACharacter`. Next we will remove another of the provided members for our own benefit. At about line 41 of the class definition will be a public `FVector` member called `GunOffset`. Remove this member and any references to it. Directly under where you removed this member, add/match the following public members:

```
/** Sound to play each time we fire */
UPROPERTY(EditAnywhere, Category = Gameplay)
class USoundBase* FireSound;

/** Sound to play each time we fire */
UPROPERTY(EditAnywhere, Category = Gameplay)
class USoundBase* PainSound;

/** 3rd person anim montage asset for gun shot */
UPROPERTY(EditAnywhere, Category = Gameplay)
class UAnimMontage* TP_FireAnimaiton;

/** 1st person anim montage asset for gun shot */
UPROPERTY(EditAnywhere, Category = Gameplay)
class UAnimMontage* FP_FireAnimaiton;

/** particle system for 1st person gun shot effect */
UPROPERTY(EditAnywhere, Category = Gameplay)
class UParticleSystemComponent* FP_GunShotParticle;

/** particle system for 3rd person gun shot effect */
UPROPERTY(EditAnywhere, Category = Gameplay)
class UParticleSystemComponent* TP_GunShotParticle;

/** particle system that will represent a bullet */
UPROPERTY(EditAnywhere, Category = Gameplay)
class UParticleSystemComponent* BulletParticle;

UPROPERTY(EditAnywhere, Category = Gameplay)
class UForceFeedbackEffect* HitSuccessFeedback;
```

Here we have declared the rest of the asset handles we are going to be using. We have two `USoundBase` handles that will be used to play sounds when a bullet is fired and when the character is hit. Following that, we have the two `UAnimMontage` asset handles that will be used to play the appropriate gunfire animations for both third and first-person perspectives. Ensure you replace any occurrences of `FireAnimation` with `FP_FireAnimation`.

We then have three `UParticleSystemComponent` handles; the first two will represent our gunshot effects. We have included a first- and third-person version as these two systems will play in different world space positions depending on the perspective through which they are viewed. The last is a particle system we will use to represent our bullet traveling through the world. This is just a particle system this time, as we will not be performing any collision on the bullet itself.

Lastly, we have a `UForceFeedbackEffect` handle. A force feedback asset is simply a curve type object that allows us to specify with detail how we would like the force feedback in a controller to play. We will use this to inform the client of a successful hit of another player! With all of our handles declared, let's initialize the corresponding components in the constructor. Navigate to `NSCharacter.cpp`; we are going to be working with the class default constructor `ANSCharacter::ANSCharacter()`. Here we have already been provided with some code that sets up our base turn rates and initializes the first person camera component, which was provided to us when we generated the project.

We need to change any `Mesh1P` references to `FP_Mesh` before we begin adding new code. You will note that when we initialize the `FP_Mesh`, we call the `SetOnlyOwnerSee()` method on the object. That will render the `FP_Mesh` invisible to anything other than the owning character. This means that anything that views this mesh from the third person won't see anything at all. You will also notice that the `FP_Gun` has been initialized for us. We have set that the owner only sees this mesh as well and we have attached the `FP_Gun` to the `GripPoint` socket found with the `FP_Mesh`. This is exactly the same code we had in the `ABMCharacter` constructor that we used in `BossMode`.

Next, we must remove the lines that initialize the `GunOffset` member as a vector. The last lines of your constructor should now look like this:

```
    FP_Gun->AttachTo(FP_Mesh, TEXT("GripPoint"),
    EAttachLocation::SnapToTargetIncludingScale, true);
}
```

Now that we have made all of the necessary modifications, we can start adding our new code to the constructor by initializing TP_Gun with the following code:

```
// Create a gun mesh component
TP_Gun = CreateDefaultSubobject<USkeletalMeshComponent>(TEXT("TP_
Gun"));
TP_Gun->SetOwnerNoSee(true);

TP_Gun->AttachTo(GetMesh(), TEXT("hand_rSocket"), EAttachLocation::Sna
pToTargetIncludingScale, true);
```

Here we have called the method SetOwnerNoSee(). This method performs the same functionality as SetOnlyOwnerSee() but the inverse. This will mean that our first person perspective of the player will not see the third-person mesh. This is very important, as the third-person gun mesh will most likely occlude some of the first person camera's view. We also attach this TP_Gun to a socket that will be found in the default skeletal mesh of this object. We have yet to assign this mesh or the socket but we will get around to doing that later when we work with the blueprint abstraction of this object. Underneath this code, add the following:

```
GetMesh()->SetOwnerNoSee(true);
```

This will ensure that our third-person character mesh cannot be seen as well. Now we can initialize our particle system components. Add the following code:

```
// Create particles
TP_GunShotParticle =
CreateDefaultSubobject<UParticleSystemComponent>(TEXT("ParticleSys
TP"));

TP_GunShotParticle->bAutoActivate = false;
TP_GunShotParticle->AttachTo(TP_Gun);
TP_GunShotParticle->SetOwnerNoSee(true);
```

Here we are initializing the third-person gunshot particle system component. We are informing the particle system that we do not wish for it to auto activate, as we only want it to play when a character fires, attaching it to the TP_Gun (as the particle effect needs to play relative to the transform of the TP_Gun mesh). We are also calling SetOwnerNoSee(). Next, add the code for the first person particle:

```
// Create particle
FP_GunShotParticle= CreateDefaultSubobject<UParticleSystemComponent>(T
EXT("FP_GunShotParticle"));

FP_GunShotParticle->bAutoActivate = false;
FP_GunShotParticle->AttachTo(FP_Gun);
FP_GunShotParticle->SetOnlyOwnerSee(true);
```

Then, finally, add the following for the bullet particle. This particle is to be seen by both third- and first-person perspectives so we needn't worry about who can see it:

```
BulletParticle =
CreateDefaultSubobject<UParticleSystemComponent>(TEXT("BulletSysTP"));
BulletParticle->bAutoActivate = false;
BulletParticle->AttachTo(FirstPersonCameraComponent);
```

That will be all we need for our constructor. Now compile the project and run; we are going to be adding some new classes using the C++ class wizard.

Player states and networking

One of the key concepts of UE4 networking is that a connection is established between a player controller and a server. This connection establishes the net role and ownership of the various network objects that are created during this relationship. However, because of this, player controllers only exist and are replicated on the owning-client (Role_AutonomousProxy) and the server (Role_Authority). The other non-owning versions of a player character do not have a replicated player controller; in fact, if you attempt to access a player controller on a non-owning client version of a character, it will return null. These non-owning clients are in fact controlled by standard AController objects.

This leaves us with an issue: where can we store a grouping of reliably replicated variables that are shared across all instances of a network character? For this, we can use APlayerState objects. Player state objects are members of standard AControllers. A APlayerState object is created for every player on a server (denoted by the number of connected player controllers). These states are replicated to all instances of a connect client and include network-relevant information about the player, such as name, score, health, team, and so on. We are going to be creating an abstraction of the UE4 APlayerState class so that we may add our own variables to that player state, which we can then replicate.

Using the C++ class wizard found under **File | New C++ class...**, create a new object that inherits from APlayerState and call it NSPlayerState. Once the class has been generated, navigate to NSPlayerState.h and modify the ANSPlayerState class definition to match the following:

```
UCLASS()
class NS_API ANSPlayerState : public APlayerState
{
    GENERATED_UCLASS_BODY()

    UPROPERTY(Replicated)
```

```
    float Health;

    UPROPERTY(Replicated)
    uint8 Deaths;

    UPROPERTY(Replicated)
    ETeam Team;


};
```

Ensure you also add #include "NSGameMode.h" to the include list, otherwise ETeam will be an unknown type. Note that we have changed GENERATED_BODY() to GENERATED_UCLASS_BODY() to take advantage of the FObjectInitializer default constructor. Under this, we have added three replicated variables, Health, Deaths, and Team. We have specified each to be Replicated via the UPROPERTY specifier. As mentioned previously, that will flag these variables for replication. Now navigate to NSPlayerState.cpp. First, we will define the default constructor as follows:

```
ANSPlayerState::ANSPlayerState(const FObjectInitializer&
ObjectInitializer)
: Super(ObjectInitializer)
{
    Health = 100.0f;
    Deaths = 0;
    Team = ETeam::BLUE_TEAM;
}
```

That will simply set the declared member variables to appropriate defaults. Next, we are going to be defining the GetLifetimeReplicatedProps() function that was mentioned previously when we covered replication. Add #include "Net/UnrealNetwork.h" to the #include list for the .cpp and then, under the constructor, add the following function definition:

```
void
ANSPlayerState::GetLifetimeReplicatedProps(TArray<FLifetimeProperty>&
OutLifetimeProps) const
{
    Super::GetLifetimeReplicatedProps(OutLifetimeProps);

    DOREPLIFETIME(ANSPlayerState, Health);
    DOREPLIFETIME(ANSPlayerState, Deaths);
    DOREPLIFETIME(ANSPlayerState, Team);
}
```

Just to reiterate, the UBT/UHT will have automatically added a function declaration for this function when it detected the `Replicated` specifier in our `UPROPERTY` macros. This may cause intelli-sense bugs as it will not think the function exists. Do not worry, this will compile fine. Within this definition, we have called the super class implementation of the `GetLifteTimeReplicatedPropers()` method; we then parse each member to the `DOREPLIFETIME` macro with the `ANSPlayerState` object type. This will flag these variables to replicate for its lifetime in memory; it will only replicate when the variable is changed to reduce network traffic.

As this is the first piece of networking code we have written, I will be explicit. These are replicated variables that are members of a replicated `AActor` object (`ANSPlayerState`). These variables will be replicated to all connected client instances of the corresponding `ANSPlayerState`. Each connected player will have its own `ANSPlayerState` that can be accessed in any of its client instances. This means that these variables will have the same value on all of the associated client instances of a particular `ANSPlayerState`. For example, computer A has a player character with an `ANSPlayerState`. If computer A's character takes damage, the server instance of computer A's character will reduce the health value stored within its `ANSPlayerState` to 90. This value will then be replicated to all other client instances of computer A's `ANSPlayerState`. This means other clients will be able to look at a non-owning client instance and still see the correct player health value (if it was displayed).

Finishing the Player class definition

Compile and run the code to ensure our new `ANSPlayerState` object compiles. We are now going to finish writing the class definition for the `ANSCharacter` object. We will start by writing the rest of the member variables we are going to be using for our character calculations. Start by adding the following members of the class definition:

```
public:
    UPROPERTY(Replicated, BlueprintReadWrite, Category = Team)
    ETeam CurrentTeam;

protected:
        class UMaterialInstanceDynamic* DynamicMat;
        class ANSPlayerState* NSPlayerState;
```

Here we have a public replicated variable to hold the current team of the player. We have a duplicate of this variable (one here and one in the `ANSPlayerState`) so we may set the team color of the character before the owning-client instance is possessed by a player controller. This again enforces the difference between player state and character state. Regardless of character, it is still important to save the team in `ANSPlayerState` in case the associated player gains control of a different game pawn.

Following this, we have a handle for a `UMaterialInstanceDynamic`; this will be used to set custom base colors on the mesh material so we can use the same material for both the blue and red teams! This will be covered later on in the chapter. We also have a handle to the character's `ANSPlayerState` that we will obtain when the player character is possessed by a player controller.

Ok, now we can define the rest of our methods for the `ANSCharacter`. Following the variables we just declared, add the following:

```
public:
    class ANSPlayerState* GetNSPlayerState();
    void SetNSPlayerState(class ANSPlayerState* newPS);
    void Respawn();
```

Here we have an accessor method for the `ANSPlayerState` so that it can be called by external objects. We also declare a setter method for the `ANSPlayerState` as well. We then declare a respawn method that we will use to inform the game mode of this character's need to respawn. Following this, we will append to the already existing protected methods. In the following code, I have removed the comments that were provided by the FPS C++ template. Ensure that each of these functions is present:

```
void OnFire();
void MoveForward(float Val);
void MoveRight(float Val);
void TurnAtRate(float Rate);
void LookUpAtRate(float Rate);

// will be called by the server to perform raytrace
void Fire(const FVector pos, const FVector dir);
```

The only new method here is the `Fire()` method that will be called by the server when a ray-trace is needed. Under this, we can add our protected methods that override functions that exist in the `APawn` interface:

```
// APawn interface
virtual void SetupPlayerInputComponent(UInputComponent*
InputComponent) override;

virtual float TakeDamage(float Damage, struct FDamageEvent const&
DamageEvent, AController* EventInstigator, AActor* DamageCauser)
override;

virtual void BeginPlay();
virtual void PossessedBy(AController* NewController) override;
```

`SetupPlayerInputComponent()` will have been provided by the template. The other three methods will be used to drive how the player is damaged, player initialization at begin play, and what happens when an owning-client character is possessed. Under this, in the class definition, you will have the two `FORCEINLINE` public functions provided by the template. Leave these unchanged. We can now finally add our RPCs for this object!

Writing the ANSCharacter RPCs

Compile and run the code before you continue. Ensure there are no compilation errors; you will receive a few linker errors, however, as we are yet to define some of the functions we overrode from the `APawn` interface. We are now going to be writing the network remote procedure calls that will drive the networked functionality of our character. For this project, we are going to have a few interactions that take place between the owning client and server. Thankfully, the replication of the player's movement state is handled for us by the replicated `APlayerController`. We are only responsible for providing the RPCs that will drive any custom functionality.

Add the following to the `NSCharacter` class definition:

```
    /** REMOTE PROCEDURE CALLS */
private:
    // Peform fire action on the server
    UFUNCTION(Server, Reliable, WithValidation)
    void ServerFire(const FVector pos, const FVector dir);

    // Multicast so all clients run shoot effects
    UFUNCTION(NetMultiCast, unreliable)
    void MultiCastShootEffects();

    // Called on death for all clients for hilarious death
    UFUNCTION(NetMultiCast, unreliable)
    void MultiCastRagdoll();

    // Play pain on owning client when hit
    UFUNCTION(Client, Reliable)
    void PlayPain();

public:
    // Set's team colour
    UFUNCTION(NetMultiCast, Reliable)
    void SetTeam(ETeam NewTeam);
```

The previous RPCs are responsible for the following:

- `ServerFire()`: This RPC has been specified as a Server RPC, meaning it will be called from the owning client instance and performed on the server. We have also specified that this RPC be called with validation. The purpose of this RPC is to inform that the client has fired its gun and the server instance needs to perform the raytrace to check for a successful hit. We take in a position and direction for the ray trace to this method. We do this as the position and direction of the raytrace will be heavily dependent on the player's mouse position and current camera view information that is only known by the owning-client thus we are parsing this info across the network to the server.

- `MultiCastShootEffect()`: This NetMultiCast RPC will be used to inform all connected client instances to play their shoot effects. Remember, `NetMultiCasts` have to be called on the server, otherwise only the local client instance will invoke the function. This method will be responsible for invoking the third-person effect assets we declared in the class definition earlier. We have specified this as unreliable as this is a non-crucial network call. If it fails, it will have a marginal effect on gameplay.

- `MultiCastRagdoll()`: This RPC, also specified as `NetMultiCast`, will be used to set the 3rd person character mesh to ragdoll on all clients when a player is killed (which will be carried out on the server).

- `PlayPain()`: This RPC will be called on the server when it detects that a player has taken damage. As this method is specified as a Client RPC, the function will only execute on the owning client version of the character that has taken damage.

- `SetTeam()`: This RPC is the only RPC that is declared as public as it will be invoked by another object (the game mode, but we will get to that later). This has been specified as multicast as we will want all of the connected clients' instances of an `ANSCharacter` to update its base mesh color to the provided team color.

Defining the ANSCharacter functions

Now that we have declared everything we are going to need for this object, let's provide these declarations definitions. We will start by adding the required `GetLifetimeReplicatedProps()` definition. Make sure you also add `#include "Net/UnrealNetwork.h"` to the `#include` list, as well as `#include "NSPlayerState.h"`, and add the following under the `SetupPlayerInputComponent()` definition:

```
void ANSCharacter::GetLifetimeReplicatedProps(TArray<
FLifetimeProperty > & OutLifetimeProps) const
```

```
{
    Super::GetLifetimeReplicatedProps(OutLifetimeProps);

    DOREPLIFETIME(ANSCharacter, CurrentTeam);
}
```

Underneath that, we can add the definition for BeginPlay():

```
void ANSCharacter::BeginPlay()
{
    Super::BeginPlay();

    if (Role != ROLE_Authority)
    {
        SetTeam(CurrentTeam);
    }
}
```

Here we have called to the super class implementation of `BeginPlay()`. Then we have performed a check on the network role of the character. Every `AActor` has the member `Role`. This member holds one of the network role states. In this case, we are checking whether this current `ANSCharacter` is not the authority instance (it is either the owning-client or non-owning client). If so, we want to set the team to whatever value is currently held in `CurrentTeam`. By now, this variable will have been set to whatever exists on the server instance of this object. We will cover how that works later on in the chapter when we write our game mode. This will ensure that all connected clients share the same material instance.

Dynamic materials and material parameters

Following this, we might as well define our `SetTeam()` RPC method as this is the only place that it is called in this object. Following the `BeginPlay()` method, add the following code:

```
void ANSCharacter::SetTeam_Implementation(ETeam NewTeam)
{
    FLinearColor outColour;

    if (NewTeam == ETeam::BLUE_TEAM)
    {
        outColour = FLinearColor(0.0f, 0.0f, 0.5f);
    }
    else
    {
        outColour = FLinearColor(0.5f, 0.0f, 0.0f);
    }
```

```
if (DynamicMat == nullptr)
{
    DynamicMat = UMaterialInstanceDynamic::Create(
    GetMesh()->GetMaterial(0), this);

    DynamicMat->SetVectorParameterValue(
    TEXT("BodyColor"), outColour);

    GetMesh()->SetMaterial(0, DynamicMat);
    FP_Mesh->SetMaterial(0, DynamicMat);
}
}
```

As stated previously, we must define this function as `SetTeam_Implementation` as the UBT will automatically replace the function definition with the appropriate versions based on of the `UFUNCTION` specifiers. Within this method, we are checking what team type has been parsed. We then set a `FLinearColor` with the appropriate color values, `0.5f` in the blue channel for `BLUE_TEAM` and `0.5f` in the red channel for `RED_TEAM`.

Next, we do something very interesting. Do you remember when we worked with materials in the previous chapters and we created `VectorParameter` and `TextureParameter` nodes in our materials? The previous code shows you how to access those parameters by name and set custom values to them via C++.

To do this, however, we must first make a dynamic instance of the base material. Assuming we set the proper material in the blueprint abstraction of this class, we use the `UMaterialInstanceDynamic` static method `Create()` to initialize a dynamic instance of whatever base material is applied to our character mesh and save it into the `DynamicMat` handle we declared in the class definition earlier. We then use this handle to call `SetVectorParameterValue()`. This method takes in an `FName` holding the name of the parameter and a vector value to set to it. In this case, we are parsing a linear color. After this, we set the new dynamic material to be that of the 3rd person and first-person meshes. This will ensure that the character meshes (both 1st and 3rd person) will be colored according to their current team.

Getting the player to shoot… online

Ok, now we can define how our player is going to shoot. What we are going to do is add some functionality to the `OnFire()` method that is currently executed when a player registers input mapped to the `Fire` action mapping. In our case, this is either the LMB or left trigger on a controller. As this method will only execute on the **owning-client**, we must invoke any effects we want played on the owning client (1st person) then inform the server of the fire event.

Modify the `OnFire()` method to match the following:

```
void ANSCharacter::OnFire()
{
    // try and play a firing animation if specified
    if(FP_FireAnimaiton!= NULL)
    {
        // Get the animation object for the arms mesh
        UAnimInstance* AnimInstance = FP_Mesh->GetAnimInstance();
        if(AnimInstance != NULL)
        {
            AnimInstance->Montage_Play(FP_FireAnimaiton, 1.f);
        }
    }

    // Play the FP particle effect if specified
    if (FP_GunShotParticle != nullptr)
    {
        FP_GunShotParticle->Activate(true);
    }
```

As you can see, we have removed the play sound at the location call from the provided definition as we need that sound to play on all clients when a fire event is registered, not just the owning-client. We then inform the `FP_GunShotParticle` to play. Ok, now add the following code to the definition:

```
FVector mousePos;
FVector mouseDir;

APlayerController* pController = Cast<APlayerController>(GetControll
er());

FVector2D ScreenPos = GEngine->GameViewport->Viewport->GetSizeXY();

pController->DeprojectScreenPositionToWorld(ScreenPos.X / 2.0f,
ScreenPos.Y / 2.0f,
mousePos,
mouseDir);
mouseDir *= 10000000.0f;

ServerFire(mousePos, mouseDir);

} // <-- closes ANSCharacter::OnFire()
```

This code will look very similar to the code we used to perform the tracking ray trace in BossMode! We are de-projecting the mouse position from screen space to world so we have a position and a direction for our fire ray trace. We scale the direction by a very large amount as there is no range limit on our gunshot. If you wanted to drive weapon range, it would be done here, by changing this amount we scale the mouse direction. Finally, we parse this information to the server via the ServerFire() RPC we declared earlier. Again, we might as well define this RPC now. Underneath this code, add the following:

```
bool ANSCharacter::ServerFire_Validate(const FVector pos,
    const FVector dir)
{
    if (pos != FVector(ForceInit) && dir != FVector(ForceInit))
    {
        return true;
    }
    else
    {
        return false;
    }
}


void ANSCharacter::ServerFire_Implementation(const FVector pos, const
FVector dir)
{
    Fire(pos, dir);
    MultiCastShootEffects();
}
```

Here we have included the definition for the validation for this RPC. We have included this to ensure that we are not wasting bandwidth on calls that would be incorrect. It is important to note that it is with these validate functions that you would probably implement anti-cheating measures. You can do this by doing various checks on the input to the method. If anything looks off, you can return false and the RPC will not be invoked. Here we are simply checking that if the vectors provided equal the default initialized vector (0, 0, 0), they must be incorrect, therefore we reject the RPC.

Within the RPC itself, we call the Fire() method we declared earlier that will do the actual ray trace. As we specified that this method is to be a Server RPC, we can ensure that this Fire() method will only be invoked on the server. Following this, we then call the MultiCastShootEffect() MultiCast RPC. The MultiCast RPC will be used to invoke all of the effects that should be seen on all clients (3rd person effects).

Let's define the `MultiCastShootEffect()` and `Fire()` methods now. Starting with the MultiCast RPC, add the following code to the `.cpp`:

```
void ANSCharacter::MultiCastShootEffects_Implementation()
{
    // try and play a firing animation if specified
    if (TP_FireAnimaiton != NULL)
    {
        // Get the animation object for the arms mesh
        UAnimInstance* AnimInstance = GetMesh()->GetAnimInstance();
        if (AnimInstance != NULL)
        {
            AnimInstance->Montage_Play(TP_FireAnimaiton, 1.f);
        }
    }

    // try and play the sound if specified
    if (FireSound != NULL)
    {
        UGameplayStatics::PlaySoundAtLocation(this, FireSound,
        GetActorLocation());
    }

    if (TP_GunShotParticle != nullptr)
    {
        TP_GunShotParticle->Activate(true);
    }

    if (BulletParticle != nullptr)
    {
        UGameplayStatics::SpawnEmitterAtLocation(GetWorld(),
        BulletParticle->Template, BulletParticle->
        GetComponentLocation(), BulletParticle->
        GetComponentRotation());
    }
}
```

This method is going to be executed on all connected clients so we need to ensure that we only activate the effects that can be seen by everyone. In the previous method, we are informing the anim instance associated with the default character mesh object to play the `TP_FireAnimation`. This will result in all of the non-owning client instances of the character to animate some recoil from the gunshot. Following this, we then play the fire sound at the location of the client instance so that attenuation and 3D sound modulation plays as intended. We then activate the `TP_GunShotParticle` so that other clients will see a small blast effect at the barrel of the `TP_Gun` mesh.

Finally, we are spawning a new emitter at the location of the `BulletParticle` component found within the character. We are spawning a new emitter instead of activating the `BulletParticle` component so we can have multiple instances of the particle system active at any one time. Activate would cause the particle to reset every time the character fires. We do not want this, as we want each bullet particle effect to play for its intended lifetime. Now it is time to define the `Fire()` method; add the following code below `MultiCastShootEffects()`:

```
void ANSCharacter::Fire(const FVector pos, const FVector dir)
{
    // Perform Raycast
    FCollisionObjectQueryParams ObjQuery;
    ObjQuery.AddObjectTypesToQuery(ECC_GameTraceChannel1);

    FCollisionQueryParams ColQuery;
    ColQuery.AddIgnoredActor(this);

    FHitResult HitRes;
    GetWorld()->LineTraceSingleByObjectType(HitRes, pos, dir,
    ObjQuery,
    ColQuery);

    DrawDebugLine(GetWorld(), pos, dir, FColor::Red, true, 100, 0,
5.0f);

    if (HitRes.bBlockingHit)
    {
            ANSCharacter* OtherChar = Cast<ANSCharacter>(HitRes.
            GetActor());

        if (OtherChar != nullptr &&
            OtherChar->GetNSPlayerState()->Team !=
            this->GetNSPlayerState()->Team)
        {
            FDamageEvent thisEvent(UDamageType::StaticClass());
            OtherChar->TakeDamage(10.0f, thisEvent, this->
            GetController(), this);

            APlayerController* thisPC = Cast<APlayerController>(GetCo
            ntroller());

            thisPC->ClientPlayForceFeedback(HitSuccessFeedback,
    false, NAME_None);
        }
    }
}
```

Again, this code will look very familiar to that of the code we used in `BossMode` for our tracking ray cast. In this instance, we are looking for objects that are part of `ECC_GameChannel1`. This is the custom game channel that we will be using to create the character collision channel. This is specified by the `FCollisionObjectQueryParams` struct. We then specify that the line trace should ignore the actor this function is being called from via the `this` keyword. We then perform the ray trace by calling `LineTraceSingleByObjecType()`. This method will take in our collision query parameter `struct`s. This will return a positive hit on the first object that is collided with that meets the query parameters.

We then check the `bBlockingHit` member of the `FHitResult` return type. If a blocking hit is found, we then do a few things. First, we cast the `HitActor` member of the `FHitResult` struct to an `ANSCharacter`. If this cast is successful, we then check that the team of the hit actor and the team of the current actor differ. If this resolves as true, we inform the hit actor to take 10.0f health damage. As we have overridden the `TakeDamage` function in our `ANSCharacter` class definition, we will be able to define how this damage is interpreted. Finally, we inform the owning-client of the shooting character of a successful hit via the `ClientPlayForceFeedback()` method of `APlayerController`. This will cause the character's owning-client to play the force feedback asset we are going to store in the `UForceFeedbackAsset` handle declared earlier.

Taking damage and UE4 timers

Now, let's define how our character is going to take damage. Add the following function definition to the `.cpp`:

```
float ANSCharacter::TakeDamage(float Damage, struct FDamageEvent
const& DamageEvent, AController* EventInstigator, AActor*
DamageCauser)
{
    Super::TakeDamage(Damage, DamageEvent, EventInstigator,
    DamageCauser);

    if (Role == ROLE_Authority &&
        DamageCauser != this &&
        NSPlayerState->Health > 0)
    {
        NSPlayerState->Health -= Damage;
        PlayPain();

        if (NSPlayerState->Health <= 0)
        {
            NSPlayerState->Deaths++;
```

```
            // Player has died time to respawn
            MultiCastRagdoll();

            ANSCharacter * OtherChar =
            Cast< ANSCharacter >(DamageCauser);

            if (OtherChar)
            {
                OtherChar->NSPlayerState->Score += 1.0f;
            }

            // After 3 seconds respawn
            FTimerHandle thisTimer;

            GetWorldTimerManager().SetTimer<ANSCharacter>
            (thisTimer,
            this, & ANSCharacter::Respawn, 3.0f, false);

        }
    }

    return Damage;
}
```

Here we are calling into the super class implementation of `TakeDamage()`. We then check that this character meets some requirements before taking damage. This method must be executed on the `ROLE_Authority`, the damage causer must not be itself, and the current health of the character must be above 0. If all of these conditions are met, we then subtract the damage amount from the health value stored in the `ANSPlayerState`. As this is a replicated value and it is being set on the server (`ROLE_Authority`), all other instances of this `ANSPlayerState` will have the health value update appropriately. We then inform the client to play a pain sound effect via the client `PlayPain()` RPC.

Following this, we check whether the player's health has fallen below zero. If so, we need to handle player death. The first thing we do is increment the number of deaths on the damaged actor. We then call the `MultiCastRagdoll()` method so that all connected clients witness the death via a ragdoll animation. We then check that the other actor is of type `ANSCharacter` via casting. If the cast is successful, we increment the score of the other player as they just killed an enemy.

Now we need to be able to respawn the character that was just set to ragdoll in 3 seconds. We do this using the `FTimerManager`, much like we did in Bounty Dash when we were working the object and coin spawners. We create a timer that will execute the respawn function after 3 seconds have passed. This will ensure we have plenty of time to witness the enemy character's mesh ragdoll after death before being respawned. Next, we will be defining the various functions that are referenced in the `TakeDamage()` function definition. First, we will define the client `PlayPain` RPC:

```
void ANSCharacter::PlayPain_Implementation()
{
    if (Role == ROLE_AutonomousProxy)
        {
            UGameplayStatics::PlaySoundAtLocation(this, PainSound,
            GetActorLocation());
        }
}
```

This simply plays the pain sound we specify via the handle at the owning-client's actor location. We can ensure that this sound is only played on the owning client via the `Role == ROLE_AutonomousProxy)` if statement. Under this, add the following method definition:

```
void ANSCharacter::MultiCastRagdoll_Implementation()
{
    GetMesh()->SetPhysicsBlendWeight(1.0f);
    GetMesh()->SetSimulatePhysics(true);
    GetMesh()->SetCollisionProfileName("Ragdoll");
}
```

This is the multicast RPC that will set the dead character's mesh to ragdoll on all connected clients. It simply uses the `GetMesh()` method to get a handle to the character mesh and call the appropriate functions. Now we need to define the respawn function for our character; this will be quite simple for now, as the main respawn functionality will take place in the `ANSGameMode` object, functionality we have yet to specify. For now, add the following definition:

```
void ANSCharacter::Respawn()
{
    if (Role == ROLE_Authority)
    {
        // Get Location from game mode
        NSPlayerState->Health = 100.0f;
            /* Cast<ANSGameMode>(GetWorld()->
            GetAuthGameMode())->Respawn(this); */
        Destroy(true, true);
    }
}
```

Here we are simply checking that this function is being executed on the authority instance, then destroying the current actor. As you can see, there is a commented line of code invoking the respawn function on the game mode. We will be defining this function later and un-commenting this line.

Cleaning up shop

The last few methods we have to define are the `GetNSPlayerState()`, `SetNSPlayerState()`, and `PossessedBy()` methods. Let's start with `PossessedBy()`:

```
void ANSCharacter::PossessedBy(AController* NewController)
{
    Super::PossessedBy(NewController);

    NSPlayerState = Cast<ANSPlayerState>(PlayerState);

    if (Role == ROLE_Authority && NSPlayerState != nullptr)
    {
        NSPlayerState->Health = 100.0f;
    }
}
```

All we are doing here is ensuring that when a character is possessed by a new controller, we get a handle to the `ANSPlayerState`. For this to work, we must also ensure we specify that `ANSPlayerState` is the default player state class for this project. I will cover how we do this in the game mode later. If we are the authority and there is a successful cast to the `ANSPlayerState` class, we also set the player health to be 100.0f. Now the `GetNSPlayerState()` definition:

```
ANSPlayerState* ANSCharacter::GetNSPlayerState()
{
    if (NSPlayerState)
    {
        return NSPlayerState;
    }
    else
    {
        NSPlayerState = Cast<ANSPlayerState>(PlayerState);
        return NSPlayerState;
    }
}
```

This simply returns the `ANSPlayerState` if it is not null. If it is, we are to cast the current player state handle (replicated to all `AActors`) to an `ANSPlayerState`. Lastly, we have the setter for the `ANSPlayerState`; it appears as follows:

```
void ANSCharacter::SetNSPlayerState(ANSPlayerState* newPS)
{
    // Ensure PS is valid and only set on server
    if (newPS && Role == ROLE_Authority)
    {
        NSPlayerState = newPS;
        PlayerState = newPS;
    }
}
```

Compile and run our code! You should encounter no build errors or warnings.

Preparing the ANSCharacter blueprint

Ok, now that we have our character's base code set up, we can modify the blueprint abstraction of the `ANSCharacter` class to meet our requirements. During this section of the book, we will be creating all of the engine-side assets that we need for our `ANSCharacter` Blueprint. This includes the force feedback asset, adding a socket to the 3rd person skeletal mesh, creating the custom collision channel, and I will also show you the vector parameter we are changing from within `ANSCharacter::SetTeam()`.

Start by importing the `BulletParticle.uasset` included with this book. You can do this by either using the in-editor import options or copy and pasting the file into the NS content folder directory. Unfortunately, there is not enough time in this book to cover the creation of particle effects as it is a very in-depth and complex topic. If you wish to learn more about creating particle systems with the UE4 particle editor, go to `https://docs.unrealengine.com/latest/INT/Engine/Rendering/ParticleSystems/index.html`.

Preparing the third-person Mesh

Before we start modifying any blueprints, let's prepare the assets we are going to be using. Navigate to **UE4_Mannequin_Skeleton** in **/Game/AnimStarterPack/UE4_ Mannequin/Mesh/** in the **Content Browser**. With the skeleton open, you will be able to see a large list of all of the bones within the skeleton on the left-hand side of the window:

```
root
  pelvis
    spine_01
      spine_02
        spine_03
          clavicle_l
            upperarm_l
              lowerarm_l
                hand_l
                  index_01_l
                    index_02_l
                      index_03_l
                  middle_01_l
                    middle_02_l
                      middle_03_l
                  pinky_01_l
                    pinky_02_l
                      pinky_03_l
                  ring_01_l
                    ring_02_l
                      ring_03_l
```

Right-click on the hand_r bone found about one-third of the way down the list and select **Add Socket**. This will create a socket called hand_rSocket. We now need to position the socket via the in-viewport window transform so it sits in the center of the palm, as so:

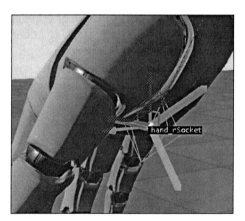

It is with this socket that we are attaching our 3rd person version of the gun mesh. We do this so the gun mesh position will update with the transformation of this bone.

Creating the force feedback asset

Force feedback assets are very easy to create, as they are essentially curves that dictate the strength of a given vibration motor in a controller. Navigate to /Game/ FirstPersonCPP/Blueprints/ and right-click in the **Content** browser and, under the **Miscellaneous** section, select **Force Feedback Effect**:

Call this new **Force Feedback Effect** HitMarkerEffect then open the asset. The editor is quite simple; it boasts a single details panel with some expandable sections. Expand the channel details section now. This will present you with four Boolean flags that represent which motors to affect, and then a curve that is how much you want the motors to vibrate over time.

We want our vibration to affect all motors and we want it to be a short 0.1-second burst of vibration. To dictate how this will work on the curve, we can right-click anywhere on the curve to add a key. Keys are time/value combinations that let us modify the curve itself. Add a curve key at 0.0 seconds, at 0.02 seconds, and at 0.1 seconds. You can simply add keys then modify the time values in the boxes provided with the key selected (it will be yellow):

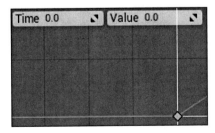

Have the value of the first key be 0, the second key be 10, and the third key be 0. If your values are too small or too varied to see the curve properly, you can hit the expand to fit horizontally and expand to fit vertically buttons found on the curve editor:

The curve should appear like this:

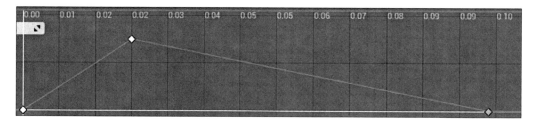

This will be a short burst of vibration power to the controller that will inform the client of a successful hit.

Custom collision channel

Just like we did in `BossMode`, we need to add a custom collision channel for our raycast collisions against the player. Luckily, the template has already added one for us. If you navigate to **Edit | Project Settings | Collision** under the **Object Channels** section, you will see **Projectile**. Simply select this collision channel then hit edit and call it `Character`!

Highlighting the VectorParameter that drives team color

Now let's look at the vector parameter node that we are modifying at runtime via the `ANSCharacter::SetTeam()` method. Navigate to `/Game/AnimStarterPack/UE4_Mannequin/Materials/` and open the `M_UE4Main_Body` material. Find the `BodyColor VectorParameter` node. It appears as follows in the graph:

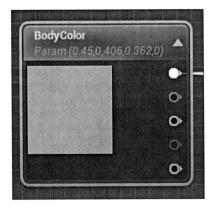

Currently set to an off-beige, we are going to be accessing this parameter by its name (**BodyColor**) and setting it to either red or blue based off of the team. As this parameter node is plugged into the calculations for the rest of the material, we are able to manipulate this one parameter so it has a drastic effect on the material appearance.

Making the fire montage assets

The last thing we need to make is the `anim` montage assets that will be used for the 1st and 3rd person fire animations. The first person montage has already been made for us and set on the character. We just need to deal with the `Fire_Rifle_Hip` animation found at `/Game/AnimStarterPack/`. Navigate to this asset now then right-click in the **Content** browser and make a new **Montage** asset. When prompted, select to base this asset on `UE4_Mannequin_Skeleton` and name it `HipFireMontage`. Open the montage asset and click and drag the `Fire_Rifle_Hip` animation from the **Asset List** on the right-hand side of the window onto the montage timeline. The final timeline should appear as follows:

Montage						
Montage Group: 'DefaultGroup'						
Default						
Fire_Rifle_Hip						DefaultGroup.DefaultSlot ▾

Now address the **Anim Asset Details** panel. Change the **Blend In Time** to `0.0` and the **Blend Out** to `0.0`. We need to do this as our animation is so short that having a blend in and out would remove a lot of the animation's articulation. The last thing we need to do is make some modifications to UE4ASP_HeroTPP_AnimBlueprint. This file can be found under `Game/AnimStarterPack/`. Navigate to and open this file now. Navigate to the **Anim Graph** for this Anim BP and modify it so it matches the following:

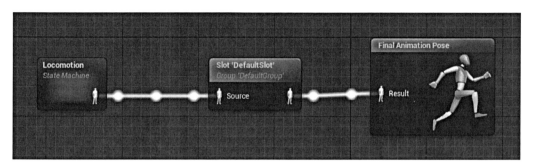

Tying it all together

With all of our assets prepared, we can now construct the physical arrangement of our character's components in a blueprint abstraction of ANSCharacter. Thankfully, one has already been created for us; navigate to the FirstPersonCharacter Blueprint at `/Game/FirstPersonCPP/Blueprints/`. Open the Blueprint now.

First off, select the mesh component and address the **Details** panel. Ensure that the SK_Mannequin mesh is set as the SkeletalMesh property of the **Mesh** section, and that the **Anim Blueprint Generated Class** is set to UE4ASP_HeroTPP_AnimBlueprint under the **Animation** section. Then ensure the **Transform** matches this:

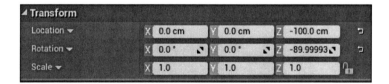

This will include and position our 3rd person mesh so it appears as follows:

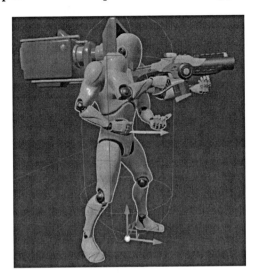

As you can see, the head of this mesh is occluding much of what the camera can observe. This is why we have set it so that the owner of the mesh cannot see it, otherwise their view would be filled with their own character's head. Next, select the TP_Gun component and ensure the SkeletalMesh property is set to SK_FPGun, and ensure that the **Transform** of the component matches the following:

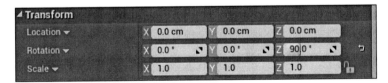

Now we can add the 3rd person gunshot particle. Select the TP_GunShotParticle and address the **Components** panel. Under the **Particles** section, set the **Template** to P_Explosion. We will also temporarily set the **Auto Activate** property under the **Activation** section to true so we can test our particle changes. What we need to do is scale and position this particle system so it plays at the tip of our 3rd person gun and is the right size. We can do this by matching these transform properties in the **Transform** section of the following **Details** panel:

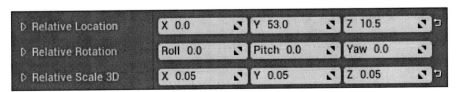

Next, we can do the same with the FP_GunShotParticle but this time we need to position this system so it exists at the tip of the 1st person gun mesh instead. We do this because if you only used the 3rd person particle effect when the owning-client shot a bullet, it would look as though the projectile explosion is coming from his hips. To position and scale this system correctly, match the following transform:

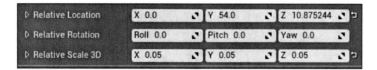

Before moving on, be sure to set the **Auto Activate** property to false on both particle systems as we only want them to activate on command. Finally, we can set the BulletParticle to be the P_BulletLine particle effect imported to the project. Then set the transform to match the following:

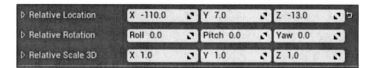

This will position the particle system so the visual effect begins its lifetime right at the start of the barrel! The last thing we need to do is populate the asset handles with the assets we just made. In the **Components** panel select the **FirstPersonCharacter(self)** component. Under the **Gameplay** section, match the following properties:

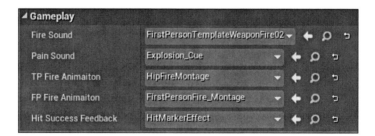

The last thing we need to do is ensure our custom collision channel is set on our capsule. Select the **Capsule Component** and address the **Details** panel, and ensure the **Collision** section matches the following:

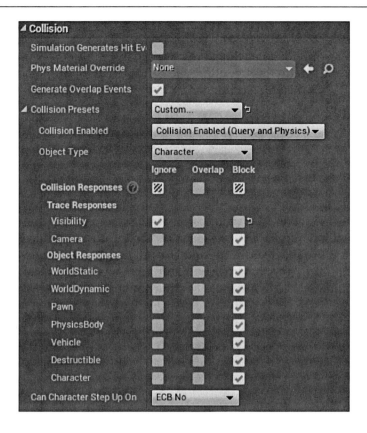

Now we can test our player! Run a PIE session and run around, jump, and shoot! All of our effects and animations play in first person just great. You will also notice a big red debug line to show that our shot has been performed on the server (as there is only one PIE session running, you are the server). You should see something similar to this:

Testing the multiplayer with a PIE session!

Unreal Engine has provided us with a great way to test multiplayer projects within the editor itself. We can do this by setting the editor to run multiple players when we press **Play**. We do this by selecting the dropdown next to the play button and changing the number of players to three:

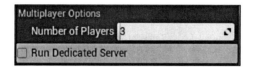

This will give us one server (the main editor window) and two clients (the two windows that will pop up). There is even an option to run a dedicated server turning the editor also into a client. With this arrangement, we can now test all of the functionality required, as we have a server authority, an owning-client autonomous proxy, and a simulated proxy instance! Try this now:

You may notice that the server instance, that being the editor window itself, has the players still colored white! That is because we have yet to set the team color on the server. We specified in the `BeginPlay()` of `ANSCharacter` to only call `SetTeam()` if the role of the character was not `Role_Authority`. As every one of the character instances on the server is the authority instance, none of them will be colored. Now, here is another cool test. You will notice that if you fire on the server, a red line will appear (being the debug line that was included in the raytrace code). However, if you fire on one of the clients, it will not. That is because our raytrace code is only taking place on the server. What you will notice, however, is that when a client fires, the debug line is still drawn on the server! That is because the code is being executed on the server instance of the game client, thus the debug line code is being hit.

Here is an example screenshot:

The previous screenshot is a view of the same game state; however, we can now see all of the fired shots from the clients. With all of the clients now on screen, we can also test our 1st and 3rd person visual assets. We can see that the fire animation and fire particles are playing appropriately.

Spawn points and spawning the players

With every multiplayer game, there is always going to be the need to spawn players at some point. We are going to need spawn points that can act as word space locations for the game mode to identify to be used as player spawn locations. We are also going to require these spawn points to identify with a team color so only the blue team gets spawned at one set of points, and the red team at another. The other hitch is that this spawning must only take place on the server, but we can handle that from the game mode code object. For now, open up the C++ class wizard and create a code object called NSSpawnPoint that inherits from AActor.

Defining the ANSSpawnPoint class

Navigate to NSSpawnPoint.h, add #include "NSGameMode.h", and ensure the class definition matches the following:

```
UCLASS()
class NS_API ANSSpawnPoint : public AActor
{
    GENERATED_BODY()
```

```
public:
// Sets default values for this actor's properties
    ANSSpawnPoint();

    // Called every frame
    virtual void Tick( float DeltaSeconds ) override;

    virtual void OnConstruction(const FTransform& Transform) override;

    UFUNCTION()
        void ActorBeginOverlaps(AActor* OtherActor);

    UFUNCTION()
    void ActorEndOverlaps(AActor* OtherActor);

    bool GetBlocked()
    {
        return OverlappingActors.Num() != 0;
    }

    UPROPERTY(EditAnywhere, BlueprintReadOnly)
    ETeam Team;

private:

    UCapsuleComponent* SpawnCapsule;

    TArray<class AActor*> OverlappingActors;
};
```

Here we have overridden the `Tick()` method so we can execute custom tick functionality. Then we have overridden a function we have yet to work with, the `OnConstruction()` method. This is used to execute any functionality that you want to take place after the item has been constructed. What this lets us do is modify the object when one of the default properties is edited in the editor, or the object is placed in the scene. We will use this to color the spawn point based off of the team color!

Following this, we have two `UFUNCTIONS` that will be parsed to the begin and end overlap delegates. We then have a short `GetBlocked()` method that will tell us whether the spawn point is currently blocked by anything. We will use this to check whether a spawn point is valid for a character spawn. Following our `public` methods, we have one `public` and two `private` members. We have a public `ETeam` member that will be used to hold the current team of the spawn point, a `private` `UCapsuleComponent` handle that will be used to initialize the collider for this actor, and a `private` `TArray` of `AActors` that represents any actors that are blocking the spawn point.

ANSSpawnPoint function definitions

The definitions for the spawn point are fairly simple. We simply need to initialize our actor properly in the default constructor, color the capsule in the OnConstruction() method, then detect when an actor is overlapping with the collider. Let's begin with the default constructor. Navigate to the NSSpawnPoint.cpp and add the following:

```
ANSSpawnPoint::ANSSpawnPoint()
{
    // Set this actor to call Tick() every frame.  You can turn to
    this off to
    improve performance if you don't need it.
    PrimaryActorTick.bCanEverTick = true;

    SpawnCapsule = CreateDefaultSubobject<UCapsuleComponent>
    (TEXT("Capsule"));
    SpawnCapsule->SetCollisionProfileName("OverlapAllDynamic");
    SpawnCapsule->bGenerateOverlapEvents = true;
    SpawnCapsule->SetCollisionResponseToChannel(ECC_GameTraceChannel1,
    ECollisionResponse::ECR_Overlap);

    OnActorBeginOverlap.AddDynamic(this,
    &ANSSpawnPoint::ActorBeginOverlaps);
    OnActorEndOverlap.AddDynamic(this,
    &ANSSpawnPoint::ActorEndOverlaps);
}
```

The only thing of note here is that we are setting the collision response to our custom channel. Using SetCollisionRepsonseToChannel(), we can ensure that SpawnCapsule will have an overlapping relationship with our custom character collision channel. Without this, the default behavior to assume would be block (as that is what we specified in the custom channel settings). Following this, let's add the OnConstruction() method definition:

```
void ANSSpawnPoint::OnConstruction(const FTransform& Transform)
{
    if (Team == ETeam::RED_TEAM)
    {
        SpawnCapsule->ShapeColor = FColor(255, 0, 0);
    }
    else // (Team == ETeam::BLUE_TEAM)
    {
        SpawnCapsule->ShapeColor = FColor(0, 0, 255);
    }
}
```

This method will be called whenever a default property is changed. In our case, that will happen when we toggle the value stored at `Team`. We have specified that this member be editable anywhere so that we can do this. We simply set the shape color to be red if the spawn point is part of the red team, otherwise we set the color to be blue. Following this, define the `Tick()` method as follows:

```
// Called every frame
void ANSSpawnPoint::Tick( float DeltaTime )
{
    Super::Tick(DeltaTime);
    SpawnCapsule->UpdateOverlaps();
}
```

The only thing we are doing in this method is forcing the spawn capsule to update its overlapping information. We do this as we will be teleporting characters to the spawn point location, and this may void the overlap detection initially. After this, define the two overlapping functions as follows:

```
void ANSSpawnPoint::ActorBeginOverlaps(AActor* OtherActor)
{
    if (ROLE_Authority == Role)
    {
        if (OverlappingActors.Find(OtherActor) == INDEX_NONE)
        {
            OverlappingActors.Add(OtherActor);
        }
    }
}


void ANSSpawnPoint::ActorEndOverlaps(AActor* OtherActor)
{
    if (ROLE_Authority == Role)
    {
        if (OverlappingActors.Find(OtherActor) != INDEX_NONE)
        {
            OverlappingActors.Remove(OtherActor);
        }
    }
}
```

Whenever an overlap is detected, we use the `Find()` method of the `TArray` object to ensure that the offending actor does not already exist in the overlapping actors. We do this by ensuring the index returned is `INDEX_NONE`, meaning nothing was found. Whenever an actor registers an end overlap event, we do the opposite. Checking that in fact this actor does exist in the array, if so we will remove the actor. Compile and run this code; we are about to delve into the world of game modes and servers!

Game modes and servers

Alright, finally we can create our game mode. For this network shooter, our game mode is going to control traveling between levels, assigning teams, and spawning/respawning players. To do this, our game mode is going to have to detect a few things. Firstly, we are going to have to override how the game mode detects a new player joining the server session. We also have to make sure we assign this new player a team and spawn them properly. We already have a GameMode generated for us that was created with the template.

Game mode class definition

Navigate to NSGameMode.h and modify the class definition underneath our ETeam enum so it matches the following:

```
UCLASS(minimalapi)
class ANSGameMode : public AGameMode
{
    GENERATED_BODY()

public:
    ANSGameMode();
    virtual void BeginPlay() override;
    virtual void Tick(float DeltaSeconds) override;
    virtual void PostLogin(APlayerController* NewPlayer) override;
virtual void EndPlay(const EEndPlayReason::Type EndPlayReason)
override;

    void Respawn(class ANSCharacter* Character);
    void Spawn(class ANSCharacter* Character);

private:
    TArray<class ANSCharacter*> RedTeam;
    TArray<class ANSCharacter*> BlueTeam;

    TArray<class ANSSpawnPoint*> RedSpawns;
    TArray<class ANSSpawnPoint*> BlueSpawns;
    TArray<class ANSCharacter*> ToBeSpawned;

    bool bGameStarted;
    static bool bInGameMenu;
};
```

Here we have overridden a few of the functions found in the `AGameMode` interface. `BeginPlay()` is going to let us initialize some of the default behaviors for the game mode, such as find all available spawn points. `Tick()` will let us check for input and spawn any queued characters. `PostLogin()` is the method that will be called whenever a client joins the server session; this method takes in handle to the `APlayerController` of the client that just joined. It is with this function that we will execute functionality on the player controller so we can prepare that player for play. `EndPlay()` will be called when a game session is ended; we will be able to interpret how to treat `ANSGameMode` static members when this happens.

Following our virtual functions, we have `Spawn()` and `Respawn()`. These methods will all be used to spawn players; the respawn method is the one referenced in the `ANSCharacter` that must be uncommented. The members of this object include five arrays that we will use to store characters from both teams, spawn points from both teams, and any characters that are queued to be spawned by the game mode. Lastly, we have some Boolean flags that will determine the state of the game, one of them being declared as static as we wish this Boolean to remain in memory during server travel, which we will cover later.

Construction the Game mode and Finding Spawn points

Navigate to `NSGameMode.cpp` now and ensure the include list at the top of the file matches the following:

```
#include "NS.h"
#include "NSGameMode.h"
#include "NSHUD.h"
#include "NSPlayerState.h"
#include "NSSpawnPoint.h"
#include "NSCharacter.h"
```

Let's start defining our game mode functions with the constructor. Modify the generated code present in `NSGameMode.cpp` to the following:

```
bool ANSGameMode::bInGameMenu = true;

ANSGameMode::ANSGameMode()
    : Super()
{
    // set default pawn class to our Blueprinted character
static ConstructorHelpers::FClassFinder<APawn>
PlayerPawnClassFinder(TEXT
```

```
("/Game/FirstPersonCPP/Blueprints/FirstPersonCharacter"));

    DefaultPawnClass = PlayerPawnClassFinder.Class;
    PlayerStateClass = ANSPlayerState::StaticClass();

    // use our custom HUD class
    HUDClass = ANSHUD::StaticClass();

    bReplicates = true;
}
```

The most important point to note about this definition is the initialization of our
static `bool bInGameMenu`. This `bool` has been declared as static so that its state
will persist through server travels to new maps. As you can see, we have had to
initialize this static memory as you normally would. Within the game mode itself,
we simply set the default pawn class to whatever generated class is found at our
`FirstPersonCharacter` Blueprint location. We then set the player state class and
HUD class to the appropriate defaults then set the game mode to replicate. Ensure
you add #include. Now let's work with `BeginPlay()`:

```
void ANSGameMode::BeginPlay()
{
    Super::BeginPlay();

    if (Role == ROLE_Authority)
    {
        for (TActorIterator<ANSSpawnPoint> Iter(GetWorld()); Iter;
        ++Iter)
        {
            if ((*Iter)->Team == ETeam::RED_TEAM)
            {
                RedSpawns.Add(*Iter);
            }
            else
            {
                BlueSpawns.Add(*Iter);
            }
        }

        // Spawn the server
        APlayerController* thisCont = GetWorld()->
        GetFirstPlayerController();

        if (thisCont)
        {
```

```
            ANSCharacter* thisChar = Cast<ANSCharacter>(thisCont->
            GetPawn());

            thisChar->SetTeam(ETeam::BLUE_TEAM);
            BlueTeam.Add(thisChar);
            Spawn(thisChar);
        }

    }
}
```

Even though the game mode will only exist on the server, it is still important to check authority. We are iterating over all `ANSSpawnPoint` objects in the scene via an `ActorIterator` template class. We then check each spawn point to see which team it is associated with, then sort it into the appropriate array. We do this so we can perform generic spawn logics on both containers. Finally, we spawn the server character; we have to do this manually as the server will not connect to itself, thus a post-login call will not be made. It is also important to note that there will be no `Role_Autonomous` proxy instance for this character as there is no owning-client, which would be the server itself.

Ending the Game and ticking the game mode

Next, we must provide a definition for the virtual `EndPlay()` method:

```
void ANSGameMode::EndPlay(const EEndPlayReason::Type EndPlayReason)
{
if (EndPlayReason == EEndPlayReason::Quit ||
    EndPlayReason == EEndPlayReason::EndPlayInEditor)
    {
        bInGameMenu = true;
    }
}
```

Here we simply ensure that play is not being ended for map traveling reasons and that it is in fact either a definite quit event or end PIE session event. If so, we are to reset our static Boolean so the game always starts in menu. Following this, we will be defining our `Tick()` method. This method will handle checking whether there are any players that need to be spawned and whether the *R* key has been pressed. If so, we will travel the server sessions to the map we have been working from. Add the following code to the `.cpp`:

```
void ANSGameMode::Tick(float DeltaSeconds)
{
```

```
    if (Role == ROLE_Authority)
    {
        APlayerController* thisCont = GetWorld()->
        GetFirstPlayerController();

        if (ToBeSpawned.Num() != 0)
        {
            for (auto charToSpawn : ToBeSpawned)
            {
                Spawn(charToSpawn);
            }
        }

        if (thisCont != nullptr && thisCont->IsInputKeyDown(EKeys::R))
        {
            bInGameMenu = false;
            GetWorld()->ServerTravel(
            L"/Game/FirstPersonCPP/Maps
            FirstPersonExampleMap?Listen");
        }
    }
}
```

Here we can see that we check again to ensure this is executing on only the authority, even though the game mode itself should only ever exist on the server. The first thing we do is retrieve the player controller from the game world. We then check whether our ToBeSpawned container is not empty. If so, we iterate over all characters to be spawned and invoke the Spawn() function. This will ensure that any characters that need to spawn that round will do so. We are doing this check in the tick to ensure that any spawns rejected due to blocked spawn points will still be spawned eventually.

After this, we then check that the player controller we obtained is valid and that the server player has pressed the R key. If so, we wish to travel the server. We are doing this by calling the method ServerTravel(). This method will travel the server to the provided map URL; it will also travel all connected clients to the map. You may have noticed that we have appended the map URL with ?Listen. This is an extra command that ensures that the map the server is traveling to will accept connecting clients.

The important thing to note is that, when the server travels the player states, player controllers and game states all persist through traveling.

For more on traveling within networked multiplayer games, visit https://docs.unrealengine.com/latest/INT/Gameplay/Networking/Travelling/.

Connecting players

We are now about to write how we handle players connecting to our game session. Whenever a new player joins the game, we want to assign that player a team and ensure that the new player is queued to spawn. This spawning will take place on the server as replicated actors should only be created/destroyed by the server. We are going to do this via the `PostLogin()` method we declared earlier. As stated previously, this method will be called whenever a new client joins the server session and will parse the new `PlayerController` that has connected. Add the following function definition to the .cpp:

```cpp
void ANSGameMode::PostLogin(APlayerController* NewPlayer)
{
    Super::PostLogin(NewPlayer);

    ANSCharacter* Teamless = Cast<ANSCharacter>(NewPlayer->GetPawn());
    ANSPlayerState* NPlayerState = Cast<ANSPlayerState>(NewPlayer->
    PlayerState);

    if (Teamless != nullptr && NPlayerState != nullptr)
    {
        Teamless->SetNSPlayerState(NPlayerState);
    }
    // Assign Team and spawn
    if (Role == ROLE_Authority && Teamless != nullptr)
    {
        if (BlueTeam.Num() > RedTeam.Num())
        {
            RedTeam.Add(Teamless);
            NPlayerState->Team = ETeam::RED_TEAM;
        }
        else if (BlueTeam.Num() < RedTeam.Num())
        {
            BlueTeam.Add(Teamless);
            NPlayerState->Team = ETeam::BLUE_TEAM;
            }
        else // Teams are equal
        {
            BlueTeam.Add(Teamless);
            NPlayerState->Team = ETeam::BLUE_TEAM;
        }

        Teamless->CurrentTeam = NPlayerState->Team;
        Teamless->SetTeam(NPlayerState->Team);
```

```
            Spawn(Teamless);
        }
    }
```

Here we are ensuring that the character type that is owned by the parsed controller is of type `ANSCharacter`; we also ensure that the player state of the controller is also of type `ANSPlayerState`. We do this via casting both and checking that the casts were valid. Following this, we simply assign the new player state to the connected character. We then check the size of the red and blue team arrays. If one is smaller than the other, they will be assigned the new player, and the player will have its team flag set in both the character and the player state. If the teams are the same size, the player will be given to the blue team. Lastly, we pass the newly connected character to the `Spawn()` function.

Spawning the players

Our spawn functionality will be fairly simple; we do not have to do anything special to spawn networked characters. We are simply going to check the team of the player to be spawned, ensure the spawns for that team are unblocked, and spawn a player. Add the following function to the `.cpp`:

```
void ANSGameMode::Spawn(class ANSCharacter* Character)
{
    if (Role == ROLE_Authority)

        // Find Spawn point that is not blocked
        ANSSpawnPoint* thisSpawn = nullptr;
        TArray<ANSSpawnPoint*>* targetTeam = nullptr;

        if (Character->CurrentTeam == ETeam::BLUE_TEAM)
        {
            targetTeam = &BlueSpawns;
        }
        else
        {
            targetTeam = &RedSpawns;
        }

        for (auto Spawn : (*targetTeam))
        {
            if (!Spawn->GetBlocked())
            {
                // Remove from spawn queue location
```

```
            if (ToBeSpawned.Find(Character) != INDEX_NONE)
            {
                ToBeSpawned.Remove(Character);
            }

            // Otherwise set actor location
            Character->SetActorLocation(Spawn->
            GetActorLocation());

            Spawn->UpdateOverlaps();

            Return;
        }
    }

    if (ToBeSpawned.Find(Character) == INDEX_NONE)
    {
        ToBeSpawned.Add(Character);
    }
  }
}
```

Here we again check authority. We then declare two handles, one for an
`ANSSpawnPoint` and another for a `TArray` that contains `ANSSpawnPoint` handles. We
then assign the address of the appropriate spawn array based off of the player's team
type. We then iterate over that array and check whether the spawn is not blocked. If
we find a non-blocked spawn, we check whether the player is contained within the
`ToBeSpawned` array. If so, we remove from the array before spawning, as this means
it was blocked from spawning at the last attempt.

The act of spawning is very simple, as the character will have already been created
in memory when the client joined; we simply set the actor location to be that of the
spawn point. We then update the overlaps on the spawn to ensure it detects the new
actor. We then return out of the function to cease any further execution.

If the function continues, this means the player was not spawned and should be
added to the `ToBeSpawned` array. We check that the player does not already exist
in the array and add it.

Respawning the player

Respawning will be a little different, as we need to be able to reset not only the player states, but also the states of the components on ALL clients. When dealing with things such as ragdoll, this can lead to some serious desynching of assets. Instead we will be creating brand new objects and destroying the old ones. Note that this does incur a cost on respawn and may be undesirable for more complicated memory-intensive actors, but works just fine for our needs. We will do this with the `Respawn()` method that is called internally by the `ANSCharacter`. Add the following function definition to the .cpp:

```
void ANSGameMode::Respawn(class ANSCharacter* Character)
{
    if (Role == ROLE_Authority)
    {
        AController* thisPC = Character->GetController();
        Character->DetachFromControllerPendingDestroy();

        ANSCharacter* newChar = Cast<ANSCharacter>(GetWorld()->
        SpawnActor(DefaultPawnClass));

        if (newChar)
        {
            thisPC->Possess(newChar);
            ANSPlayerState* thisPS = Cast<ANSPlayerState>(newChar->
            GetController()->PlayerState);

            newChar->CurrentTeam = thisPS->Team;
            newChar->SetNSPlayerState(thisPS);

            Spawn(newChar);

            newChar->SetTeam(newChar->GetNSPlayerState()->Team);
        }
    }
}
```

The important thing to remember when addressing this function is that everything between an owning-client and server is invoked through the player controller. This means, as long as we have a handle to the player controller of the connected client, we can inform changes to the player. For example, we can now spawn a new character on the server and assign it to the player controller. This will shift the ownership for the character spawned on the server to be that of the player controller (and the owning client). The server will still be the authority for this new player.

In the previous function, we ensure that the current role is authority. If so, we are to respawn the provided character. We then get the controller from the character to be spawned and then call `DetachFromControllerPendingDestroy()`. This will detach the old character pawn from the player controller, this will flag that old pawn for destroy and free up the controller for a new character. This will also occur on the client, so be warned, if for some reason the new character is not spawned and assigned to the controller, the client will be left characterless!

Following this, we then spawn a new `ANSCharacter` via the game world and parse the default pawn class to the `SpawnActor()` method (this will ensure that our blueprint abstraction is spawned and not the base class). If this character was spawned successfully, we then ensure that the player controller possesses this new `ANSCharacter` and that we assign the `ANSPlayerState` to a new character. This will guarantee that the values saved in the player state are accessible by the new character. Following this, we call `Spawn()` on this new character so that it is positioned properly, then call `SetTeam()` on the new character so that the mesh materials are colored properly.

Now, quickly navigate back to the `NSCharacter.cpp` and go to the `Respawn()` method and uncomment the previously commented respawn line. It will appear as follows:

```
void ANSCharacter::Respawn()
{
    if (Role == ROLE_Authority)
    {
        // Get Location from game mode
        NSPlayerState->Health = 100.0f;
        Cast<ANSGameMode>(GetWorld()->GetAuthGameMode())->
        Respawn(this);

        Destroy(true, true);
    }
}
```

Preparing our game map

For now, the map is only going to work as a `testbed` for our multiplayer implementation. We need to add our spawn point objects to the map, configure their team colors, and remove any unwanted actors from the scene. As it currently stands, there is a high volume of cube physics actors. We do not want all of these actors updating over the network, as that would increase network traffic; we might as well remove them. Compile and run the code now and address the editor **World Outlier**.

Under the subfolder **Cubes**, remove all cube actors from the scene by highlighting all of the `EditorCubes`:

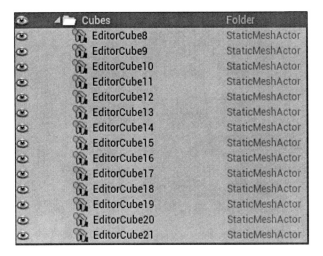

With the cubes selected, press the *delete* key. Next we are going to place our spawns! Create a new Blueprint actor that inherits from `NSSPawnPoint` called **Spawn Point**. Open the generated BP now, select **SpawnPoint(self)** from the **Components** panel, and address the **Details** panel. Under the **Replication** section, untick the `NetLoadOnClient` flag, as only our server is concerned with spawning the players. This object does not need to exist on the client. Now let's place these spawns in the scene!

Place six of these new blueprints in the scene in rows of three; set half of the spawns to be `BLUE_TEAM` and the other to `RED_TEAM`. The property will be found in the **Details** panel under the `NSSPawnPoint` section. I place the spawns here on the following map:

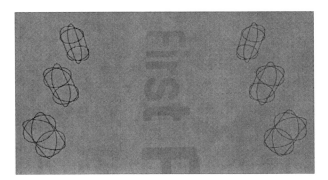

Now when you start a PIE session with multiple clients, the spawns/teams will be assigned properly. Try a PIE session with four players; you will see something like this:

Testing our game functionality

Ok, now we have two teams, both with players that can shoot. Let's try shooting a player on the enemy team and see what happens. It is advised that you set it up so you can see both the editor viewport and two of the client viewports so you can be sure that everything is working as intended. Hopefully you will find that if you shoot an enemy player 10 times (100 - 10*10 == 0), you will then see that character ragdoll! And after three seconds, respawn!

Ensure that this is viewable on all clients and the server, especially that the player is reset properly on respawn!

Drawing the HUD and preparing the lobby

Ok, the last thing we need to do is provide each player with an accurate readout of their own score/deaths! We will then also set up a pseudo multiplayer lobby by showing who is connected to the game, and that we are waiting on the server to initiate travel to the main multiplayer map. This, however, is going to require that we have information from the GameMode replicated to all clients, namely when the game has started. We already have a static bool present in the game mode that we can use, but we now need to replicate the value of this bool to all clients. The only way we can do that is with a GameState.

Creating the GameState

In a very similar way to PlayerStates of the PlayerController, we have GameStates for game modes. They are replicated objects that are replicated on all connected clients. We can use this game state to store variables pertaining to the game world within this state. Game states, by default, contain information on all of the currently connected players via player states, how long the game has been running, and other game state variables.

We are going to be creating a very simple game state that contains a single Boolean. Open the **C++ class wizard** and create an object that inherits from GameState. Call this object NSGameState. Once the code for this object has been compiled, navigate to NSGameState.h. Modify the class declaration to match the following:

```
UCLASS()
class NS_API ANSGameState : public AGameState
{
    GENERATED_BODY()

public:
    ANSGameState();

UPROPERTY(Replicated)
    bool bInMenu;
};
```

Here we are simply declaring a default class constructor and a Boolean flag that will inform the player's HUD if the game is still in the menu, and yet to be run by the server. Navigate to `NSGameState.cpp` now and add the following code:

```
ANSGameState::ANSGameState()
{
    bInMenu = false;
}


void
ANSGameState::GetLifetimeReplicatedProps(TArray<FLifetimeProperty>&
OutLifetimeProps) const
{
    Super::GetLifetimeReplicatedProps(OutLifetimeProps);

    DOREPLIFETIME(ANSGameState, bInMenu);
}
```

Ensure that you also add `#include "Net/UnrealNetwork.h"` to your `.cpp` include list. The previous code will simply set that, by default, the game is not in the menu and then ensures that we replicate that variable over its lifetime whenever it is changed. Now navigate to your `NSGameMode.cpp` and address the constructor. We need to inform the game mode of its new game state class. We can do this by adding the following line to the `ANSGameMode` constructor:

```
GameStateClass = ANSGameState::StaticClass();
```

Be sure to also include `#include "NSGameState.h"` in the `.cpp` include list.

Drawing in the HUD

Ok, now we can do some basic information drawing in the HUD! We are going to be using basic text and colors to create our HUD readout. Alright, let's start by modifying the already generated ANSHUD class. Navigate to NSHUD.cpp now. We are not going to be removing any functionality from the DrawHUD() method, we are simply going to be appending to it. Before we begin, be sure to modify the include list of this .cpp to include the following:

```
#include "NSCharacter.h"
#include "NSGameState.h"
#include "NSGameMode.h"
#include "NSPlayerState.h"
```

The first thing we need to do is query the `ANSGameState` we just created if the game is in fact still in the menu. If so, we want to be able to draw the name of each connected client underneath their respective teams:

```
ANSGameState* thisGameState = Cast<ANSGameState>(GetWorld()->
GetGameState());

    if (thisGameState != nullptr && thisGameState->bInMenu)
    {
        int BlueScreenPos = 50;
        int RedScreenPos = Center.Y + 50;
        int nameSpacing = 25;
        int NumBlueteam = 1;
        int NumReadTeam = 1;
```

The first thing we do is get our game state from the game world. We have to use the game world here as the game mode itself is not replicated. If we successfully get the game state, we then check whether the Boolean value is contained within. If this resolves to true, we now know we must draw the in-menu HUD. We then declare all of the logic variables we are going to need. We have specified where the blue team list will start and where the red team list will start. Each name will be 25 units apart and we have then declared two counters that will be used to increment where we draw team names.

Following this, add:

```
FString thisString = "BLUE TEAM:";
DrawText(thisString, FColor::Cyan, 50, BlueScreenPos);

thisString = "RED TEAM:";
DrawText(thisString, FColor::Red, 50, RedScreenPos);
for (auto player : thisGameState->PlayerArray)
{
    ANSPlayerState* thisPS = Cast<ANSPlayerState>(player);

    if (thisPS)
    {
        if (thisPS->Team == ETeam::BLUE_TEAM)
        {
            thisString = FString::Printf(TEXT("%s"), &(thisPS->
            PlayerName[0]));

            DrawText(thisString, FColor::Cyan, 50,
            BlueScreenPos + nameSpacing * NumBlueteam);
```

```
                        NumBlueteam++;
            }
            else
            {
                    thisString = FString::Printf(TEXT("%s"), &(thisPS->
PlayerName[0]));

DrawText(thisString, FColor::Red, 50, RedScreenPos + nameSpacing *
NumReadTeam);

                    NumReadTeam++;
            }
        }
    }
```

The previous code starts by drawing either BLUE TEAM: or RED TEAM: at the previously mentioned screen positions. We then iterate over all of the player states that exist in the GameState base class. This array will contain the player states of all connected clients. This means we can use this container as a go-to when wanting information from every connected client. Then we check which team the player state is associated with. We then draw the name of that player state by getting the player name member and drawing it, in the right color at the team screen position, plus the 25-unit offset multiplied by the number of names already drawn. The final thing we need to do for this is inform the clients that they are waiting on the server to start the game, and inform the server to press *R* if they wish to travel:

```
if (GetWorld()->GetAuthGameMode())
{
    thisString = "Press R to start game";
    DrawText(thisString, FColor::Yellow, Center.X, Center.Y);

}
else
{
    thisString = "Waiting on Server!!";
    DrawText(thisString, FColor::Yellow, Center.X, Center.Y);
}
} <-- closes if (thisGameState != nullptr && thisGameState->bInMenu)
```

Instead of checking authority, we can check whether a given HUD object is not the server by seeing whether we can get access to the Game Mode! As only the server will have a valid game mode, this will return null for all other net roles. Here we check whether the return is valid. If so, we draw the server message; if not, we draw the client message. This closes the functionality for when the clients are still in-menu.

Now we must write the accompanying `else` for the `if` statement:

```
else
{
ANSCharacter* ThisChar = Cast<ANSCharacter>(UGameplayStatics::GetPlaye
rPawn(GetWorld(), 0));

    if (ThisChar != nullptr)
    {
        if (ThisChar->GetNSPlayerState())
        {
            FString HUDString = FString::Printf(TEXT("Health: %f,
            Score: %d, Deaths: %d"), ThisChar->GetNSPlayerState()->
            Health, ThisChar->GetNSPlayerState()->Score, ThisChar->
            GetNSPlayerState()->Deaths);

            DrawText(HUDString, FColor::Yellow, 50, 50);
        }
    }
}
```

Here we simply get the player state from the player and draw the health, score, and deaths to the screen in yellow in the top left-hand corner.

Now navigate back to NSGameMode.cpp, we have to add this line:

```
Cast<ANSGameState>(GameState)->bInMenu = bInGameMenu;
```

in `NSGameMode::BeginPlay()` within the true scope for the role authority check, and after we have traveled the server in `ANSGameMode::Tick()`.

Testing our Game

Alright! That is everything we are going to be implementing in this chapter. Build and run the code now. The last thing we have to do is set the default map to be a blank map, this will act as a temporary menu map. Let's do this now. With the editor open, go to the **File** dropdown and select **New Level...**, then select **Empty Level**. Now simply save this level and call it **Menu Map**. Then navigate to **Edit | Project Settings | Maps and Modes**. Under the **Default Maps** section, change both **Game Default Map** and **Editor Startup Map** to **Menu Map**.

Once this is done, simply start a PIE session; I chose one with three players. The server will see this:

And the clients will see this:

As you can see, both display the teams and connected players! The numbers that are underneath the team names represent the players. We currently have three players connected, 265, 266, and 267. As you can see, the game mode has correctly filtered the players into the appropriate teams. Ok, now select the server window and press R. This will travel the server session to our multiplayer map. This will also transport all clients and if you see the HUD now, it will appear as follows:

LIGHTING NEEDS TO BE REBUILT (1 unbuilt object(s))
Health: 100.000000, Score: 2.000000, Deaths: 1

You will also notice that if you die or kill players, your scores, deaths, and health will also update!

Summary

Alright! Congratulations, you survived your first encounter with UE4 networking! We have learnt so much during this chapter. We have learnt about networking basics, replication, client/server networking patterns, RPCs, player states, game state, and so much more. This is the capping of your Unreal education. In the next chapter, we are going to be covering how we can improve the client-side representation of our FPS characters by looking into Aim Blendspaces and blueprint-based replication! We will also be packaging our project so we can give this project to our friends to play. This will be the last chapter in this book and I am extremely excited to finish this Unreal journey with you.

10
Goodbyes and Thank yous

Welcome to the final chapter of *Unreal Engine By Example*. To wrap up our journey we are going to look into how we can package our project into a binary executable! You will be able to give this executable and asset package to your friends to test the Network Shooter project together on different computers! Before we finish our education with UE4 I will quickly cover how we can get verbose profiling information from our projects. Finally, we will go over a brief recap of the book so we can revisit some of the learning experiences that we had during this UE4 journey!

We will cover:

- The UE4 packaging process
- Aim offsets and how to use them
- Testing packaged networking builds via console commands
- Profiling and debugging via console commands
- Unreal by example recap!

Packaging a project

Now that we have finished writing the code for NS we need to be able to test its network capabilities by packaging the project. This will produce a binary and asset package. Together these form the game files that will be installed or downloaded on a user's PC.

Build Targets

UE4's packaging system supports a wide range of development platforms. We are able to build to Android, IOS, Windows, Linux, HTML5 (web) and even PS4 or Xbox One. The latter two require development licenses, and are already installed on your PC. Preparing your project for the various build platforms is very easy and can be done via a simple dropdown. First we must describe some of the various options that will be used when packaging a project.

Build configuration

Build Configurations dictate the type of package that will be produced. Each type will control how many of the debug features available to UE4 developers are built into the packaged binary. This means we can include debugging and profiling features in our binary packages that can be used to collect data and logging when testing. When developing with a large team, regular, well-tested builds are essential for creating a quality development product. Build configurations are a great way to be able to retain debugging functionality that usually gets built out when packaging a project. The three build types we are concerned with are shipping, debug game and development. Each build type can be described as follows:

- **Debug Game**: This is the package that will include the most debugging functionality and test features. You will have full access to console commands (from within your project) and verbose logging will take place.

- **Development**: A development package is the ideal build configuration when producing a build that will be scrutinized for testing by your development team. This will remove much of the debugging functionality from the build for the sake of performance, however, you will still have access to some console commands and simple logging.

- **Shipping**: Shipping has no debugging or testing functionality and will be the build configuration that is used when producing the final product!

Compiler specific building to configuration

We are able to use `#ifdef` to dictate which of our own code is included when building for these various configurations. If you wish for a certain section of code to be compiled out depending on build configuration, you can do something like this:

```
#ifdef UE_BUILD_DEBUG
    // Code that you wish to only be present in test build
#endif // UE_BUILD_ DEBUG
The #defines are all defined as UE_BUILD_DEBUG, UE_BUILD_SHIPPING and
UE_BUILD_DEVELOPMENT.
```

Packaging NS

OK, let's make our first package for the NS project. Open the project now and, with the main editor window open, navigate to the **File** dropdown and select **Package Project**:

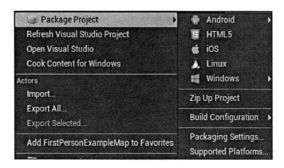

Here you can see we are presented with the various build platforms. You may notice that Xbox One and PS4 are missing. This is due to the absence of the platform development licenses on my computer. Underneath this we have **Zip Up Project**, **Build Configuration**, **Packaging Settings...** and **Supported Platforms**.

Zip Up Project is what I used to provide my completed projects to you for the purposes of this textbook! **Build Configuration** allows us to swap our build configuration from this dropdown. **Supported Platforms** is used to define which platforms our given project supports. Finally, **Packaging Settings...** lets us define how we wish our project to package. Select this now and you will be presented with the **Project Settings** window at **Project – Package**.

Here you can specify what **Build Configuration** you would like to use by default, an output path for the build (known as the staging directory), whether you would like the package to perform a full rebuild, whether the package is going to be used for distribution and whether the package should include debug files. For this package, set the **Build Configuration** to **Debug Game** and set the **Staging Directory** to be somewhere on your computer that has enough space for the package. It is important to note that the **For Distribution** option is used when you are creating applications for the IOS or Android storefronts. Your settings should appear as follows:

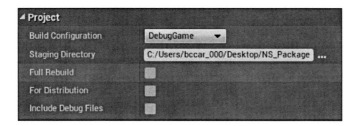

`C:/Users/bccar_000/Desktop/NS_Package` should be set to your own file path. After you have selected the correct settings, return to the **Package Project** dropdown and hover over the **Windows** option. From this select **Windows (64-bit)**; this will then prompt you to select a folder (with the staging directory specified as default). Select **Ok** and start the build! You will see this popup in the bottom right hand side of the main editor window:

You can select **Show Output Log** to see the runtime logging output from the package:

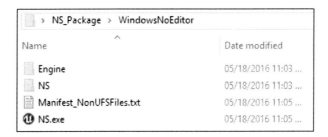

Once the package is finished, the popup will change to a message saying **Package Complete**! accompanied by a short alert noise to signify the build's success. Now navigate to the staging directory you specified. Inside you will find a folder titled `WindowsNoEditor` with the following contents:

Name	Date modified
Engine	05/18/2016 11:03 ...
NS	05/18/2016 11:03 ...
Manifest_NonUFSFiles.txt	05/18/2016 11:05 ...
NS.exe	05/18/2016 11:05 ...

Here we have an **Engine** folder that will contain assets specific to the editor. We then have a **NS** folder which will contain another instance of the build binary as well as the `.pak` file that contains all of our assets for the package. We also have a manifest file that denotes the contents of the engine folder and another instance of the `NS.exe` binary. Run the `NS.exe` now!

You will see our game running in its own window, standalone. You may also have noticed that the game currently thinks this is a server instance. That is because there is no networking session currently active, so the role of our character will be `ROLE_Authority` by default.

Testing the NS package

Ok, now we need to be able to run multiple instances of the NS.exe and have them join a common server instance. This means we need to establish one of the running NS.exe instances as a listen server. We can do this via the command line argument ?Listen.

Creating the listen server instance

We can utilize command line arguments without the command prompt by editing shortcut paths to include any command line arguments we want. Do this now by right clicking on NS.exe and selecting **Create shortcut**. This will create a shortcut to this executable called **NS.exe - Shortcut**. Now right click this shortcut and select **Properties** from the provided dropdown. Here you will see a Target field that contains the file path for the target .exe of this shortcut file. At the end of this path after .exe, add ?Listen to the Target field as follows:

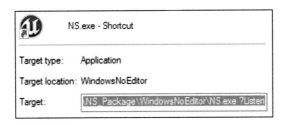

When you run this file it will launch our NS.exe as a listen server that other clients can connect to! The absence of this command line argument in our standard .exe means we are able to use that for all other clients. Launch an instance of NS.exe and an instance of **NS.exe - Shortcut** now!

When working on a Windows platform, I like to use Windows Key + left arrow or Windows Key + Right arrow to positon my dual game play instances on either side of my monitor.

Console commands

One of the main debugging toolsets for a UE4 developer is the in-play console. We can do things like invoke game travel to different maps, flag various profiling and statistical captures and change render settings at run-time. In this chapter we will look at how we can connect to listen servers via the console, as well as some of the great rendering and profiling settings we can invoke. It is important to note that all of these commands are available in editor and can be very useful from within the editor as well.

Connecting to the local host

Right now your two game clients will both state "**Press R to start game**" as they are currently not part of an online session, therefore their net role will default to ROLE_Authority. With the NS.exe instance selected, press the tilde key; this will open the console as follows:

This console, much like every text-based search in UE4, does include an auto complete feature. It will suggest various actions that include some/all of the letters already typed. Now type **Open** into the console. You will be presented with the following list:

```
Open <MapName> (Opens the specified map, doesn't pass previously set options)
open 127.0.0.1 (opens connection to localhost)
OpenGL.BindlessTexture
OpenGL.MaxSubDataSize
OpenGL.RebindTextureBuffers
OpenGL.SkipCompute
OpenGL.UBODirectWrite
OpenGL.UBOPoolSize
OpenGL.UseEmulatedUBs
OpenGL.UseMapBuffer
OpenGL.UseSeparateShaderObjects
OpenGL.UseStagingBuffer
OpenGL.UseVAB
> open_
```

Here we can see that the generated list has suggested most of the commands available with open included in the command. The one we are concerned with is open 127.0.0.1. as we are attempting to connect to a server running on the same PC as the client we want to connect to the localhost. If you are attempting to connect to another PC over LAN you would need to replace 127.0.0.1. with the IP of that computer. With the open 127.0.0.1 command open in the console press enter to execute the command! The client will now connect to the server!

As you can see, we have connected to the server! You can do this for as many clients as you would like!

 If you want to see a complete list of console commands, type DumpConsoleCommands into the console and press enter. If you press the key again to expand the console, you will see the list of all console commands.

Profiling using the console commands

The console is exceptionally useful for getting runtime information about your game's performance. We can leverage some of the statistic capture commands and visual outputs to test the performance of our NS project! With either the client or the server selected type stat into the console, you will be presented with all of the available stat commands that can be used to get runtime information from the project:

```
Stat ThreadPoolAsyncTasks
Stat Threads
Stat Tickables
Stat TickGroups
Stat UI
Stat UNIT (Shows hardware unit framerate)
Stat UnitGraph (Draws simple unit time graph)
Stat UObjectHash
Stat UObjects
stat_
```

The entry point for any profiling is to know what your average frame per second is. We can achieve this by bringing up a simple FPS value by typing `stat fps` into the console.

The next thing we would probably like to know is where our frame cost is going. Thankfully, UE4 records the `ms` time for each of the major threads running: Game, Draw and GPU. Each thread can be described as follows:

- **Game**: This will be the total cost of all game-based processes; this includes physics calculations, blueprints, and anything else that would be considered on the CPU apart from draw instructions being sent to the GPU. You may find this has a high value when you are running inefficient code, running a scene with a high number of actors, or when the game world has not been optimized to work well with the garbage collection system in UE4.

- **Draw**: The draw thread is indicative of the runtime cost that is incurred by batching and sending instructions to the GPU. This value will be high when transferring information from the CPU to the GPU numerous times per frame.

- **GPU**: The GPU thread shows you the amount of time it takes for all of the drawing to take place within your scene. This value will increase as graphical fidelity increases, and can be directly controlled by reducing the visual quality of your project.

It is important to know where most of the processing time is taking place in your projects so you can direct your optimization efforts towards the right areas. It is important to note that the Game thread can be capped by the render thread so that, when Vsync or smooth frames is enabled, the Game thread will wait on the render thread. Therefore, when profiling, these two threads will appear to have the same frame time cost. It is important to disable both vsync and frame smoothing via the editor settings when making builds to be scrutinized for profiling.

We can get access to this thread information from our NS.exe by typing stat unit into the console. Do this now:

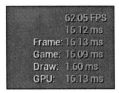

We can see here that our Draw thread is only taking 1.60 ms as we are not sending much information to the GPU every frame. I took this capture with Vsync enabled to demonstrate that our Game thread is bound to the GPU thread. They both read ~16.0ms where in reality, for this current project, they should be much smaller. As a comparison, here is the same capture made with smooth frames turned off and Vsync disabled:

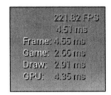

This will make your frame readings more erratic but also more accurate as well. Vsync can be disabled by typing r.Vsync 0 into the console and smooth frames can be found within the project settings at **General Settings | FrameRate**:

Another thing we can do is view a histogram of our frame rate over the last hundred frames or so. This is can be achieved by typing stat `unit graph` into the console. This will bring up the following graph:

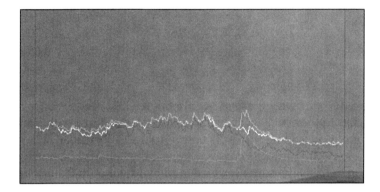

You will notice that once this graph is activated, the various thread stats on the right hand side of the screen will become color coded. This is so you can scrutinize those threads with the information in this graph. The green line will represent the total frame cost. The yellow is the GPU thread, the blue is the Draw thread, and the red is the Game thread.

Unfortunately, we do not have the time left in this book to go into profiling in depth, but this link is a great place to start at `https://docs.unrealengine.com/latest/INT/Engine/Performance/`.

The documentation details profiling the CPU via the front end session manager or GPU using the graphic profiler as well as some other stat commands that give you runtime information on the current memory cost of your scene!

Console visualizations

There are various visualization modes you can activate via the console. These modes will provide you with visual information about the various rendering and game processes within the game scene. These visualizations are a great way to identify rendering costs within your scene or to identify how prominent a given effect is in your scene (such as SSR reflections, for example). If you are scrutinizing your project from within the editor, you will be able to utilize this great rendering debug feature.

First off, run the project again from within the editor, then use the console command `ShowFlag.VisualizeBuffer`. This will add several new buffer views to your current viewport, each with their own name. This is a great way to dissect the rendering scene within your project.

Another great command is `ShowFlag.ShaderComplexity`. To see if any particle effects or materials within the scene are costing too much. Each pixel will be colored from green to red (then to white), which will represent the cost of that particular pixel. Our current project has very cheap materials, so, when activated, we simply see the following:

I would strongly encourage you to explore each of these visualization options so you may learn what each do. The profiling link above also describes some of the uses of this visualization tool!

Wrapping up the NS project

Ok, now we are done with this NS project! Great job on working through all of that networking code. This marks the last piece of learning in this book. Obviously all of the projects we have worked on are far from being commercial game titles, and could all be taken to greater heights! You could add different types of obstacles to Barrel Hopper, you could make different powerups and terrain types for `Bounty Dash`. For `BossMode` and NS you could expand on what we have already done and create fully fledged game prototypes. You could even combine the two for some co-op boss action! Now, let's have a quick look at what we have learnt!

What we have learned so far

Wow! We finally made it. Thank you very much for making it through the book. I have nothing left to teach you within the scope of Unreal Engine By Example! We have covered so much in our journey thus far. From making a `Hello Sphere` using only the editor, to creating missile launching boss AIs and networked first person characters! We have covered a lot in this book, but I thought it would be a good idea to summarize some of the core learning concepts we covered.

The Editors

We are now very familiar with the multiple editors of UE4, each following a fairly similar structure. We know to look at the **Details** panel when we wish to edit or inspect specific elements of a selected object. We know we can construct our objects via the viewport and viewport widgets. We have also learned to expose various properties of our own objects so we may tweak them via the numerous editors found within the engine. The most important thing we learned, however, is that the editor will be the window through which game designers and artists view your work. As a programmer, one of the best things you can bring to a development team is a quality of life usability for the objects and processes you create.

We have learnt about using BSP brushes to approximate level geometry and how to convert our brushes into a consolidated static mesh. We have also dabbled with placing in-game markers in the form of scene actors. Then using those markers as positional references from code to assist with our obstacle-spawning in `Bounty Dash`!

Blueprints

Blueprints was the main focus for the first third or so of this book, and, despite not featuring very much in the later chapters, is still a very powerful tool that can be leveraged by developers to create quick and effective prototypes. We learnt how to create our own blueprints from objects that already exist in the editor as well as from scratch. We have learnt how to use the context-sensitive search to find various blueprint nodes, and we also learnt about Blueprint functions, macros and delegates!

One of the more important things we learnt is that blueprints and C++ code can work together very well via UPROPERTY and UFUNCITON specifiers. This became particularly useful when we began to work with Unreal Engine's AI systems that require a nice merger of in-editor work and C++.

The speed at which we were able to create `Barrel Hopper` is a testament to how robust blueprint is as a development tool. I would strongly encourage using blueprint as your go-to prototyping tool going forward (if you are not using C++ that is!).

Unreal animation

We briefly looked at the animation pipeline for Unreal. I wish we had time to cover all of the facets of unreal in great detail; you never know maybe it will be in the next book. We did cover the basics though: We have learnt how to get our characters to articulate and move within the game world via animation blueprints and animation state machines! We explored the uses of skeletons and sockets for binding external assets like guns or equipment to specific bones so they will move and update with the character. We even covered how to play animations from C++!

C++

One of the most powerful things we covered in this book was the use of C++ with UE4. As the engine is written in C++, it is the primary tool for creating content that works seamlessly and easily with the UE4 backend. We have learnt how to inherit from and expand the UE4 base objects like `AActor` and `ACharacter` to create our own custom characters and actors that still use all of Unreal Engine's underlying systems. We have learnt how to use the reflection system UE4 has provided with the UBT and UHT via Macros like UPROPERTERY, UFUCNITON and UCLASS. We have learnt how to communicate between our project's underlying code and the editor via macro specifiers.

Using C++ outside of UEmay feel strange now that we have had delegates and a robust template library at our fingertips for so long. Learning how to leverage these systems provided with UE has been a fantastic addition to your toolset as a developer. Hopefully going forward you will defer to using C++ in your UE projects.

Artificial Intelligence

The Artificial Intelligence system in Unreal Engine is robust and deep; it provides us with a great template upon which we can build elaborate and complicated AI. During this book we learnt how to leverage this template to create a boss AI that used both editor based AI assets and C++ services. We learnt how to create custom nav meshes for our large floating boss. We learnt about UE4s behavior tree system, creating our own AI tree and using decorators to dictate logic flow. We created blueprint and C++ tasks that can be executed to have the AI perform some custom functionality. We combined all of this knowledge to create a boss that changes through three different states of behavior and fires missiles!

Unreal Rendering

Unreal boasts a very robust and feature-rich renderer. Again this is a whole other ball game when it comes to information we did not cover. I would strongly suggest that you look up more resources on the Unreal Engine rendering and material layers if you wish to continue developing your rendering skills with Unreal Engine. Having said that, we learnt how to leverage this through Unreal Engine materials! We have learnt about texture UV's and normal maps to create minute details and bumps on a surface. We have learnt about the main material node and all of the different input channels and how to leverage them to create cool effects like emissive glows! We have also just learnt how to profile our graphics scene so we can get a rough idea of how much pain we are putting our gpus through!

Unreal networking!

The last feature we learnt about was that of the Unreal Engine networking layer! Congratulations on creating your very own networked first person shooter. We learnt about networking protocols, like peer 2 peer or client server. We learnt about networking roles and how we can change our logic so that it functions with server authority in mind. We leveraged this networking role knowledge to then implement our own RPCs that invoked specific functionality on either the client or server. We learnt how to replicate information between networked objects via the replicated specifier and GetLifetimeReplicatedProps().

The most important thing we learnt about networking is how to construct our backend game code to accommodate for the various networking roles. If you wish to continue to learn about and use Unreal Engine as a networking platform I would strongly suggest looking into the networking interpolation functionality included in the UMovementComponent. It is there that you will begin to find out how UE4 deals with lag in games!

Summary

There we have it. You have finished *Unreal Engine By Example*! I hope you have enjoyed the journey through the pages of this book. Congratulations, by the way; you are now ready to take your own UE projects regardless of genre and required feature set. You now have the toolset to utilize UE4, and if you come across any gap in your knowledge the documentation is hosted online and can always be accessed.

Congratulations on finishing the book, and I look forward to guiding you through more UE experiences in the future!

Index

H

header file
breaking down 114
default constructor 114
include list 115
parent, calling 115, 116
virtual functions 115, 116
Hello Sphere Blueprint
Blueprint Graphs, working with 20-22
Blueprint palette, utilizing 25
Blueprints, compiling 23
Blueprint Variables, using 24
meta-data 26, 27
modifying 19, 20
string manipulation 26, 27
Hello World, for C++
3D text, adding 123
about 111
code, building 120
components, adding 116-118
construction helpers 118, 119
delegates 124, 125
delegates, reference link 126
events 124-126
events, receiving through delegates 122
Fire Particles, adding 120
first code class, exploring 112
header file, breaking down 114
Hello Sphere 127
Hello world text 122
Hot Compilation, adding 120
object creators, adding 116, 117
object finders 118, 119
Unreal Build Tool, accommodating for 113
high-detail levels
blocking geometry 41, 42
building 39
camera tips 40
creating 41
tricks 40
Hot Compilation 122
HUD 33

I

input events
character movement component,
tweaking 37, 38
creating 34, 35
receiving 34-36
inputs, branch node
class 51
Collision Handling Override 51
instigator 51
Spawn Transform 51

K

key frames 71

L

level to support AI, modifying
about 324
navigation mesh 325
NavMesh generation settings,
adjusting 325, 326
NavMesh, placing 326, 327
line trace
creating 330-333
listen server
about 395
instance, creating 461
logical node 51
looping 80

M

material
applying, to Boss 387
material editor
about 356
Base material node 358-360
Details panel 362
Graph panel 358-360
Palette 362
stats panel 362
Toolbar panel 356, 357
Viewport 357, 358

CPSIA information can be obtained
at www.ICGtesting.com
Printed in the USA
FSOW02n1657310716
23287FS